Reciprocity, Truth, and Gender
in Pindar and Aeschylus

Reciprocity, Truth, and Gender in Pindar and Aeschylus

Arum Park

UNIVERSITY OF MICHIGAN PRESS

ANN ARBOR

For questions or permissions, please contact um.press.perms@umich.edu

Published in the United States of America by the
University of Michigan Press
Manufactured in the United States of America
Printed on acid-free paper
First published May 2023

A CIP catalog record for this book is available from the British Library.

Library of Congress Cataloging-in-Publication data has been applied for.

ISBN 978-0-472-13342-0 (hardcover : alk. paper)
ISBN 978-0-472-90386-3 (open access ebook)

DOI: https://doi.org/10.3998/mpub.11853864

The University of Michigan Press's open access publishing program is made possible thanks to additional funding from the University of Michigan Office of the Provost and the generous support of contributing libraries.

Cover illustration: Attic red figure calyx krater with the killing of Agamemnon, 460 BCE, by the Dokimasia Painter. Courtesy William Francis Warden Fund, 63.1246, Museum of Fine Arts, Boston.

For Ellen

Contents

Acknowledgments

This book represents the end of a very long and trying journey. In the time it took to bring this book to print, my two children were born, my father passed away, and a global pandemic crisis descended upon us. Needless to say, there were many moments of difficulty along the way, and I contemplated throwing in the towel more than once. But in August of 2020, I happened to revisit my campus office for the first time since the COVID-19 pandemic began and saw two notes waiting for me in my mailbox, from students who had graduated with their MAs several months prior. They thanked me for my support and encouragement; one of them said how much it meant to her, as a woman of color, to see another one in the field of Classics. These notes reminded me that my work means something, that its impact is not limited to those who read my publications. I finished this book not only for myself but for the people I could help by continuing my work as a scholar and teacher of Classics. To everyone who helped me with this book, thank you. Whether you intended to or not, you were helping an Asian American woman secure a foothold in a field that has not historically been populated by people like me, and by extension you were helping anyone I could help as a Classicist of color.

Thanks are owed to my mentors at the University of North Carolina at Chapel Hill, especially to Peter Smith, who directed the doctoral dissertation that formed the starting point for this book; to Rebekah, who ensures that I stay in touch; and to Sharon James and Jim O'Hara, who are always willing to read my work and offer incisive critiques. Thanks as well to other members of my Chapel Hill family: to Chris Polt for providing feedback on my proposal and readers' reports; to Joy Reeber, who also read and commented on my readers' reports, as well as parts of the manuscript; to Jeff Beneker for reading large chunks of the full manuscript; and to Sarah Bond, Kinitra Brooks, and T. H. M. Gellar-Goad, who offered me clarity and support throughout the revision process.

My University of Arizona colleagues also made this book possible. Thanks to Rob Groves and Phil Waddell for providing feedback on my book proposal; to Courtney Friesen for sagely telling me to just send the proposal already without waiting for even more feedback; to Sarah McCallum for helping me understand the readers' reports; and to my mentors Karen Seat, Bill Simmons, and Marilyn Skinner, who lifted my spirits when they were low. I cannot overstate the extent of Marilyn's generosity and help in particular. After reading my book proposal, sample chapters, readers' reports, and then the entire revised manuscript, Marilyn understood what I was trying to say better than I did and helped me conceptualize and frame my argument. This book is a more refined and articulate one thanks to her.

I am grateful also to my many friends from previous institutions, including Ed Sacks, who hired me for my very first job in Classics and has always been beyond generous with his time and resources, and my Brigham Young University writing buddies Matt Ancell, Robert Colson, Marlene Esplin, Seth Jeppesen, Nate Kramer, Mike Pope, and Carl Sederholm, who had such unwavering faith in my potential as a scholar that I eventually became one. Thanks also to the Center for Hellenic Studies, which supported this project in its early stages.

This book is also the product of my beloved family. My mother, Youngtae Shin, read through the entire manuscript and helped me rewrite its most crucial parts. My late father, Chung Shin Park, was always a scholarly role model. I could not have survived graduate school or the years since then without the love of my husband, David Carlisle. Our sons Desmond and Wallace are almost as proud of me as I am of them; I am grateful to them as well as to everyone who took care of them, particularly in their earliest years: Yellow Brick Road, Adventure Time, Makaela Townsend, the Tucson Jewish Community Center, and Catalina Methodist Day School. Dawn Park Hamilton has always been the best sister anyone could have; among other things, she gave me the idea years ago for a system to keep my work on track, and I still use it to this day. My friends are my family too, but I will limit myself to listing only my longest friendships, Akilah Stewart, Rungthip Choensookasem, and Carmen Korehbandi. There are so many more people in my life for whom I am grateful, but I will just have to write more books to thank them all.

Finally, thanks to both people who played official editorial roles in this process, Lauren Apfel and Ellen Bauerle. I am proud to call Lauren, an inspiring writer and scholar, my first friend in Classics and my trusty editor; with her incisive mind and precise wordsmithing, I managed to get a handle on the many unwieldy tentacles of this book. I am also grateful for the criticisms from the anonymous peer reviewers that resulted in a much-improved book. And of course, my deepest gratitude to Ellen Bauerle at the University of Michigan Press, who secured these readers in the first place. I will forever be in her debt for her unflagging dedication to this project. Despite the significant setbacks that presented themselves, Ellen never wavered in her conviction that my book was a worthwhile endeavor, and I doubt that many editors would have shown me the kind of patience and grace that she did. I dedicate this book to Ellen and all editors like her, who tirelessly bolster the efforts and confidence of first-time authors.

Contexts for Complementarity

This book is a comparison of Pindar and Aeschylus.[1] It relies on the utility of comparison to uncover insights otherwise hidden from view. Comparisons are critical to how we make sense of our world; they inform our perceptions, our beliefs, our behaviors, our choices. Even in mundane acts like choosing an item of clothing, an entree from a restaurant menu, or a place to live, we make comparisons either consciously or unconsciously between the available options. Comparisons inform not only our choices but also our intellectual reactions and assessments more generally. By considering similarities and differences between two (or more) things, we enrich our understanding of those things, and we are able to categorize them and make sense of them in context. An art critic, for example, in analyzing a work of art, likely relies on her knowledge of other art to inform her understanding of the present work. A literary critic would engage similar processes. All our assessments or analyses are shaped in some way by what we have previously seen, experienced, or learned, and we rely on the illuminative power of comparison to form a comprehensive view.

This book takes a comparative approach to identify the relationships between truth, reciprocity, and gender in the works of Pindar and Aeschylus. It argues that each poet engages with similar reciprocity principles to frame his poetry; that each depicts truth in a way that is specific to those reciprocity principles; and that their depictions of gender, too, are shaped by this intertwining of truth and reciprocity. Though these intertwinings may be discernible in a

---

1. Here and henceforth, my use of any poet's name designates the poetic persona perceptible in their poems rather than the actual, historical poet.

single-poet study, they are more sharply illuminated and vivified by a comparative approach. What emerges through this dual-poet study is a thematic complementarity between Pindar and Aeschylus, a complementarity that encompasses both their similarities and differences. To view Pindar and Aeschylus in terms of complementarity allows us to understand each poet in light of the other. It is by examining them together that we can see the three concepts that anchor this book—truth, reciprocity, and gender—as intertwined and interrelated. And the interpretive benefits of this examination flow both ways: just as seeing Pindar and Aeschylus as complements helps reveal the interrelationship of truth, reciprocity, and gender in their poetry, so too does recognizing this interrelationship shed light on the thematic similarities between Pindar and Aeschylus and suggest the poetic culture they share.

Pindar and Aeschylus were contemporaries. Both were born in the last quarter of the sixth century BCE, Aeschylus in 525/4 BCE in Eleusis, and Pindar less than a decade later in Thebes.[2] Their poetic careers each spanned the first half of the fifth century. Aeschylus first competed in the City Dionysia in 499 BCE,[3] and his final production, the *Oresteia*, was staged in 458 BCE. Though younger than Aeschylus, Pindar began his career around the same time, toward the beginning of the fifth century BCE, when he would have been only about twenty years old. His first epinician ode dates to 498 BCE, and the last of his datable odes to 446 BCE.[4] From the perspective of the modern scholar, the poetic careers of Pindar and Aeschylus bridge the Archaic and Classical periods, having started before the Persian invasions of Darius and Xerxes and continuing long afterward. Aeschylus is even said to have fought in the pivotal battles of Marathon in 490 BCE and Artemisium and Salamis in 480 BCE and deemed these actions more significant than his poetry (Paus. 1.14.5).

In other words, Pindar and Aeschylus were composing their poetry during a time of historical and political transformation. Both were young men when the Persian invasions changed the Greek speaking world forever and catalyzed self-examination on what it meant to be Greek and what it meant to be from a particular Greek city. The cities with which they were associated, Athens and Thebes, represented contrasting political orientations. Both were cities whose reputation and status in the Greek world were shaped by their roles in the Per-

---

2.   Likely 518 BCE, though some scholars favor a date of 522; see Race 1986, 1, for discussion.
3.   Sommerstein 2010a, 3 and 15n7, citing *Suda* α1357 and π2230.
4.   *Pythian* 10 and *Pythian* 8, respectively. This dating is based on the ancient commentaries, though Race 1986, 131n5, cautions against overreliance on them.

sian Wars: Athens' naval strength and leadership in resisting the Persians gave rise to her growing hegemony; Thebes, by contrast, had submitted to Xerxes (Hdt. 7.132), was continually shifting in her alliances, and had an increasingly contentious relationship with Athens (see, e.g., Hdt. 6.108.4–6, Th. 1.108). Aeschylus lived through the Athenian expulsion of tyranny in 510 BCE, Cleisthenes' introduction of democracy shortly thereafter, and the continuing evolution of Athenian democracy, which paralleled its rising prominence in the Greek world at large.[5] But Pindar was famous for a career that depended on wealthy, aristocratic patronage, and he was hired to celebrate tyrants more than once. He produced poetry that, unlike tragedy, was designed to mute political conflict rather than explore it.[6]

In light of the historical and political moment they represent, it makes sense to examine Pindar and Aeschylus together. The two poets have been compared on the basis of their mythological content and their respective genres.[7] On the surface their poetic forms of epinician and tragedy are radically different, not least for the contrasting ideologies and time periods with which they are associated.[8] Tragedy is treated as a hallmark of the Classical period and of Athenian democracy.[9] Epinician is often seen as an homage to the aristocratic culture and conservatism of the Archaic era. Pindaric epinician may even reflect the aristocracy's oppositional reaction to the rise of Athenian democracy.[10] It is conventional, then, to view Pindar and Aeschylus as a sort of Janus figure, to borrow a Roman image: Pindar, the poet of tyrants and aristocrats, looking

---

5. On which, see Finley 1955, 179–81; Herington 1985, 87–97; Sommerstein 2010a, 3–6.

6. Kurke 1991, 6–7.

7. Foster 2017; Griffiths 2014; Herington 1984; Kurke 2013; Nagy 2000; Sailor and Stroup 1999, 160–71; Steiner 2010; Swift 2010, 104–72. On the generic interactions between lyric and tragedy more generally, see Andújar, Coward, and Hadjimichael 2018. On identifying and conceptualizing "genre" in Archaic Greek poetry, see Davies 1988; Ford 2006; Harvey 1955; Nicholson 2016, 29–30, 46–50, 51–52; Silk 2013. Pindar's Fragment 128c (Sn.-M.) lists several types of songs, suggesting the poet's awareness of poetic genre and function, as he describes the "seasonableness" of paeans (Ford 2006, 292). On epinician genre more specifically, see Maslov 2015, 276–87; Nagy 1990, 412–37; Nicholson 2016, 52–77, 229–32, 309–18; Spelman 2018, 183–214.

8. Of course, their association with these genres is a function of their works that survive into modernity. The Alexandrian scholars collected Pindar's works into books of paeans, dithyrambs, prosodia, partheneia, hyporchemata, encomia, threnoi, and epinicians, only the last of which survive. Aeschylus, of course, composed satyr plays as well as tragedies.

9. Uhlig 2019, 4–7, summarizes the binary that typifies scholarship contrasting Pindar and Aeschylus and argues against the tendency to segregate the two poets on the basis of genre.

10. See Kurke 1991, 6, on epinician as an intermediary between sympotic and tragic poetry, and 258–59 on epinician as "a kind of counterrevolution on the part of the aristocracy." See also Rose 1992, 141–84, who complicates but seems ultimately to endorse this view. See also Rose 1982, 55, criticized by Thomas 2007, 141–43. LeVen 2014 examines lyric from the Late Classical period, thus complicating the identification of the form with earlier eras.

backward to an idealized Archaic past of aristocratic virtue and Panhellenism;[11] Aeschylus looking forward, an avatar of the innovative, disruptive, interrogative spirit of Athenian democracy.[12]

Though the faces of Janus look in opposite directions, they have something in common, a shared headspace. This metaphor helps us view the similarities as well as the differences between Pindar and Aeschylus, and to see the two poets as halves of a whole, each needing the other to be comprehensible. We might alternatively make use of Anna Uhlig's strategy of "imagining a conversation" between them.[13] Both metaphors allow us to see the two poets as distinctive, yet occupying the same poetic ecosystem. As John Herington has compellingly argued, tragedy was born not in an Athenian democratic vacuum but in a literary culture that permeated the Greek speaking world from the Archaic period until the death of Pindar. Tragedy emerged in a world in which performed poetry was the primary communicative medium.[14] Such a view accords well with the Alexandrian inclusion of Pindar (and Bacchylides) in the same canon as lyric poets of the Archaic period, and it helps situate Aeschylus in the same poetic world as Pindar. The lives of the two poets may even have intersected.[15] The ancient biographical tradition tells us that Pindar received some of his training in Athens;[16] likewise, Aeschylus had been to Sicily more than once at the invitation of the same tyrants whom Pindar celebrates in several of his victory odes. One of these tyrants, Hieron of Syracuse, had supposedly invited both Pindar and Aeschylus to his court in the 470s BCE and commissioned them to celebrate his rule.[17]

Their shared poetic culture is mirrored by common ground in the otherwise contrasting political ideologies associated with epinician and tragedy.[18] It

---

11. For a recent study of epinician's political associations, see Nicholson 2016.
12. See Finley 1955, 4–7. Rose 1992, 142, summarizes the scholarly tendency to view Pindar as a "tail-end figure . . . of a temporal span beginning with Archilochus" and as "unambiguously backward-looking and irretrievably archaic." See also Rose 1992, 185, on the contrasts between Pindar and Aeschylus. Thomas 2007, 141–44, succinctly presents the scholarly views on epinician's traditionalism and notes where it converges with the ideals of democratic Athens.
13. Uhlig 2019, 1–9.
14. Herington 1985, 3–5, differentiates between the "song culture" that predominates the Greek speaking world from Homer through the death of Pindar, and the "book culture" that emerges in the late fourth century BCE.
15. See Uhlig, 2019, 1–19, on "imagining a conversation" between Pindar and Aeschylus.
16. *Bios Pindarou* 11–15 in Drachmann 1997 vol. 1, 1. On Pindar's relationship to Athens and Athenians, see Hornblower 2004, 248–61.
17. As noted by Finley 1955, 3; Race 1986, 2; Uhlig 2019, 1.
18. As Thomas 2007, 142 writes, "It is clear that the Pindaric victory ode is a phenomenon mainly devoted to the aristocratic and wealthy elite of Greece, and celebrates what are essentially aristo-

should not be forgotten that Aeschylus was born in the latter years of tyranny; so too was his genre of drama, the City Dionysia having been established by the Peisistratids in the second half of the sixth century. Attic tragedy as we know it now may have flourished in democracy, but the form got its start in tyranny.[19] In the same vein, epinician lyric is a more recent genre than it presents itself to be and must continually rely on older forms to appease its audiences.[20] Both Pindar and Aeschylus were traditionalists in that they were working in genres established before they started their careers, but they were also innovators in that they were influential in shaping their relatively new forms.[21]

When we consider them together as participants in the same poetic culture, we can see that they figure reciprocity into their poetry in different but complementary ways.[22] Pindar represents his relationship with his patron as one premised on poet-patron reciprocity and allegorizes this relationship and its ideals in his mythic exemplars. In like manner Aeschylean tragedy centers on reciprocal action, whether of an amicable or hostile variety. Aeschylean plots engage the action-reaction pattern and temporal continuity of reciprocity. This pattern is particularly foregrounded in extant Aeschylean tragedy, which emphasizes the intergenerational scope of reciprocity and revenge more so than other extant Attic tragedy does.

Pindar and Aeschylus also figure reciprocity into their constructions of truth and gender. Both truth and gender are highly contextual; that is to say, their meanings and the ways they operate are dependent on the contexts in which they appear. In Archaic and Classical Greek poetry, words for truth often signal some kind of objective reality, but at the same time, their poetic contexts

---

cratic values, *aretē*, beauty, athletic prowess. But it is worth remembering that the Athenian people applied just the same set of aristocratic ideals to itself, the democratic *dēmos*." See also Thomas 1989, 213–21.

19. See Rose 1992, 185–94, on the ideological underpinnings of the tragic form. He also suggests that tyranny and democracy were not direct antitheses, given tyranny's empowerment through the peasantry: "Tyranny . . . is best understood as a consequence of the hoplite revolution. Newly empowered peasants were able to assert their power only indirectly through a champion, who himself was usually of the aristocratic class, but was prepared to check the worst abuses of the aristocracy in the name of some newly broadened conception of the political community (the polis)" (Rose 1992, 186).

20. Kurke 1991, 259; Spelman 2018, 185.

21. Spelman 2018, 179, makes a similar point about Pindar's poetry as both forward- and backward-looking. See also Spelman 2018, 185: "Like tragedy, epinician is a relatively young type of poetry that is generically capacious and voracious." Thomas 2007 explores the origins of epinician, which she argues stretches far back into the sixth century BCE.

22. Reciprocity, of course, is a pervasive concept in ancient Greek thought. See, e.g., Blundell 1989; Cook 2016; Donlan 1982; Gill, Postlethwaite, and Seaford 1998; Herman 1987; Kurke 1991; Lyons 2012; MacLachlan 1993; Rabinowitz 1993; Reden 1995; Seaford 1994; Wohl 1998.

shape their meanings. Similarly, whether and what behaviors and attitudes are coded by gender depends on the aims or purposes of the poem. Poems representing various types of relationships or conflicts may refract them through male-female dynamics. These constructions of gender are often intertwined with constructions of truth, particularly in Greek poetry. In the works of Pindar and Aeschylus, the concept of reciprocity provides a stable vantage point from which to consider truth, gender, and the interplay between the two. Pindar's references to truth are embedded in these frameworks of reciprocity, and his depictions of deceptive female figures emphasize their harm to reciprocal relationships. Likewise, Aeschylus often codes his reciprocal patterns with terms for truth, using such terms to designate the inevitability of reciprocity. Gender operates within the Aeschylean intertwining of truth and reciprocity in that by and large it is through his female characters that the force of reciprocity is expressed. In both Pindar and Aeschylus, then, female figures somehow foreground the mechanisms of reciprocity and truth that drive their poetry, though in different ways.

There are a number of entwined oppositions at play here, involving the temporal dimension of reciprocity, the relationship of female figures to truth, and the role of female figures in reciprocity. Pindar's depictions of reciprocal relationships tend to focus on the immediacy of relationships between, say, guest-friends, rather than the intergenerational continuity of such relationships.[23] Aeschylean tragedy, on the other hand, features reciprocity as a continuously repeating pattern that spans past, present, and future. Pindar's female figures, through their deceptive tendencies, disrupt reciprocal relationships. By contrast, Aeschylus' female characters, while they may be deceptive, ultimately do serve to articulate truth as a phenomenon of intergenerational reciprocity. Pindar's and Aeschylus' female figures, in inverse ways, illuminate the intertwining of truth and reciprocity. These entwined oppositions emerge through comparison of the two poets, which reveals the interplay of truth, reciprocity, and gender more than a single-poet study would.

---

23. Sigelman 2016, 73. This is not to say that Pindar has no sense of temporal progression whatsoever; as Spelman 2018 argues, Pindar is mindful of past, present, and future and makes his poetry accessible to audiences across time and space. See also Foster 2017; Kurke 1991, 69–70 and 80–81; Kurke 2013, 132–33; Rose 1992, 185; and Uhlig 2019, 200–217, who discuss the theme of generational continuity in some of Pindar's myths. I am merely pointing out that depictions of reciprocal relationships in Pindar tend to focus on the immediate relationship between its participants rather than future or past iterations of it.

The Structure of the Book

Over the course of this book I present detailed examinations of this interplay. Chapter 1 examines reciprocity and the function of alētheia in articulating it in Pindar and Aeschylus. I discuss definitions of reciprocity as well as Pindar's and Aeschylus' complementary configurations of it. Further, I make the case that both poets present alētheia in ways that reflect their conceptions of reciprocity. Chapter 2, which explores reciprocity and truth in Pindar's myths, updates arguments that I first advanced in 2013.[24] I argue that Pindar harmonizes the potential conflict between his obligation to tell the truth and his obligation as a xenos to his patron. I further argue that he presents epinician—a type of poetry defined by reciprocity between poet and patron—as the most truthful kind of poetry. His references to truth signal their epinician context and in effect ground truth in the reciprocity frameworks of his victory odes. Chapter 3 argues that Pindar's deceptive female figures must be understood within such frameworks. Pindar deploys negative stereotypes of women as false, deceptive, or seductive to emphasize the harm such women inflict specifically on male exchange relationships. Furthermore, they perform a metapoetic function in that their stories and actions call attention to poetic activity as well as to the reciprocity principles fundamental to epinician poetry.

The remaining chapters explore how this entwining of reciprocity, truth, and gender appears in *Seven against Thebes*, *Suppliants*, and the *Oresteia*.[25] Like Pindar's female characters, Aeschylus' signal the reciprocity principles that govern the stories in which they exist. While Pindar depicts female deception as detrimental to reciprocal relationships, Aeschylus shows how female characters express and perpetuate cycles of reciprocal action as truth. Chapter 4 examines the distinct and diverse ways of accessing and understanding the truth in *Seven against Thebes*. The Chorus of Theban Women trust in a type of truth that is constructed from interpretations of what they can see and hear from a distance. Further, they understand this truth in terms of reciprocity and temporal continuity: past, present, and future are intertwined and based on action-reaction patterns. They designate this pattern as "truth" when they articulate the House

---

24. Park 2013. Some of this material also appears in chapter 1.
25. My decision not to include *Persians* and *Prometheus Bound* in my study is based on their various outlier qualities: as a historical play not staged as part of a trilogy, *Persians* falls outside the scope of this book, while the questions of authorship that surround *Prometheus* (on which, see Herington 1970 and Griffith 1976) excessively complicate the validity of the kinds of conclusions I can make about Aeschylean truth, gender, and reciprocity.

of Laius myth as an intergenerational narrative of action and response (720–91). They thus, more than the other characters of *Seven*, demonstrate a keen perception and a long view of the story in which they exist. Chapter 5 explores how the temporal aspects of reciprocity figure in *Suppliants*. I argue that the Danaids envision, affect, and effect the plot, essentially forging their own truth. They imagine a future they desire, and they enact it through male agents whom they must enlist to their cause. They are able to do so by articulating a shared future with them, one based on and responsive to their shared past and one that implies a continued trajectory of reciprocal obligation. The Danaids' ability to envision their future and engage male allies to enact it reflects their attempt at narrative control. Chapter 6 explores truth, reciprocity, and gender in the *Oresteia*. In *Agamemnon* Clytemnestra and Cassandra share an ability to envision their own experiences and actions as part of a larger narrative. Both understand this narrative as ongoing and inevitable, and they designate it as "truth" (ἀλήθεια; *A.* 1241, 1567). They possess the same imaginative ability of the Chorus of *Seven*, along with their understanding of the temporal continuity of reciprocity. Furthermore, their visions anticipate the plot of *Choephori* and thus afford the audience a glimpse of how the trilogy will unfold. The conclusion to the *Oresteia*, however, complicates the intertwining of truth, reciprocity, and gender that was established in *Agamemnon*.

Throughout the book, I show how reciprocity informs Pindar's and Aeschylus' representations of truth and gender. By recognizing the complementary patterns that play out in Pindar's and Aeschylus' works, I hope to shed light on each poet individually and in relation to one another. Comparing their respective treatments of truth, reciprocity, and gender can help us understand the similar positions they occupy in the ancient Greek poetic tradition, despite the stark differences between their respective genres and performance contexts. The conceptual framework I use here may be useful for other authors too. Certainly reciprocity is a ubiquitous principle in Greek thought, as is the complexity of gender and truth. I can imagine intellectually fruitful studies of reciprocity, gender, and truth in, for example, Archaic epic, or in Attic tragedy more broadly, or in Herodotean historiography. While the interrelationship of truth, reciprocity, and gender may not be unique to Pindar and Aeschylus, it is a particularly helpful tool for exploring their complementarity, as it helps us see these two ostensibly very different poets as two sides of the same historical and poetic coin.

CHAPTER 1

Reciprocity and Truth in Pindar and Aeschylus

Reciprocity

Reciprocity is a core feature of Pindar's and Aeschylus' poetry, as it was in the ancient Greek world more broadly. It figured into gift exchange, kinship relations, marriage contracts, mortal-divine relations, and quintessentially Greek ideals or practices like xenia, supplication, and charis.[1] Social scientists have observed reciprocity norms operating at every level of society and have even asserted the universality of reciprocity as a principle integral to social relations and stability.[2] As the anthropologist Marshall Sahlins asserts,

> the connection between material flow and social relations is reciprocity. A specific social relation may constrain a given movement of goods, but a specific transaction—"by the same token"—suggests a particular social relation. If friends make gifts, gifts make friends. A great proportion of primitive exchange, much more than our own traffic, has as its decisive function this latter, instrumental one: the material flow underwrites or initiates social relations. Thus do primitive peoples transcend the Hobbesian chaos. For the indicative condition of primitive society is the absence of a public and sovereign power. (Sahlins 1972, 186)

---

1. For a summary of the scholarship on exchange in ancient Greece, see Lyons 2003, 94 and Lyons 2012, 7–21. On supplication, see Crotty 1994 and Naiden 2006. On charis, see MacLachlan 1993. For a definition of guest-friendship, see Herman 1987, 10: "For analytical purposes ritualized friendship [i.e., xenia] is here defined as a bond of solidarity manifesting itself in an exchange of goods and services between individuals originating from separate social units."
2. Fry 2006, 400, citing Brown 1991, 139; Gouldner 1960, 171.

What Sahlins articulates so effectively is that the exchange of material goods parallels and indeed is premised on social bonds between the parties involved. Furthermore, this relationship is a circular and mutually reinforcing one: material exchange strengthens social bonds just as social bonds precipitate material exchange. The social expectations underlying these practices essentially possess a kind of governing force, especially in societies without a recognized ruler.[3]

References to reciprocity in this book denote what is implicit in the circularity between exchange and social relations, namely, the expectation that any action will be met with an equal and corresponding response or reaction, whether immediately or in the future. This expectation is key to all manner of relationships and practices in the ancient Greek world. The exchange of armor between Glaucus and Diomedes in *Iliad* 6, for example, symbolizes and reifies the bond of xenia between them that was established by their ancestors several generations prior (*Il.* 6.119–236). The exchange itself reflects their mutual observance of the xenia established by their ancestors and the expectation of harmonious and mutually supportive relations between their two families. The poet's comment on the unevenness of the exchange—Glaucus giving gold in return for Diomedes' bronze—makes clear that parity is presumed, though not upheld: ἔνθ᾿ αὖτε Γλαύκῳ Κρονίδης φρένας ἐξέλετο Ζεύς, | ὃς πρὸς Τυδεΐδην Διομήδεα τεύχε᾿ ἄμειβε | χρύσεα χαλκείων, ἑκατόμβοι᾿ ἐννεαβοίων ("then Zeus the son of Cronus took away the mind of Glaucus, who gave gold arms to Diomedes, son of Tydeus, in exchange for bronze, a hundred oxen's worth in exchange for nine," *Il.* 6.234–36). Within interpersonal relationships, the expectation of reciprocity amounts to an obligation or even debt. This is what we will see in Pindar's epinician poetry. Furthermore, the indebtedness generated in reciprocity can be balanced in the future, whether by the original debtor or by someone else. It can expand beyond the bounds of a relationship between two people to a general expectation that actions will be repaid in kind—whether for good or ill—at some point. This conception of reciprocity as a kind of cosmic force is particularly apparent in Aeschylean tragedy.

The sense of reciprocity that predominates in my discussions is one that carries with it an inherent responsiveness and symmetry: there should be a

---

3. Claude Lévi-Strauss' seminal *The Elementary Structures of Kinship* (1966) similarly shows how expectations of reciprocity dictate social norms and behavior in ancient societies. See also Seaford 1998, 1: "It is well known that . . . reciprocity is in general a more central value and practice in the economic, political, and interpersonal processes of pre-state societies than it is in those of modern industrial societies." See van Wees 1998, for a survey of the scholarship in anthropology that comes to this consensus.

response to an action that is commensurate with the original action. By the same token, reciprocity involves a presumption of mutual benefit in the actions and responses performed within this system. For example, if I give food to a hungry friend, I do so because the norms of friendship would dictate such an act of kindness, but also because under these same norms, I would stand to benefit in kind from the friend I served, either immediately or in the future. Perhaps I provide food to my hungry friend and assume the same treatment would be forthcoming from them if I ever experienced hunger. Or I might provide food for a meal we shared while he provided drink. In each scenario, both my friend and I would have provided equal and mutually beneficial sustenance to the other. Of course, this simple assumption of parity can prove misplaced, as in the above example of Glaucus and Diomedes. Social scientists have accounted for such imbalances by considering variations of reciprocity involving uneven or even completely one-sided exchange.[4] But for the most part, reciprocity norms are premised on the expectation of equal and mutual benefit.[5]

Expectations of reciprocity animate the earliest Greek myths, suggesting the pervasiveness of the reciprocity principle in ancient Greek thought. The Trojan War is premised on Paris' abduction of Helen, which violates two types of reciprocity (xenia and marriage), catalyzes a war of retaliation, and makes female gender the source of that conflict through the figure of Helen.[6] The *Iliad* illustrates the sacrosanctity of reciprocity in numerous episodes: the truce between Glaucus and Diomedes that I mention above demonstrates the force of ancestral xenia in overcoming wartime enmity; Achilles' rejection of Agamemnon's gifts in *Iliad* 9 illustrates their shared understanding of the power imbalance the gifts signify;[7] and the final interaction between Priam and Achilles reveals the symbolic and emotional undercurrents of physical transactions (*Il.*

---

4. E.g., Gouldner 1960, 165, and Sahlins 1965, 144 and 1972, 195–96, who discuss uneven or even completely one-sided reciprocity ("negative reciprocity," in Sahlins' words) wherein someone tries to get something for nothing, possibly resorting to violent methods to do so.

5. Fry 2006, 401–2, summarizes Sahlins' three types of reciprocity ("generalized," "balanced," and "negative"), which constitute a continuum of behaviors from altruism to mutual exchange to theft. Fry concludes convincingly that only the middle type ("balanced reciprocity") involves two-way exchange and is thus the only type that involves actual reciprocity. Even Gouldner 1960 acknowledges the potential for imbalance but assumes *eventual* equivalence in reciprocity, following Malinowski 1932, 39. See Liapis 2020, 22, for an exploration of Sahlins' generalized reciprocity principle operating in *Olympian* 10.

6. Blondell 2013 and Edmunds 2016 are the most recent extensive examinations of Helen.

7. See Wilson 1999 and Postlethwaite 1998, for examinations of the social and economic concerns at play in this episode.

24.468–88).[8] Reciprocity is at the center of the *Odyssey* too, in the suitors' violation of xenia and in the various episodes of Odysseus' return journey that exemplify either improper or ideal guest-host situations.[9]

In this chapter I examine Pindaric and Aeschylean presentations of reciprocity and argue for their complementarity. I will discuss Pindar's constructions of poet-patron relationships in epinician poetry and explore the language he uses to articulate the reciprocity in these relationships. Pindar emphasizes parity and symmetry between poet and patron and between their actions. I will further investigate Pindaric alētheia to argue that the reciprocity principle is so pervasive that it comes to be articulated as truth. Indeed, the use of alētheia in contexts emphasizing reciprocity even suggests that truth is a function of reciprocal parity. As I turn the discussion to Aeschylus, I will examine how Aeschylean tragedy is animated by similar articulations of parity, not so much on parity between individuals in sacrosanct relationships like xenia, but rather on the overarching principle that actions will be met by corresponding reactions. As I will point out, the principles of reciprocity that permeate tragedy in general are such that reciprocity is configured as a general law of payback, whether for good or ill. While Pindar's emphasis is on amicable reciprocity, Aeschylus is just as likely to present the good with the bad, returning a good for a good or retaliating with a bad for a bad. In either case Aeschylus' rhetoric of reciprocity aligns with Pindar's expressions of poet-patron reciprocity, and viewing the two poets alongside one another is mutually illuminating. As I will go on to show, their parallel uses of alētheia in contexts emphasizing reciprocity further illustrate this complementarity. Aeschylus, like Pindar, uses alētheia to denote generally "what happens," and in the context of Aeschylean tragedy and Pindaric epinician, what happens is dictated by the reciprocity principle. Like Pindar, Aeschylus conceives of reciprocity as a force governing human behavior and the unfolding of events, and he marks this sovereignty with alētheia. Truth, for both poets, denotes the power of reciprocity, whether in the relationship between poet and patron in Pindaric epinician or in the interconnectedness between events in Aeschylean tragedy.

---

8.   Zanker 1998 examines this episode, arguing that it presents Achilles as going above and beyond the poem's norms of reciprocal parity.
9.   The bibliography on Homeric reciprocity is vast, but good places to start are Beidelman 1989; Cook 2016; Donlan 1982 and 1997; Finley 1954, 46–113; Seaford 1994, 1–90; Reden 1995; and Wilson 1999 and 2002.

Reciprocity and Truth in Pindaric Epinician

Poetry and Reciprocity in Pindar

Reciprocity serves as the framework for Pindar's epinician poetry, which casts the poet-patron relationship as one of mutual exchange and parity.[10] Pindar conceives of his poetry as a good he provides to his patron (typically the athletic victor he is praising) in return for what he receives. He depicts his patron as a partner in a reciprocal relationship akin to friendship, guest-friendship, or marriage exchange (*O*. 4.4, 1.103, 7.1–10, 10.6; *P*. 4.299; *P*. 10.64; *N*. 7.61–62, 9.2) and allegorizes such relationships in his mythological digressions.[11] He constructs, then, a poet-patron relationship based on kindness, willing reciprocity, mutual respect, and parity.

This relationship is encapsulated in terms or concepts like charis and xenia, and in language emphasizing parity between poet and patron along with symmetry between their actions. Pindaric constructions of reciprocity are characterized by repetitive language and references to payment and repayment or action and return action. For example, the poet uses such language in describing his relationship to his patron Thorax in *Pythian* 10:

πέποιθα ξενίᾳ προσανέι Θώρακος, ὅσπερ ἐμὰν ποιπνύων χάριν
τόδ᾽ ἔζευξεν ἅρμα Πιερίδων τετράορον,
φιλέων φιλέοντ᾽, ἄγων ἄγοντα προφρόνως. (*P*. 10.64–66)

I trust in the soothing *guest-friendship* of Thorax, who labored *for my sake* and yoked this four-horse chariot of the Pierian Muses, *as a friend to a friend, kindly guiding the guide.*[12]

The poet casts Thorax and himself as xenoi, and he asserts the equivalence between their roles to one another through the use of polyptoton (φιλέων φιλέοντ᾽, ἄγων ἄγοντα, 66). This kind of language is what we will see in

---

10. See Kurke 1991 for a thorough analysis of the social dimension of Pindar's odes and pp. 85–134 in particular for models of exchange relationships operating in Pindar's epinician.
11. On the convention of guest-friendship in Pindar, see Bundy 1986, 24–26; Race 1986, 90–91; Hubbard 1985, 156–62; and Kurke 1991, 135–59.
12. Text of the Snell-Maehler Teubner. Translations here and elsewhere are my own unless otherwise indicated. Published translations that I have found particularly helpful for my own are listed in the bibliography.

Aeschylus' articulations of reciprocal action too, as I will discuss below. Furthermore, Pindar characterizes this relationship as a willing and mutually affectionate one by using the terms charis and prophrōn, which typify Pindar's poetics of reciprocity—language of sameness and equality is couched in language of friendship and favor.[13]

Similar assertions of parity occur in *Olympian 7*, in which Pindar likens the poet-patron relationship to the mutually beneficial partnership between households that marriage establishes. The poet compares his poem to a bridegroom gift:

Φιάλαν ὡς εἴ τις ἀφνειᾶς ἀπὸ χειρὸς ἑλών
ἔνδον ἀμπέλου καχλάζοισαν δρόσῳ
<u>δωρήσεται</u>
νεανίᾳ γαμβρῷ προπίνων <u>οἴκοθεν οἴκαδε</u>, πάγχρυσον, κορυφὰν κτεάνων,
συμποσίου τε χάριν κᾶδός τε τιμάσαις ἑόν, ἐν δὲ φίλων
παρεόντων θῆκέ νιν ζαλωτὸν ὁμόφρονος εὐνᾶς·
καὶ ἐγὼ νέκταρ χυτόν, Μοισᾶν <u>δόσιν</u>, ἀεθλοφόροις
ἀνδράσιν πέμπων, γλυκὺν καρπὸν φρενός,
ἱλάσκομαι,
Ὀλυμπίᾳ Πυθοῖ τε νικώντεσσιν· ὁ δ᾽ ὄλβιος, ὃν φᾶμαι κατέχωντ᾽ ἀγαθαί.
    (*O.* 7.1–10)

As when someone takes from his wealthy hand a golden bowl—the crown of his possessions, splashing with the dew of wine—offers a toast *from house to house*, *gifts* it to a young bridegroom in honor of his own marriage connection and the glory of his symposium, and makes him envied in the presence of his friends for his harmonious marriage, I too send flowing nectar, *gift* of the Muses, sweet fruit of my heart, to victors at Olympia and Pytho and appease them. Happy is he whom good reports possess.

As in guest-friendship, the marriage contract involves exchange that symbolizes the amicable relationship now established between two parties; the focus is on the male participants in this exchange rather than the bride.[14] Pindar com-

---

13. Kurke 1991, 141–42.
14. The bride is presumably considered one of the objects exchanged, as is typical of ancient Greek marital practices. See Lyons 2012, 22–52, for the often elaborate exchanges involved in ancient Greek marriage, and the gendered implications of such exchanges. When the bride exercises her

pares himself to a father-in-law welcoming a new son-in-law, while the athletic victors he praises are cast as recipients of a gift-offering. He envisions his poetry as a golden cup lifted for a toast in a symposium, a symbol of a relationship forged between two allies, whose parity and partnership are expressed in the phrase "from house to house" (οἴκοθεν οἴκαδε).[15] Again, Pindar's language emphasizes the symmetry of the exchange.

Casting this relationship in such terms may seem contradictory to the realities of epinician poetry, which is by nature a commercially oriented genre: the poet is commissioned to compose a poem for a particular occasion and is promised payment for his work. Indeed, Pindar openly refers to payment for poetry, for example, in *Pythian* 11: Μοῖσα . . . εἰ μισθοῖο συνέθευ παρέχειν | φωνὰν ὑπάργυρον ("Muse, if you undertook to provide your voice inlaid with silver for a fee," 41–42). The transactional nature of Pindaric poetry may seem more akin to a system of commodities exchange than gift exchange: monetary payment is rendered for goods or services provided and is not contingent on a personal relationship between two parties.[16] But as Leslie Kurke has demonstrated, Pindar's poetry blends a Homeric aristocratic ideology of exchange with the realities of a society in which money now exists.[17] Thus, the language of favor and reciprocity exists side by side with the language of monetary exchange, for example, in *Isthmian* 2, where Pindar invokes a "mercenary Muse,"[18] or in *Pythian* 1, where he refers to the gratitude he will receive for his poem as a payment: ἀρέομαι | πὰρ μὲν Σαλαμῖνος Ἀθαναίων χάριν | μισθόν ("From Salamis I will gain *favor* from the Athenians as a *reward*," 75–77).[19] Furthermore, he speaks of his poetry as an obligation or even debt, both of which typify systems of reciprocity premised on continuing cycles of obligation (e.g., *O.* 1.103, 3.7, 8.74, 10.3–8; *P.* 4.1–3, 8.33, 9.104; *I.* 1.43, 3.7–8, 6.20).[20] His construc-

---

own agency in a marriage contract, mayhem ensues, as I will discuss in chapter 3.

15. On the significance of the cup in this passage and the relationship between material and voice, see Uhlig 2019, 101–2.

16. Kurke 1991, 93, citing Mauss 1967, 34–35, and Bourdieu 1977, 171. This type of transaction typifies Karl Polanyi's concept of a "disembedded" economy in which commercial exchange is not "embedded" in a network of social relationships; see Kurke 1991, 166–67.

17. See Kurke 1991, 85–107 and 240–56, for arguments that Pindar reconciles gift and commercial exchange.

18. For the phrase, see Woodbury 1968. In *Isthmian* 2, Pindar refers to a Muse who was formerly "not yet a lover of gain nor working for hire" (ἁ Μοῖσα γὰρ οὐ φιλοκερδής πω τότ᾽ ἦν οὐδ᾽ ἐργάτις, 6).

19. See also *N.* 7.61–63 for a comparable blend of friendship and payment language.

20. See Bundy 1986, 10–11, on "the necessity or propriety that determines the relationship between song and merit." Bundy cites μισθός, χρῆσις, χρή, χρέος, πρέπει, τέθμιον, τεθμός, ὀφείλω, πρόσφορος, and καιρός as examples of terms marking the obligation of epinician poetry. On debt and obligation in reciprocity, see Gouldner 1960, 174–75.

tions of reciprocity and monetary exchange are vital to understanding how he conceives of his poetry as grounded in reciprocal obligation between poet and patron. This conception of his poetry informs his presentation of truth, as I will discuss below and in the next chapter, and it also shapes his use of gender, as I will discuss in chapter 3.

Alētheia and Poetic Reciprocity

In Pindar the models of reciprocity that frame his epinician poetry are discernible in his uses of alētheia. Indeed, the sacrosanctity of reciprocity is bolstered by the language of truth. At this point I should concede that the semantic ranges of Greek alētheia and English "truth" are not equivalent; for one thing, alētheia does not have the same positive connotations that English "truth" does. But the two terms are not mutually exclusive either, and there is enough overlap between them that for simplicity's sake, I may at times use "truth" as a synonym for alētheia.[21] Pindar's references to alētheia reflect both his obligation to his patron as well as his duty to tell the truth. The symmetry of reciprocity I discuss above parallels the symmetry between reality and account for which Pindar strives. Ultimately, as I will argue in the next chapter, alētheia cleaves so closely to poetic reciprocity that epinician is even presented as the kind of poetry most suited to telling the truth. Pindar can make this argument by stressing obligation as an aspect of both alētheia and reciprocity.

An examination of alētheia from its earliest uses illuminates its idiosyncrasies and complexities in Pindar's epinician contexts. Compared to previous poets, Pindar's use of the term is more expansive and encompasses his adherence to reciprocity principles. Homeric alētheia has largely to do with spoken utterances, as scholars point out and as its entry in LSJ ("opposite to a lie") would suggest.[22] Although the epic context may indicate a desire for sincerity or authenticity, these senses do not inhere in alētheia itself.[23] Post-Homeric

---

21. Cf. Adkins 1972, who argues in part that Homeric alētheia is not very different from a modern conception of truth.

22. LSJ, s.v. "ἀλήθεια," I.1. See Luther 1966, 30–40, for more on Homeric truth, particularly its visual aspects. See also Starr 1968, 349 and Cole 1983, 9, who observe that alētheia/alēthēs in Homer refers to spoken truths. It seems commonplace to think of truth as something spoken: as Lamarque and Olsen (1994, 6–8) note, Aristotle's dictum on truth at *Metaph.* 1011b25–8 ("to say of what is that it is, and of what is not that it is not, is true") similarly implies "that truth is a property of *sayings* or *something said*" (8). But such a conception of truth, unlike Pindar's, does not take into account unspoken qualities of truth such as trust or reliability.

23. Cf. Adkins 1972, 5–18, who examines Homeric situations of truth-telling and concludes that

uses demonstrate its opposition to mere appearance, hence designating reality or a speaker's tendency to express what he believes (truthfulness or sincerity).[24] The evolution of alētheia has largely to do with the ambiguity of its etymology: the lēthē-root negated by alētheia has been taken to refer either to persons ("forgetfulness") or things ("hiddenness") and therefore has a both subjective and objective dimension.[25] Whether alētheia negates λανθάνομαι ("I forget") or λανθάνω ("I escape notice") is a subject of much debate, but in some part the meaning depends on the type of poetry in which it appears.

William J. Slater's *Lexicon to Pindar* defines alētheia (Doric ἀλάθεια) simply as "truth," but it is incumbent on us to examine what additional nuances "truth" carries in the contexts under consideration.[26] It has been argued that in epinician poetry, where alētheia often refers to the persistence of something in memory and its disclosure in "the immortal poetic tradition," alētheia usually negates λανθάνω.[27] But Pindar's uses of alētheia represent a wider range of meaning beyond its already complex associations with memory or memorialization. As Anna Komornicka explains, Pindaric alētheia has at least eight main aspects, which include reality and authenticity, and thus encompasses a significantly broader range than in earlier poetry.[28] Unlike his predecessors and contemporaries, Pindar speaks of truth outside of contexts of verbal accuracy and personal disposition. He proposes a reality that is antecedent and external to its verbal accounts (e.g., τελεύταθεν δὲ λόγων κορυφαί | ἐν ἀλαθείᾳ πετοῖσαι,

---

pleasantness, indicated by phrases like κατὰ κόσμον, is a more valued component of truthful speech than alētheia and may even denote truthfulness or veracity. One example Adkins cites is Odysseus' praise of Demodocus' song in *Od.* 8.487–91.

24. LSJ, s.v. "ἀλήθεια," I.2. On accuracy and sincerity, see Williams 2002, 11, who identifies them as "the two basic virtues of truth . . . you do the best you can to acquire true beliefs, and what you say reveals what you believe."

25. Cole 1983, 7–8, summarizes the argument of Snell 1975, 9–17 thus: "the *lēthē* excluded by *a-lētheia* is something found in persons rather than things: forgetfulness rather than hiddenness or being forgotten." Krischer 1965, 161–74, argues that the perspective of the speaker inheres in ἀληθής, which describes an utterance devoid of (the speaker's) forgetting. See also Detienne 1996, 64–65, and Heitsch 1963, 36–52.

26. Slater 1969, s.v. "ἀλάθεια."

27. Cairns and Howie 2010, 214–15 *ad* 3.96–98. See also Cairns and Howie 2010, 245–46 *ad* 5.187–90, 264 *ad* 9.85, and 326–27 *ad* 13.199–209; Bremer 1976, 161n144; Heitsch 1962, 24–33; and Woodbury 1969, 331–35.

28. As Komornicka 1979, 252–53 notes, "1) le réel, 2) l'authentique, 3) l'essentiel . . . , 4) le vrai dans toute oeuvre poétique qui s'appuie sur l'imitation de la réalité (opposé à fiction pure), 5) le vrai sur le plan moral de la véracité (sincère, véridique, fidèle) par rapport à l'homme, à ses paroles et à ses actes et par rapport à la divinité, 6) le vrai c'est-à-dire ce qui est proper, correct (right, appropriate), 7) le vrai, ce qui est verifiable, ce qui se laisse prouver par rapport . . . , 8) le vraisemblable" are all aspects of alētheia in Pindar. See also Komornicka 1972, 235–53 and Komornicka 1981, 81–89.

"The chief points of the words fell *on truth* and were brought to completion," *O.* 7.68–69; νῦν δ᾿ ἐφίητι <τὸ> τὠργείου φυλάξαι | ῥῆμ᾿ <u>ἀλαθείας</u> ≤ ⌣ —> ἄγχιστα <u>βαῖνον</u>, | "χρήματα, χρήματ᾿ ἀνήρ" ὃς φᾶ κτεάνων θ᾿ ἅμα λειφθεὶς καὶ φίλων, "And now she commands us to pay heed to the Argive's saying *as it comes closest to truth*: 'Money, money is man,' said the one who was bereft of his possessions and friends at the same time," *I.* 2.9–11).[29]

Furthermore, he uses the adjective alēthēs to describe both statements (or metaphors for statements) and speakers' dispositions, thus meaning both "true" and "truthful" and conveying accuracy as well as sincerity, both of which are part and parcel of his epinician purpose.[30] These two applications need not be mutually exclusive since alēthēs tends to be used in contexts where Pindar claims to speak the truth, thus suggesting his disposition toward true reportage. For example, when he expresses his hope that his "true words" will help him evade Boeotian stereotype, he claims both that his words are true and, implicitly, that he is truthful (ἀρχαῖον ὄνειδος ἀλαθέσιν | λόγοις εἰ φεύγομεν, Βοιωτίαν ὗν, "if we flee with true words the old reproach 'Boeotian pig,'" *O.* 6.89–90).

While Pindar's priority is to praise his patron, he nevertheless validates his praise by casting truth as something specific to his epinician purpose. When he invokes Olympia in *Olympian 8*, he stresses the importance of truth to his particular task and situates it within a larger obligation:

Μᾶτερ ὦ χρυσοστεφάνων ἀέθλων, Οὐλυμπία,
δέσποιν᾿ ἀλαθείας, ἵνα μάντιες ἄνδρες
ἐμπύροις τεκμαιρόμενοι παραπειρῶνται Διὸς ἀργικεραύνου,
εἴ τιν᾿ ἔχει λόγον ἀνθρώπων πέρι
μαιομένων μεγάλαν
ἀρετὰν θυμῷ λαβεῖν,
τῶν δὲ μόχθων ἀμπνοάν.
ἄνεται δὲ πρὸς χάριν εὐσεβίας ἀνδρῶν λιταῖς. (1–8)

---

29. Maslov 2015, 185–86, makes a related point when he refers to alēthēs/alētheia as connoting "access to the past" and comprising one aspect of "veridiction" or "authoritative speech." See also Nagy 1996, 122–27, on the distinction between alētheia and muthos in Pindar. See Segal 1986a, 73–77, on the imagery of falling in *O.* 7.68–69.

30. Pindar applies the adjective once to the herald's shout as a "true witness under oath" (ἀλαθής . . . ἔξορκος, *O.* 13.98–99), which demonstrates the first application of alēthēs to the accuracy of a report. By contrast, Pindar describes his disposition rather than his words as alēthēs in *O.* 2.92 (ἀλαθεῖ νόῳ, "with a true mind," *O.* 2.92).

Mother of the contests crowned with gold, Olympia, queen of truth, where men
who are seers make judgments by burnt sacrifices and make trial of Zeus of the
flashing thunderbolt, to see whether he has a prophecy about men who seek to
win great glory and respite from their toils with their bravery. There is accomplishment through prayers, in gratitude for the piety of men.

The truth sought by seers at Olympia involves the outcome of athletic contests,
which will be determined by Zeus.[31] By identifying Olympia both as "mother of
contests" (Μᾶτερ . . . ἀέθλων, 1) and "queen of truth" (δέσποιν' ἀλαθείας, 2), the
poet locates alētheia in the domain of athletic ability. He introduces the Olympic victory of his laudandus as a manifestation of truth, thus aligning the story
of the laudandus with truth and communicating his devotion to this truth
simultaneously. He situates alētheia, which according to William Race "denotes
'how something actually turns out to be,' a sense it *always* has in Pindar,"[32]
within its specific context of athletic competition.

Furthermore, he ties that truth to principles of reciprocity when he presents
Olympic victory as something that occurs "in gratitude" (πρὸς χάριν, 8) for
men's piety. In so doing he casts athletic victory as the gods' reciprocation for
prayers and thereby lays the groundwork for associating alētheia with reciprocity. Athletic achievement is a responsive gift, one granted by the gods in
exchange for something given to them. By extension, truth, too, is an act of
reciprocation, given that athletic victory is a manifestation of truth. By locating
both athletic victory and truth in Olympia, he conjoins them, and he caps this
message with an aphorism about reciprocity. In this compressed nexus of concepts, reciprocity becomes the framework within which truth exists. What the
passage suggests is that Pindaric alētheia is couched in the particular kind of
poetry Pindar writes, namely, athletic praise poetry. Therein lies the further
suggestion that Pindaric alētheia will be embedded within the constraints of
that poetry as well, namely, the constraints of reciprocity.

Truth Personified: Fragment 205 and Olympian 10

Pindar's personifications of alētheia too reflect the reciprocal obligations of epinician poetry. As a praise poet, Pindar presents his task as twofold: he must

---

31. See Komornicka 1972, 238, and Slater 1969, s.v. "δέσποινα." Both explain Olympia's epithet as
   stemming from the function of the Olympic games as the true proof of athletic ability.
32. Race 1990, 144.

fulfil his obligation to his patron, and he must also represent events accurately. He thus speaks of truth both as an aim of his epinician agenda and as a reality external to and independent of that agenda. There is a possible conflict between these two conceptions of truth since praise may not always cleave to objective reality. Pindar resolves this conflict in part through the mechanisms of personification, which can invoke multiple aspects of an abstract concept like alētheia. Pindar's personifications of alētheia endow it with agency while simultaneously presenting it as a passive concept: truth guides his poetry, and in turn his poetry will tell the truth. This compression of the active and passive dimensions of alētheia activates a reciprocity between the poet and truth in which each is bound to serve the other. The mutually reinforcing relationship between the poet and truth in turn provides a basis or model for the obligations between poet and patron. The contexts, too, in which personifications of alētheia appear further call up and reinforce the poet-patron reciprocity that is central to epinician poetry.

Pindar personifies alētheia in Fragment 205 and *Olympian* 10, both of which convey the conventional meaning of alētheia as "reality" but also signal praise and obligation, thus demonstrating the multiple applications of alētheia in epinician poetry. In Fragment 205, Pindar invokes Alatheia and calls up the themes of obligation and reciprocity that thread through his epinician poetry:

Ἀρχὰ μεγάλας ἀρετᾶς,
ὤνασσ᾽ Ἀλάθεια, μὴ πταίσῃς ἐμάν
σύνθεσιν τραχεῖ ποτὶ ψεύδει.[33]

Beginning of great excellence, Queen Truth, do not cause my good faith to stumble on a harsh lie.

While we have no context for these lines, the reference to "great achievement" (μεγάλας ἀρετᾶς) evokes similar phrases that appear in epinician contexts[34] and probably refers to athletic achievement and its subsequent poetic praise or to some mythical event that validates the athletic victory, just as it does in

---

33. Stob. *ecl.* 3.11.18 (3.432 Wachsmuth-Henze).
34. E.g., *O.* 11.6 (πιστὸν ὅρκιον μεγάλαις ἀρεταῖς) and *N.* 1.8–9 (ἀρχαὶ δὲ βέβληνται θεῶν | κείνου σὺν ἀνδρὸς δαιμονίαις ἀρεταῖς); lack of context impedes absolute certainty, but the similar language suggests that Fragment 205 too was part of an epinician poem. On areta and poetry, see Norwood 1945, 49: "[Pindar] uses [ἀρετά] both of excellence and of the success won thereby." See also Race 1986, 64: "Song needs deeds to celebrate, and success needs song to make the ἀρετά last."

Olympian 8.6–7. This, along with its expression of obligation, makes the original context of these lines very likely an epinician ode.[35]

As Bonnie MacLachlan notes, Pindar adopts the stance of a truth-teller by
expressing reverence for a goddess who will aid his truthfulness: "As *alatheia*
served the sovereign Olympia in proving/revealing victors (*O.* 8.1–2), so the
poet serves the queen *Alatheia* in giving an accurate testimony of the victory
event."[36] By referring to Alatheia as the beginning, Pindar situates truth as ante-
cedent to his poetry, and by requesting her assistance, he presents truth as an
entity with agency.[37] Furthermore, the request in this passage suggests that it
has been composed with the aid of, and thus *in obligation to*, truth. Though
brief, the fragment encapsulates the slippage between the active and passive
aspects of truth: truth encompasses both the force that shapes the poet's words
as well as the words themselves that he will speak. In this slippage lies an
implied relationship of mutual obligation and reciprocity, as Pindar is beholden
to the truth, but in turn the truth relies on the poet to be told.

These active-passive circularities between Pindar and Alatheia are reminiscent of the relationship between Hesiod and the Muses of the *Theogony*:

"ποιμένες ἄγραυλοι, κάκ' ἐλέγχεα, γαστέρες οἶον,
ἴδμεν ψεύδεα πολλὰ λέγειν ἐτύμοισιν ὁμοῖα,
ἴδμεν δ᾿, εὖτ᾿ ἐθέλωμεν, ἀληθέα γηρύσασθαι."
ὡς ἔφασαν κοῦραι μεγάλου Διὸς ἀρτιέπειαι·
καί μοι σκῆπτρον ἔδον, δάφνης ἐριθηλέος ὄζον
δρέψασαι θηητόν· ἐνέπνευσαν δέ μοι αὐδὴν
θέσπιν, ἵνα κλείοιμι τά τ᾿ ἐσσόμενα πρό τ᾿ ἐόντα,
καί με κέλονθ᾿ ὑμνεῖν μακάρων γένος αἰὲν ἐόντων,
σφᾶς δ᾿ αὐτὰς πρῶτόν τε καὶ ὕστατον αἰὲν ἀείδειν. (Hesiod, *Th.* 26–34)

"Agrarian shepherds, wretched disgraces, mere bellies, we know how to speak
lies like true things, and we know, when we wish, how to speak true things." So
the daughters of great Zeus, with their quick voices, spoke. And they plucked

---

35. Cf. MacLachlan 1993, 101–2, who includes Fr. 205 in her discussion of epinician poetry and Gen-
     tili 1981, whose comparisons between Fr. 205 and several of Pindar's epinician odes suggest a
     similar assumption.
36. MacLachlan 1993, 101.
37. I am using female gendered pronouns to reflect the grammatical gender of Alatheia, but I do not
     mean to consider truth as a woman, as Nietzsche proposes at the beginning of *Beyond Good and
     Evil* (Nietzsche 2017, 9).

and gave me a staff, a marvelous branch of flourishing laurel; and they breathed a divine voice into me, so that I might tell of the future and the past, and they ordered me to hymn the race of the blessed, eternal gods, but to always sing the Muses first and last.[38]

In this passage Hesiod makes the Muses not only the source, but almost the sole creators—the arbiters—of poetry and its truths and falsehoods.[39] Their reference to shepherds as "mere bellies" evokes passive conduits through which the Muses transmit their truths and falsehoods, inscrutable to both shepherds and their audiences.[40] Further, Hesiod does go on to do their bidding, beginning his song with them as they have directed (Μουσάων ἀρχώμεθα, "let us begin from the Muses," 36).

But Hesiod's claim that the Muses breathed a divine voice into him, thus empowering him to sing of the future and the past (31–32) counters this image of simple passivity, for what he receives from them affords him some degree of agency, even as he must conform to their commands. Indeed, his charge to celebrate the future and the past (ἵνα κλείοιμι τά τ' ἐσσόμενα πρό τ' ἐόντα, 33) anticipates the kinds of utterances he explicitly attributes to the Muses themselves, who additionally can speak of the present (εἰρεῦσαι τά τ' ἐόντα τά τ' ἐσσόμενα πρό τ' ἐόντα, "saying the present, the future, and the past," 38). The verbal repetitions blur the distinction between poet and Muse. As Shaul Tor observes, "We would be wrong to ask here for a clear and precise demarcation between divine influence and human agency."[41] Indeed, the parallels between Muses and poet as creative figures make it difficult to determine who precisely is responsible for the words the poet utters. While Hesiod relies on the Muses for his content and creative capacity, the Muses' depiction rests in his hands. Pindar's relationship to truth is analogous and similarly complicated, thanks to the ambiguities activated in the personification of Alatheia. The kind of active-

---

38. Text of the Oxford Classical Text of Solmsen, Merkelbach, and West.
39. See Katz and Volk 2000, 122 and n. 1 for a concise summary of the scholarship on *Th.* 27–28. For further discussions of the relationship between truth, falsehood, and poetry implied in these lines, see Belfiore 1985, 48; Bowie 1993, 20; Finkelberg 1998, 157; Latte 1946, 159; Luther 1966, 41–42; Michelini 1987, 65 and n. 62; Pucci 1977, 36n11; Puelma 1989, 74–79; Sikes 1931, 5–6; Tor 2017, 61–84; Verdenius 1972, 234.
40. Simonides later reflects this idea, describing a poet's reception of truth from the Muses: ὃς παρ' ἰοπλοκάμων δέξατο Πιερίδων | πᾶσαν ἀληθείην ("who received all truth from the violet-haired Pierians," Fr. 11 W²). The whole fragment is published in Obbink 2001, 68.
41. Tor 2017, 80. Tor does go on to argue for the poet's "epistemic dependence on the content provided by the Muses" (81).

passive circularity between Hesiod and his Muses is present between Pindar and truth, and the circularity parallels and perhaps fosters the symmetry on which relationships of reciprocal obligation are premised. Pindar constructs a relationship of mutual benefit between himself and truth in which truth steers his poetry and in return he will, presumably, tell the truth.

The term σύνθεσις is key to this circularity. It has been variously interpreted as "my good faith,"[42] "pledge,"[43] and as a reference to the poet's commission for composing a victory ode.[44] At least two possible meanings consequently emerge from these varying readings: σύνθεσις refers either to the poet's promise to produce an ode or to the ode itself as a particular object pledged. As the entity invoked to guide his σύνθεσις, then, Alatheia is both a testament to the poet's reliability in keeping his obligations and an assurance that the words of his poem are true, and thus works on two levels, to ensure the composition of the promised poem and to guarantee its veracity.[45] The fragment is suggestive of the poet's dual obligations to truth and to his patron, obligations that he will have to navigate and harmonize in his praise poetry.

Pindar personifies truth as an entity to whom he is subordinate. Truth is autonomous, unlike in Hesiod's *Theogony*, where the Muses' caprices determine the veracity of their utterances (26–28). By contrast, Pindar presents his own poetry as explicitly aspiring to tell the truth, a theme that appears in several other odes.[46] Attribution of agency to inanimate concepts is well attested in Pindar and illuminates the striking degree to which he differs from other poets, previous or contemporary.[47] It is particularly unusual to personify alētheia— only Parmenides and Bacchylides also do so, but their personifications do not present the complexities or circularities between active agent and passive concept that are encapsulated in Pindar's Alatheia.[48] Pindar's personification fully

---

42. Slater 1969, s.v. "σύνθεσις."

43. Farnell 1932 vol. 2, 452.

44. MacLachlan 1993, 101; Gentili 1981, 219–20.

45. Pindar is known for his double meanings, particularly in his gnomes. For example, *N.* 10.54, where the gnome (καὶ μὰν θεῶν πιστὸν γένος, "And indeed, the race of gods is trusty") refers back to the Tyndaridae's historically favorable treatment of the victor's family (10.49–54), while also anticipating the theme of loyalty that pervades the rest of the poem.

46. See my discussion of *Olympian* 1 and *Nemean* 7 in the next chapter.

47. For example, Pindar makes chronos the active subject of a verb in *O.* 6.97, *O.* 10.7, *O.* 10.53–55, *N.* 1.46, *N.* 4.43, *Pae.* 2.27, and *Fr.* 159. For further discussion see Gerber 1962; Komornicka 1976; Kromer 1976; Segal 1986a, 69–70; Tatsi 2008; Vivante 1972. For a philosophical approach to time in Pindar, see Theunissen 2000.

48. Parmenides, Fragment 1.28–30 (χρεὼ δέ σε πάντα πυθέσθαι | ἠμὲν Ἀληθείης εὐκυκλέος ἀτρεμὲς ἦτορ | ἠδὲ βροτῶν δόξας, ταῖς οὐκ ἔνι πίστις ἀληθής, "It is proper that you should learn all things, both *the unshaken heart of well-rounded Truth*, and the opinions of mortals, in which there is no

integrates alētheia into the particular aims of his praise poetry and harmonizes their dual purposes.

While interpretation of Fragment 205 is hindered by its fragmentary nature, the other Pindaric personification of alētheia appears in a complete ode and con-firms what Fragment 205 suggests, namely, that Alatheia is bound by the obliga-tions of guest-host reciprocity that Pindar uses to frame his epinician poetry:

Τὸν Ὀλυμπιονίκαν ἀνάγνωτέ μοι
Ἀρχεστράτου παῖδα, πόθι φρενός
ἐμᾶς γέγραπται· γλυκὺ γὰρ αὐτῷ μέλος ὀφείλων ἐπιλέλαθ'· ὦ Μοῖσ', ἀλλὰ σὺ
καὶ θυγάτηρ
Ἀλάθεια Διός, ὀρθᾷ χερί
ἐρύκετον ψευδέων
ἐνιπὰν ἀλιτόξενον.
ἔκαθεν γὰρ ἐπελθὼν ὁ μέλλων χρόνος
ἐμὸν καταίσχυνε βαθὺ χρέος. (*Olympian* 10.1–8)

Read aloud to me the Olympic victor, son of Archestratus, where it has been inscribed on my soul.[49] For I have forgotten that I owe him a sweet song. Muse, you and the daughter of Zeus, Truth, with a straight hand put a stop to the guest-friend harming reproach of falsehoods. For future time has come from afar and shamed my deep debt.

Just as in Fragment 205, the poet invokes divine Truth and gives her the dual function of presiding over his obligation to the victor and ensuring the accu-racy of his words, as indicated by the juxtaposition of truth and falsehood (ψευδέων, 5). He expresses his regret for neglecting his duties to the victor Hag-esidamos and invokes the Muse and Alatheia to rectify his mistakes.[50]

---

true reliance"). Bacchylides, 13.204–5 (ἁ δ'ἀλαθεία φιλεῖ | νικᾶν, "The truth loves to be victori-ous") and Fragment 57 (Ἀλάθεια θεῶν ὁμόπολις | μόνα θεοῖς συνδιαιτωμένα, "Truth alone, inhabiting the same city as the gods").

49. On the addressee of ἀνάγνωτε, see Verdenius 1988, 55 ("the imperative is used 'absolutely' and has rhetorical force"); Hubbard 1985, 67, who says the imperative is addressed to the audience; and Kromer 1976, 423, who speculates that the addressees are "someone else." On the imagery of reading and writing, see Nagy 1990, 171: "the image of reading out loud can even serve as the metaphor for the composition itself. Moreover, the image of writing here conveys the fixity of the composition in the mind of the composer"; see also Nicholson 2016, 119, who in turn cites Fearn 2013, 247–50, Steiner 2004, 282, and Wells 2009, 35–36. On the image of writing on the mind, see Steiner 1994, 100–115.

50. Kromer 1976, 422. Lines 1–3 are usually taken as a reference to the poet's composition of *Olympi-ans* 1, 2, and 3.

What is key here is that the personification of alētheia conflates or combines two aspects of truth: (1) the sincerity of his promise to the patron and (2) the accuracy of the content of his ode. This conflation allows the poet to observe the strictures of guest-friendship that introduce *Olympian* 10 while also telling the truth. The wordplay between ἐπιλέλαθ' and Ἀλάθεια brings out the opposition between truth and forgetfulness, of course.[51] But more significantly, it hints at the symmetry of reciprocal relationships that the poet is in danger of violating—a theme that will permeate the myth of Heracles and Augeas, as I will discuss in the next chapter.

The poet makes clear his concerns for xenia in line 6 (ἀλιτόξενον). When he invokes the Muse and Alatheia to protect this relationship, he presents truth as an entity concerned with guest-host reciprocity. He further reinforces this construction with his multilayered use of pseudea (ψευδέων, 5), which refer broadly to falsehoods but more specifically to the poet's failure to keep his promise to produce an ode.[52] His invocation of the Muse and Alatheia to ensure and validate his guest-friendship is unprecedented. Indeed, Alatheia's placement in an interpersonal relationship of any sort has only one known precedent, in Mimnermus (ἀληθείη δὲ παρέστω | σοὶ καὶ ἐμοί, πάντων χρῆμα δικαιότατον, "Let the truth be present between you and me, the most just possession of all," Fr. 8 West). Her connection to xenia helps shed light on the designation "daughter of Zeus" (θυγάτηρ Ἀλάθεια Διός, 3–4) since Zeus is the patron god of the guest-host relationship. The concern for xenia infuses the ode with epinician ideals of reciprocity: poet and patron have a relationship of obligatory yet willing exchange.

Further, the ambiguity of ἀλιτόξενον brings out the parity between poet and patron: "put a stop to the guest-friend harming reproach of falsehoods" (ἐρύκετον ψευδέων | ἐνιπὰν ἀλιτόξενον, 5–6). These lines ostensibly refer to the poet's potential harm against his patron; as William Race renders them: "ward off from me the charge of harming a guest-friend with broken promises."[53] Race's translation effectively transfers ἀλιτόξενον to ψευδέων (ἀλιτοξένων

---

51. A number of additional oppositions further define alētheia and preclude a simple equation between truth and memory. See Pratt 1993, 119: "Here Pindar clearly plays on a notion of aletheia as a kind of unforgetting. But this passage does not make truth synonymous with memory, for Pindar also opposes lies (pseudea) to truth here." Furthermore, the Muse more than Alatheia is an aid to memory (see *I.* 6.74–5, *N.* 1.12, and *Pae.* 14.35). For the respective roles of the Muse and Alatheia, see Gildersleeve 1885, 214; Nassen 1975, 223; Verdenius 1988, 56. For truth and memory in praise poetry, see Detienne 1996, 47–49.

52. See Gildersleeve 1885, 214; Kromer 1976, 422; Pratt 1993, 119–20.

53. Race 1997 vol. 1, 163. The scholia too note that ἀλιτόξενον refers to Pindar's wrongdoing against his xenos but take the xenos to be Archestratus rather than Hagesidamus (Schol. Pind. *O.* 10.4b).

ψευδέων, "falsehoods that harm guest-friends") and decodes the presumed hypallage of ἐνιπὰν ἀλιτόξενον.[54] But if left as is, ἐνιπὰν ἀλιτόξενον ("guest-friend harming reproach") activates an ambiguity between poet and patron: the xenos harmed could just as easily be the poet, whose reputation stands to suffer if he becomes known as a liar or promise-breaker. Such an ambiguity brings out the symmetry between poet and patron that typifies Pindar's expressions of their reciprocal relationship, a symmetry that finds expression in the mythological digression, as I will discuss in the next chapter.[55]

By construing Truth as a deity that opposes lies and governs his relationship to his patron, and by defining this relationship as a guest-friendship, Pindar depicts himself as beholden to the truth while also maintaining his obligation to praise. As the ode continues, he further reconciles the two potentially opposing obligations to truth and praise by harmonizing contractual duties with friendship.[56] He juxtaposes references to obligation, debt, and repayment (ὀφείλων, 3; ἀλιτόξενον, 6; χρέος, 8; τόκος, 9; τείσομεν, 12) with the language of ungrudging friendship (φίλαν . . . ἐς χάριν, 12),[57] even using the term charis, which Leslie Kurke asserts "designates a *willing* [emphasis mine] and precious reciprocal exchange."[58] The emphasis on willingness in relationships of obligation recurs when Pindar reminds Hagesidamus to give thanks to his trainer (χάριν, 17), just as Patroclus did to Achilles.[59] By asking Alatheia in particular to guide this friendship, Pindar infuses loyalty into his relationship with his patron while authenticating the content of his ode,[60] thus reconciling any potential

---

54. On the hypallage, see Gildersleeve 1885, 214.
55. See Liapis 2020, 11–12, on Atrekeia (O. 10.13) and the homology between poet and athlete that emerges therefrom.
56. On the alignment of commodity exchange and gift exchange, see Kurke 1991, 225–39 and Nicholson 2016, 143. Similarly, on harmonizing "contractual obligation and the relationship of friendly reciprocity," see Liapis 2020, 7, following Kromer 1976, 421–22.
57. To this list of terms for payment, Liapis would add ψᾶφον (9), which ambiguously means "pebble" or more specifically "counter" (Liapis 2020, 6). On the economic metaphors of *Olympian* 10, see Kurke 1991, 233–35.
58. Kurke 1991, 67. For a discussion of epinician charis, see MacLachlan 1993, 87–123, where she discusses charis in epinician poetry as the gratification of the victor.
59. Nicholson 1998, 28, similarly notes the personal tone of Pindar's truth-telling rhetoric, focusing on the pederastic imagery of the odes: "any suggestion . . . that this truth is the production of a disinterested eyewitness is belied by the strongly pederastic flavor of Pindar's epinician poetry . . . [In O. 10.99–105] Pindar's testimony is, as Pratt observes, validated by his status as an eyewitness (*eidon*, 'I saw'), but this is not the testimony of a dispassionate observer. Far from being the truth of a modern court, Pindar's truth is implicated in his adoption of a pederastic persona."
60. See Adkins 1972, 17, on comparable truth-telling in Homer: "Truth-telling—the telling of desired, useful truths, at all events—is to be expected only from φίλοι, those who are for one reason or another within the same cooperative group; and even there it is only to be told when ἀρετή and status-considerations do not forbid it."

conflict between obligatory and veridical praise. Truth becomes both an expression of accuracy as well as an aspect of reciprocal obligation. And as I will discuss in the next chapter, Pindar's mythological digressions similarly uphold alētheia and symmetry as the twin ideals of epinician reciprocity, even conflating alētheia with reciprocity.

Pindar employs principles of reciprocity to define the relationship between poet and patron, a relationship that entails reciprocal exchange: the poet provides the ode, the patron provides payment. The language he uses emphasizes the obligation between poet and patron and the symmetry in their treatment of one another. Furthermore, he characterizes this relationship as one governed by alētheia, his constructions of which encompass both the sincerity of his own part in the relationship as well as the accuracy of his praise. In other words, alētheia authenticates both poet-patron reciprocity as well as the content of his ode. While alētheia represents the poet's duty to the truth, it also reflects the promises of reciprocity within the relationship between patron and epinician poet. He reconciles the two by producing an accurate representation of praiseworthy events. When he invokes Alatheia (*Olympian* 10.4, Fragment 205), he refers to accuracy both in his poetry and in his promise to the laudandus. He presents his duties to his patron and to truth as his foremost concerns, but he takes measures to define the one in terms of the other, using frameworks of reciprocity to accomplish this task.

Reciprocity, Revenge, and Truth in Aeschylus

As we turn to Aeschylus, we will see that symmetry similarly permeates Aeschylean notions of reciprocity and truth. Reciprocity is central to Greek tragedy as a whole, which is often animated by the violation or perversion of amicable reciprocity, a phenomenon that Elizabeth Belfiore labels "problematic reciprocity."[61] As she points out, ancient Greek tragedy revolves around hostility within friendships, kinships, marriages, or other relationships whose presumed bases are kindness and mutual, beneficial exchange.[62] Others have

---

61. Belfiore 1998, 140.
62. Belfiore 1998, 140. See also Belfiore 2000, 13–20, for a discussion of violations of philia (a term she uses broadly to characterize any personal and affectionate relationship, both kin-based and extrafamilial) in tragedy; Belfiore 2000, 123–60, for a list of tragedies whose plots center on violence within relationships of philia. See also Blundell 1989, who examines the ethics of reciprocity in Sophoclean tragedy.

pointed out the centrality of corrupted xenia in the *Oresteia* in particular.[63] Froma Zeitlin articulates tragic reciprocity as a kind of zero-sum game: "But in drama every transaction must be reciprocal and every loss to one side must be balanced out by some gain."[64] Exchange relationships involving female characters as objects of exchange between male characters can be particularly conducive to drama when these exchanges are disrupted.[65]

Revenge is another way for tragedy to present perversions of reciprocity. Ancient Greek literature in general often treats revenge or retribution as analogous to the kinds of friendly exchanges we see in Pindaric reciprocity.[66] In the *Odyssey* the cowherd Philoetius refers to a vengeful, retributive action ironically as a "guest-gift" (ξεινήϊον, 22.290), thus comparing mutually beneficial exchange between xenoi to the vengeful actions inflicted among enemies.[67] Jesper Svenbro even argues that revenge was just as systematized for the ancient Greeks as gift exchange.[68] Reciprocity and revenge share the same basic principle of responsive and equal exchange: if we define revenge as an action an individual takes to punish a perceived wrong—an action intended to respond in equal measure to that perceived wrong—its similarity to reciprocity is clear. Social scientists sometimes refer to the inclination to vengeance as the "negative reciprocity norm," suggesting that reciprocity and revenge are easily analogized.[69] Richard Seaford seems to take this analogy for granted when he succinctly and almost off-handedly defines reciprocity as "a system of exchange in which the return of benefit *or harm* [emphasis mine] is compelled neither by law nor by force."[70]

---

63. See Sailor and Stroup 1999, 154–57; Roth 1993.
64. Zeitlin 1996, 168.
65. As scholars have noted, e.g, Belfiore 1998, 140 and Wohl 1998, xiv. Tragedy often dramatizes the high exchange value of figures like Iphigenia and Cassandra, whose entry into marriage is thwarted or corrupted; see Wohl 1998, 71–82 and 110–17. See also Lévi-Strauss 1966, 63–68 and 134–45; Lyons 2003, 109; and Rubin 2011, esp. 42–47; all three discuss the dual status of women as objects of exchange, yet as subjects with their own (albeit limited) agency. See also Seaford 1987, 106: "Wedding ritual in tragedy tends to be subverted." Ormand 1999 and Rabinowitz 1993 have taken similar approaches to Sophoclean tragedy and Euripidean tragedy, respectively, exploring what the depiction of women as objects of exchange reflects about attitudes toward women among the male audiences of Attic tragedy.
66. See Black-Michaud 1975; Donlan 1982, 142–43; Gernet 1981, 149; Seaford 1994, 25–29; Svenbro 1984.
67. See Svenbro 1984, 54.
68. Svenbro 1984.
69. Barclay, Whiteside, and Aquino 2014, 15, following Gouldner 1960, 172.
70. Seaford 1994, xvii. See also Fry 2006, 399–400, who summarizes various scholarly analogies between kindly and resentful payback, including Westermarck 1906 and Killen and de Waal 2000.

There are some potential differences between reciprocity and revenge, which Aeschylean tragedy often presents but also complicates. As the adage "an eye for an eye" suggests, revenge often presumes equivalence in the responsive action, which can raise logistical and moral problems that are not as present or fraught in "amicable" reciprocity whose intended outcome is mutual benefit.[71] For example, a farmer might supply a baker with grain, to which the baker might respond in kind with a gift of bread; their gifts would not be equivalent in form, but they would be in value and thus would confer mutual and equal benefit.[72] In a revenge scenario, by contrast, equivalence in form is more likely, as the point is to ensure equivalent harm. This can present a logistical problem of agency. For a theft to be repaid by another theft, or a physical injury by the same injury and so on, the agent of revenge can simply be the originally injured party, but in the case of homicide, the avenging agent *must* be different from the original victim—a murder victim cannot avenge their own death. Instead, it must be avenged by someone else, such as a bereft family member or friend. This difference in agency can but does not have to occur in amicable reciprocity. The aforementioned farmer, for example, might receive bread from the baker's son instead of the baker himself, but this particular kind of exchange does not necessitate a new agent to perform the reciprocating act. Aeschylus prompts consideration of this problem in *Eumenides*, where Clytemnestra's ghost goads the Furies to avenge her death, thus complicating the issue of agency in murder-vengeance.

The specific example of homicide raises the further issue of magnitude, both of harm and of consequences. For homicide, an equivalent retaliatory action would necessarily entail a further loss of life, a consequence not all are willing to accept. An eye for an eye is one thing, but a life for a life is another. There is anthropological evidence to suggest that while the reciprocity principle—a good for a good, a bad for a bad—is for the most part universal, situations involving lethal violence give pause. Societies built on nonviolent principles do not engage so readily in vengeance-killing, and other social conditions, too, like how a society is organized, can minimize or mitigate violence of any kind, much less of a retaliatory nature. Social pressures can affect the likelihood

---

71. Seaford 1994, 7, uses the terms "amicable" and "hostile" to designate the two types of reciprocity.
72. See Gouldner 1960, 172, for the distinctions between equivalence in value and equivalence in form, and the significance of the latter in revenge scenarios. Gouldner goes on to discuss the role of the reciprocity norm in preserving social systems (Gouldner 1960, 172–76).

and acceptability of retaliatory violence; an individual taking violent revenge into his own hands may meet with the disapproval of his community, but the community itself might undertake retaliatory violence as a form of socially sanctioned punishment. In the simplest terms, the reciprocity of revenge is far from a universal principle when it comes to lethal aggression, possibly because the hesitation to take a life—even if someone else did it first—is itself a universal.[73] Indeed, the *Oresteia* explores the moral dimension of homicide revenge as the characters in *Eumenides* disagree so starkly about the nature of various crimes and their appropriate punishments.

Finally, reciprocity and revenge can have different temporal dimensions. There is a potential for immediacy in amicable reciprocity that does not exist for revenge. In gift exchange, for example, reciprocity could occur simultaneously; that is to say, both parties could exchange gifts on the spot, as Glaucus and Diomedes do in *Iliad* 6. Pindaric constructions generally reflect this expectation of immediate reciprocity.[74] Reciprocity *can* be extended over some period of time—indeed, sometimes the indebtedness generated during such delays of repayment can even help stabilize social systems.[75] But it does not *have* to. Revenge, by contrast, is by its very nature sequential and predicated on a prior action. A wrong such as homicide, *must* be committed first before it can precipitate a retaliatory response. Aeschylus both brings out and complicates this difference too, through the figure of Cassandra, who articulates past, present, and future but compresses them and sees them as one and the same.

Aeschylus treats revenge in ways comparable to Pindar's depictions of amicable reciprocity. Like Pindaric epinician, Aeschylean tragedy also articulates the expectation of reciprocity with language emphasizing parity, this time between action and response more so than between agents. But Aeschylus puts greater focus on the temporal dimension of reciprocity and revenge, their repetitions over time. Characters like Cassandra and the Choruses of *Seven, Suppliants*, and *Choephori* perceive and articulate the repeating and intergenera-

---

73. See Fry 2006, 406–417, for an examination of the reciprocity of revenge and the likelihood of lethal aggression.

74. As Sigelman 2016, 73, notes, "The relationship of *xenia* between the poet and his addressees is *instantaneously* reciprocal."

75. Gouldner 1960, 170 and 174–75. Liapis 2020, 19–20, has argued compellingly that Pindar's *Olympian* 10, an ode composed to repay a debt, confers nonmaterial benefits that transcend the transactional arrangement from which the debt and ode originate; thus the ode continues the cycle of debt and repayment by generating a new kind of debt. Ultimately his argument is consistent with my closed-loop understanding of Pindaric reciprocity as he argues that Pindar's ode generates a new kind of debt that can never be repaid.

tional patterns of reciprocity, whether in its amicable or hostile variation. They thus reflect the convergence of revenge with certain systems of what social scientists call "indirect" or "generalized" reciprocity wherein benefits are essentially paid forward over time rather than back to the original do-gooder.[76]

The Language of Reciprocity in Aeschylus

Aeschylus' language of revenge and reciprocity resonates with Pindar's in that it emphasizes the symmetry intrinsic to reciprocity, whether in its amicable or hostile instantiation. Like Pindar, Aeschylus refers to payment and repayment and employs repetition reflecting parity, mainly between action and reaction.[77] In some instances this principle is identified with dikē. In *Seven against Thebes*, for instance, the Scout reports that Polyneices expects payment from Eteocles for perceived wrongs:

> σοὶ ξυμφέρεσθαι καὶ <u>κτανὼν θανεῖν</u> πέλας
> ἢ ζῶντ' ἀτιμαστῆρα τὼς ἀνδρηλατῶν
> φυγῇ <u>τὸν αὐτὸν τόνδε τείσασθαι τρόπον</u>. (*Th.* 636–38)

> [Polyneices prays] to engage with you, and to *kill* you, then *die* beside you, or, if you live, *to exact the same manner of payment from you*, banishing you who dishonored him with exile.

Polyneices' plan is premised on sameness in retaliation (τὸν αὐτὸν τόνδε τείσασθαι τρόπον, "to exact the same manner of payment," 638). Furthermore, his convictions about parity run so deep that he even entertains the possibility of dying with Eteocles (κτανὼν θανεῖν, 636), using polyptoton to reinforce his point.

Eteocles counters with language even more marked by symmetry: <u>ἄρχοντί</u> τ' <u>ἄρχων</u> καὶ <u>κασιγνήτῳ κάσις</u>, | <u>ἐχθρὸς</u> σὺν <u>ἐχθρῷ</u> στήσομαι ("I will stand, *ruler*

---

76. Such systems are fundamental to social solidarity. See Molm, Collett, and Schaefer 2007, citing Lévi-Strauss 1969 (=revision of 1966); Malinowski 1922; Mauss 1925; and Sahlins 1965. See also Gouldner 1960, 170 and 174–75, for the comparable point that indebtedness generated during delays of repayment can help stabilize social systems.

77. This kind of language is present in other tragedy as well, but not emphasized to the same degree. In Sophocles' *Ajax*, Tecmessa asserts that "kindness always engenders kindness" (χάρις χάριν γάρ ἐστιν ἡ τίκτουσ' ἀεί, 522). Ajax may use similarly repetitive language to express the hostile counterpart to this principle (S., *Aj.* 839–42, bracketed in the Oxford Classical Text of H. Lloyd-Jones and N. G. Wilson).

against ruler, brother against brother, enemy against enemy," 674–75). Furthermore, while the Scout describes parity between events, Eteocles' articulation adds
the dimension of parity between parties. His deliberate repetition signals the
ideas and expectations of symmetry and requital that he and his brother share;
their similar rhetoric presents a negative counterpart to the type of amicable reciprocity intrinsic to Pindaric epinician, which, as I discuss above, uses repetitive
language to emphasize parity between partners in a reciprocal relationship. Pindar even uses the same rhetoric of symmetry for both friendship and enmity,
thereby succinctly analogizing the two: φίλον εἴη φιλεῖν· | ποτὶ δ' ἐχθρὸν ἅτ'
ἐχθρὸς ἐὼν λύκοιο δίκαν ὑποθεύσομαι ("Let me be a *friend to a friend*; and as *an
enemy to an enemy* I will ambush him like a wolf," P. 2.82–84).[78]

The Scout's report concludes with a description of Polyneices' shield, which
depicts Dikē personified, presumably to legitimize his payback agenda. Eteocles, of course, denies the legitimacy of his claim to dikē (662–71), thus raising
the question of what dikē is and who possesses it.[79] Eteocles' and Polyneices'
mutual situation of dikē in this context of symmetrical retaliation at the very
least suggests that whatever their disagreements, they both conceive of dikē as
part and parcel of the broader system of reciprocity that they hold sovereign.
Other Aeschylean characters, too, express dikē as an expectation of reciprocity
and payment in kind—indeed, Aeschylean tragedy is premised on this kind of
quid pro quo expectation. The Chorus of *Choephori*, for example, employ similar constructions in their invocation of Dikē:

ἀντὶ μὲν ἐχθρᾶς γλώσσης ἐχθρὰ
γλῶσσα τελείσθω· τοὐφειλόμενον
πράσσουσα Δίκη μέγ' αὐτεῖ·
ἀντὶ δὲ πληγῆς φονίας φονίαν
πληγὴν τινέτω. δράσαντα παθεῖν,
τριγέρων μῦθος τάδε φωνεῖ. (*Ch.* 309–15)

Let *evil tongue be paid for evil tongue.* In doing what is due Justice cries loudly,
"Let one *pay bloody stroke for bloody stroke.*" "That the doer suffer" is a story
thrice-told.

---

78. Pindar's rhetoric here substantiates the claims of Seaford (1994, 25) and Svenbro (1984, 54), that
    hostile and amicable reciprocity share the same terminology.
79. Cf. Gagarin 1976, 137, on general tendencies in Aeschylean tragedy: "each side has some validity,
    each individual claims the support of *dikē*, each feels he is right and his adversary wrong."

As Michael Gagarin observes, both the diction and the syntax clearly communicate the expectation of parity: "It is hardly necessary to list in detail the strong verbal balances within the clauses beginning *anti men* and *anti de* and the parallels between these two clauses, all of which emphasize the content of the message."[80] Again, this passage resonates with Pindaric constructions of reciprocity, both for its repetitive language (ἐχθρᾶς . . . ἐχθρὰ; πληγῆς . . . πληγὴν; φονίας φονίαν) and its references to payment or repayment and debt (τελείσθω; τοὐφειλόμενον; τινέτω). While Pindar emphasizes repayment for gift-giving, the Aeschylean passages describe retaliation for harms, but the same rhetoric is used for both, reflecting the two sides of reciprocity that Pindar and Aeschylus represent. Furthermore, the position of Dikē as the entity governing this system of debt and repayment suggests that dikē can encapsulate the kinds of expectations of reciprocity we see in Pindar.

Reciprocity and Truth? The Danaids' Ode to Zeus

What further demonstrates the similarities between Aeschylean and Pindaric constructions of reciprocity is the embedding of alētheia within such constructions. In an ode to Zeus delivered by the Chorus of *Suppliants*, Aeschylus situates reciprocity and truth together. As the daughters of Danaus express gratitude for the asylum they have just been granted in Argos, they invoke Zeus Xenios—a telling attribute in a play where "Zeus figures . . . for the most part in his aspect as Hikesios, the protector of suppliants."[81] By calling on Zeus in his role as protector of xenia, the Danaids conflate supplication with guest-host friendship and ultimately subsume the former under the latter. They cast their Argive saviors as partners in xenia and thereby elevate their own status from suppliants to guest-friends and balance the power between themselves and the Argives.

This new balance of power is reflected in the language of symmetry and is punctuated by alētheia:

ἄγε δὴ λέξωμεν ἐπ᾽ Ἀργείοις
εὐχὰς <u>ἀγαθὰς ἀγαθῶν ποινάς·</u>

---

80. Gagarin 1976, 66.
81. Winnington-Ingram 1983, 63. He points out the double occurrence of Zeus Xenios in 627 and 672, proposing that "just as Zeus Hikesios presides over *Supplices*, so did Zeus Xenios over *Aegyptii* [i.e., the second play of the Danaid trilogy]." He further argues that the murder of the Egyptians in that second play is a violation of xenia, since the Aegyptiads would have been deemed guest-friends of the Argives.

Ζεὺς δ᾽ ἐφορεύοι <u>ξένιος ξενίου</u>
στόματος τιμὰς †ἐπ᾽ ἀληθείᾳ
τέρμον᾽ ἀμέμπτων πρὸς ἅπαντα† (625–29)

Come, indeed, and let us speak *good* prayers for the Argives, *returns for good
deeds*. May Zeus, god of *strangers*, look upon offerings from a *stranger's* mouth,
in truth, in service to every goal of the blameless.[82]

The phrase ξένιος ξενίου (627) mimics the polyptoton in the previous line
(ἀγαθὰς ἀγαθῶν), thus implicating the Argives too in a relationship that presumes reciprocity between partners.[83] These polyptota recall similar repetitions
in epinician contexts and reflect Pindar and Aeschylus' shared rhetorical strategies for expressing the principles of reciprocity.

What the Danaids pointedly offer the Argives are ποιναί ("returns," 626), a
term that further signals reciprocity and exchange and, like reciprocity in general, can have both an amicable and a hostile dimension. As Donna Wilson
explains, poinē in Homer denotes compensation paid specifically for a loss; this
can be payment amicably rendered in exchange for merchandise, or retaliation
taken for wrongs inflicted.[84] Walter Donlan observes that acceptance of this
type of compensation "for someone killed has as its primary purpose the main-
tenance of peaceful relations" and is thus a component of what Marshall Sahlins
would call "balanced reciprocity."[85] In other words, the compensatory practices
encapsulated in poinē are akin to gift exchange and xenia in that they are not
merely acts between individuals but aspects of formal structures designed to
preserve social stability.[86]

---

82. The translation of ἐπ᾽ ἀληθείᾳ is difficult and various translations have been proposed, e.g., "in
true frankness" (Bernardete in Grene and Lattimore 1991, 28) or "to the achieving of truth (sc.
'that they may come true!')" (Friis Johansen and Whittle 1980 vol. 2, 515 *ad* 628, citing Theocritus
7.44 for comparison). My own translation is meant simply to convey the range of associations
with reciprocity and poetry that I argue are encompassed in Pindaric and Aeschylean alētheia.
Similarly, textual difficulties plague line 629 and render it impossible to translate with any accuracy. See Friis Johansen and Whittle 1980 vol. 2, 515–17 *ad* 629 and West 1990b, 149, for extensive
discussion.
83. Sommerstein 2019, 265 *ad* 626, also notes the polyptoton and how it "emphasizes the principle of
reciprocity." See also Bowen 2013, 280: "The juxtaposition of ἀγαθὰς ἀγαθῶν is echoed at once by
Ξένιος ξενίου."
84. Wilson 1999, 138–39; when Zeus takes Tros' son Ganymede, his compensatory offer of horses is
called a poinē (*Il.* 5.266); Patroclus' slaughter of Trojans for the wrongs they have inflicted is also
designated poinē (*Il.* 16.398). See also Wilson 2002, 38–39. Cf. Arthur 1982, 66, who articulates the
"basic sense" of poinē as "harm returned for harm, violence for violence."
85. Donlan 1982, 144. On balanced reciprocity, see Sahlins 1972, 194–95 and 219–30.
86. Donlan 1982, 144–45.

The Danaids' use of poinē here suggests gratitude in return for a previous kindness rather than compensation for a loss. This sense of poinē is unique to Aeschylus and Pindar and is rare even in these two poets.[87] Friis Johansen and Whittle consider its use here "secondary and to be due to the semantic influence of τιμή."[88] Their dismissiveness is understandable given that every other instance of poinē in Aeschylus has the sense of "punishment," more akin to "revenge."[89] Indeed, poinē is twice used specifically to characterize dikē in its retributive sense (Ch. 936, Eu. 543). But the seemingly atypical use of poinē as "reward" actually suggests a conception of reciprocity as existing on a spectrum that encompasses both amicable and hostile instantiations. Pindar and Aeschylus treat reciprocity and revenge as synonymous in their use of poinē to designate reward, redress, or punishment. Its idiosyncratic use in the Danaids' song indicates the continuum of Aeschylean reciprocity, which implies that the principles of exchange apply both to acts of gratitude as well as to acts of retaliation. Pindar's uses of poinē reinforce this point that reciprocity is a double-edged sword: it is used just as much for "recompense" or "reward" (P. 1.58–59, N. 1.70) as for "compensation for a loss" or "penalty" (O. 2.58, Fr. 133.1).

The appearance of alētheia in this context is suggestive, as it associates truth with reciprocity. Admittedly, it appears within a problematic portion of the text, and some editors replace it with ἀλητείας ("wandering").[90] But most editors propose some reading of alētheia, and at least one edition deems it uncontroversial.[91] Its proximity to hallmarks of reciprocity, such as the invocation to Zeus Xenios, the reference to poinē, and the use of repetitive language emphasizing the symmetry of reciprocal relationships (ἀγαθὰς ἀγαθῶν, 626; ξένιος ξενίου, 627), recall the associations documented in Pindar's epinician, where, as I have shown, alētheia is situated in frameworks of reciprocity. We see, then, a likely instance of Aeschylean alētheia that is analogous to Pindaric truth in that

---

87. It appears in A., Ch. 792–93 as well as Pi., P. 1.58–59 and N. 1.70 (Friis Johansen and Whittle 1980 vol. 2, 514 ad 626 and Sommerstein 2019, 265–66 ad 626).

88. Friis Johansen and Whittle 1980 vol. 2, 514 ad 626.

89. As instances of ποινή designating punishment, Italie 1955 cites: A. 1223 and 1340; Ch. 936; Eu. 203, 323, 464, 543, and 981; Pr. 112, 176, 223, 268, 564, and 620. Italie also cites Ch. 947 as an instance of Poiná personified as a goddess.

90. E.g., Sommerstein 2019; see discussion in Sommerstein 2019, 266 ad 628–29.

91. The text I quote reflects Page's Oxford Classical Text and West's Teubner, based on manuscript M. The same text but with the daggering isolated to ἀμέμπτων πρὸς ἄπαντα, thus excluding ἐπ' ἀληθείᾳ from textual controversy, appears in Bowen 2013 and Friis Johanssen and Whittle 1980 vol. 1. Indeed, Bowen 2013, 280, even asserts, "there seems no reason to doubt ἐπ' ἀληθείᾳ." One proposed alternative still favors a reading of alētheia (ἀληθείας, Burges), while West's discussion of these lines focuses on the problems of line 629, for which he proposes τέρμον' πρὸς πάντας ἀμέμπτως and suggests ἀλητείας in line 628 primarily to accommodate this reading (West 1990b, 149, followed by Sommerstein 2019, 266 ad 628–29; cf. West 1990a, 159).

it is tinged by reciprocity. This association, as I will discuss below, is a common and natural one in Aeschylus.

Truth as "What Happens"

In the Danaids' ode alētheia is embedded in a context that emphasizes balance and reciprocity. The natural question now becomes, what is alētheia for Aeschylus? As I noted above, the earliest uses of alētheia and its cognates tend to designate the veracity of a verbal statement. Homer typically situates words for truth as the direct object of a verb of speaking (e.g., ὡς μεμνέῳτο δρόμους καὶ ἀληθείην ἀποείποι, "so that he might remember the races and speak the truth," *Il.* 23.361; ὦ Νέστορ Νηληϊάδη, σὺ δ᾽ ἀληθὲς ἐνίσπες, "Nestor, son of Neleus, tell the truth," *Od.* 3.247). Aeschylean uses of alētheia follow suit in that they refer mainly to verbal statements. When the Herald of *Persians*, for example, concludes his report on the Battle of Salamis, he says, "These things are *true*, but as I speak I leave out many of the evils a god hurled against the Persians" (ταῦτ᾽ ἔστ᾽ ἀληθῆ, πολλὰ δ᾽ ἐκλείπω λέγων | κακῶν ἃ Πέρσαις ἐγκατέσκηψεν θεός, *Pers.* 513–14).

In acknowledging the incompleteness of his report, the Herald's statement raises the question of whether alētheia can extend beyond the scope of what the speaker says and what his audience knows. This potential expansiveness of alētheia is crucial to Aeschylean storytelling, as I will explore in subsequent chapters. The Herald of *Agamemnon* raises an adjacent point when he speaks to the Chorus about the whereabouts of Menelaus. They use terms for truth and falsehood to differentiate what he knows to be accurate and what they hope to be so:

> Κη. οὐκ ἔσθ᾽ ὅπως λέξαιμι τὰ ψευδῆ καλά,
> ἐς τὸν πολὺν φίλοισι καρποῦσθαι χρόνον.
> Χο. πῶς δῆτ᾽ ἂν εἰπὼν κεδνὰ τἀληθῆ τύχοις;
> σχισθέντα δ᾽ οὐκ εὔκρυπτα γίγνεται τάδε.
> Κη. ἀνὴρ ἄφαντος ἐξ Ἀχαιικοῦ στρατοῦ,
> αὐτός τε καὶ τὸ πλοῖον· οὐ ψευδῆ λέγω. (*A.* 620–25)

> HERALD: There isn't a way for me to say *false things as if they are good* for
> friends to enjoy for a long time.

CHORUS: How might you chance to speak *true things that are also joyful*! But it is not easy to conceal when these things are split.

HERALD: The man has disappeared from the Achaean army, he and his ship. I do not speak *lies*.

Both the Chorus and the Herald emphasize the difference between what happened and what the Chorus *want* to have happened.[92] The syntax adheres to what we see in Homer: words for truth and its opposite appear as direct objects of verbs of speaking (τὰ ψευδῆ, 620; τἀληθῆ, 622; ψευδῆ, 625). At first glance, truth appears as a quality of speech, an appraisal of how accurately such speech represents what has happened. The Herald goes on to describe the stormy waters that destroyed countless Greek ships on their return journey from Troy.

But as the Herald concludes his report, he reveals that there is more to alētheia than the accuracy or comprehensiveness of his report:

καὶ νῦν ἐκείνων εἴ τις ἐστὶν ἐμπνέων,
λέγουσιν ἡμᾶς ὡς ὀλωλότας· τί μήν;
ἡμεῖς τ᾽ ἐκείνους ταῦτ᾽ ἔχειν δοξάζομεν.
γένοιτο δ᾽ ὡς ἄριστα. Μενέλεων γὰρ οὖν
πρῶτόν τε καὶ μάλιστα προσδόκα μολεῖν·
εἰ δ᾽ οὖν τις ἀκτὶς ἡλίου νιν ἱστορεῖ
καὶ ζῶντα καὶ βλέποντα, μηχαναῖς Διὸς
οὔπω θέλοντος ἐξαναλῶσαι γένος,
ἐλπίς τις αὐτὸν πρὸς δόμους ἥξειν πάλιν.
τοσαῦτ᾽ ἀκούσας ἴσθι τἀληθῆ κλύων. (A. 671–80)

And if any of them is now breathing, they are saying that we have perished; well, what of it? We imagine that they suffer the same things. May the best possible things happen! Therefore first and foremost expect Menelaus' arrival. And if some ray of sun observes him alive and well, by the designs of a Zeus not yet willing to destroy his line, there is some hope that he will come back home. Know that having heard so much, you hear *the truth*!

---

92. See Goldhill 1984, 57: "In other words, this construction both asserts a wish (that the messenger might speak both good and true things) and puts its possibility under question."

His claim to accuracy is a common trope of messenger speeches (e.g., *Th.* 66–68, 651–52, *Supp.* 931–32).[93] What is puzzling is that his claim includes his wishes for Menelaus' safe return, despite his earlier caution about truth and hope. Reasoning that because he and his shipmates are safe, he posits that the same may be true of Menelaus, and he marks his entire report, including this supposition, with alētheia. Though careful at first not to conflate truth with hope, his optimism about Menelaus' return does just that. His speech thus suggests that alētheia can encompass more than verified facts. It can include what *should* happen, as inferred from reasonable and optimistic best guesses.

These exchanges tell us that in Aeschylus truth can be associated with the unknown; its applications are not limited to verbal reports that represent the whole of reality. The Heralds of *Agamemnon* and *Persians* both acknowledge that truth can encompass more than what they themselves are reporting or perhaps are capable of reporting. The Herald of *Agamemnon* hints, further, that there is more to come—this is central to tragedy, in which incremental revelation prompts further action. To be clear, the two Heralds' statements are not equivalent: the Herald of *Persians* seemingly withholds nonessential details while the Herald of *Agamemnon* simply does not know them. But what their speeches have in common is that their reports are explicitly incomplete yet still described as "true." They suggest that alētheia has a significance that goes beyond merely designating factual, comprehensive verbal reports. The Herald of *Agamemnon*, in particular, acknowledges that alētheia encompasses things beyond the scope of his knowledge or the knowledge of his immediate addressees. The truth can be reported in parts even if its full scope is inscrutable. Additionally, the Herald of *Agamemnon*'s speech suggests a temporal dimension to truth: what he reports on is in the past, as per his capabilities. But information yet to be discovered—which includes future events—can also be true. And as I will discuss further, this temporal dimension of Aeschylean truth is congruent with the reciprocity themes that permeate his tragic plots, whose action-reaction patterns can be characterized as alētheia.

Truth in Untruth: Clytemnestra

The inscrutability of truth is what comes to the fore in Clytemnestra's ironic claims to fidelity, which she marks as alētheia:

---

93. The Herald of the Aegyptiads in *Suppliants* even explicitly states that the duty of a herald is to report precisely and completely (931–32).

γυναῖκα πιστὴν δ᾽ ἐν δόμοις εὕροι μολὼν
οἵανπερ οὖν ἔλειπε, δωμάτων κύνα
ἐσθλὴν ἐκείνῳ, πολεμίαν τοῖς δύσφροσιν,
καὶ τἄλλ᾽ ὁμοίαν πάντα, σημαντήριον
οὐδὲν διαφθείρασαν ἐν μήκει χρόνου·
οὐδ᾽ οἶδα τέρψιν οὐδ᾽ ἐπίψογον φάτιν
ἄλλου πρὸς ἀνδρὸς μᾶλλον ἢ χαλκοῦ βαφάς.
τοιόσδ᾽ ὁ κόμπος, <u>τῆς ἀληθείας γέμων</u>,
οὐκ αἰσχρὸς ὡς γυναικὶ γενναίᾳ λακεῖν. (A. 606–14)

May he come and find a trustworthy wife at home, just the sort of woman he left behind, a guard-dog of his home, good to him, hostile to his enemies, and in all other ways the same woman who has destroyed no seal over time. I know neither pleasure nor blaming speech from another man any more than I know how to temper brass. Such is my boast, *replete with truth*, not shameful for a noble woman to shout.

Clytemnestra's speech is most astonishing for her profoundly dishonest claims of trustworthiness and loyalty and for her bald declaration that such patently false statements are "replete with truth" (τῆς ἀληθείας γέμων, 613).[94] Simon Goldhill has written that this phrase "implies the possibility of its opposite, that the language may have no truth content—as indeed in this case it has not."[95] At first glance Clytemnestra's attachment of the term alētheia to such a completely false statement seems simply a symptom of her character's duplicity.

But these lines are rich with irony that reveals truths underlying her mendacity. She is, for example, almost certainly "just the sort of woman he left behind" (οἵανπερ οὖν ἔλειπε, 607), her diction emphasizing her bold falseness.[96] So too is she the "watch-dog of the home" (δωμάτων κύνα, 607)—but

---

94. There is some debate about the speaker of lines 613–14, which belong to the herald in the manuscripts (Fraenkel 1950 vol. 2, 305 *ad* 613–14). But we must view it in light of previous lines, in which Clytemnestra has earlier mocked the Chorus for faulting her female credulousness and reclaimed female-gendered tendencies as positive characteristics (A. 587–97). Further, assigning the lines to Clytemnestra would be in keeping with her character, which is built on how brazenly deceptive she is. Most scholars (e.g., Fraenkel, West, Wilamowitz), following Hermann, give them to Clytemnestra, but at least one argues that the reference to female gender makes no sense from Clytemnestra's mouth (Thomson 1966 vol. 2, 54–55 *ad* 613–16).

95. Goldhill 1984, 56. He makes the same point in Goldhill 1986, 8: "'loaded with truth' . . . suggests the marked possibility of its opposite, that words can be emptied, unloaded of truth."

96. Raeburn and Thomas 2011, 132 *ad* 607: "-περ and οὖν both strengthen the pronoun (Denniston 421) and underline Clytemnestra's dissimulation."

she has appropriated Agamemnon's home for herself. Further, her claim of truth appears within a speech that does make reference to some of the complexities of truth in Aeschylus. However duplicitous, she hints at the reciprocity themes that permeate the *Oresteia*, and she situates alētheia within these themes. When she speaks of being good to Agamemnon and hostile to his enemies (ἐσθλὴν ἐκείνῳ, πολεμίαν τοῖς δύσφροσιν, 608), she is not merely being dishonest; she is also evoking the reciprocity expectations that I discussed above.[97] As she pledges her allegiance to reciprocity—both amicable and hostile—she obliquely foreshadows the vengeful actions she will take later, thus, in a perverse way, communicating a truthful intention.

By couching alētheia in this context, Clytemnestra infuses it with layers of meaning. On one level alētheia is merely "what happened," and her use of it here demonstrates her mendacity as she claims so falsely to be truthful. But beneath this ostensible meaning lies another: her speech alludes to the larger truth of the trilogy, the reciprocity and revenge patterns governing the plot, and the vengeful actions she herself intends to take. At first her claims of alētheia simply ring false to the audience. But her speech articulates the payback principle that we later learn will inform her murderous actions. Her use of alētheia within this context alludes to an overarching truth about the governing principle of reciprocity. As I have noted above, the idea of repayment—whether a good for a good or a harm for a harm—permeates Greek tragedy. The use of alētheia to connote this reciprocity principle links specifically Aeschylus to Pindar. Furthermore, Clytemnestra's application of truth in this ironic way has the effect of conflating truth and falsehood and putting them both in service to reciprocity. The truth of reciprocity underlies the untruth of Clytemnestra's words, thus making her claim to be "replete with alētheia," on some level, true.

The Truth of Reciprocity

Clytemnestra refers to reciprocity expectations that are central to Aeschylean tragedy and are blended with revenge or retribution. She caps her whole speech with a claim to alētheia, which, as I have suggested, can signal not just spoken truths in Aeschylus but also something more. As in Pindar, alētheia can connote a principle of reciprocity intrinsic to his poetry. Pindaric truth emphasizes

---

97.   See Pindar, *P.* 2.83–84 (φίλον εἴη φιλεῖν· | ποτὶ δ' ἐχθρὸν ἅτ' ἐχθρὸς ἐὼν λύκοιο δίκαν ὑποθεύσομαι, "Let me be a friend to a friend; and as an enemy to an enemy I will ambush him like a wolf"). Cf. E., *Med.* 809 (βαρεῖαν ἐχθροῖς καὶ φίλοισιν εὐμενῆ, "severe to enemies, kind to friends").

the reciprocity of amicable and willing exchange that underscores the poet's obligation to his patron. Telling the truth for Pindar involves both documenting what happened and reciprocating what he has been given by his patron, thus harmonizing truth with the obligations of reciprocal relationships. Aeschylean truth, analogously, emphasizes the repetitive and responsive nature of reciprocity, whether that be retribution or recompense. What is "true" in his tragedies involves "what happened" and "what will happen"—a series of events that correspond to one another as action and reaction and occur along a timeline. While both Pindar and Aeschylus use alētheia to encapsulate the symmetry of reciprocity, Aeschylus takes the further step of using alētheia to emphasize the repetition of reciprocity over time.

Many applications of alētheia in Aeschylus apply specifically to this aspect of reciprocity: action followed by commensurate reaction, whether amicable or hostile. Just as Pindaric epinician centers on reciprocity—specifically reciprocity between poet and patron—so too does Aeschylean tragedy. But Aeschylus more conspicuously conflates reward with retribution as two sides of the same coin.[98] "That the doer suffer," famously uttered by the Chorus of *Choephori* (δράσαντα παθεῖν, 314) is often taken to be the defining principle of the *Oresteia*, and of tragedy more broadly.[99] While this principle of retribution makes occasional appearance in Pindar (*N.* 4.32: ἐπεί ῥέζοντά τι καὶ παθεῖν ἔοικεν, "Since it is fitting that the one who does something also suffer"[100]), it, along with the conflation of amicable and hostile reciprocity, becomes the animating principle of Aeschylean tragedy.

The striking parallel between Aeschylean tragedy and Pindaric epinician is the enfolding of truth within the principles of reciprocity. Aeschylus stresses the repeating patterns and temporal continuity of reciprocity, casting it as a self-perpetuating phenomenon.[101] The sovereignty and certainty of such reciprocity is articulated with alētheia. In *Agamemnon*, for example, Clytemnestra confirms certain predictions of retribution:

---

98. See Kurke 1991, 6–7, for a discussion of the similarities and differences between epinician and tragedy.

99. Blundell 1989, 29: "The talio appears at its most general in the formula 'the doer suffers,' which we associate particularly with Aeschylus' *Oresteia*, but which is echoed in many other sources."

100. Blundell 1989, 29n21 notes this parallel.

101. See Podlecki 1966, 70 and 74, on the "never-ending" justice (i.e., revenge) in *Agamemnon* and *Choephori*, justice that he describes as "endless" but also "self-defeating" (70). Podlecki argues that conversion of retributive justice to its "higher," court-based form in *Eumenides* is anticipated in the previous plays of the trilogy as well.

Χο. ὄνειδος ἥκει τόδ᾽ ἀντ᾽ ὀνείδους,
   δύσμαχα δ᾽ ἐστὶ κρῖναι.
   φέρει φέροντ᾽, ἐκτίνει δ᾽ ὁ καίνων·
   μίμνει δὲ μίμνοντος ἐν θρόνῳ Διὸς
   παθεῖν τὸν ἔρξαντα· θέσμιον γάρ.
   τίς ἂν γονὰν ἀραῖον ἐκβάλοι δόμων;
   κεκόλληται γένος πρὸς ἄτᾳ.
Κλ. ἐς τόνδ᾽ ἐνέβης ξὺν ἀληθείᾳ
   χρησμόν. (A. 1560–68)

CHORUS: This *reproach* has come to answer *reproach*, and it is difficult to judge.
Someone robs the robber, and the killer pays the penalty. It *awaits* the
doer to suffer while Zeus *awaits* on his throne, for it is the way things
work. Who would throw the accursed seed from the house? The race has
been affixed to ruin.

CLYTEMNESTRA: You came upon this prophecy *with truth*.

In the aftermath of Agamemnon's murder, this exchange between Clytemnestra
and the Chorus posits a cosmic system of reciprocity with Zeus as the overseer of
such a system. As in Pindar, the language signals expectations of equal repayment, but here it characterizes retributive violence rather than mutually beneficial exchange (ὄνειδος . . . ὀνείδους, 1560; ἐκτίνει, 1562; φέρει φέροντ᾽, 1562; μίμνει
δὲ μίμνοντος, 1563). Furthermore, Aeschylean tragedy emphasizes the temporal
dimension of reciprocity and payment/repayment—repayment occurs at some
point in the future.

As Clytemnestra acknowledges the inevitability of what the Chorus predict, her use of alētheia essentially reflects the plot of *Choephori*. There is an
extradramatic dimension to alētheia here, in that it signals what the truth
looks like not just for the characters within the drama but to the audience
observing it. The audience, familiar with the full myths, typically know more
about what will happen to the characters than they themselves do. But with
her admission here, Clytemnestra suggests that she possesses similar knowledge. This is a tendency of Aeschylus' female characters, as I will discuss in
subsequent chapters. I will explore further in chapter 6 how this passage
demonstrates the intersection of truth, gender, and reciprocity: a female
character articulates reciprocity emblematic of Aeschylean tragedy, which
she perceives and articulates as truth.

Conclusion

Both Pindar and Aeschylus stress the governing force of reciprocity in their works. They emphasize different aspects of reciprocity, but the language they use to articulate it is strikingly similar and reflects complementarity in their concepts of reciprocity despite their ostensibly contrasting poetic purposes. Pindar's focus is on the amicable reciprocity that governs his relationship to his patron, while Aeschylus' tendency is to conflate reciprocity with revenge and primarily focus on the latter—unsurprising, given tragedy's preoccupation with retaliation. But they each present reciprocity as a sovereign principle of their poetry and plots, and they use alētheia to mark this sovereignty. For both poets, alētheia denotes "what happens" and is intrinsically linked to reciprocity.

Pindar's uses of alētheia stress general principles of obligation that operate between poet and patron, as well as between the poet and truth. He presents alētheia as an entity with whom he has a mutually obligatory but also mutually beneficial relationship: the truth will guide his poetry, and he will tell the truth. This construction parallels the poet-patron relationship: the patron will provide payment, and in return Pindar will provide an ode. Furthermore, the patron must not only provide payment but also must perform a feat meriting the poet's praise. Thus the poet-patron relationship becomes intertwined with the poet-truth relationship, given that the poet must then depict the patron's accomplishment accurately as he praises it.

While both poets stress the symmetry and parity of reciprocal acts, Aeschylus puts greater emphasis on the similarities between amicable and hostile reciprocity. Just as Pindar uses repetitive language to focus on mutually beneficial partnerships, Aeschylus uses similar language to describe reciprocal violence. Furthermore, Aeschylus brings out the temporal continuity of reciprocity more so than Pindar does, and he uses alētheia to mark the reliability of the action-reaction pattern to occur over time. He can do so because, like Pindar, he uses alētheia to designate not only the accuracy of a speaker's account but also, more expansively, what happens over time, whether or not it is known or expressed by the speaker or addressee. The temporal dimension of alētheia is also causal. Present and future respond to the past as reactions do to previous actions. In Aeschylus, this temporal-causal sequence is articulated by the language of reciprocity and truth. When the Chorus warn Clytemnestra that she will suffer equivalent consequences for her actions, she acknowledges this prediction as alētheia. And when the Danaids construct their ode to Zeus Xenios, they, too, designate the ideals of reciprocal exchange as alētheia.

In the chapters that follow, I will continue to trace the interrelatedness of reciprocity and truth in Pindar and Aeschylus. I will also discuss gender and its significance for truth and reciprocity. In different but complementary ways Pindar and Aeschylus present their female characters as having creative functions that parallel poetic creativity. Furthermore, the creativity of these female characters is tied to the principles of reciprocity and truth that permeate the works of both poets. In Pindar female figures exhibit creative agency that puts them at odds with the ideals of reciprocity and truth governing the poet-patron relationships of epinician poetry. In Aeschylus female figures serve to articulate expectations of reciprocity in a way that makes them mouthpieces for a truth governed by reciprocity principles. Though they serve contrasting functions, ultimately female figures in both poets' works serve to shed light on the interrelationships between reciprocity and truth that animate Pindaric epinician and Aeschylean tragedy.

CHAPTER 2

The Truth of Reciprocity in Pindar's Myths

In this chapter I examine how Pindar's mythological digressions interact with the intertwining of reciprocity and truth in the outer praise narratives.[1] Such digressions reinforce the primary praise purpose of his odes, which is in part built on mutually beneficial reciprocal exchange between poet and patron.[2] As I discussed in the previous chapter, both Pindar and Aeschylus stress parity in their configurations of reciprocity. For Pindar, this parity is between participants in reciprocal relationships and between their deeds, while Aeschylus focuses more on symmetry of action and corresponding reaction. Pindar stresses reciprocity in both the outer praise narratives as well as his mythological digressions. Likewise, alētheia too runs through the mythological content of Pindar's epinicians, as a term that reflects and reinforces epinician reciprocity. Reciprocity and truth could present a conflict for the poet: his obligation to praise his patron and his claims to tell the truth might operate at cross-purposes.[3] According to one critic, Pindar reconciles this conflict by casting his relationship to the patron as one of guest-friendship: when he declares himself a guest-friend of the victor, he agrees to the obligation "(a) not to be envious of his *xenos* and (b) to speak well of him. The argumentation is: *Xenia* excludes envy, I am a *xenos*, therefore I am not envious and consequently praise

---

1. On the interactions between encomium, myths, and maxims in epinician poetry, see Felson 1984, 378–83.
2. As Bundy famously wrote, "there is no passage in Pindar and Bakkhulides that is not in its primary intent encomiastic—that is, designed to enhance the glory of a particular patron" (1986, 3).
3. Pratt 1993, 115, notes that epinician poetry claims to be truthful. See Lefkowitz 1991 and Morrison 2007, esp. 36–102, for a comprehensive discussion of the persona of Pindar.

honestly."[4] These observations show how Pindar prevents the potential charge of *anti*-patron bias. But the guest-friendship construction gives rise to the problem of *pro*-patron bias: does the poet's friendship with—and obligation to—his patron produce praise at the expense of truth?

Pindar resolves this potential conflict by making the case that truth and praise not only complement but also mutually reinforce one another.[5] As I discussed in the previous chapter, Pindar harmonizes his dual devotions to his patron and to truth by defining both his relationship to his patron and his duty to the truth in terms of reciprocal obligation. The models of exchange that ground the poet-patron relationship also provide the basis for the relationship between the poet and truth. Furthermore, Pindar harnesses the ambiguities of alētheia to intertwine his two obligations to praise and to truth. He presents his praise as truthful not only in spite of his obligation to the victor but even *because* of it, and thus fulfills his encomiastic duties while making a claim to veracity.

To make this argument Pindar deploys his mythological exempla both to reinforce his models of reciprocity and truth and to provide contrasting negative examples. Reciprocity and truth are especially foregrounded in the mythological digressions of *Olympian* 10, *Olympian* 1, and *Nemean* 7. In *Olympian* 10, the themes of reciprocity, obligation, and symmetry are laid out in the poem's invocation and echoed in the myth of Heracles and Augeas, which illustrates by negative example the sanctity of reciprocity. In *Olympian* 1 Pindar uses the myth of Tantalus and Pelops to present complicated ideas about the relationship between poetry and truth. Ultimately he adopts a critical attitude toward falsehood and deception and equates praise with truth. The chapter culminates in a reading of *Nemean* 7, which presents an argument that epinician, because it is shaped by the reciprocal obligations between poet and patron, accommodates truthful discourse more readily than other types of poetry.[6] Pindar takes a critical attitude to poets—specifically Homer—who do not serve truth and

---

4. Slater 1979, 80.
5. Segal 1986a, 66, informed by Detienne 1967, 24–26. Segal observes that Pindar "strives to create a poetry of truth and praise," but focuses less on the difficulty of reconciling praise and truth and more on myths of creation as metaphors for poetic art.
6. Nicholson 2016, 8–10, also notes that *Nemeans* 7 and 8 and *Olympian* 1 are similar in their criticisms of other poetic traditions. Most of the material in this chapter comes from my 2013 article in *Classical Quarterly*, revised and updated for this book. In the time since then, Dr. Nicholson and I have become more acquainted with each other's work, which has been mutually enriched as a result (Nigel Nicholson, e-mail message to author, June 17, 2018).

praise.[7] He implies that because they are not bound by obligation to a patron, such poets irresponsibly privilege audience reaction over accuracy. Ultimately Pindar presents an equivalence between truth and praise that is a function of the reciprocal relationship between the poet and his patron, one that obligates the poet to praise.

Olympian *10: Truth, Obligation, and Reciprocity*

As I discussed in the previous chapter, Pindar lays out the importance of symmetry and parity in the invocation to *Olympian* 10. The ode celebrates Hagesidamus for his 476 BCE victory in boys' boxing, and, if we are to believe these opening words, it is overdue.[8] Pindar assumes a compensatory, reparative stance, presenting the ode as an apology and form of redress for the laudandus whom he casts as a guest-friend (ἀλιτόξενον, 6). He invokes Alatheia (4) as a corrective force against his forgetfulness (ἐπιλέλαθ᾽, 3), capitalizing on their shared root (lath-) and on the parity implied in xenia to bring out the symmetries that animate the ode, symmetries between poet and patron and between truth and poetic representation of it. This kind of wordplay typifies both Pindar's and Aeschylus' presentations of reciprocity as they emphasize the correspondence between action and reciprocal reaction. Here Pindar presents reciprocity as a framework that will structure his praise poem in such a way that both his patron and truth will be served.

A negative example for these symmetries and the dual obligations they reflect comes out in the embedded myth of Augeas and Heracles, in which Pindar presents a corrupted version of the xenia he shares with his patron.[9] The relationship between Augeas and Heracles is supposedly premised on xenia but quickly unravels thanks to Augeas' failure to uphold the principles of truth and truthfulness that are fundamental to reciprocal relationships. According to Pin-

---

7. Gentili 1981, 219. Gentili, apropos of Fr. 205, concludes that the poet-patron relationship does not preclude an absolute respect for truth but welcomes silence over unpleasant truths. I would argue more forcefully for Pindar's truthful stance, since he presents epinician as an inherently more truthful genre because of the relationship between poet and patron. Pindar does seemingly evade telling the truth in N. 5.16–18, but as I will argue in chapter 3, he does not reject alētheia but rather refrains from excessive detail.

8. The ode may also engage polemically and intertextually with an oral tradition celebrating a more famous victor; see Nicholson 2016, 99–149.

9. For discussion of various other connections between the mythological digression and Pindar's poetics, see Spelman 2018, 196–203.

dar, Augeas withholds payment from Heracles (λάτριον . . . μισθόν, "servile pay," 29), thus undermining the guest-host relationship between them by deceiving him (ξεναπάτας, "guest-friend betrayer," 34).[10] The presence of deception within such a relationship is a theme that also resounds in many of Pindar's depictions of mythical female figures, as I will discuss in the next chapter. Augeas illustrates the importance of the ideals presented in the ode's opening by undermining them. That he reneges on payment recalls the poet's references to his debt and repayment to his patron (ὀφείλων, 3; τόκος, 9). Similarly, Pindar's characterization of Augeas' broken promise resonates with the accusations against himself that he hopes to deflect: both are cast as violating guest-friendship (ξεναπάτας, 34; ἀλιτόξενον, 6). The resonance activates a contrast between Augeas, who deceives his guest-friend, and the poet, who balks at charges of doing so and brings truth into his guest-host relationship. Like the poet and his patron, Heracles and Augeas are xenoi whose relationship is premised on parity and on payment in good faith, and their relationship suffers in the violation of these ideals. The poet's earlier invocation of Alatheia (4) for her protective guidance can now be read as an element missing from the relationship between Augeas and Heracles.

Pindar reinforces this contrast by faulting Augeas not only for his failure to pay but also for his *unwillingness* to do so, juxtaposed against Heracles' own willingness to perform the task: ὡς Αὐγέαν λάτριον | ἀέκονθ' ἑκὼν μισθὸν ὑπέρβιον | πράσσοιτο ("so that [Heracles], a *willing* man, might exact his payment for service from Augeas, *unwilling* and *powerful*," 28–30). This sentiment recalls the spirit of willingness with which Pindar has defined his own relationship with his patron (φίλαν . . . ἐς χάριν, 12), while the adjective ὑπέρβιον echoes an earlier characterization of Heracles (τράπε δὲ Κύκνεια Μάχα καὶ ὑπέρβιον Ἡρακλέα, "The battle with Cygnus turned back even *powerful* Heracles," 15). Here, its application is ambiguous: it refers to Augeas or to the pay he owes Heracles (μισθόν),[11] thus characterizing Augeas either directly or metonymically. The use of this term for both Heracles and Augeas stresses the association between them and indicts the latter all the more for his mistreatment of the former.[12] Likewise, the wordplay in ἀέκονθ' ἑκὼν parallels the wordplay of

---

10. Detienne 1996, 107–34, notes that Pindar's poetic contemporaries were beginning to make a conscious choice between alētheia and apatē.
11. Fitzgerald 1987, 119–20, cited and discussed by Nicholson 2016, 117n48 and 129n90. The term ὑπέρβιος appears in the odes only in *O.* 10, although, as Nicholson points out, it is one of many ὑπερ- adjectives in Pindaric epinician (2016, 62n39).
12. In the context of Nicholson's argument, the description of Heracles as "overmighty" is part of

ἐπιλέλαθ' and Ἀλάθεια in the ode's opening (3–4) and underscores the expected parity and the actual disparity between Heracles' and Augeas' dispositions. The phrase evokes but adapts instances of polyptoton that emphasize reciprocity, as I have discussed, thus elucidating both the symmetrical reciprocity expected of a guest and host and the failure of Augeas to fulfill this expectation.[13] Augeas is the archetypal corrupted guest-friend who is unwilling to keep promises to a friend of equal stature and whom Pindar hopes not to emulate.

Through the myth of Heracles and Augeas Pindar illustrates a commitment to xenia, the obligations of which are not only between guest and host but also, and more importantly, to the gods who govern this system of hospitality. Augeas' disregard of xenia results in the destruction of his homeland and his death at the hands of Heracles (*Olympian* 10.34–42), who later establishes a precinct for Zeus in Augeas' former kingdom (43–45). The establishment of this sacred precinct is the ultimate response to Augeas' guest-cheating and signals the triumph not only of Heracles, but also of Zeus, whose concern for xenia is implied in the opening invocation to his daughter Alatheia as someone who will protect the poet from charges of guest-cheating (4–6). Furthermore, Pindar connects Heracles' actions to alētheia, when he proclaims Time as a witness and characterizes it as the "sole tester of genuine truth" (ὅ τ' ἐξελέγχων μόνος | ἀλάθειαν ἐτήτυμον, 53–54).[14] He goes on to credit Time with telling the story of Heracles' founding of the Olympics (57–59), thus associating truth with the athletic contest he celebrates in this ode.[15] Furthermore, he casts the games as an act of reverence for Zeus and by extension for the principles of xenia that Zeus protects. He thus brings alētheia once again under the umbrella of reciprocity, a relationship that he sets forth in the invocation to Alatheia and reinforces with the mythological digression here.

The collocation of xenia, truth, and Zeus further connects the mythological digression to the outer praise narrative, which mutually reinforce one another. While the poet's duties are ostensibly to his patron first and foremost, his invo-

---

Olympian 10's largely critical stance toward him (Nicholson 2016, 129n90), an interpretation that is attractive but with which I do not fully accord, as my discussion in this chapter makes clear.

13. E.g., φιλέων φιλέοντ', ἄγων ἄγοντα προφρόνως, *Pythian* 10.66; ἄρχοντί τ' ἄρχων καὶ κασιγνήτῳ κάσις, | ἐχθρὸς σὺν ἐχθρῷ στήσομαι, A., *Th.* 674–75.

14. On the significance of ἔτυμος and ἀλήθεια here, see Nicholson 2016, 120, who follows Nagy 1990, 421–22 in arguing that the collocation of the two terms "preserves and merges the local and the Panhellenic." Cf. Kurke 2013, 139, on Pindar's general concern to preserve local specificities. On the role of time with respect to the two types of truth in *Olympian* 10, see Kromer 1976, esp. 433. See also Gerber 1962 on time in Pindar.

15. Comparable to *O.* 8.1–2, discussed in the previous chapter.

cation to Alatheia implies an obligation partly to her, thus opening the possibility of obligations other than those to the laudandus.[16] Later in the ode he names
Zeus as his motivation for singing: ἀγῶνα δ' ἐξαίρετον ἀεῖσαι θέμιτες ὦρσαν
Διός ("The ordinances of Zeus prompt me to sing the choice contest," 24). His
obligation to his patron is set by divine rule (θέμιτες) governed by Zeus himself
and is therefore part of a duty larger than the reciprocity between poet and
laudandus, since failure to uphold this obligation is tantamount to defiance of
Zeus. The specific relationships between Zeus, xenia, and themis are laid out in
Olympian 8.21–30:

> ἔνθα σώτειρα Διὸς ξενίου
> πάρεδρος ἀσκεῖται Θέμις
> ἔξοχ' ἀνθρώπων. ὅ τι γὰρ πολὺ καὶ πολλᾷ ῥέπῃ,
> ὀρθᾷ διακρῖναι φρενὶ μὴ παρὰ καιρὸν
> δυσπαλές· τεθμὸς δέ τις ἀθανάτων καὶ τάνδ' ἁλιερκέα χώραν
> παντοδαποῖσιν ὑπέστασε ξένοις
> κίονα δαιμονίαν—
> ὁ δ' ἐπαντέλλων χρόνος
> τοῦτο πράσσων μὴ κάμοι—
> Δωριεῖ λαῷ ταμιευομέναν ἐξ Αἰακοῦ.

[Aigina,] where Savior Themis, the partner of Zeus Xenios is honored more
than among other men. For when much swings in the balance in many directions, it is difficult to judge appropriately with a straight mind. Some ordinance
of the gods set even this sea-girt land for strangers of all kinds as a divine
pillar—and may time as it rises up not grow weary of doing this—a land kept in
trust for the Dorian people since the time of Aeacus.

Themis personified is the associate of Zeus Xenios. These lines explain xenia as
a system instituted by gods for men, whose careful observation of xenia-
relationships constitutes service to the gods Themis and Zeus.[17]

This structure of obligation reinforces the opening of *Olympian* 10, where

---

16. MacLachlan 1993, 101, senses a similar servile tone toward Alatheia in Fr. 205: "As *alatheia* served
    the sovereign Olympia in proving/revealing victors (*O.* 8.1–2), so the poet serves the queen
    Alatheia in giving an accurate testimony of the victory event."

17. In the context of *Olympian* 8, these associations have the additional significance of invoking the
    victor's home of Aegina, renowned for its hospitality. See Athanassaki 2010 for an argument situ-
    ating this ode in the context of the rivalry between Athens and Aegina.

Pindar calls on Alatheia as Zeus' daughter to oversee his poetic and personal responsibilities. Alatheia presides over the poet's many interconnected obligations, to the victor and to Zeus, while also validating the content of his ode. In balancing truth and reciprocal obligation, *Olympian* 10 harmonizes dual and potentially conflicting duties and intertwines truth with reciprocity. The myth of Heracles and Augeas serves as an illustrative example of the violation of this ideal. Through the figure of Augeas Pindar shows us the archetypal bad xenos, one who cheats his fellow xenos and suffers the consequences therefrom. Heracles' destructive actions are a retaliatory response to this violation, while his establishment of a precinct for Zeus restores the respect for xenia that Augeas disregarded. Associating the founding of this precinct with the truth revealed by time (53–59) collocates alētheia with xenia just as the opening invocation to Alatheia did, blending truth and reciprocity as mutually reinforcing principles.[18] Pindar's personification of truth as the overseer of his duties creates a poetic framework in which he can fulfill his duty to produce a praise poem while precluding any charges of bias toward his patron, thus presenting a true account. The myth of Heracles and Augeas reinforces this harmonization.

Truth, Praise, and Poetic Obligation in Olympian 1

Olympian 1 also presents the potential conflicts of truth and praise and resolves them by situating both under the umbrella of reciprocity. One of the most famous of Pindar's odes, *Olympian* 1 celebrates Hieron of Syracuse's 476 BCE victory in the single-horse race. In the ode Pindar suggests that truth and praise are complementary and analogous to one another. He does so through the embedded myth of Tantalus and Pelops, which he revises from its traditional version that Tantalus slaughtered Pelops and and served him to the gods (36, 46–52).[19] Instead he claims that Pelops was abducted by a besotted Poseidon, at a dinner hosted by Tantalus to which the gods were invited (25–27, 40–41). What Pindar foregrounds in his alternative myth is a celebration of reciprocity, here between god and mortal: Tantalus' dinner is repayment for a similar kindness (ἀμοιβαῖα θεοῖσι δεῖπνα παρέχων, "providing dinner for the gods in

---

18. See Liapis 2020, 16, for the relationship between time and truth in *Olympian* 10 and the evolution of time as an "integrative force."
19. On Pindar's revisions in *Olympian* 1, see Howie 1983; Hubbard 1987; McLaughlin 2004; Morgan 2015, 234–50; Nagy 1986.

return," *O.* 1.39). This reciprocity parallels the reciprocity between the poet and his patron Hieron, whom he describes as a host (ξένον, 103) at whose hearth and table poets congregate (10–17).[20]

Within these intertwined narratives of reciprocity, between gods and mortals in myth and between poets and patrons in praise odes, Pindar embeds a complicated argument about reciprocal obligation and truth. He asserts that accounts constrained by concerns for one's host can nevertheless coexist with truth. The truth he presents is shaped by the obligations of reciprocity, between his mythical characters and between poet and patron. This may seem like a less than satisfactory conception of truth, but in showing us how reciprocity governs it, Pindar resolves the potential conflicts between obligatory praise and truthful account.

Pindar rewrites the myth of Tantalus and Pelops in such a way as to claim that truthful accounts can accord with pious ones. He prompts us to draw parallels between the obligation to the gods of the mythological digression and the obligation to his patron that stems from their relationship as xenoi and forms the basis of his praise narrative. Thus he invites us to derive conclusions about the congruence between truth and praise informed by his claims about truth and piety. Piety and epinician praise are analogous. Both involve expressing reverence and avoiding offense lest goodwill—the gods' or the patron's—be lost. Both piety and praise are, in Pindar's presentation, communicated by poets. Finally, both present the poet with potentially conflicting obligations between reverence and truth that he must negotiate: his poem will be ineffective and unbelievable if it appears to worship or praise blindly at the expense of truth. Pindar presents a case that the obligations stemming from poet-patron reciprocity do not hinder his depiction of truth but, rather, reinforce it. In part he is able to make this questionable argument by acknowledging that the aesthetic aspects of poetry are not inherently conducive to truth-telling and in fact may lend themselves to the opposite. By expressing awareness of this potential pitfall Pindar implicitly provides assurance that his own poetry will avoid it. He thus builds credibility for his own poetry as a vehicle for truth.

Pindar's reference to alētheia occurs in the mythological digression on Tantalus and Pelops, through which he raises complicated points about poetic aesthetics and truth that are applicable to the obligations of both piety and praise.

---

20. For rich discussion of the various and intertwined reciprocities that operate in *Olympian* 1, see Burgess 1993 and Morgan 2015, 223–25.

The way Pindar presents this myth privileges piety above all else, but in such a way that piety and truth complement one another. The myth enables the poet to make a case that piety and truth can work in tandem. This argument in turn has implications for the outer praise narrative. The harmony of truth and piety that Pindar presents in this myth resonates with the delicate balance he must strike in the outer praise narrative between lauding his patron and presenting a true account.

Pindar asserts that the traditional version has been shaped by the mortal tendency to believe what is pleasant:

τοῦ μεγασθενὴς ἐράσσατο Γαιάοχος
Ποσειδάν, ἐπεί νιν καθαροῦ λέβητος ἔξελε Κλωθώ,
ἐλέφαντι φαίδιμον ὦμον κεκαδμένον.
ἦ θαύματα πολλά, καί πού τι καὶ βροτῶν φάτις ὑπὲρ τὸν ἀλαθῆ λόγον
δεδαιδαλμένοι ψεύδεσι ποικίλοις ἐξαπατῶντι μῦθοι·
Χάρις δ᾽, ἅπερ ἅπαντα τεύχει τὰ μείλιχα θνατοῖς,
ἐπιφέροισα τιμὰν καὶ ἄπιστον ἐμήσατο πιστὸν
ἔμμεναι τὸ πολλάκις·
ἁμέραι δ᾽ ἐπίλοιποι
μάρτυρες σοφώτατοι. (*Olympian* 1.25–34)

The mighty Earth-holder Poseidon fell in love with him when Clotho took him out of the pure cauldron, distinct for his gleaming ivory shoulder. Indeed, there are many wonders, and somehow the speeches of mortals, stories, have been embellished beyond the true account and deceive with intricate falsities;[21] for Charis, who provides mortals with all pleasant things, often makes something untrustworthy credible by bringing honor. But future days are the most skilled witnesses.

Pindar's alternative version has Pelops born from a cauldron with an ivory shoulder; these details allude to the more traditional one, that Pelops had been butchered and boiled in a cauldron but was almost completely reconstructed by

---

21. As many scholars have argued, pseudos can refer to fiction in the sense of an authorial creation that seems feasible but is known not to have happened. The extent to which the concept of fiction existed during this period is a matter of some debate. For further discussion see Finkelberg 1998; Gill and Wiseman 1993; Konstan 1998, 3–17; Lowe 2000, 259–72; and Rösler 1980, 283–319. On these lines in particular, see Ledbetter 2003, 68–70, who argues that "Pindar decidedly lacks any notion of poetic fiction" (69).

the gods but for his shoulder, which had to be replaced with ivory. The enmesh-
ing of the two versions sets the stage for what follows. Pindar distinguishes the
traditional version from the "true account" (τὸν ἀλαθῆ λόγον, 28) and suggests
that the traditional version originated from embellishments of the true account
that accrued over time. In so doing he posits a filiation between falsehood
(ψεύδεσι, 29) and truth. The wordplay in ἄπιστον . . . πιστόν ("[makes] something untrustworthy credible," 31) further suggests this filiation, the alpha-
privative bringing out both the directly oppositional nature of the terms as well
as their shared root.

He attributes the credibility of these false accounts to the power of Charis,
a personification of grace or charm.[22] Here the associations of charis with perception and reputation are suggestive of the aesthetically compelling aspects of
poetry.[23] As critical readers would observe, these lines thus present a problem
for the poet since they assert that poetic skill can "bring honor" (ἐπιφέροισα
τιμάν, 31) to something that does not merit it. Pindar could be perceived as
praising poetry's potential to deceive. As Douglas Gerber notes, "Even though
Pindar is critical of the false tales recorded by earlier poets, he is at the same
time praising the power of poetry to make 'the unbelievable believable.'"[24]
Indeed, Pindar provides little explicit assurance that his own poetry does not
also espouse persuasion and artistry at the expense of truth; these lines could
be read as a playful, even noncommittal, attitude to the truth, akin to what
Hesiod's Muses convey in *Th.* 26–28.[25]

But Pindar's recognition of the deceptive potential of charis along with his
implied criticism of poets who might exploit it provides assurances of his own
credibility. By stressing the singularity of "the true account" (τὸν ἀλαθῆ λόγον,
28) with the definite article τόν, he communicates his own knowledge of such
an account and his ability to discern what is true from what is false. Likewise,
his explanation of how poetry elicits belief demonstrates his awareness of its
rhetorical powers and suggests his intention not to capitalize on them for
untruthful ends.

---

22. Slater 1969, s.v. "χάρις," 2.a.
23. Gildersleeve 1885, 132 *ad* 30; Instone 1996, 101 *ad* 30; Kirkwood 1982, 52; Verdenius 1988, 20 *ad*
    30. I should note that Pindar attributes the false Pelops myth to two parties: here he faults his
    poetic predecessors for embellishment to the point of falsehood; later he charges intentional
    falsehood on the part of Pelops' envious neighbors (46–51). And as Morgan 2015, 236, points out,
    even in this passage, although Pindar must at least partially be referring to poetry, he does not do
    so explicitly, instead generalizing to mortal speech more broadly.
24. Gerber 1982, 59. See also Pratt 1993, 124.
25. See Athanassaki 2004, 339–41, who similarly sees these lines as responsive to Hesiod's Muses.

His reference to charis, too, hints at the argument he will ultimately make, that the obligations of reciprocity serve to ground poetry from straying into falsehood. Not only does charis designate poetry's charms, it also signals the spirit of mutual goodwill fundamental to relationships of reciprocity (e.g., *O.* 8.8, 10.12; *P.* 1.76, 2.17). Leslie Kurke asserts that charis always designates a willing, reciprocal exchange.[26] Such a meaning explains its function here: poetry's charms are part of its gift, both to its subject and to its audience. Reinforcing this implication of reciprocity is the wordplay of ἄπιστον . . . πιστόν (31), which parallels similar wordplays that emphasize reciprocity, its expectation of parity, and the actual disparity that occurs in corrupted reciprocity (see *O.* 10.29, discussed above). With the multiple evocations of charis, these lines hint at the potential conflict between reciprocal obligation and truth, the potential of poetry to distort, and—the argument Pindar ultimately makes—the potential of reciprocity to clarify.

The next sentence provides further suggestions about Pindar's perceived role: ἔστι δ' ἀνδρὶ φάμεν ἐοικὸς ἀμφὶ δαιμόνων καλά· μείων γὰρ αἰτία ("It is fitting for a man to say good things about the gods, for the blame is less," 35). His rather blunt prioritizing of the gods' approval seems to conflict with his earlier reverence for the true account (τὸν ἀλαθῆ λόγον, 28). Yet both concerns, for piety and for truth, govern his poetry and are connected by the interceding aphorism about the revelatory effects of time (ἀμέραι δ' ἐπίλοιποι | μάρτυρες σοφώτατοι, "future days are the most skilled witnesses," 33–34). The conjoining of these two concerns suggests that a true account is ultimately controlled by the gods it portrays, since Pindar expresses the dual motivations of providing a true account while simultaneously pleasing the gods. Line 35 has been interpreted as Pindar's unwillingness to privilege truth-telling above piety.[27] This reading seems fitting in light of Pindar's later refusal to speak ill of the gods for the lack of gain he will incur for it (ἐμοὶ δ' ἄπορα γαστρίμαργον μακάρων τιν' εἰπεῖν· ἀφίσταμαι· | ἀκέρδεια λέλογχεν θαμινὰ κακαγόρους, "It is impossible for me to say that any of the blessed gods is gluttonous—I hold back; lack of gain often obtains slanderers as its lot," 52–53). But this statement must be read in light of this earlier passage that conjoins truth and praise, thus precluding

---

26. Kurke 1991, 67. See also Nagy 1990, 198, who describes charis as "a beautiful and pleasurable reciprocity that is simultaneously material and transcendent in nature."

27. Pratt 1993, 126: "Here again Pindar does not justify his refusal to speak ill of the gods by appealing to the truth or to what the gods deserve." See also Burgess 1993, 38–39. See Köhnken 1974 for an argument that Pindar's innovations stem from concerns about poetic composition rather than religious piety.

possible tension between the two.[28] His criticism of inaccuracy in others' poetry makes it unlikely that he would risk inviting such criticism of his own. Rather, it is more likely that he conceives of his own poetry as a balance and integration of truth and piety, thus implying that truth coincides with what is appropriate to say about the gods.[29]

Further, Pindar does not actually omit the traditional version entirely but incorporates it into his account.[30] In doing so, he adopts a stance like that of Stesichorus, whose alternative Helen myth allows for a double-truth:

οὐκ ἔστ᾽ ἔτυμος λόγος οὗτος·
οὐδ᾽ ἔβας ἐν νηυσὶν εὐσέλμοις
οὐδ᾽ ἵκεο πέργαμα Τροίας. (Plato, *Phaedrus* 243a = Finglass 91a = *PMG* 192)

This story is not true. You did not go in well-benched ships, nor did you arrive at the towers of Troy.

According to Plato's *Phaedrus*, the source for this fragment, Stesichorus had been blinded for an earlier poem telling the traditional tale of Helen. Upon recanting that earlier version, he regains his sight.[31] Other fragmentary evidence tells us that the *Palinode* proceeded to detail the real Helen's departure

---

28. Pratt 1993, 126–27, cites this passage as well as *O.* 9.35–41 and *N.* 5.14–17 as further evidence that Pindar values tact and appropriateness above truth. At *O.* 9.35–41 Pindar asserts that to slander the gods is hateful and inappropriate (παρὰ καιρόν, *O.* 9.38), which I would argue reinforces my interpretation of *O.* 1.28–35: Pindar construes piety and truth-telling as complementary and uses the language of tact (ἐοικός, καιρός) to bridge the potential gap between the two. I discuss the *Nemean* 5 passage in the next chapter.

29. A similar point is made by Ledbetter 2003, 70: "in the divine realm, what is morally appropriate coincides with what is true." Hubbard 1987, 14–15, too, sees Pindar's presentation of poetry as positive here, given its "polymorphic transformative potential"; he sees the cooking of Pelops as a metaphor for the poetic process (16).

30. Köhnken 1974, 200–201, observes that Pindar goes into significant detail about Tantalus' meal to the gods. See Nagy 1986, who argues that the juxtaposition of the two myths signals that both are traditional.

31. Isocrates gives us further information about the tradition surrounding the *Palinode* (Isocrates, *Helen* 64 = Davies and Finglass 91c = *PMG* 192) and suggests that it was part of a longer ode that included the traditional Helen myth (i.e., Stesichorus' *Helen*); see Kannicht 1969 vol. 1, 28–29; Kelly 2007; Pratt 1993, 134n6; Sider 1989; Woodbury 1967, 168n24; *contra* Finglass 2015, 93–96. D'Alfonso 1993–1994 reconciles the two views. Another source indicates that Stesichorus composed not just one but two *Palinodes*, blaming Homer and Hesiod, respectively, for their faulty accounts of the Helen myth (P.Oxy. 2506 fr. 26 col. 1 = Davies and Finglass 90 = *PMG* 193); see Cingano 1982 and Massimilla 1990; *contra* Bowie 1993, 24–25; Kelly 2007; Leone 1964; Podlecki 1971, 321–25; Woodbury 1967, 158–60.

for Egypt while an image (eidōlon) of her goes to Troy in her stead.[32] Stesichorus initiates (or perhaps simply takes advantage of) an alternative mythological tradition later adapted by Euripides in *Helen* and by Herodotus as well (2.113–20).

Like *Olympian* 1, the *Palinode* raises questions about the nature of truth and its relationship to poetry. Helen herself is said to have restored Stesichorus' sight after he denies the truth of the traditional (Homeric) version (οὐκ . . . ἔτυμος), which has angered her. Thus what the poet labels as true and not true is shaped by Helen's concern for her reputation—truth is informed not primarily by objective accuracy but rather by what is pleasing or acceptable to its subject. In other words, the suitability for its particular context can affect whether a poem is deemed true.[33] Furthermore, the *Palinode* is not a wholesale dismissal of the Homeric account; Stesichorus does not claim that the Trojan War never occurred at all, just that it revolved around an illusion rather than the real Helen. By replacing Homer's Helen with a cloud, Stesichorus provides an explanation for how both his own account and the events at Troy could have occurred simultaneously.[34] His alternative tradition thus provides a way for both versions of the Helen myth to be valid in some way.[35] Likewise, in *Olympian* 1 Pindar enfolds the traditional version of the Pelops myth into his own, thus acknowledging the greater familiarity of the former while preserving the validity of the latter, which is tightly circumscribed and specific to his praise purposes.[36] For both Stesichorus and Pindar, their proposed alternatives do not completely replace previous ones, yet both poets claim veracity for their alternatives. Finally, for both poets, their alternative truths allow them to remain pious, thus

32. For a summary of the sources, see Bassi 1993, 52. For the probable content of Stesichorus' *Helen* poems see Kelly 2007 and Finglass 2015, 93–96.

33. See Beecroft 2006, 48–49, who argues that the first line of the fragment "situates the *Palinode* within a complex network of ideas concerning truth and lies, fictionality and narrative . . . [it] is deceptively simple, and each word within this line, when understood within the context of the song culture of which it is a part, is freighted with programmatic significance." Beecroft continues with an analysis of each word in the line, including *etētumos*, which denotes statements whose truth-value reflects efficaciousness in local myth and ritual (Beecroft 2006, 66); see also Nagy 1990, 421–92.

34. Bassi 1993, 58. See also Woodbury 1967, 165–68, who sees the *Palinode* as a way of reconciling the Homeric tradition, which presents Helen in a sympathetic light, with the emerging view castigating Helen for her responsibility in causing the war.

35. For further discussions of the *Palinode* and its implications for truth and poetry, see Austin 1994, 2–17 and 90–117; Bassi 1993; Beecroft 2006; and Park 2017.

36. See Morgan 2015, 235: "The introductory sentence accommodates both versions of the myth. It seems at first to conform to the cannibalistic version, but in retrospect we can understand it (if we choose) as part of the purified version."

benefiting poets and poetic subjects alike. They balance their own welfare with that of the subjects of their poetry.

For Pindar this balance ultimately lends credibility to his praise of the laudandus. He harmonizes his allegiance to truth with his desire not to offend the gods. Defining truth in such a way may not be believable or satisfactory to modern readers, as other critics have pointed out.[37] But it allows for poetic obligation to coincide with truthful reporting. Thus Pindar creates a context in which truth and piety can coexist. These juxtaposed claims of truth and piety have implications for Pindar's similar declaration of loyalty to his laudandus Hieron, since they suggest that loyalty to one's subject provides a basis for a true account.[38] The poet's admonishments about Charis, pseudos, and embellishment reflect a consciousness of poetry's persuasiveness and assure us that his poem will not deploy them to the same effect.

He is consequently able to characterize his own ode as an embellishment of Hieron's qualities with no loss of credibility:

ἐμὲ δὲ στεφανῶσαι
κεῖνον ἱππίῳ νόμῳ
Αἰοληΐδι μολπᾷ
χρή· πέποιθα δὲ ξένον
μή τιν' ἀμφότερα καλῶν τε ἴδριν ἅμα καὶ δύναμιν κυριώτερον
τῶν γε νῦν κλυταῖσι δαιδαλωσέμεν ὕμνων πτυχαῖς. (100–105)

I must crown that man with a horse-melody in the Aeolic mode. I trust that there is no xenos alive today to embellish with glorious folds of songs who is both knowledgeable of good things and more authoritative in power.

The language of embellishment (δαιδαλωσέμεν, 105) recalls his characterization of deceptive stories (δεδαιδαλμένοι, 28), but his poetry fundamentally differs in that it is composed in full awareness of its powers and its aims. Because he is mindful of charis and its effects and he composes poetry with a concern for his xenos-patron, Pindar is safe from the pseudea that riddle other accounts. Whereas false accounts are created and propagated by those who are not similarly conscious of poetry's effects nor loyal to their subject, Pindar openly

---

37. Pratt (1993, 123–26) discusses the problems of Pindar's claims in O. 1 and argues, along with Gerber (1982, 59–60), that Pindar's praise of poetry's power to persuade, albeit by deception (1.28–32) suggests that his own poetry could be persuasive but untrue.
38. Burgess 1993, 41, reads Hieron as a direct parallel for the gods.

expresses his obligations to his patron Hieron (χρή, 103; ξένον, 103) just as he has to the gods (ἔστι δ᾿ ἀνδρὶ φάμεν ἐοικὸς ἀμφὶ δαιμόνων καλά· μείων γὰρ αἰτία, 35); these obligations will keep his poetry grounded in and centered on its epinician purpose rather than distracted by aesthetic concerns. The reference to Hieron as a xenos caps the argument the poet has thus far been implying, that reciprocity can foster truth and is indeed conducive to doing so.

Olympian 1 suggests how epinician poetry might fashion a distinctive means for representing the truth. Alētheia informs the poet's duty to his subject matter, and his statements about poetry intertwine truth with reciprocal obligation and reconcile—indeed, even equate—the two. Olympian 1 presents a Pindaric notion of truthfulness that balances external reality—that is, an empirically verifiable circumstance or event—with internal, subjective concerns by claiming that a true account must take into consideration one's obligation to one's subject. In his praise Pindar combines truth and reciprocity as two objectives of epinician truth-telling, thus lending authority to his praise poetry. He declares his devotion to his patron while mitigating his pro-patron bias, incorporating both reciprocal obligation and objectivity into his poetic program.

Parity, Reality, and Poetry: Nemean 7

While *Olympian* 1 presents truth and reciprocal obligation as complements, *Nemean* 7 presents reciprocal obligation as necessary for producing truthful accounts. The ode, of unknown date, celebrates the victory of Sogenes in the boys' pentathlon and digresses to the contest between Odysseus and Ajax over Achilles' arms and to the story of Achilles' son Neoptolemus. Pindar lays out an explicit call for parity between word and deed that parallels the symmetry between poet and patron xenoi. Both in the outer praise narratives and in the embedded myth of Odysseus and Ajax, the poet urges symmetry between reality and its verbal representation; the suicide of Ajax exemplifies the deadly consequences when such symmetry is absent. Furthermore, Pindar intertwines this symmetry with poet-patron parity, making the case that poet-patron reciprocity is what produces true and accurate poetry. As in *Olympian* 1, he draws a contrast between his own poetry and that of others, specifically Homer's, which he criticizes for its skewed priorities.[39] *Nemean* 7 presents the duty of

---

39. Spelman 2018, 217 and 277, argues that references to Homer in *Nemean* 7 belong in the larger context of Pindar's presumption of his audience's knowledge of poetic precedent.

poetry to represent reality and proposes the reciprocity-bound obligations of epinician poetry as the best conditions for this purpose.[40]

In *Nemean 7* Pindar calls for a correspondence between word and deed that reflects and is even embedded in the symmetry of reciprocity, or, more precisely, in the configurations of reciprocity typical of Pindaric epinician and Aeschylean tragedy. Pindar avoids ostensible bias and validates his truth-telling claims partly by intertwining the reciprocal obligations of the poet-patron relationship with an obligation to represent the truth. He makes numerous claims to truth (68–69, 77–79), all the while openly expressing his duties to the laudandus (33–34, 61, 75–76). He is able to reconcile his obligation to the victor with his truth-telling rhetoric by making the case that the poet's obligation to his patron coincides with the obligation to truth that should inform poetry. Poet-patron reciprocity is what yields truth.

Nemean 7 begins with an invocation to Eleithyia as the goddess who enables human existence, which is described in terms of light and darkness (ἄνευ σέθεν | οὐ φάος, οὐ μέλαιναν δρακέντες εὐφρόναν | τεὰν ἀδελφεὰν ἐλάχομεν ἀγλαόγυιον Ἥβαν, "Without you, neither light nor black night do we see, nor do we receive your beautiful-limbed sister Hebe," 2–4).[41] Thus begins the pervasive language of vision in the poem, which is connected to the poet's message about the effects of poetry. The poet later describes its illuminative function:

εἰ δὲ τύχῃ τις ἔρδων, μελίφρον' αἰτίαν
ῥοαῖσι Μοισᾶν ἐνέβαλε· ταὶ μεγάλαι γὰρ ἀλκαί
σκότον πολὺν ὕμνων ἔχοντι δεόμεναι·
ἔργοις δὲ καλοῖς ἔσοπτρον ἴσαμεν ἑνὶ σὺν τρόπῳ,
εἰ Μναμοσύνας ἕκατι λιπαράμπυκος
εὕρηται ἄποινα μόχθων κλυταῖς ἐπέων ἀοιδαῖς. (12–16)

If someone happens to do well, he throws a pleasing cause in the streams of the Muses, for great, valiant actions have much darkness when they lack songs. We know the mirror of good deeds through one means only, if, by the will of Mnemosyne with her bright headband, someone finds reward for his toils in the famous songs of poetry.

---

40.   Nicholson 2016, 8–10, too observes that *Nemeans* 7 and 8 and *Olympian* 1 are critical of the oral tradition and its ability to represent the truth.

41.   See Young 1970, 633–43, for the function of Eleithyia in *Nemean 7*. Young argues that the opening of this ode is a typically Pindaric type whereby the poet introduces a universal human experience before moving to the specific case of the laudandus.

The alignment of light with poetry and of darkness with the absence of poetry anticipates similar statements about truth and memory that will appear later in the poem, where light and darkness reappear as metaphors for knowledge and the lack thereof.

As Pindar delineates familiar relationships between poetry, accomplishment, and memory, he describes how athletic accomplishment relies on poetry for its glorification.[42] As recompense for accomplished athletes (ἄποινα, 16), poetry is an act not only of memorialization but also of reciprocal obligation, without which notable deeds effectively cease to exist.[43] This conception of poetry as memory evokes alētheia's etymology and points up the poet's duty to the laudandus. The opening lines describe the universality of birth and existence, which poetry then has the pivotal role of memorializing through accurate representation. When Pindar later describes blame as dark (σκοτεινόν, 61), he recalls the obfuscation that poetry ought to prevent. The invocation to Eleithyia and the image of a mirror point to two distinct but intertwined truths about poetry, that it is at once an act of creation by the poet and an obligatory act of reflection on a deed already performed.[44]

As both something new and a representation of something old, poetry must balance its novelty with its accuracy. This sentiment is echoed in *Nemean* 8.20–22, an echo that anticipates further resonances between the two odes that in concert serve the poet's overarching message about truth, poetry, and reciprocity:

πολλὰ γὰρ πολλᾷ λέλεκται, νεαρὰ δ' ἐξευρόντα δόμεν βασάνῳ
ἐς ἔλεγχον, ἅπας κίνδυνος· ὄψον δὲ λόγοι φθονεροῖσιν,
ἅπτεται δ' ἐσλῶν ἀεί, χειρόνεσσι δ' οὐκ ἐρίζει.

For many things have been said in many ways, and when someone finds new things and puts them to the test on the touchstone, it is a danger in every respect; words are relish for the envious, and envy always takes hold of good men but has no beef with lesser men.

---

42. Many scholars discuss the relationship between poetry and memory. E.g., Bundy 1986; Detienne 1996, 48–49; Kurke 1991; and Pratt 1993, 115–29.
43. On ἄποινα, see Finley 1981, 241; Kurke 1991, 108–34; and Wilson 1999, 136–38.
44. For the poetics of creation in Pindar, see Segal 1986a, esp. 69 for *N.* 7 specifically. This conception of poetry anticipates what eventually becomes a commonplace about literature in general, that it has both imaginative and mimetic dimensions. See Lamarque and Olsen 1994, 261–67, for further reflections on this literary convention.

Ideas about poetic novelty, truth, and envy are compressed within these few lines, which subsequently transition to the suicide of Ajax as the lamentable result of envy. The metaphor of the touchstone evokes truth and verification, which novel words must undergo to attain validity.[45] Such verification, however, can trigger envy; the implication is that praise, when accurate, can incur ill will. The silver lining, however, is that envy itself is proof of someone's value and the validity of praising him since envy is never directed at an inferior person. Implicit in all of this is that Pindar's own praise is accurate, given that his susceptibility to attack by envious people marks his membership among the good (ἐσλῶν, 22). Pindar thus constructs a situation in which praise and truthful rhetoric are synonymous, for if envy comes only to men who are esloi, the attacks of envy are actually proof of a man's laudability.

The dual conception of poetry as a both creative and reflective medium lies at the heart of Pindar's criticism of Homer in *Nemean 7*. Specifically, Pindar faults Homer for falsely presenting Odysseus' story, to disastrous ends for Ajax. Odysseus, although objectively Ajax's inferior, nonetheless is awarded the arms of Achilles. Pindar attributes this miscarriage of justice to Homer's artificial—and thus deceitful and noxious—inflation of Odysseus' heroism:

ἐγὼ δὲ πλέον' ἔλπομαι
λόγον Ὀδυσσέος ἢ πάθαν διὰ τὸν ἀδυεπῆ γενέσθ᾽ Ὅμηρον·
ἐπεὶ ψεύδεσί οἱ ποτανᾷ <τε> μαχανᾷ
σεμνὸν ἔπεστί τι· σοφία δὲ κλέπτει παράγοισα μύθοις. τυφλὸν δ᾽ ἔχει
ἦτορ ὅμιλος ἀνδρῶν ὁ πλεῖστος. εἰ γὰρ ἦν
ἓ τὰν ἀλάθειαν ἰδέμεν, οὔ κεν ὅπλων χολωθεὶς
ὁ καρτερὸς Αἴας ἔπαξε διὰ φρενῶν
λευρὸν ξίφος. (7.20–27)

I expect that Odysseus' story has become greater than his experience on account of sweet-talking Homer, since something majestic lies upon his falsehoods and his soaring resourcefulness. Skill deceives and misleads with stories. The majority of men have a blind heart, for if it were possible for them to see the truth, mighty Ajax, angered over the arms, would not have stuck a smooth sword through his heart.

---

45. For a discussion of the touchstone metaphor in Greek literature, see duBois 1991, 9–34.

Homer has not failed in the creative aspect of poetry, as his skill with words is demonstrable and laudable (ἀδυεπῆ, 21; ποτανᾷ τε μαχανᾷ, 22; σεμνόν, 23).[46] But the aesthetic quality of his poetry distracts the audience from the truth (τὰν ἀλάθειαν, 25) and obscures his own divergence from it. Homer's poetry thus fails in its reflective duty by presenting Odysseus in a manner disproportionate to his experiences (πλέον᾽ . . . λόγον Ὀδυσσέος ἢ πάθαν, 21).

The contrast between verbal and visual modes further emphasizes this asymmetry. Pindar praises Homer's creativity in terms of speech (λόγον, ἀδυεπῆ, 21) but uses visual language for Ajax (τυφλόν, 23; ἰδέμεν, 25), a contrast that points up the disparity between Homer's words and the truth.[47] Furthermore, the discrepancy between Odysseus' experience and its account (λόγον . . . ἢ πάθαν, 21) conflicts with the prescribed symmetry between deeds and their reportage evoked by the earlier image of the mirror (14). Pindar criticizes Homer for lacking such symmetry, which, in Pindar's presentation, is the duty of poetry. His opening lines prescribe a combination of creation and representation in poetry, a combination he deems absent in Homer.

Pindar's criticism suggests indirection rather than actual lying since pseudos can designate a number of things, for example, a perceiver's misapprehension, a speaker's intentional deception, fiction, or some combination of these meanings.[48] The ambiguous focalization of terms like pseudos—does it refer to the speaker's intentional deception or simply the listener's misapprehension?—does not mean the speaker is absolved from blame. As Bernard Williams observes, patently true statements still have the potential to deceive by producing a misapprehensive disposition in the hearer.[49] If a person goes through another's mail then claims, "someone has been opening your mail," he does not lie, but he does falsely suggest a culprit other than himself. This scenario depicts deception as any communication that fosters misapprehension and thereby violates a tacit agreement of trust between speaker and listener. In any case Pindar faults Homer for producing a narrative that elicits inaccurate perceptions of events.

---

46. As Pratt 1993, 127, notes: "Pindar here slyly praises Homer's ability to confer more fame on Odysseus than he deserved as a positive attribute of poetry, a quality that a patron might well appreciate."

47. As Nagy 1990, 422–23, puts it: "[Pindar's] tradition . . . puts a strong emphasis on its association with the visual metaphor, as distinct from the auditory metaphor that marks the Homeric tradition, and an equally strong emphasis on the truth-value of local traditions grounded in cult, as distinct from the synthetic complexities attributed to Homer."

48. "Fiction," per the translation of Race 1997 vol. 2, 73.

49. Williams 2002, 96.

He seems at first to distinguish between Homer's account of Odysseus (λόγον Ὀδυσσέος, 21) and the truth (τὰν ἀλάθειαν, 25), thus pointing out an instance in which poetry has shaped memory falsely. His comments on deceptive skill (σοφία δὲ κλέπτει παράγοισα μύθοις, 23) and the blindness of men (τυφλὸν δ' ἔχει | ἦτορ ὅμιλος ἀνδρῶν ὁ πλεῖστος, 23–24) are directed to an audience external to but familiar with Homer's poetry. But the next sentence (εἰ γὰρ . . . λευρὸν ξίφος, 24–27) indicates an internal audience. The aphorism about blindness blends Homer's audience with Ajax's[50] and thus expands the sphere of relevance for truth and falsehood beyond the confines of the myth. While alētheia here designates the reality of Ajax's superiority, its context points to the need for poetry to preserve this reality; it refers to both an objective reality as well as the poet's duty to the truth. As a poet, Pindar serves to foreground truths that will otherwise disappear and to bring praiseworthy events to the attention of his audience so that his victor will not suffer the same fate as Ajax.

Ajax's suicide is the extreme consequence of deception, as we see more clearly in *Nemean* 8.24–34:

ἦ τιν' ἄγλωσσον μέν, ἦτορ δ' ἄλκιμον, λάθα κατέχει
ἐν λυγρῷ νείκει· μέγιστον δ' αἰόλῳ ψεύδει γέρας ἀντέταται.
κρυφίαισι γὰρ ἐν ψάφοις Ὀδυσσῆ Δαναοὶ θεράπευσαν·
χρυσέων δ' Αἴας στερηθεὶς ὅπλων φόνῳ πάλαισεν.
ἦ μὰν ἀνόμοιά γε δάοισιν ἐν θερμῷ χροΐ
ἕλκεα ῥῆξαν πελεμιζόμενοι
ὑπ' ἀλεξιμβρότῳ λόγχᾳ, τὰ μὲν ἀμφ' Ἀχιλεῖ νεοκτόνῳ,
ἄλλων τε μόχθων ἐν πολυφθόροις
ἁμέραις. ἐχθρὰ δ' ἄρα πάρφασις ἦν καὶ πάλαι,
αἱμύλων μύθων ὁμόφοιτος, δολοφραδής, κακοποιὸν ὄνειδος·
ἃ τὸ μὲν λαμπρὸν βιᾶται, τῶν δ' ἀφάντων κῦδος ἀντείνει σαθρόν.

Yes, in deadly strife obscurity takes hold of someone tongueless but valiant in heart; the greatest honor is held up to fickle falsehood. For in secret ballots the Danaans devoted themselves to Odysseus, but Ajax, robbed of the golden weap-

---

50. Pratt 1993, 128, also makes this observation. She notes the ambiguity of the pronoun οἱ in verse 22, taking it, correctly I think, as a reference to Homer rather than Odysseus. See also Segal 1967, 442; and Most 1985, 150–51, for discussion of the close association between Homer and Odysseus in these lines. See Morgan 2015, 236–37, on the similarities between this passage and *Olympian* 1.28–34, both of which conflate poetry and nonpoetic mortal speech.

ons, wrestled with death. Truly they struck unequal wounds in the warm bodies of the enemy, as they drove them back with their helpful spears, both over freshly killed Achilles and in the destructive days of other toils. Indeed, there was hateful deception even long ago, the fellow traveler of flattering stories, wily, a maleficent disgrace, which violates the luminous and upholds the unwholesome renown of those who should not be seen.

This passage ostensibly explains Odysseus' offense in *Nemean* 7.20–27.[51] But in neither ode does Pindar explicitly name Odysseus as the agent of pseudos (25) and parphasis (32).[52] He focuses not on Odysseus but on the deception itself, which results in the inaccurate bestowal of praise and blame. The reference to inequality between Odysseus' and Ajax's achievements (ἀνόμοια, 28) evokes *Nemean* 7's emphasis on parity between reality and verbal accounts of it and further links Odysseus and Ajax's story to messaging about the purpose of poetry.

The language used of Odysseus in *Nemean* 8 (ψεύδει, *Nemean* 8.25; πάρφασις, 32; αἱμύλων μύθων, 33) echoes language describing Homer in *Nemean* 7 (ψεύδεσι, 22; κλέπτει παράγοισα μύθοις, 23) and thus likens Odysseus' rhetoric to untruthful poetry.[53] But by understating Odysseus' agency, Pindar generalizes praise as determined by an audience susceptible to verbal manipulation.[54] The Greeks misjudge the relative merits of Ajax and Odysseus despite Ajax's clear superiority, the self-evidence of which is emphasized again by the language of vision: Ajax is "the luminous" (τὸ μὲν λαμπρὸν, 8.34) whereas men like Odysseus are "the invisible" (τῶν δ' ἀφάντων, 8.34).[55] Since the audience is not prone to seeing even obvious truths, the implication is that poets

---

51. For the various accounts about Achilles' arms, see Most 1985, 153. Most 1985, 150, diverges from the traditional view that *N.* 7.20–23 refer to the judgment on Achilles' arms, arguing instead that "Pindar may be suggesting that Homer, instead of inquiring whether Odysseus' narrative was truthful or not, simply repeated Odysseus' report in his own words." Although I do not go as far as Most does, I do see merit in his idea that Pindar merges Homer's and Odysseus' characteristics here.

52. As Most 1985, 152, observes: "Pindar is careful here [in *N.* 7] and elsewhere to avoid making the explicit claim that Achilles' arms were awarded to Odysseus only because Odysseus deceived and cheated the Greeks."

53. See Miller 1982, 118, on the function of Odysseus as "corrupt or perverse rhetorician." Carey 1976, 31, points out that Odysseus traditionally has an unfair advantage over Ajax, but his use of deceit is a Pindaric innovation. See also Nisetich 1989, 22.

54. Nicholson 2016, 9, makes a similar point about the conflation between myth and poetry in *Nemean* 8; he notes that while *N.* 8.32–34 at first glance refers to Ajax's poor rhetoric, "the broader oral tradition seems the likely target."

55. Bremer 1976, 307, makes a similar point.

must represent events in accordance with reality. This sentiment resonates with *Nemean 7*, where Pindar presents a similar contrast between how Ajax was perceived and what he actually did, terming the latter situation "the truth" (τὰν ἀλάθειαν, 7.25).

Although Pindar criticizes Homer in *Nemean 7*, in *Isthmian* 4.37–39 he lauds Homer for duly glorifying Ajax.[56] These puzzlingly divergent attitudes can be explained through consideration of the mirror in *Nemean* 7.14. Pindar criticizes Homer's poetry not for failing in its creative or aesthetic aspects, but for inconsistently fulfilling its reflective duty. Homer sometimes, but not always, upholds symmetry between poetry and reality as he praises appropriately in some cases but not in others. His glorification of Odysseus is disproportionate to the reality and thus diminishes the credibility of his praise. A possible cause of this inconsistency is that his primary concern is not praise but art, so his poetry shows no particular allegiance to his subject or to the truth.

By contrast Pindar identifies his own praise in terms of the obligations of poet-patron reciprocity:

ξεῖνός εἰμι· σκοτεινὸν ἀπέχων ψόγον,
ὕδατος ὥτε ῥοὰς φίλον ἐς ἄνδρ' ἄγων
κλέος ἐτήτυμον αἰνέσω· ποτίφορος δ' ἀγαθοῖσι μισθὸς οὗτος.
ἐὼν δ' ἐγγὺς Ἀχαιὸς οὐ μέμψεταί μ' ἀνὴρ
Ἰονίας ὑπὲρ ἁλὸς οἰκέων, καὶ προξενίᾳ πέποιθ', ἔν τε δαμόταις
ὄμματι δέρκομαι λαμπρόν, οὐχ ὑπερβαλών,
βίαια πάντ' ἐκ ποδὸς ἐρύσαις. (*Nemean* 7.61–67)

I am a *xenos*. As I hold off dark blame and lead genuine fame like streams of water to a man who is my *friend*, I will praise; this is suitable *payment* for good men. An Achaean man being nearby and living over the Ionian Sea will not find fault with me.[57] I trust in *hospitality*, and I look brightly among my townsmen since I do not overstep the mark and I have removed all force from my path.

---

56. Spelman 2018, 277, dismisses this discrepancy to claim that the significant point is that "both these passages presuppose that Homeric epic is widely known, as it was"; cf. Spelman 2018, 217, where he reads *N.* 7.14–16 as reference to shared knowledge of poetic precedent. See Fitch 1924, 57–65 and Nisetich 1989 for an explanation of the body of texts encapsulated by Pindar's use of the name "Homer." Nisetich 1989, 9–23, argues that Pindar's varying attitudes toward Homer stem from the varying contexts and occasions in which the various odes were composed. Perhaps so, but I would also add that Pindar finds certain aspects of Homer more laudable than others.

57. On the expansiveness of Pindar's imagined audience in these lines, see Spelman 2018, 120–23.

The comparison of his poetry to streams of water (ῥοάς, 62) recalls his earlier reference to the Muses' streams (ῥοαῖσι, 13) and verbally links Pindar's praise with the opening message about the reflective duty of poetry. Likewise, the language of light and vision (ὄμματι δέρκομαι λαμπρόν, 66) evokes the prescriptive opening of the ode as well as the digression about Ajax.[58] As in *Olympian* 10.3–12, Pindar engages the various spheres of guest-host obligation, friendship, and monetary exchange (μισθός, 63) to characterize and emphasize the reciprocal relationship between poet and patron.[59] He praises his patron (here, the victor's father Thearion) as a friend (φίλον, 62) but makes clear that this friendship is couched in xenia (ξεῖνος, 61; προξενίᾳ, 65), which obligates the praise poet to protect his patron from blame (ἀπέχων ψόγον, 61). This obligation does not preclude the accuracy of his praise, which the poet describes as "genuine" (ἐτήτυμον), thus asserting both sincerity and accuracy.[60]

The key difference between Pindar and Homer, then, is that Pindar's poetry reflects an obligation both to his subject and to reality. This obligation is comparable to his stance of piety toward the gods in *Olympian* 1.28–35, where he expresses obligation and accuracy as joint and complementary concerns. In *Nemean* 7 he presents a more convincing argument that poetry unrestrained by obligations of reciprocity and unconcerned with parity between poet and patron cannot properly reflect reality. His criticism of Homer suggests that a truthful account is born of a relationship of obligation between poet and patron, absent in Homer's poetry, and adheres to praise that accurately reflects the kleos of the laudandus.

Kurke has argued that Pindar's description of poet-patron guest-friendship involves reciprocity tantamount to equality.[61] I would add that *Nemean* 7 goes so far as to propose a parallel parity between poetry and its subject matter. At least two levels of obligation are outlined in *Nemean* 7: there is an obligation to reflect deeds accurately since poetry is their only "mirror," the *sole* means for

---

58. On the associations between light, truth, and poetry in Pindar, see Bremer 1976, 296–314, esp. 301–14.

59. See Kurke 1991, 93, who relies on Bourdieu to argue that this metaphor of payment does not suggest an impersonal monetary exchange; rather, the values of the archaic guest-host relationship continue in Pindar's time, even though the language has broadened to reflect the increased use of real rather than symbolic currency.

60. See Kurke 1991, 136 (citing Slater 1979, 80), who argues that "The bond of *xenia* authenticates the poet's encomium, but it also participates in a precise social context." On ἐτήτυμον, see Carey 1981, 159: "ἐτήτυμον emphasizes the truth of Pindar's words (in contrast to Homer and ὅμιλος ἀνδρῶν ὁ πλεῖστος)."

61. See Kurke 1991, 140–41, where she discusses O. 1.103–5 and P. 10.63–65. Both passages mention guest-friendship in a way similar to N. 7.65 (προξενίᾳ πέποιθ').

knowledge of great deeds (ἔργοις δὲ καλοῖς ἔσοπτρον ἴσαμεν ἑνὶ σὺν τρόπῳ, 14), and there is the obligation that the poet has to his patron-host. Finally, Pindar takes the argument further to propose, surprisingly, that praise poetry, because its purpose is most closely tied to such obligations, is best suited to communicating the truth. His promise not to "overstep the mark" (ὑπερβαλών, 66) recalls his concern for symmetry between event and record, which Homer, in presenting a λόγος that exceeds Odysseus' πάθα (21), has failed to achieve.

Conclusion

As I argued in the previous chapter, Pindar situates alētheia within epinician poetry, which is premised on reciprocity and obligation between poet and patron. He thus embeds truth within the obligations of reciprocal relationships. While alētheia represents the truth, it also reflects the promises of reciprocity within the relationship between patron and epinician poet. He reconciles his obligation to his patron with his duty to the truth by producing an accurate representation of praiseworthy events. Moreover, the poet contends that praise poetry, bound by its duties to the laudandus, is inherently more truthful than poetry driven by aesthetic concerns. The formulations of alētheia, reciprocity, and obligation that ground Pindar's outer praise narrative are reinforced by his mythological digressions, which provide exempla for the importance of intertwining reciprocity and truth.

Through the myths of Heracles and Augeas, Tantalus and Pelops, and Odysseus and Ajax, Pindar reinforces the ground rules of truth and poetry that he sets forth in his praise. Through lying and cheating, Augeas violates his reciprocal arrangement with Heracles and undermines the expected parity between them. He thus runs counter to the ideals of alētheia and poetry that Pindar lays out in the opening of the ode and in this respect is similar to the female figures I will examine in the next chapter. In *Olympian* 1 Pindar takes aim at other poets for prioritizing aesthetics over truth and holds up the traditional story of Tantalus and Pelops as an example. He proposes his own alternative, which exemplifies the harmony between truth and piety. By comparing his praise aims with piety, Pindar suggests that his own poetic agenda, though hampered by the constraints of reciprocity and obligation, nevertheless can coexist with truth. *Nemean* 7, too, presents Pindar's criticism of poets who are not bound to a program of accurate representation. Pindar faults Homer for praising Odysseus to a degree disproportionate to reality. He then suggests a parallel between the reflective relationship between poetry and truth and the parity between poet and patron. The primary difference between Pindar and poets like Homer is the role xenia plays in shaping their poetry. What this criticism suggests is that a poet's obligation to the patron must be associated with truth but, counterintuitively, poetry composed outside the bounds of this obligation can yield falsehood and deception. The reciprocal exchange relationship is the specific hallmark of epinician poetry: as a guest-friend to the laudandus, Pindar is able to provide a more accurate and balanced account than a poet not constrained by such reciprocal obligations.

Taking note of the ways in which Pindar incorporates truth and falsehood in his mythological digressions allows for fuller comprehension of his poetic aims. His statements about truth and verbal expression connect his myths to the outer praise narratives in which they are embedded. The priority of poet-patron reciprocity informs the poet's conception of truth, both in his praise and in his promise to his patron. These concerns are reflected in Pindar's mythological digressions, which illustrate the ideals of reciprocity and truth that inform his praise poetry. His statements about truth and verbal expression within his myths are informed by the reciprocity frameworks in the outer praise narrative: both are premised on correspondence and symmetry, between word and deed and between poet and patron.

Pindar conveys the impression that his commitment to praising the victor will yield a true account and that his commitment to the laudandus is part of a broader commitment to the truth. It has been observed that Pindar presents truth-telling as the purpose of poetry.[62] What has gone unnoticed is how Pindar employs the various epinician aspects of obligation and reciprocity to put forth an aesthetic that not only balances truth and praise but equates them and presents praise as a mode uniquely suited to presenting the truth. Such an equation is premised on the sanctity of reciprocity and truth as conjoined ideals. This integration of truth with the reciprocity that defines his poetry is reflected in Pindar's treatments of female figures and deception as well, which, as I discuss in the next chapter, evoke existing stereotypes but are adapted for messaging specific to epinician poetry. In Pindar's presentation female deception undermines the delicate harmony of reciprocity and truth; thus, deception, as practiced by female figures, is antithetical to the very reciprocal relationships

---

62. Ortega 1970, 353–72.

on which epinician poetry itself is premised. Just as the mythological digressions in the present chapter reflect the poet's aims in regard to reciprocity and truth, so too do his deceptive female figures shed similar light. And as we shall see in later chapters, Aeschylean tragedy presents an intertwining of reciprocity, truth, and gender that complements Pindar's, wherein female figures articulate in various ways the tight connections between reciprocity and truth.

Indeed, the explorations I have conducted here ultimately serve my larger aim of situating Pindar and Aeschylus in relation to one another in terms of the conceptual frameworks their poetry reflects. In both Pindar's expressions of praise and in his mythological exempla, concerns for reciprocity shape alētheia, which in turn reinforces the ideals of reciprocity. This interrelationship between reciprocity and truth puts Pindar on the same page as Aeschylus. As I have discussed and will discuss further, Aeschylean configurations of reciprocity complement Pindar's in their emphasis on symmetry; the kind of language each poet uses to emphasize this symmetry is strikingly similar. Moreover, Aeschylus, like Pindar, incorporates alētheia into many of his articulations of reciprocity, thus demonstrating the comparability of the two poets' visions of reciprocity and truth.

CHAPTER 3

Gender, Reciprocity, and Truth in Pindar

In previous chapters I argued that reciprocity governs Pindar's use of alētheia, which in turn helps to delineate reciprocity. The term alētheia is presented in ways that are specific to the frameworks of reciprocity governing the poet-patron relationship of epinician poetry. We can see these tendencies in both the sections of Pindar's epinician odes explicitly devoted to praise, as well as the mythological digressions that reinforce them. Pindar's alētheia is a hybrid that connotes both objective reality as well as the reciprocity-bound obligations of the epinician poet. On the flip side, as the example of Augeas in *Olympian* 10 tells us, deception and falsehood undermine this relationship.

This chapter explores the role of female gender in this intertwining of reciprocity and truth. It examines several female figures who are, on the surface, configured as antitheses to truth and reciprocity. The deceptive female figures of Pindar's myths damage relationships of (male) reciprocity and obligation similar to the ones examined in previous chapters.[1] These relationships reflect an expectation of mutual exchange and benefit and are fundamental to epinician poetry. Pindar often conflates any female activity—especially seduction—with deception, and his versions of myths magnify the specifically deceptive role of the female characters within them. In this respect his configurations of female characters reflect a general tendency of ancient Greek literature.[2] But he

---

1. This is not to say that Pindar depicts all female characters negatively; for example, the portrayals of Evadne in *Olympian* 6 and Medea in *Pythian* 4 are largely positive.
2. As Worman 1997, 154–55, notes: "In the ancient texts . . . bodies depicted as dangerously desirable, bodies whose possession is elusive, bodies that impede knowledge (by veiling, deceiving, etc.) tend to be female." She makes similar points in Worman 2002, 83–85.

also embeds such depictions within larger narratives of reciprocity, showing how female deception damages reciprocal relationships specifically. These acts of female deception are metaphorically significant for epinician poetry itself, which is built on reciprocity and truth.[3] Simply put, deceptive female figures are in the same company as Augeas in that they help Pindar illustrate, by negative example, the delicacy of reciprocal relationships built on trust and truthfulness.

Further, the deceptive female figures examined in this chapter are more complicated than Augeas in that they mirror, in ways that he does not, some of the gray areas of poetry's functions. The deceptions they enact or embody overlap with some aspects of poetry, such as creativity or artistic skill. As in *Olympian* 1, where Pindar's poetry shares aesthetic qualities with false but persuasive accounts, the crafty and creative capacities of his deceptive female characters parallel his own poetic traits. And as in *Nemeans* 7 and 8, where Odysseus' and Ajax's audience overlaps with that of the poet who tells their story, the depictions of the female characters in this chapter have implications not only for the characters within the myth but also for Pindar's reality as an epinician poet. In effect, these female figures embody an acknowledgment of poetry's potential for harm, and they communicate Pindar's implicit assurance that his own poetry will avoid the pitfalls they represent. Ultimately, then, the way Pindar deploys such deceptive female characters has specific implications for his own poetry, as he situates them within contexts that emphasize reciprocity and depicts their actions as distorted reflections of his own. This chapter examines how Pindar participates in a tradition of refracting truth and poetry through gendered dynamics, in a way that is specific to epinician reciprocity. Subsequent chapters will examine similar functions of female characters for Aeschylean truth and reciprocity.

In this chapter I conduct a brief examination of gender and its significance for ancient Greek poetry. I then turn to three female figures in Pindar's odes who illustrate how Pindar's myth-making incorporates gendered configurations to serve his poetic program. The Hera-cloud in the Ixion-myth of *Pythian* 2, Coronis in *Pythian* 3, and Hippolyta in the myth of Peleus in *Nemean* 5 demonstrate the conflation of specifically female seduction with deception and the

---

3.   His treatment of divine rape is comparable. As De Boer 2017 has persuasively argued, Pindar sanitizes accounts of divine rape by reformulating them into "stories of affection and marriage" (1–2); he does so in order to reinforce the pious stance he projects in his poetic program.

implications thereof for Pindar's conception of his poetry.[4] Through these female figures, cast as deceptive ones, Pindar presents the harms of deception to relationships of reciprocity. Just as he frames truth in its specificity to the reciprocity governing epinician poetry, so too does he present deception as harmful to it. Furthermore, by channeling deception through female figures, he deploys motifs we see in previous poets' configurations of female figures, whose creative activities are ambiguously true or false or both. I will conclude with an exploration of male seduction in Pindar to show its relative innocuousness compared to female seduction.

The Significance of Gender

Ancient Greek literature reflects a perception of gender difference. In the *Iliad*, for example, Hector "assures" Andromache of his safety in part by telling her to tend to her housework and leave the business of war to men (6.490–93). The *Odyssey*'s Calypso protests the unfair treatment of goddesses who engage in sexual relationships with mortals, thus implying a double standard for gods and goddesses (5.118–29). Often gender is articulated through consideration of the feminine as the "other" against which the normal is defined.[5] For example, Semonides' Fragment 7 is devoted to listing different female—but not male—types; the Chorus of *Agamemnon* criticize Clytemnestra's specifically female credulity (483–87); Orestes mocks Aegisthus for having a woman's heart (θήλεια γὰρ φρὴν, "for his heart is womanly," *Ch.* 305). This is not to say that stereotypes about masculinity are never expressed: various characters do remark on Clytemnestra's masculine temperament (ἀνδόβουλον ἐλπίζον κέαρ, *A.* 11; κατ' ἄνδρα σώφρον', 351). But articulations of feminine traits, on the whole, are more common.[6]

Of course, "male" and "female" are neither stable nor monolithic categories, and the degree to which they are considered oppositional varies with time,

---

4. Ahlert 1942, 58, points out that these myths center on transgressive love, from which Aphrodite is absent.
5. Zeitlin 1996, 1–15.
6. Particularly in tragedy, which is rife with them, along with characters and situations that undermine them; e.g., the Chorus of Danaids claim a feminine lack of bellicosity (A., *Supp.* 748–49); Ismene says something similar about the impropriety or inability of women to resist men (S., *Ant.* 61–62); Medea lists a litany of woes unique to women (E., *Med.* 230–51).

place, and society.[7] Furthermore, perspectives on gender can vary with schol-arly discipline. Biologists and evolutionary psychologists, for example, start with the physical and biological manifestations of gender—sex organs and hor-mones—to approach gender as something innate ("gender essentialism"). Social theorists and anthropologists, on the other hand, view behaviors and perceptions associated with gender as products of cultural and social forces; they differentiate "sex" and "gender," using the former for biological phenom-ena and the latter to signify social constructs and expectations, but the sex/gender binary too has its own flaws.[8]

Gender is dynamic, shaped by different cultures and their histories.[9] Thus, considerations of gender and gendered constructs can shed light on the social and historical contexts in which they appear. As Joan Wallach Scott notes, "gen-der is a primary way of signifying relationships of power."[10] The implicit hierar-chical nature of gender relations makes gender an illuminating lens through which to view many other types of relationships as well: "When historians look for the ways in which the concept of gender legitimizes and constructs social relationships, they develop insight into the reciprocal nature of gender and soci-ety and into the particular and contextually specific ways in which politics con-structs gender and gender constructs politics."[11] In other words, gender can be a mirror. Its ubiquity means that it can reflect many kinds of relationships or power dynamics, even those that are not ostensibly or strictly about gender per se.

What Scott observes about gender and historical analysis is also useful in the study of ancient Greek poetry, in which gender and gendered relationships parallel and help define poetic ones. Perceived gender and gender difference can coincide with and thus help us understand many kinds of hierarchies and constructs in Greek poetry. For example, scholars have written about the male-female oppositions at the basis of the *Theogony* myth, oppositions that mirror the various power dynamics threading through the poem.[12] Similarly, as Kirk

---

7. Once treated synonymously with biological sex, gender is increasingly understood as a product of a number of factors, biological, cultural, and social. Thinkers from Simone de Beauvoir to Michel Foucault to Judith Butler have helped us understand this complexity. See Robson, Rabinowitz, and Masterson 2014, 2–3.

8. See Foxhall 2013, 2–4, for a summary of various approaches to gender. See Holmes 2012, 47–48, for a summary of the sex/gender binary and its controversies.

9. Such considerations are particularly valuable for understanding the structures of ancient Greek societies, whose extreme paucity of texts by women speaks volumes about the status of women in such societies. See Lardinois and McClure 2001.

10. Scott 1986, 1067.

11. Scott 1986, 1070.

12. E.g., Arthur 1982; Park 2014; Sussman 1978. Burke 1966, 129, makes a similar point about

Ormand observes, "Recent feminist scholars have [discussed] the ways in which tragedy uses the hierarchy of gender in ancient Greece as a literary device. They productively suggest that the gender conflict in ancient tragedy stands in for various other conflicts in the Athenian state: humans versus gods, private versus public, past versus present, etc."[13] Of course, when we examine poetry through the lens of gender, we must understand that poetic references to gender do not have an absolute basis in biology, nor do they necessarily reflect the historical reality of men and women in ancient Greece.[14] But they do shed light on ancient *ideas* about gender, which are often premised on a male-female binary, with all its inadequacy and instability.[15]

For my purposes, gender matters because gender difference can be embedded in conceptions of Greek poetry and its relationship to truth. For example, Hesiod's interactions with the Muses can be understood in terms of male-female difference and hierarchy, and their concomitant complexities, circularities, or inconsistencies:

"ποιμένες ἄγραυλοι, κάκ᾽ ἐλέγχεα, γαστέρες οἶον,
ἴδμεν ψεύδεα πολλὰ λέγειν ἐτύμοισιν ὁμοῖα,
ἴδμεν δ᾽, εὖτ᾽ ἐθέλωμεν, ἀληθέα γηρύσασθαι."
ὣς ἔφασαν κοῦραι μεγάλου Διὸς ἀρτιέπειαι·
καί μοι σκῆπτρον ἔδον, δάφνης ἐριθηλέος ὄζον
δρέψασαι θηητόν· ἐνέπνευσαν δέ μοι αὐδὴν
θέσπιν, ἵνα κλείοιμι τά τ᾽ ἐσσόμενα πρό τ᾽ ἐόντα,
καί με κέλονθ᾽ ὑμνεῖν μακάρων γένος αἰὲν ἐόντων,
σφᾶς δ᾽ αὐτὰς πρῶτόν τε καὶ ὕστατον αἰὲν ἀείδειν. (Hesiod, *Th.* 26–34)

"Agrarian shepherds, wretched disgraces, mere bellies, we know how to speak lies like true things, and we know, when we wish, how to speak true things." So

---

Aeschylus' *Oresteia*: "Women, socially submerged . . . may thus come to stand for nearly all submerged motives."

13. Ormand 1999, 3. With citations to Bergren 1992, Foley 1981 and 1992, Katz 1994, Zeitlin 1992.
14. But as Lin Foxhall points out, both texts and archaeological remains "are the product of social and political expectations and ideologies," thus suggesting that what is reflected in literary and material evidence sheds some light on historical "reality" (Foxhall 2013, 21).
15. Whether biologically or socially based, transgender or intersex identifications defy simple binaries between male and female or between sex and gender and show that sex/gender is perhaps best conceptualized as a spectrum or continuum rather than an either/or distinction. See Butler 1993 and 1999 (cited in Foxhall 2013, 12). See also Bordo 1993; Grosz 1994; Laqueur 1990 (cited in Masterson et al. 2014, 2); Fausto-Sterling 1993 (cited in Holmes 2012, 50).

the daughters of great Zeus, with their quick voices, spoke. And they plucked and gave me a staff, a marvelous branch of flourishing laurel; and they breathed a divine voice into me, so that I might tell of the future and the past, and they ordered me to hymn the race of the blessed, eternal gods, but to always sing the Muses first and last.

As I noted in chapter 1, Hesiod and the Muses are entangled with one another, and their power dynamic is circular. The poet relies on the Muses for giving him his voice, but the voice he receives from them enables him to exercise his own creative agency. Likewise, the Muses are the sources of Hesiod's poetic power and content, yet they are also dependent on him to actualize their existence within poetry. Furthermore, the Muses' authorial function is akin to the poet's own even as he differentiates himself from them. Thus the binary and hierarchy between active female Muses and passive male poet are subverted from their very inception.

Stesichorus' Helen occupies a similar position in his *Palinode* (Plato, *Phaedrus* 243a = Finglass 91a = *PMG* 192). As I explained in the previous chapter, the tradition of the *Palinode* involves Stesichorus' loss of sight and its subsequent restoration, presumably by Helen, who punishes Stesichorus for his earlier poetry about her and rewards him when he recants. Thus, she exerts some control over the content of his poems about her even as she is at the mercy of his depictions. Granted, her influence is reactive rather than contemporaneous—she cannot shape his content as he produces it but only afterward. But broadly speaking, she resembles Hesiod's Muses in her (limited) capacity to influence poetic speech.[16] This is not surprising given the association of Helen (real or imitation) with creativity and poetry: in *Iliad* 3.125–29 her woven depiction of the Trojan War mirrors the poem in which she herself is situated.

Figures like Hesiod's Muses and Stesichorus' Helen reveal a circularity of active and passive when it comes to gender, truth, and poetry. They are female figures inscribed in poetry by male poets. Yet they are depicted as wielding power over verbal and narrative expression, along with the perceived truth or falsehood of it. Their gendered depictions have metaphorical significance for how poetry works: the oppositions, complexities, and inconsistencies of gender

---

16. See Bassi 1993; Bergren 2008; Blondell 2013. Blondell 2013 and Edmunds 2016 are the most recent extensive examinations of Helen, specifically.

map onto and are reflected in the complicated relationship between poets and their subject matter. Hesiod's Muses and Stesichorus' Helen anticipate the kinds of female figures we will see in Pindar and Aeschylus, figures that articulate the complexities of truth and poetic creativity. In Pindar and Aeschylus these female characters call attention specifically to reciprocity as a force that defines truth in their poetry.

The Hera-Cloud of Pythian 2

Pythian 2 provides an illustrative example. One of several odes addressed to Hieron, tyrant of Syracuse, *Pythian* 2 celebrates a victory in a chariot race whose date is unknown.[17] Like many of the epinician odes, its beginning names the victor, his city, and his event, before transitioning to a myth presumably meant to allegorize the praise of his laudandus in some way. Pindar refers to his poetry as a "paid recompense" to kings in return for their excellence (βασιλεῦσιν ὕμνον ἄποιν᾽ ἀρετᾶς, *P.* 2.14), holds up the mythical king Cinyras as one such example of paid excellence (15–17), and caps the section with an aphorism about gratitude (ἄγει δὲ χάρις φίλων ποί τινος ἀντὶ ἔργων ὀπιζομένα, "Respectful gratitude for someone's friendly deeds is a guide in some way," 17). The poet thus establishes reciprocal gratitude (charis) as the framework for his poetry before turning to the mythical Ixion as a negative example.

Pindar depicts Ixion as someone who has failed to show gratitude, specifically to Zeus. A mortal man who has enjoyed the rare privilege of living among the gods (25–26), Ixion loses this privilege through his own error and suffers the torment of being permanently bound to a spinning wheel in the Underworld. Pindar tells us of two specific crimes that result in Ixion's eternal damnation: the murder of a family member and the attempted rape of Hera (31–34). In retaliation for the latter Zeus fashions a false Hera, a cloud bearing the appearance and sexual allure of the real one. Ixion couples with her and begets Centaurus, who in turn becomes the eponymous forebear of the half-man, half-horse creatures familiar from mythology.[18] The usual story of Ixion is that he

17. On the date and occasion of *Pythian* 2, see Duchemin 1970, 82–83; Gantz 1978b; Kirkwood 1982, 141–42; Lloyd-Jones 1973, 118; and Morgan 2015, 172–75. Morgan goes so far as to conjecture that the ode may not even be an epinician, but I see in the ode the same ideals about reciprocity and exchange that are intrinsic to Pindar's epinician poetry. On the relevance of *Pythian* 2 to Sicily, see Duchemin 1970; Morgan 2015, 163–208.

18. Stamatopoulou 2017, 94, notes that the figure of Centaurus as an intermediate generation between

reneges on his promise of gifts to his father-in-law and murders him; he is subsequently overcome by madness. Zeus purges him of bloodguilt and invites
him to Olympus, only to expel him for attempting to rape Hera.[19] While Pindar
makes specific reference to both of Ixion's crimes, his reference to the murder is
vague and presupposes a precise familiarity with the rest of the myth.[20] Details
of Ixion's bloodguilt are omitted or downplayed in Pindar's version.[21]

Instead, Pindar focuses on Ixion's violation of his reciprocal relationship
with Zeus, in accordance with the ode's overall message about the importance
of gratitude to a benefactor.[22] Ixion's attempted rape of Hera inverts Homer's
presentation, where it is Zeus who couples with Ixion's wife (*Il.* 14.317). Further,
Pindar presents Zeus more than Hera as Ixion's primary victim; Hera is merely
a possession of her husband: Ἥρας ὅτ' ἐράσσατο, τὰν Διὸς εὐναὶ λάχον |
πολυγαθέες ("When he developed lust for Hera, who was the property of Zeus'
pleasing marital bed," *P.* 2.27–28). Pindar even casts Zeus rather than Hera as
the fashioner of the Hera-cloud, thus emphasizing that the primary conflict is
between Zeus and Ixion, rather than Hera and Ixion.[23] This framing evokes the
mythical view of Helen's abduction as a violation of xenia against Menelaus
(Herodotus 2.115.4);[24] it also reflects general ancient Greek attitudes about sexual violence as undermining male authority.[25] Ixion, too, sees his crimes in this
light: he issues warnings from his wheel of torment to "approach your benefac-

---

Ixion and the Centaurs appears to be a Pindaric innovation reflecting the influence of Hesiodic
genealogical poetry.

19. Most 1985, 77.
20. Most 1985, 81–82.
21. Morgan 2015, 183–84, suggests that Ixion's bloodguilt is presented as a pardonable offense in
order to align him with the tyrant Hieron, "who would without doubt have lived a life involving
acts of greater-than-usual cruelty and deceit." Gantz 1978b, 21–22, also sees a parallel between
Ixion and Hieron, but posits delusional inability to perceive reality correctly as their salient point
of similarity. I see Ixion more as a negative example for the poet than as a parallel for Hieron, but
given the symmetry between parties in xenia, it is quite possible for Ixion to serve both
purposes.
22. See Lloyd-Jones 1973, 121 and n. 75. This does not exclude other interpretations, but rather complements them. For example, I find compelling the argument of Morgan 2015, 163–208, that this
ode presents us with a "royal poetics."
23. This differs from another known account in which Hera creates her cloud imitation; as Christopher Carey writes (1981, 39 *ad* 40), "there was another, perhaps later, account (see RE X 1376), in
which Hera fashioned the cloud. Whether or not Pindar knew of this version, it is significant that
for Pindar Hera is the passive victim." See also Gildersleeve 1885, 260, citing Schol. Eur. *Phoen.*
1185.
24. Harris 2006, 310.
25. Such attitudes were the rationale behind many Athenian laws concerning sexual violence. See
Harris 2006, 314–16.

tor and repay him by returning gentle favors" (τὸν εὐεργέταν ἀγαναῖς ἀμοιβαῖς ἐποιχομένους τίνεσθαι, 24).[26]

The parallels between the mythological digression and the praise narrative are clear so far: Pindar will not fail Hieron the way Ixion has failed Zeus. In the myth Pindar tells, it is deception that ultimately severs the relationship between Ixion and Zeus; their story allegorically reinforces Pindar's implied promises to uphold reciprocal parity and to be truthful. He explicitly articulates his participation in reciprocity toward the end of the ode (φίλον εἴη φιλεῖν· | ποτὶ δ' ἐχθρὸν ἅτ' ἐχθρὸς ἐὼν λύκοιο δίκαν ὑποθεύσομαι, "Let me be a *friend to a friend*; and as *an enemy to an enemy* I will ambush him like a wolf," P. 2.82–84), and he implicitly assures of his truthfulness when he praises Rhadamanthys for taking no pleasure in deceptions (οὐδ' ἀπάταισι θυμὸν τέρπεται ἔνδοθεν, 74).[27] This is a fairly straightforward message, given that deception is antithetical to the spirit of alētheia fundamental to reciprocal relationships, as the example of Augeas in *Olympian* 10 tells us.

The Active-Passive Paradox: Feminizing Male Deception

What is surprising in this lesson about reciprocity is that it is not the violator, Ixion, who has committed the deception; rather, it is Zeus who enacts the deception that ultimately severs the relationship. Further, he does so by creating a female figure to embody that deception. The introduction of this kind of female figure complicates an otherwise simple picture as it creates multiple agents of deception and obscures the distinction between Ixion's crime and his punishment. These obfuscations can actually help us understand Pindar's conception of his poetry, by drawing attention to the complexities of authorial agency. Pindar's depiction of the Hera-cloud draws on gendered circularities reminiscent of Hesiod's Muses and Stesichorus' Helen. Although Zeus is unequivocally the creator of the cloud, his agency in her creation is understated as he is mentioned only twice and each time in oblique cases (Διός, 34; Ζηνός, 40) before he recedes to the background. His part in Ixion's punishment has been obscured by the language as well, which casts Ixion as the agent of his own

---

26. On the interplay between Ixion's vocal and corporeal actions and experiences, see Uhlig 2019, 211–17.
27. On Rhadamanthys and the connections between *Olympian* 2 and *Pythian* 2, see Duchemin 1970, 84–85.

torment (τὸν δὲ τετράκναμον ἔπραξε δεσμόν | ἑὸν ὄλεθρον ὅγ᾽, "This man made that four-spoked bond his own doom," 40–41).[28]

The obfuscation of Zeus' agency is possible in part through the nature of his creation. Pindar refers to the Hera-cloud as a pseudos, a word he usually reserves for verbal falsehoods:[29]

ἐπεὶ νεφέλᾳ παρελέξατο
ψεῦδος γλυκὺ μεθέπων ἄιδρις ἀνήρ·
εἶδος γὰρ ὑπεροχωτάτᾳ πρέπεν Οὐρανιᾶν
θυγατέρι Κρόνου· ἄντε δόλον αὐτῷ θέσαν
Ζηνὸς παλάμαι, καλὸν πῆμα. (P. 2.36–40)

Because he lay with a cloud, a man unwittingly chasing a sweet *lie*, for in appearance she was like the most prominent of the celestial goddesses, the daughter of Cronus, which the devices of Zeus set as a trap for him, a beautiful bane.

The pseudos of the Hera-cloud is what Zeus has fabricated as a "trap" and a "bane" for Ixion (δόλον, 39; πῆμα, 40). It represents the introduction of falsehood and deception into the relationship between Zeus and Ixion, a kind of relationship that, as we have seen in the examples of previous chapters, must be premised on alētheia. Zeus effectively ends this relationship by creating a pseudos that would be directly antithetical to it. As a pseudos, the cloud serves as an act of communication from Zeus to Ixion. Through her Zeus "speaks" to Ixion, conveying to him a false message that seduction of Hera is permissible. The Hera-cloud, then, constitutes a communicative act between two male figures, a deceptive message from Zeus to Ixion that ultimately severs relations between them.

The very nature of this imitation Hera as a manufactured cloud puts her in an intermediate position between active and passive. A cloud suggests intangibility. But she is "real" enough to engage in sexual and reproductive activity and as such she blurs the distinction between illusion and reality.[30] And although she is an ethereal pseudos concocted by Zeus, she has her own bodily reality and capabilities. A comparable phenomenon can be found in Hephaestus' female attendants, crafted from gold, who are explicitly said to have their own

28. Gantz 1978b, 23, also makes this observation.
29. See O. 1.29, 4.17, 10.5; P. 4.99, 9.42; N. 1.18, 7.22.
30. See Park 2017.

sentience and skills learned from the gods (*Iliad* 18.417–20). This active-passive intermediary position is one that is well documented in ancient Greek representations of the female, as Ann Bergren has articulated:

> Women are *like* words, they are "metaphorical words," but they are also original sources of speech, speakers themselves. They are both passive objects and active agents of linguistic exchange. . . . In this relation to the linguistic and the social system, the woman . . . is paradoxically both secondary and original, both passive and active, both a silent and a speaking sign. (Bergren 1983, 76 = Bergren 2008, 20)

Speaking to Herodotus' characterizations of women, Bergren relies in part on the work of Lévi-Strauss, who observes that in the practice of marriage exchange, women are traded between men as a communicative sign, yet themselves generate their own signs.[31] Deborah Lyons makes similar observations about archaic and classical Greek literature and culture more broadly: "As much as men may define women as exchange objects, there is always the possibility that women will find a way to express their own agency—in the Greek mythic context, usually by giving themselves away again."[32] In ancient Greek literary representations, female figures are passive objects in exchanges that communicate power relationships between men. Yet they have their own (limited) agency to act as well. This passive-active duality has implications for how we understand Pindar's conception of poetry, as I will explain further below.

The Hera-cloud exemplifies passive agency.[33] Originating as an invention of Zeus, she is capable of sexual and reproductive activity, which increasingly becomes the focus of the mythological narrative. Born as a cloud, pseudo-Hera nevertheless acquires enough tangibility to couple with Ixion and foster a line of descendants, with which the mythological digression concludes:

ἄνευ οἱ Χαρίτων τέκεν γόνον ὑπερφίαλον
μόνα καὶ μόνον οὔτ' ἐν ἀνδράσι γερασφόρον οὔτ' ἐν θεῶν νόμοις·
τὸν ὀνύμαζε τράφοισα Κένταυρον. (42–44)

---

31. Bergren 1983, 75.
32. Lyons 2012, 19.
33. Brillante 1995, 34, too, notes this intermediary real-unreal, active-passive status of the Hera-cloud. See also Gantz 1978b, 21–22, who argues that "Ixion's real transgression is his inability to perceive the realities of his situation," which results in "serious consequences" when he couples with the Hera-cloud and engenders progeny.

Without the Graces, that singular woman bore a singular, monstrous child, who was honored neither among men nor in the customs of the gods. She raised him and called him Centaurus.

At this point, Zeus' hand has completely disappeared. Even attention to Ixion, after a few reiterative words about his punishment, yields to a focus on the Hera-cloud and her progeny. The repetition of μόνα/μόνον (43) stresses the singularity of the Hera-cloud and her child Centaurus, whose isolation, as Bonnie MacLachlan observes, is further accentuated by the absence of the Graces (Charites) from the birth.[34] The lack of charis also makes the cloud and her offspring antithetical to the promise of reciprocity that permeates the poem, for example, in the poet's reverence for charis in line 17 (ἄγει δὲ χάρις φίλων ποί τινος ἀντὶ ἔργων ὀπιζομένα, "Respectful gratitude for someone's friendly deeds is a guide in some way").[35] The cloud thus becomes a distorted reflection of poetic activity; like the poet, the Hera-cloud has creative capacity, but (presumably unlike the poet) her creation is devoid of charis, which gestures both to the aesthetic qualities of poetry and to the spirit of reciprocal exchange that underlies Pindar's poetry.[36] The absence of charis from the Hera-cloud's childbirth is a telling metaphor for the poet's creative activity and how it differs from the cloud's.

The Hera-cloud, originally a passive illusion, is now an independent, discrete entity. By playing the dual roles of message and speaker, she enables a communicative act by Zeus, who in creating her as a deception, metaphorically "speaks" through her. By fashioning her, Zeus ensures punishment or retribution, but he transfers the agency of deception onto her by creating a figure who can act for herself. Deception is thus feminized, as an initially male act of falsehood is transformed into a female act of seduction.[37] This allows Zeus to achieve his purpose: to punish Ixion without directly interacting with him any further. Through the Hera-cloud Zeus can engage in a xenia-severing act of deception without being in the same category as a figure like Augeas, for he uses a female proxy to carry out this deed. Feminizing Zeus' deception in this way carries a

---

34. MacLachlan 1993, 121: "Further, he [Ixion] and his offspring are isolated from human society, from the Charites."
35. Brillante 1995, 35–36.
36. See Slater 1969, s.v. "χάρις"; see also my discussion of charis in *Olympian* 1 in the previous chapter.
37. Buxton 1982, 63–66, makes a comparable point when he suggests that seductive persuasion is the female version of dolos.

number of interrelated implications. First, the Hera-cloud reflects a general tendency in archaic and classical Greek thought of stereotyping female figures as more deceptive than male figures, a phenomenon I will discuss further in my examples of male seduction at the end of this chapter. Second, the cloud exemplifies a certain poetic convention of female depiction, as I will discuss in the next section. As Zeus' creation with her own procreative abilities, the Hera-cloud embodies a conflation of male and female creation and as such can function as a metaphor for male poetic creation of female figures. In transferring agency from Zeus to the Hera-cloud, Pindar participates in a tradition of refracting poetic creativity through female figures and thereby expressing subtle statements about creative agency. It is this complicated tradition to which I now turn.

The Hera-Cloud's Ancestors and Epinician Poetry

The Hera-cloud evokes aspects of Hesiod's Muses in the *Theogony*, which I discussed earlier in this chapter. As an illusory resemblance of something real, the Hera-cloud parallels the falsehoods of Hesiod's Muses that resemble truths (*Th.* 27), and as an invention of Zeus with her own physical capabilities, she embodies active-passive paradoxes similar to those of Hesiod's Muses. Just as Hesiod's interaction with the Muses shows the circularity between inspiration and authorship, poet and subject matter, male and female, so too does the Hera-cloud reflect the circularity of male and female agency inherent in male creation of female agents, particularly deceptive agents. Hesiod's poetry presents another analog as well: Pandora, who inaugurates the association of deception, mystery, and seduction with the female and informs the way subsequent poets conceptualize woman.[38] As punishment for the theft of fire Zeus commissions the creation of the first mortal woman (*Th.* 570; *Op.* 57), Hephaestus molds her from earth (*Op.* 60), Athena dresses her (*Th.* 576–77) and teaches her various skills (*Op.* 63–64), Aphrodite invests her with sexual charms (*Op.* 65–66), and the other gods and goddesses grant their own gifts. The resultant figure of Pandora embodies a paradox: she is beautiful but evil (*Th.* 585), a gift from the gods but a bane for man (*Op.* 81–82), a creature with *or* without whom man's life is intolerable (*Th.* 603–12). Not only is Pandora responsible for unleashing every

---

38. Loraux 1978 (translated in Loraux 1993, 72–110) demonstrates that the consistency of ancient Greek representations of women can be traced to Hesiod's Pandora myth in the *Theogony*.

possible evil into the world, she and the race of women as a whole drain all the resources of mankind (*Th.* 590–612).[39] Lyons has called her the "original dangerous gift" from the gods.[40] Traces of Hesiod's Pandora appear in later representations of female figures, suggesting that she establishes the conventions to be followed. The very notion of Pandora as a divinely created precedent is echoed by Semonides, Fragment 7, which proposes female descent from an original source, or rather, sources[41] and is in turn echoed by Phocylides (Fr. 2 Diehl).[42] Fragment 7 recalls Hesiod's Pandora at several points, first and foremost in the role of Zeus. In Hesiod Zeus is credited with (or blamed for) the creation of woman, which occurs "on account of the plans of Zeus" (Κρονίδεω διὰ βουλάς, *Th.* 572 = *Op.* 71). Semonides, too, repeatedly emphasizes Zeus' authorship in the creation of all women (Semon. 7.96–97; 7.96 = 7.115), and of the ape-woman and bee-woman specifically (71–72, 92–93).[43]

These points of verbal and thematic similarity suggest poetic conventions for the depiction of women, conventions that resurface in *Pythian* 2's Hera-cloud.[44] She too is an invention of Zeus and a "gift" to a mortal man, who then proceeds to ensnare and entrap her hapless recipient. The Hera-cloud is also a beautiful bane (καλὸν πῆμα, *P.* 2.40), a paradox that affiliates her with Pandora (καλὸν κακόν, *Th.* 585; πῆμα μέγα, *Th.* 591) and Semonides' horse-woman (καλὸν . . . κακόν, Semon. 7.67–68). Furthermore, both Pandora and the Hera-cloud have been constructed in the likeness of something else: the Hera-cloud is a resemblance of the real Hera (εἶδος . . . ὑπεροχωτάτα . . . θυγατέρι Κρόνου,

---

39. Hesiod's depiction of Pandora results in duBois declaring him the beginning of the "anti-erotic and misogynist tradition" (1992, 114). Other scholars take more ambiguous stances: Marquardt 1982, 283, argues that Hesiod's Pandora represents both the negative side of sexuality, deceptive seduction, as well as the positive, creative aspect, sexual beauty; Zarecki 2007 argues that Pandora is analogous to the Good Eris in the *Works and Days*. See Blümer 2001 vol. 2, 239–395, for other scholarship on Pandora.

40. Lyons 2003, 97–99. See also Lyons 2012, 38–45.

41. The similarities between Hesiod's Pandora and Semonides' female types have been noted by (among others) Blanchard 2003, 80–85; Brown 2018, 41; Campbell 1982, 187; Lloyd-Jones 1975, 20; Loraux 1978 (=1993, 72–110); West 1966, 326.

42. See Blanchard 2003, 85 and Loraux 1978, 57–58, 80n120, 81n126, 82n133, 84n157, 86nn188–89 (=1993, 93–96, 101n157, 104n177, 106n188, and 107n189).

43. Lloyd-Jones asserts "it is obvious that [Semonides'] poem is influenced by . . . Hesiod" and "Hesiod was certainly known to Semonides" (1975, 18 and 20; informed by resonances between Semon. 6 and Hes., *Op.* 702–3). Morgan 2005, 76, argues that Semonides' emphasis on Zeus drives home the point that "men and women are inextricably involved, and that far from being a bad thing, many women are necessary, useful, clever, or good." See also Osborne 2001, 59, who similarly argues that Semonides' poem "makes women more necessary, not less."

44. Pandora is not the only Hesiodic model for Pindar's Hera-cloud, who also mimics the Hesiodic narrative of Endymion (Stamatopoulou 2017, 96–99).

P. 2.38–39) while Pandora is made in the image of a modest maiden (παρθένῳ αἰδοίη ἴκελον, *Th.* 572 = *Op.* 71). The Hera-cloud is a "sweet lie" and a "deception" (ψεῦδος γλυκύ, 2.37; δόλον, 2.39), similar to the "sheer deception" Pandora represents (δόλον αἰπύν, *Op.* 83, *Th.* 589) and reminiscent of the conniving nature of Semonides' monkey-woman (τοῦτο πᾶσαν ἡμέρην βουλεύεται, | ὅκως τιν᾽ ὡς μέγιστον ἔρξειεν κακόν, "she plots this all day, how she might concoct the greatest evil possible," Semon. 7.81–82).[45]

Most significantly, these precursors to the Hera-cloud share her active-passive intermediary nature. As a divine creation, Pandora is a passive entity embodying the various aspects of the gods who contributed to her making (Hephaestus' craftsmanship, Athena's artistic skills, Aphrodite's beauty, and Hermes' trickery). She is also the incarnation of a message Zeus sends to mankind, a message of retribution in the form of a woman's body. But the very gifts she represents also enable her to act of her own accord. Not only is she a "steep deception" of Zeus, she is also given the capacity to speak falsehoods and deceptions herself by Hermes (*Op.* 78). It is through her contrivance (ἐμήσατο, *Op.* 95) that she opens the jar unleashing all evil onto the world (*Op.* 94–95). Yet she ultimately serves Zeus' plan (*Op.* 98–99, 105). In her the will of the gods blends with her own, a blend anticipated by Zeus' order that her face resemble those of the immortal goddesses (ἀθανάτης δὲ θεῆς εἰς ὦπα ἐίσκειν, "to make her like the immortal goddesses in her face," *Op.* 62). Even the ambiguity of her very name—"all gifts [i.e., those received from the gods]" or "all giving"— embodies this active-passive duality.[46] Semonides' Fragment 7 presents essentially the same phenomena of active passivity, but subdivided among many female characters.

While all three poets capitalize on familiar stereotypes about women to represent exchange relationships between Zeus and mortals, Pindar in particular couches them in poetry that defines itself as premised on reciprocal exchange between poet and patron. As we saw in the previous chapter, Pindar's depictions of mythical relationships of exchange and reciprocal obligation can be read as metaphors for the poet-patron relationship. The female figures I examine in this chapter serve a similar function: their incorporation in narratives of reciprocity reflects Pindar's adaptation of female stereotypes for his particular

---

45. The scholiast to Pindar similarly notes these resonances between Hesiod's Pandora and Pindar's Hera-cloud, as do modern scholars, e.g., Bell 1984, 10n27; Most 1985, 82–84; Morgan 2015, 187; Segal 1986a, 81–82; Stamatopoulou 2017, 99–102.

46. Lyons 2003, 98; Lyons 2012, 42.

poetry. As I have noted above, Pindar's references to poetry emphasize reciprocity. He refers to his work as "reward for excellence" (ὕμνον ἄποιν' ἀρετᾶς, 13) and casts it as a form of charis, a term that evokes both the aesthetic qualities of poetry and its reciprocal function (17).[47] These points are echoed within the mythological digression as well, expressed by Ixion himself (24) and reflected in the "graceless" birth of Centaurus (ἄνευ . . . Χαρίτων, 42).

The Hera-cloud is situated in such a framework of poetry and reciprocity. Glenn Most has documented the points where myth and praise overlap, noting that charis is a central concern of both the Ixion-myth and the praise of Hieron, tyrant of Syracuse, in which the myth is embedded.[48] The Hera-cloud, then, is antithetical both to the formerly healthy relationship between Zeus and Ixion as well as to the poet-patron relationship it allegorizes. There is some debate about whether Ixion functions as a negative example for Hieron or for the praise-poet.[49] But given the symmetry of reciprocity that Pindar repeatedly emphasizes, such a debate seems beside the point. It is the *relationship* between Zeus and Ixion that is key, rather than the precise analogues for its individual participants. The poet's concern is for the ideals that have been violated in this relationship, ideals that are the responsibility for all parties to uphold. The creation of a female, third-party pseudos between Zeus and Ixion sheds light on both the poet's relationship with his patron and the role of female figures in his characterizations of reciprocity and truth. In locating deception in a female figure, Pindar participates in a tradition of stereotyping deception as a female trait, and by casting the Hera-cloud as the consequence of a severed reciprocal relationship between Zeus and Ixion, he conveys the message that reciprocity excludes female participation.

Pindar also communicates subtler points about poetry, in keeping with poetic traditions of filtering the complexities of poetic creation through the complexities of gender. As the creator of the Hera-cloud, Zeus parallels poets like Pindar, who create characters that act of their own will. In this analogy Zeus' creation of pseudo-Hera can imply an acknowledgment of poetry's

---

47. See my discussion of *Olympian* 1 in the previous chapter.
48. Most 1985, 78. See also Gantz 1978b, 22, who argues for a parallel between Ixion and Hieron, who, Gantz deems, has "erred in his perception of reality"; Hubbard 1986, 57, on the relationship between the messages for Ixion and Hieron.
49. See Hubbard 1986, 55: "Critics have divided on the question of whether Ixion is an admonitory paradigm for Hieron or for the poet himself. Detailed analysis of the manner in which the myth is introduced and concluded will demonstrate that the ingratitude which Ixion exemplifies is a potential danger for both poets and kings."

deceptive potential, which resonates with the declaration of Hesiod's Muses in the *Theogony* and with Pindar's critical stance toward other poets in *Olympian* 1. That Zeus' creation has her own creative capacity blurs distinctions between creator and creation and situates the Hera-cloud in the tradition of Hesiod's Muses and Stesichorus' Helen, who similarly confound such categories; indeed, the Hera-cloud even shares the same illusory, ethereal nature of Stesichorus' Helen.[50] Pindar specifies the relevance of this tradition to his own epinician poetry. By having his Hera-cloud produce offspring devoid of charis, Pindar grounds familiar messages about gender, creation, and deception firmly within a context that consistently emphasizes the ideals of reciprocity fundamental to and defining of his own epinician poetry. The Hera-cloud is not merely a repetition or replication of previous tropes about gender, poetry, and truth, but an incorporation of them in a specifically epinician framework. Her story reflects the potential for creation to deceive and to lack charis and implies an assurance that Pindar's own poetry will differ.

Coronis in Pythian 3: *Alētheia, Myth, and Poetry*

The myth of Coronis in *Pythian* 3 also reflects a deployment of female stereotypes specific to epinician poetry, in a way that sheds light on that poetry. Through her acts of deception Coronis serves as a reminder of the epinician ideals of reciprocity and truth and the fragility of those ideals. She is not simply an antithesis to epinician poetry, however, but rather a distortion, as some of her actions overlap with Pindar's poetic activity. Like the female figures I discuss above, Coronis illustrates how gender can refract poetry. The occasion of *Pythian* 3 is the illness of Hieron that will ultimately kill him in 467 BCE, some years after the composition of this poem. It is not strictly an "epinician," as it mentions no athletic victory on Hieron's part, but it does adopt epinician conventions of praise emphasizing the importance of reciprocity.[51] The repeated message of the poem is to desire and aim for what is possible and appropriate, a message that the poet ultimately packages as alētheia: "If any of the mortals keeps in mind the path of *truth*, he must suffer well what he has obtained from

---

50. As I have discussed in Park 2017.
51. Morgan 2015, 270–71, notes the epinician conventions reflected in *Pythian* 3. For the genre of *Pythian* 3, see Wilamowitz 1922, 280–93, who argues that this and other odes constitute a genre of "poetic epistle"; see also Young 1983, who argues against this notion.

the gods" (εἰ δὲ νόῳ τις ἔχει θνατῶν <u>ἀλαθείας</u> ὁδόν, χρὴ πρὸς μακάρων | τυγχάνοντ᾽ εὖ πασχέμεν, 3.103–4). The poem centers on this message in the stories of Coronis, who overreaches in love (*P.* 3.20), and Asclepius, who revives a dead man for money (3.55–57); both suffer disastrous consequences for their crimes. The lesson is clear: one should make proper use of their lot in life, neither disregarding what the gods have given nor avariciously demanding more.[52] This lesson overlaps with *Pythian* 2's focus on gratitude; accordingly, similar language is used of Ixion and Coronis. Both Coronis' and Ixion's crimes are errors or failings (ἀμπλακίαισι φρενῶν, "by the errors of her mind," *P.* 3.13; αἱ δύο δ᾽ ἀμπλακίαι, "two faults," *P.* 2.30). Both involve inappropriate love: Coronis "was in love with what was distant" (ἤρατο τῶν ἀπεόντων, *P.* 3.20), while Ixion's lust for Hera is based on crazed irrationality (μαινομέναις φρασίν |Ἥρας ὅτ᾽ ἐράσσατο, "in his crazed mind when he developed lust for Hera," *P.* 2.26–27). Moreover, Pindar stresses their profoundly delusional mental states (ἀυάταν ὑπεράφανον, "arrogant delusion," *P.* 2.28; μεγάλαν ἀυάταν, "great delusion," *P.* 3.24).[53] Finally, Coronis' crimes, like Ixion's, also violate reciprocal relationships.

Coronis differs from Ixion in that her crimes are depicted as deceptive. In this regard, she is more akin to the Hera-cloud. Indeed, the key component of Coronis' transgressions is her deceptiveness, a character defect that pits her against the "path of alētheia" of lines 103–4 and the ideals of reciprocity underlying Pindar's poetry. Secrecy characterizes her relations with her father as well as with Apollo.[54] Having conceived the child of Apollo, Coronis falls in love with and couples with another man, Ischys, unbeknownst to her father. Apollo detects her infidelity and has Artemis kill her, but he rescues his unborn child Asclepius and gives him to Chiron to raise. Like his mother, Asclepius too dies for transgressing the limits of his role, in his case, attempting to resurrect the dead.[55]

The poet focuses on Coronis' deceptive tendencies while diluting Ischys' culpability (κρύβδαν πατρός, "secretly from her father," 13; οὐδ᾽ ἔλαθε σκοπόν,

---

52. See Uhlig 2019, 36–38, on the resonances between Apollo's speech and the ode's overall message.
53. Race 1986, 65, also notices this echo. See also Morgan 2015, 277–79, who interprets similarities among Tantalus, Ixion, and Coronis as indicators of Pindar's royal poetics.
54. See Tsitsibakou-Vasalos 2010 for an examination of how Coronis' crimes map against the themes of light and darkness that pervade the ode.
55. See Currie 2005, 345–68, for an examination of life, death, and mortal ambition in *Pythian* 3. See also Young 1968, 62–63.

"she did not escape her watcher's [i.e., Apollo's] notice," 27; ἄθεμιν δόλον, "impious deception," 32). These details contrast with an earlier version of the myth, which focuses on the rivalry between Ischys and Apollo rather than on Coronis' wrongdoing (Ἴσχυ' ἅμ' ἀντιθέῳ Ἐλατιονίδῃ εὐίππῳ, "rival to Ischys, Elatus' son delighting in horses," *h. Ap.* 210).[56] Indeed, Pindar's version renders Ischys, who is unnamed until line 31, nearly invisible and blameless.[57] But Coronis' deception is clear, as is Apollo's quick knowledge of it:

οὐδ' ἔλαθε σκοπόν· ἐν δ' ἄρα μηλοδόκῳ Πυθῶνι τόσσαις ἄιεν ναοῦ βασιλεύς
Λοξίας, κοινᾶνι παρ' εὐθυτάτῳ γνώμαν πιθών,
πάντα ἰσάντι νόῳ· ψευδέων δ' οὐχ ἅπτεται, κλέπτει τέ μιν
οὐ θεὸς οὐ βροτὸς ἔργοις οὔτε βουλαῖς. (*P.* 3.27–30)

She did not escape her watcher's notice, but in Pytho where sheep are received, Loxias, king of the temple, happened to perceive her, entrusting his judgment to his most reliable confidant, his omniscient mind. He does not embrace falsehoods, and neither god nor mortal deceives him in deed or thought.

His omniscience is another Pindaric departure from an earlier version of the myth in which a raven informs Apollo of Coronis' infidelity.[58] The intention behind this change is debatable, but Apollo's ability to detect Coronis' deception is crucial to Pindar's version, which characterizes Apollo's distance from falsehoods not as a refusal to craft them, but rather as an ability to recognize and reject them, an ability that parallels the poet's own (see my discussion of *Olympian* 1 in the previous chapter).[59]

Furthermore, Coronis' crimes are depicted as violations of reciprocity and thus as antithetical to the very principles on which Pindar's epinician poetry is based. Her actions also disrupt the relationship of xenia between Ischys and her

---

56. Gantz 1993 vol. 1, 91, even calls this allusion to Ischys a "clash between Apollo and Ischys," thus investing Ischys with a great deal more agency in the *Homeric Hymn* than he has in *Pythian* 3.
57. Stamatopoulou 2017, 74–75, also makes this observation and discusses Pindar's engagement with Hesiod here.
58. See Young 1968, 37–38, for a discussion of this divergence. Young argues that Pindar alludes to the Hesiodic tale of the raven with the word σκοπός (27), but chooses not to go into further detail, as the aetiological nature of the raven-myth does not fit into Pindar's overall scheme in *Pythian* 3. I am skeptical about the allusive nature of σκοπός, which I take to be a direct reference to Apollo's omniscience. Cf. Burton 1962, 84, who observes that the absence of the raven emphasizes Apollo's reliance on his own omniscience for the truth of Coronis' infidelity.
59. *Pace* Gildersleeve 1885, 272, who sees more ambiguity in the phrase: "Neither deceiving nor deceived."

father. The poet provides very few details about Ischys, but he does refer to him twice as a xenos (ξένου, *P.* 3.25; ξεινίαν κοίταν, 32), a significant repetition in light of the paucity of other details about him. The term ostensibly indicates his foreignness—he is from Arcadia (25) while Coronis is Thessalian. This detail seems to be a variation from the traditional myth and fits into the ode's general message to love what is near, both geographically and figuratively, as some scholars assert.[60] Crucially, it also casts Ischys and Coronis' father as xenoi and Coronis' crimes against them as corrosive to their guest-friendship and thus, by extension, to Pindar's relationship to his patron, whom he calls his "Aetnean guest-friend" (Αἰτναῖον ξένον, 69). The few references to her father Phlegyas (εὐίππου Φλεγύα θυγάτηρ, 8; κρύβδαν πατρός, 13) seem puzzlingly unnecessary unless they are understood in light of his relationship to Ischys, a relationship that Coronis damages. As Poulheria Kyriakou argues, there is no reason for Pindar to make Ischys a stranger from Arcadia, given that this detail does nothing to compound Coronis' betrayal of Apollo; it does, however, suggest that Ischys was a guest of Coronis' father.[61] As she further notes, "Ischys' secret affair with his host's daughter had perhaps more serious implications than a fatal attraction between strangers would have. In the eyes of a Greek audience Ischys transgressed the limits of ξενία and thus offended not only Apollo but also Zeus Xenios."[62]

Pindar's emphasis, however, is not on Ischys' crimes but on those of Coronis. It is she whom the poet implicates in this violation of xenia, indeed making her its primary violator. Her transgressions of xenia are mirrored by her marital crimes, which, too, demonstrate how she undermines reciprocal relationships. Her deception of Apollo causes disorder in their marriage, whose obligations and expectations of reciprocity are similar to those of xenia.[63] Marriage is analogous to xenia in that it assumes trust and truthfulness between husband and wife. Coronis' marriage to Apollo is implied by the poet's reference to her union

60. Burton 1962, 83; Young 1968, 36.
61. Kyriakou 1994, 32–35.
62. Kyriakou 1994, 34.
63. See Roth 1993, 3, on the relationship between Clytemnestra and Agamemnon in the *Oresteia*: "Aside from the fact that like Helen and the lion of the parable she [Clytemnestra] is an outsider brought into the house who with time encompasses her host's destruction, her status as a wife is analogous to that of a guest, for marriage and *xenia* were parallel social institutions. The basic function of each was to bring an outsider into the kin-group, and both forms of relationship entailed the exchanging of gifts and the formation of a hereditary bond imposing mutual obligations between families."

with Ischys as "*another* marriage" (ἄλλον . . . γάμον, 3.13).[64] Her betrayal of Apollo violates the terms of their de facto marriage; she also undermines the very practice of marriage as an exchange of women between men by contracting a marriage to Ischys without her father's consent or knowledge.[65] In exercising agency over her own marriage and taking this act of exchange into her own hands, Coronis fits the mold of a "wild woman," a term Jeffrey Carnes uses to describe a female figure who defies the practice of marriage as an act of "civilization" that suppresses "women who must be exchanged by others [i.e., men], not by themselves."[66] Her marital crimes, moreover, corrupt the guest-friendship between Ischys and her father as well, thus violating two relationships of reciprocal exchange.[67]

Coronis and Poetry

The stereotypes about deceptive and seductive women embodied in Coronis serve to expose complexities in the role and effect of poetry. Pindar's configuration of the myth of Coronis inherently encompasses reflection on poetry: it seems to engage with and correct a Hesiodic version, and the figure of Coronis herself is presented as antithetical to poetry given that her marriage to Ischys lacks a traditional wedding with song (16–19).[68] With this detail Pindar establishes "the absence of song as the primary motif in the disastrous nature of Coronis' new union."[69] Furthermore, with her deceptions and her violations of reciprocal relationships, Coronis is ostensibly antithetical to the poet of *Pythian* 3, who seeks to adhere to alētheia and preserve his reciprocal relationship to his patron.

This simple opposition between Coronis and poetry is complicated, how-

---

64. Kyriakou 1994, 35. See also Kuhns 1962, 40–41, who compares Coronis and Cassandra as brides of Apollo who betrayed him. Leahy 1969, 159, also compares Cassandra and Coronis but does not see Cassandra and Apollo's relationship as a marriage (166).

65. There is an abundance of scholarship on ancient Greek marriage, e.g., Finley 1981, 233–45; Finkelberg 2005, 90–108; Garland 1990, 210–41; Larsson Lovén and Strömberg 2010; Lyons 2012; Walcot 1987.

66. Carnes 1996, 31, discussing specifically how the marriage of Thetis to Peleus in *Nemean* 4 imposes a custom of civilization on the untamed fringes of the earth. As I have noted, similar points about women and exchange have been made by many others, e.g., Bergren 1983, 76 (= 2008, 20) and Lyons 2012, 19. See De Boer 2017, 13–17, on Coronis' agency over her own sexual choices.

67. See Herman 1987, 24–25, for the role of a xenos in contracting marriage.

68. Young 1968, 34–40, examines the Coronis myth and its significant departures from the Hesiodic version in the *Ehoiai*. More recently, Stamatopoulou 2017, 64–77, extensively explores Pindar's engagement with Hesiod in the Coronis myth.

69. Young 1968, 34–35.

ever, by the continuity or even interchangeability between Pindar, his poetry, and the myths he documents. Just as the Ixion myth of *Pythian* 2 interrogates the division between reality and illusion, *Pythian* 3 shifts back and forth between the Coronis and Asclepius myth and the poet's own reality, closing the gap between poetry and its subject matter and effectively presenting the poet as a participant in the myths he depicts. Such seamlessness is established from the very beginning, where Pindar laments that Chiron, a mythical figure, is no longer alive:

Ἤθελον Χίρωνά κε Φιλλυρίδαν,
εἰ χρεὼν τοῦθ' ἀμετέρας ἀπὸ γλώσσας κοινὸν εὔξασθαι ἔπος,
ζώειν τὸν ἀποιχόμενον. (1–3)

I wish the now deceased Chiron, son of Philyra, were alive, if it is necessary to utter this common prayer from my tongue.[70]

As the ode progresses, it becomes clear that the poet's wish stems from the illness of his patron Hieron, whom Chiron's healing powers could have helped. In other words, he wishes for something impossible, the same impulse for which he later faults Coronis and Asclepius.[71] As the moral message of the ode is revealed, it retroactively informs our understanding of the ode's beginning, which can then be understood as a way of embedding the poet himself and his poetry into the message of the ode.

The next passage that refers to Chiron similarly implicates poetry:

χρὴ τὰ ἐοικότα πὰρ δαιμόνων μαστευέμεν θναταῖς φρασίν
γνόντα τὸ πὰρ ποδός, οἵας εἰμὲν αἴσας.
μή, φίλα ψυχά, βίον ἀθάνατον
σπεῦδε, τὰν δ' ἔμπρακτον ἄντλει μαχανάν.
εἰ δὲ σώφρων ἄντρον ἔναι' ἔτι Χίρων, καί τί οἱ
φίλτρον <ἐν> θυμῷ μελιγάρυες ὕμνοι
ἀμέτεροι τίθεν, ἰατῆρά τοί κέν νιν πίθον

---

70. There are many ambiguities in this wish construction that scholars have discussed at length. By taking this statement as a real rather than merely contemplated wish, my translation runs counter to the argument of Young 1968, 28–34. For the ambiguities of lines 1–3, see also Morgan 2015, 272–75; Pellicia 1987; and Slater 1988.

71. Morgan 2015, 286–87, argues that a crucial difference between Pindar and Coronis is that Pindar situates himself within a community while Coronis goes against one.

καί νυν ἐσλοῖσι παρασχεῖν ἀνδράσιν θερμᾶν νόσων
ἤ τινα Λατοΐδα κεκλημένον ἤ πατέρος. (59–67)

It is necessary to seek from the gods what is fitting for mortal minds, knowing what is in front of our feet, of what sort of fate we are. Do not, my soul, be eager for immortal life; get everything you can out of practical resources. If wise Chiron were still inhabiting his cave and my honey-voiced songs were charming his heart, I would have persuaded him even now to provide good men with a healer from their feverish illnesses, someone called the son of either Apollo or of his father.

At this point the relevance of Chiron to the poet's own reality becomes clear. From the beginning Pindar has established a continuity between the myth of Chiron and the reality of Hieron's illness, embedding his poetry and its purpose within the message the mythological content is meant to communicate. He advises himself not to seek the impossible. Here he also refers explicitly to the persuasive function of poetry. In the Chiron-wish, he questions the efficacy and perhaps even the propriety of this function, thus making the ode's lesson about boundaries and their transgression relevant to his own reality.

Yet at the same time there is a crucial ambiguity. It is unequivocally impossible for Chiron to be alive, but if he *were* alive, the poet supposes he might have successfully persuaded him to cure Hieron. He thus situates himself on the same spectrum as the delusional or overreaching figures of Coronis or Asclepius, as Bruno Currie observes: "The laudator, in indulging his wish-fantasy that the dead Cheiron were alive so that Hieron could be cured, comes dangerously close to replicating the errors of Koronis and Asklepios."[72] Currie further notes the verbal and thematic parallels between the poet's longing for the now dead Chiron in line 3 (τὸν ἀποιχόμενον) and the way Coronis' desire is characterized in line 20 (τῶν ἀπεόντων).[73] Pindar deploys persuasion (πίθον, 65) rather than deception to achieve his aims, but persuasion is the positive sibling of deception, as in *Olympian* 1, where Pindar describes the persuasive power of both good poetry and deceptive poetry with similar language, acknowledging that both include embellishment (δεδαιδαλμένοι, 29; δαιδαλωσέμεν, 105). There is shared ground between Pindar's poetry and Coronis' actions, which

---

72. Currie 2005, 350.
73. Currie 2005, 350.

produces a tension between the negative female stereotypes the poet deploys and the poetic ideals he proposes.

It is against this complex backdrop that the Coronis digression must be considered. On the surface she simply exemplifies stereotypes about untrustworthy women. But Pindar deploys negative female stereotypes to emphasize how they undermine reciprocal relationships. These stereotypes have underlying significance for how Pindar envisions his poetry, for the reciprocal relationships threatened by Coronis metaphorically represent the poet's relationship with his patron. Further, Coronis' story is a cautionary tale about the errors and dangers of overreaching desires. This, too, is a message relevant to the poet and his work, as he ambiguously presents himself as shying away from yet also indulging in such desires when he wishes for Chiron to be alive. This tension illuminates how female gender intersects with creative expression like poetry. As with the other female figures I have discussed, Coronis sheds light on what poetry *should* do along with what poetry *can* do, for good or ill. In a number of respects, she parallels Cassandra from *Agamemnon*, whom I will discuss in chapter 6; both are former consorts of Apollo, and both, in some way, parallel the poets who tell their stories. Coronis' deceptive actions are antithetical to reciprocity and poetry, but they also overlap with persuasion, which is a positive characteristic of poetry, indeed, a way that poetry can communicate truth effectively. There is an inherent paradox in Coronis and Pindaric characters like her, for they evoke positive qualities such as intellect and creativity, as well as their potential for harm when corrupted by female sexuality.

Hippolyta in Nemean 5: Seduction, Deception, Poetry

The myth of Hippolyta, likewise, reflects the complex messages about poetry that emerge at the intersection of reciprocity, truth, and gender. She appears in *Nemean 5*, a short ode praising Pytheas of Aegina's victory in the pancratium. The victor's home of Aegina, a center of commerce and the mythical homeland of the Aeacidae, occasions reference to the myth of Peleus and Thetis and the lessons of xenia intrinsic to it.[74] Peleus' marriage to Thetis serves as the mythical paragon of harmonious relations between man and god, the forging of an

---

74. Peleus appears in many odes to Aeginetan victors, e.g., *N.* 4, *N.* 5, *I.* 8. For xenia in Aegina, see *O.* 8.20–23, *N.* 3.2, *N.* 4.12, *N.* 5.8.

alliance sanctioned by Zeus Xenios and based on Peleus' respect for xenia. Zeus' approval alone is insufficient, however, for he must obtain Poseidon's consent. The marriage of Peleus and Thetis thus represents a celebration of collaborative efforts and the culmination of Peleus' respect for the guest-host relationship, Zeus' recognition of this respect, and the cooperation of Zeus and Poseidon to reward it.

Hippolyta appears as a figure counter to these ideals. She tries and fails to seduce Peleus, falsely accuses him of rape or attempted rape, and finally recruits her husband for an act of vengeance. It is because Peleus rejects her advances out of concern for Zeus Xenios (33–34) that Zeus rewards him with marriage to Thetis. Once this decision is made, Hippolyta disappears from the narrative, and we hear nothing about her punishment or subsequent fate.[75] Her primary function is to shine a light on Peleus' virtuous respect for xenia. Unlike the other odes featured in this chapter, *Nemean* 5 does not draw explicit connections between the focus on xenia in the mythological digression and the poet-patron relationship of the outer praise narrative. The ode does make reference to alētheia, however, and relates Peleus' story to it:

στάσομαι· οὔ τοι ἅπασα κερδίων
φαίνοισα πρόσωπον ἀλάθει᾽ ἀτρεκές·
καὶ τὸ σιγᾶν πολλάκις ἐστὶ σοφώτατον ἀνθρώπῳ νοῆσαι. (*N.* 5.16–18)

I will stop: not every truth is better for showing its exact face, and often silence is the wisest thing for a man to observe.

The poet expresses reluctance to detail Peleus and Telamon's murder of Phocus, which is interpreted by some scholars as evidence of the poet's disregard for truth.[76] But it is important to note that Pindar does not reject alētheia altogether; rather, he shies away from going into excessive detail (πρόσωπον . . . ἀτρεκές, "exact face," 17).[77] Pindar does draw attention to the murder, however obliquely, thus acknowledging it but minimizing its significance to the narrative. By making clear allusions without providing full narration, the poet makes

---

75. Carnes 1996, 46, also notes this omission.
76. E.g., Pratt 1993, 126–27.
77. I print here the Teubner reading, but several editors prefer the manuscripts' ἀτρεκής, to modify ἀλάθει᾽ ("exact truth"). In either reading, the meaning is essentially same: the poet's vision of alētheia excludes unnecessary detail.

a show of tactfulness while still communicating discomforting truths. The implication of these carefully worded lines is that Pindar will adhere to alētheia, and the aspects of it he chooses to emphasize have to do with the reciprocity ideal, which Peleus upholds and Hippolyta damages.

Like Coronis, Hippolyta parallels Ixion in several key ways but diverges from him in the crucial matter of deception. Hippolyta engages in a lustful attraction that would harm a reciprocal relationship, just as Ixion and Coronis do. But the language Pindar uses to characterize Hippolyta and Coronis, unlike Ixion, emphasizes their deception:

αἱ δὲ πρώτιστον μὲν ὕμνησαν Διὸς ἀρχόμεναι σεμνὰν Θέτιν
Πηλέα θ', ὥς τέ νιν ἁβρὰ Κρηθεῖς Ἱππολύτα δόλῳ πεδᾶσαι
ἤθελε ξυνᾶνα Μαγνήτων σκοπόν
πείσαισ' ἀκοίταν ποικίλοις βουλεύμασιν,
ψεύσταν δὲ ποιητὸν συνέπαξε λόγον,
ὡς ἦρα νυμφείας ἐπείρα κεῖνος ἐν λέκτροις Ἀκάστου
εὐνᾶς· τὸ δ' ἐναντίον ἔσκεν· πολλὰ γάρ νιν παντὶ θυμῷ
παρφαμένα λιτάνευεν. (N. 5.25–31)

They [the Muses] began with Zeus, then sang first of holy Thetis and Peleus, how delicate Hippolyta, daughter of Cretheus, wanted to bind him with a trick and with elaborate plans persuaded her husband, watcher of the Magnesians, to be an accomplice; she put together a fabricated, false account that Peleus made an attempt on her bridal love in the bed of Acastus. The opposite was what happened. For she over and over begged him with her whole heart, speaking deceitfully.

Hippolyta is sneaky (δόλῳ, 26), deceitful, and seductive.[78] She is also deftly persuasive, convincing her husband to take retaliatory action based on trumped-up charges (πείσαισ' ἀκοίταν ποικίλοις βουλεύμασιν, | ψεύσταν δὲ ποιητὸν συνέπαξε λόγον, 28). These characterizations are consistent with her appearance in *Nemean* 4, where she has "deceptive crafts" (δολίαις | τέχναισι,

---

78. Miller 1982, 117, observes that the participle παρφαμένα here has the force of erotic persuasion, but notes that the other Pindaric uses of παράφημι connote misspeaking or insincere utterance. *Pace* Carnes 1996, 44, who argues that παρφαμένα refers to Hippolyta's impropriety rather than insincerity. See also Slater 1969, s.v. "πάρφαμι" and McClure 1999, 63. Ahlert 1942, 89, notes the salience of δόλος in Pindar's depiction of Hippolyta and similar women.

57–58).[79] The attribution of technē, a term elsewhere used positively of skill, illuminates the perversions and abuse of positive qualities inherent in Hippolyta's cunning.[80]

Pindar's Hippolyta narrative speaks to a well-known and wide-ranging myth tradition of the ancient Mediterranean, the motif of "Potiphar's Wife," the woman who tries to seduce Joseph in the Book of Genesis (39:5–20).[81] Having been sold into slavery by his brothers, Joseph ultimately becomes the slave of the Egyptian Potiphar, whose wife propositions and is rejected by Joseph several times. She then falsely claims he attempted to rape her and thereby brings her husband's retaliatory wrath upon him. Joseph is subsequently imprisoned. The Potiphar's-wife mytheme more generally refers to, as the folklorist Stith Thompson puts it, "A woman [making] vain overtures to a man and then [accusing] him of attempting to force her."[82] The name Hippolyta immediately evokes another Greek example, the myth of Hippolytus, who is falsely accused of rape by his step-mother Phaedra.[83] The mytheme appears in many Mediterranean traditions (e.g., Jewish, Egyptian, Islamic) and causes strife in the close relationship between two men, whether they be slaveholder and favored slave, father and son, or brothers.

In the case of Hippolyta the threatened male relationship is between two xenoi, as befits the centrality of xenia to Nemean 5 and to Pindar's epinician poetry more generally. The myth's association with xenia is somewhat anticipated by the Bellerophon myth, another Greek iteration of the Potiphar's-wife type. In Book 6 of the Iliad Bellerophon spurns the advances of his stepmother Anteia. His story ultimately forges a guest-friendship between his descendant Glaucus and Diomedes, whose ancestor was Bellerophon's xenos. In the Pindaric context the link between the Potiphar's-wife figure and xenia is more direct in that Hippolyta's actions immediately threaten the relationship between two guest-friends.

Hippolyta's impact on xenia situates her alongside the Hera-cloud and Coronis. Each is the instrument of corrupted relations between guest and host,

---

79. This similarity appears to be one of the few between the two treatments of the Peleus and Thetis myth in Nemeans 4 and 5. See Carnes 1996 for an examination of how the two odes and their differing emphases work together.
80. Positive depictions of technē appear in O. 7.35, O. 7.50, P. 12.6. For other examples, see Slater 1969, s.v. "τέχνα."
81. Carnes 1996, 15.
82. Quoted in Goldman 1995, 31.
83. But we have little evidence that this myth was well known before the time of Sophocles and Euripides; see Gantz 1993 vol. 1, 285–88.

even when it is a male figure like Ixion who first violates xenia. Furthermore, in enacting or even embodying falsehood these female figures shed light on the interrelationship of reciprocity and alētheia, for in undermining the latter, they also undo the former. Thus they also call attention to the poetic context in which they appear, for, as I have discussed, the intertwining of reciprocity and truth is endemic to Pindar's conception of epinician poetry. The very context in which Hippolyta is introduced calls attention to poetry. She is mentioned by the Muses, who name her while singing at the wedding of Peleus and Thetis (22–26), a wedding that itself is the subject matter of their song. The Muses entangle their song in the occasion for it, looping the one into the other so that the song's content and occasion mirror one another. There is an additional thread to this increasingly complicated web: the Muses are the source of a song that is embedded in Pindar's poem. He ventriloquizes them, merging his voice with theirs.[84] Thus does Pindar invite reflection on the nature of poetry through the figure of Hippolyta: she is situated in a song that calls attention to the occasion of its performance and is itself nested within another song.

The associations between Hippolyta and poetry are further implied in the language describing her deceits, language that evokes or even mirrors language the poet uses elsewhere to describe poetry and its potential pitfalls. Her "elaborate" plans and "false, fabricated account" with which she persuades her husband (πείσαισ᾽ ἀκοίταν ποικίλοις βουλεύμασιν, | ψεύσταν δὲ ποιητὸν συνέπαξε λόγον, 5.28–29) resonate with the poet's descriptions of his own poetry and accompanying music as "elaborate" (ποικίλων . . . ὕμνων, N. 5.42; ποικίλον ὕμνον, O. 6.87; ποικίλον κιθαρίζων, N. 4.14), as well as with his criticism of poetry misused for falsehood (ψεύδεσι ποικίλοις, O. 1.29). Hippolyta's brand of deception evokes poetry's potential to deceive, and recalls the fine line between pleasure and falsehood that I discussed in the previous chapter. She and characters like her are a foil for Pindar's ideal poetry. It is no surprise that Pindar makes use of negative female stereotypes in his mythological digressions—these caricatures of women as dangerously seductive and deceptive have a long history dating to the earliest Greek poetry, as I have discussed. What is important to understand here is Pindar's deployment of these tropes to emphasize the threat female figures pose to the systems of reciprocity that frame his poetry. All three of the female characters I have examined inflict demonstrable harm to

---

84. This evokes what occurs with embedded speech in Pindar, which, as Anna Uhlig discusses, blends the voices of primary and secondary speakers (Uhlig 2019, 43–60).

male exchange relationships, and, by extension, to the very foundation of epinician poetry itself.

Further, Pindar's depictions of such figures are negative on the surface, but they also call attention to the ways deception overlaps with poetic function. Implicit in these subtle messages is an assurance that Pindar's own poetry will adhere to the positive aspects of what these figures do, so that the sacrosanctity of reciprocal relationships like xenia will be preserved. Pindar's depictions of female gender occur within frameworks of reciprocity, as they integrate female stereotypes into contexts that reflect epinician structures. He thus refracts his poetry through the female characters of his myths. The ways in which he casts them as harmful to the reciprocity principles of his poetry call attention to the qualities they have that actually overlap with poetry. Thus his depictions of such figures are not merely critical; they also convey subtle messages about the purpose and effect of epinician poetry.

Male Seduction

Only female seduction has this conspicuous association with deception in Pindar. His consistent pairing of female seduction with deception has some precedent (Pandora, for example), and provides a model against which to view the marriage of praise, truth, and xenia by which he defines epinician poetry. I have shown how Pindar employs the trope of the deceptive female figure to emphasize her damage to reciprocal relationships like xenia and marriage. This harm to exchange relationships has implications for poetry, which, in Pindar's conception, is premised on socially sanctioned expectations of reciprocity. Poetry itself is an object of exchange in such relationships between poet and patron, a relationship that excludes falsehood. Pindar uses female figures to highlight the delicacy underlying such relationships. The system he presents, in other words, capitalizes on traditional gender stereotypes to make a specific point about reciprocity and poetry, a system in which *female* seduction can have no part.

Male seduction, on the other hand, tells a different story. In Pindar's version of the Tantalus and Pelops myth (*O.* 1.40–45), Poseidon's abduction of Pelops is violent but not deceptive. Similarly, neither of the examples I examine below, Aegisthus' seduction of Clytemnestra in *Pythian* 11 and Jason's of Medea in *Pythian* 4, is portrayed in the same negative, specifically deceptive light as the seductive actions of Hippolyta, Coronis, or the Hera-cloud. Granted, the two models of seduction represented by Aegisthus and Jason fundamentally differ from each other in that one disrupts a marriage while the other forges one. But both further demonstrate that Pindar does not cast male seduction as deception nor does he depict it as dangerous to truth, xenia, and poetry itself.

Aegisthus and Clytemnestra in *Pythian* 11

The case of Clytemnestra in *Pythian* 11 shows Pindar's alignment of deception with female gender, even in clear cases of male seduction and treachery. Clytemnestra here is a target of seduction rather than herself a seductress, yet she is the one characterized as destructive and deceptive while her male seducer Aegisthus has neither of these traits. Thus she follows her Homeric depiction, which casts her as the foil for the model wife Penelope. She is guilty of trickery (*Od.* 3.235, 4.91–92), she is a partner in Agamemnon's murder (*Od.* 3.232–35), and she is also blamed for Cassandra's death (*Od.* 11.405–34). But Homer places equal if not greater blame on Aegisthus, who steals the wife of another man before killing him, explicitly disregarding the advice of Hermes (*Od.* 1.32–43). Clytemnestra is in nowise blameless, but Aegisthus' culpability is equally stressed.[85]

Pindar's version of the myth differs from Homer's by giving prominence to Clytemnestra's role in the destruction of Atreus' house.[86] He accomplishes this in part through a ring-structured narrative that begins *in medias res* with the death of Agamemnon, then recounts the rescue of Orestes and the death of Cassandra:[87]

τὸν δὴ φονευομένου πατρὸς Ἀρσινόα Κλυταιμήστρας
χειρῶν ὕπο κρατερᾶν ἐκ δόλου τροφὸς ἄνελε δυσπενθέος,

---

85. By contrast, iconographic evidence of the seventh and sixth centuries BCE shows Clytemnestra playing a central role in Agamemnon's death. Several terra cotta plaques from Gortyn and shield-bands from Aegina and Olympia depict her wielding the murder weapon, whereas Homer faults her for her treachery, but not for committing the act itself. See Gantz 1993 vol. 2, 668–69. See also Prag 1991, 243n3, for a list and fuller description of the material representations.
86. Gantz 1993 vol. 2, 672, claims that *Pythian* 11 is the "first literary source to move Clytemnestra fully to center stage, making the initiative and control of the situation hers (as well as the deed?), with Aigisthos reduced to a supporting role"; he acknowledges, however, the uncertainties underlying this position. Prag (1991) notes there is conjecture that Stesichorus' *Oresteia* first promotes Clytemnestra to central status, on which, see Mueller-Goldingen 2000, 8. For arguments dating *Pythian* 11 after Aeschylus' *Oresteia*, see Kurke 2013, with additional citations in Kurke 2013, 102n2.
87. See Finglass 2007, 35–36, for a tidy presentation of the events of the Agamemnon myth, both in chronological order and in the order presented by *Pythian* 11.

ὁπότε Δαρδανίδα κόραν Πριάμου Κασσάνδραν πολιῷ χαλκῷ σὺν
    Ἀγαμεμνονίᾳ
ψυχᾷ πόρευ' Ἀχέροντος ἀκτὰν παρ' εὔσκιον
νηλὴς γυνά. (P. 11.17–22)

[Orestes] whom indeed, when his father was murdered, the nurse Arsinoe took
from under Clytemnestra's mighty hands[88] away from her grievous treachery
when she with a gray sword[89] made the Dardanian daughter of Priam, Cassandra, go to the shadowy promontory of Acheron with the soul of Agamemnon,
pitiless woman.

This order of presentation foregrounds Clytemnestra's culpability for mistreat-
ing Orestes and for killing Cassandra and Agamemnon and justifies her depiction as guileful (ἐκ δόλου . . . δυσπενθέος, 18) and pitiless (νηλὴς γυνά, 22).

A subsequent rhetorical question poses alternative explanations for Clytemnestra's violence:

πότερόν νιν ἄρ' Ἰφιγένει' ἐπ' Εὐρίπῳ
σφαχθεῖσα τῆλε πάτρας ἔκνισεν βαρυπάλαμον ὄρσαι χόλον;
ἢ ἑτέρῳ λέχεϊ δαμαζομέναν
ἔννυχοι πάραγον κοῖται; (P. 11.22–25)

Did Iphigenia, slaughtered at the Euripus far from her homeland, goad her to
awaken her heavy-handed anger? Or did nightly couplings seduce her, conquered by the bed of another?

Having previously painted Clytemnestra as a treacherous woman, Pindar suggests motherly revenge as a motivation for her violence. Maternal concern,
however, is incongruous with the danger she poses to Orestes, which Pindar
describes in the previous lines (P. 11.17–18). The clear "correct" answer is in the

---

88. Or "as his father was being slaughtered by the mighty hands of Clytemnestra" (Finglass 2007, 65).
The ambiguity of the phrase χειρῶν ὕπο κρατερᾶν—does it refer to Clytemnestra's slaying of
Agamemnon or to her near murder of·Orestes?—suggests Clytemnestra's culpability for both
crimes. Pace Ahlert 1942, 86, who seems to see her agency deemphasized in these lines, in keeping
with Pindar's preference for "neutral expressions when he has to talk about crime" ("Auch an
diesem Wort [κρατεραί] zeigt sich Pindars Vorliebe für neutrale Ausdrücke, wenn er von Ver-
brechen reden muß").
89. There has been some debate about whether Clytemnestra's murder weapon was a sword or an axe.
See Prag 1991 for a summary of arguments on either side of this debate. See also Davies 1987.

second question—Clytemnestra succumbed to adultery. The word initiating these rhetorical questions, πότερον, signals the imminent appearance of an alternative, the enticements of adultery.[90]

But Pindar diminishes Aegisthus' agency in this act of adultery, essentially presenting a female victim of seduction without a male seducer. He uses the language of seduction in the verb πάραγον (25), whose prefix πάρ- denotes something done "'amiss' or 'wrongly,'" as in πάρφαμι, used of Hippolyta's beguiling speech at Nemean 5.32 (παρφαμένα λιτάνευεν, 32).[91] Yet the language focuses on Clytemnestra's experiences rather than any person responsible for causing them. Clytemnestra is seduced by "nightly couplings" (ἔννυχοι . . . κοῖται, 25) rather than by Aegisthus, who is not even named as the agent of her seduction or domination (δαμαζομέναν, 24). To emphasize her culpability further, Pindar refers to her adultery as the "most hateful fault of young wives" (τὸ δὲ νέαις ἀλόχοις | ἔχθιστον ἀμπλάκιον, 25–26), painting Clytemnestra's crime as a typically female one and even using the same term for it as for Coronis' (ἀμπλάκιον, P. 11.26; cf. ἀμπλακίαισι, P. 3.13). This indictment is confusing at best, as it suggests Clytemnestra is a new bride and identifies her solely in terms of her marriage.[92]

In Pindar's Oresteia Aegisthus' seduction is not portrayed as deceptive. Instead, the manner of his seduction is dominance rather than trickery (δαμαζομέναν, 24), a characterization that paradoxically presents Clytemnestra both as powerless as well as culpable. She is a far cry from Homer's Clytemnestra, who initially resists Aegisthus' advances, succumbing only when her guardian is slain (Od. 3.263–75). Aegisthus is by no means blameless, but Pindar's focus is on Clytemnestra, on whom he places most of the culpability for death and destruction. The example of Clytemnestra in Pythian 11 suggests that Pindar presents female seducers and seduced alike as equally guilty of deception and treachery. Pindar's Oresteia complements Aeschylus', both of which foreground Clytemnestra and her deceptiveness. But Pindar's Clytemnestra is simply deceptive and a fragmenter of her marriage and her family, a hallmark of

---

90. See Finglass 2007, 96 ad 22 (πότερον). See also Ahlert 1942, 87, who also sees the second of the two alternative questions as salient; for him Pindar suggests that the real reason for Clytemnestra's crime is adultery. Kurke 2013, 122–25, presents a nuanced reading of the intertextual interactions between this passage and Aeschylus' Agamemnon, to support her argument that Pythian 11 reflects a generic dialogue between epinician and tragedy.
91. Miller 1982, 117.
92. Kyriakou 1994, 48–49.

the closed temporal loop of Pindar's myth.[93] Aeschylus' Clytemnestra, on the other hand, deploys deception to serve a reciprocity-driven narrative, one of repeated retaliation that she envisions. Like her *Pythian* 11 twin, her narrative focuses on reciprocity of a different sort, but she has a longer view and further-reaching impact in Aeschylus' iteration.

Jason and Medea in *Pythian* 4

The account of the Jason and Medea myth in *Pythian* 4 likewise absolves a male seducer from charges of deception. Indeed, Jason's seduction of Medea is depicted as helpful, even necessary, to his mission. It is a legitimate means of securing her aid and bears none of the deception and trickery that mark female seduction. Medea, too, enjoys a positive depiction. Unlike Euripides, Pindar focuses on Medea as an unequivocally helpful figure in *Pythian* 4; she is also lauded in *Olympian* 13.53–54 for choosing a husband in defiance of her father.[94] What catalyzes her helpfulness is her seduction by Jason, whose depiction lacks the marks of trickery ascribed to the female seducers of Ixion and Peleus.

A key difference between Jason and the female seducers I have discussed above lies in the role of Aphrodite, who instigates and aids Jason's seduction of Medea.[95] She provides him with a love-charm (*P.* 4.213–16) along with the language to use it (λιτάς τ' ἐπαοιδάς, "supplicatory enchantments," 217), which removes Medea's filial piety and instills in her a longing for Greece (ὄφρα Μηδείας τοκέων ἀφέλοιτο αἰδῶ, ποθεινὰ δ' Ἑλλὰς αὐτάν | ἐν φρασὶ καιομέναν δονέοι μάστιγι Πειθοῦς, "so that he might rob Medea of her reverence for her parents, and a longing for Greece would shake her with the whip of Persuasion as she burned in her mind," 218–19).[96] The love charm is effective not through deception but through "the whip of persuasion" (μάστιγι Πειθοῦς), which is depicted as forceful, rather than mendacious or misleading. Persuasion and deception may share a goal of steering someone from one course of action to another, but persuasion—even violent persuasion—does

---

93. In terms of intergenerational continuity, Pindar prefers to foreground inherited excellence rather than the cross-generational enmity generated by kin-murder; see Foster 2017 and Kurke 2013, 132–33.

94. Arguably, however, even Euripides' Medea is motivated by principles of reciprocity. See Gill 1996, 154–74 and Mueller 2001.

95. On the absence of Aphrodite from the transgressive love of Ixion, Coronis, and Hippolyta, see Ahlert 1942, 58.

96. On the iynx-love-charm, see Gow 1934 and Faraone 1993.

not have the same negative associations with lying.[97] The appearance of Peitho here typifies Pindar's use of it in association with sexuality and reciprocity markers like xenia or charis.[98]

Jason's seduction of Medea further differs from seductions by female figures in that it serves a larger quest, namely, for the golden fleece. To serve this quest Aphrodite and Jason replace Medea's familial loyalties with allegiance to a foreign land. The immediate result of Medea's seduction is a desire just as much for Jason as for a new home and homeland. Her seduction is framed as a conversion to hellenophilism rather than as a deception enacted merely for sexual conquest. Aphrodite's aid to Jason parallels Hera's earlier motivation of the Argonauts:

τὸν δὲ παμπειθῆ γλυκὺν ἡμιθέοισιν πόθον ἔνδαιεν Ἥρα
ναὸς Ἀργοῦς, μή τινα λειπόμενον
τὰν ἀκίνδυνον παρὰ ματρὶ μένειν αἰῶνα πέσσοντ', ἀλλ' ἐπὶ καὶ θανάτῳ
φάρμακον κάλλιστον ἑᾶς ἀρετᾶς ἅλιξιν εὑρέσθαι σὺν ἄλλοις. (P. 4.184–87)

Hera kindled that wholly persuasive sweet desire in the demigods for the ship Argo so that no one would be left behind to stay with his mother and nurse a risk-free life, but would discover with his other comrades, even at the price of death, the most beautiful medicine in his achievement.

The conjoining of persuasion and desire outlined here (παμπειθῆ γλυκὺν . . . πόθον, 184) resembles the experience of Medea (ποθεινὰ δ᾽ Ἑλλὰς αὐτάν | ἐν φρασὶ καιομέναν δονέοι μάστιγι Πειθοῦς, 218–219). Just as Hera instills in the Argonauts "all-persuasive longing" for the Argo rather than their parents, so the love-charm of Aphrodite dissolves Medea's filial ties and fills her instead

---

97. See Buxton 1982, 63–66, who examines the ambiguous distinction between peitho and dolos in Greek tragedy and points out that peitho tends to be characterized by frankness, whereas dolos subverts the normal values of the polis.

98. See Fr. 122.1–2 (Πολύξεναι νεάνιδες, ἀμφίπολοι | Πειθοῦς ἐν ἀφνειῷ Κορίνθῳ, "Young women who welcome many strangers, attendants of Persuasion in rich Corinth") and Fr. 123.14 (ἐν δ᾽ ἄρα καὶ Τενέδῳ | Πειθώ τ᾽ ἔναιεν καὶ Χάρις | υἱὸν Ἀγησίλα, "In Tenedos Persuasion and Charis inhabit the son of Hagesilas"). See also P. 9.39, where Chiron puts lovemaking in the domain of Persuasion. Pindar adheres to Archaic Greek uses of peitho personified, as Braswell 1988, 304 ad 219 (d) notes: "In early Greek the special field of Peitho is clearly that of sexual passion (relevance to the political and other spheres is, however, also recognized; cf. e.g., Anacr. PMG 384, Hdt. 8.111.2). According to Plu., Moralia 264b, Peitho is one of the five gods required by people getting married."

with a yearning for Hellas.[99] The efficacy of Hera's influence stems from elicit-
ing the same reactions of sexual desire: dismissal of what one would normally
espouse in favor of something unknown and potentially dangerous. Aphrodite's
and Hera's analogous actions equate Medea's seduction with the call to the
Argonauts. Unlike the deceptive seductions by, for example, Coronis and Hippolyta, persuasion is not employed here for the sole or primary goal of an individual act of sexual conquest. The result of persuasion is an incorporation of
Medea's and the Argonauts' skills into the larger goal of Jason's quest.

Persuasion, unlike deception, changes Medea's perspective but does not put
her on uneven footing with Jason. They enter into a partnership whose mutual-
ity and parity are stressed by language of sharing and reciprocity: καταίνησάν
τε κοινὸν γάμον | γλυκὺν ἐν ἀλλάλοισι μεῖξαι ("And they *agreed* to contract
with one another a sweet marriage *by mutual consent*," 222–23). This idea of
consensual seduction is subsequently reiterated when the poet says that Jason
"stole Medea *with her own help*" (κλέψεν τε Μήδειαν σὺν αὐτᾷ, 250). When
Pindar describes Medea's help for Jason's encounter with the fire-breathing
bulls, he refers to Medea as a xenē (πῦρ δέ νιν οὐκ ἐόλει παμφαρμάκου ξείνας
ἐφετμαῖς, "The fire did not cause him to waver because of the commands of the
host-woman, all-powerful in magic," 233), a clear reference to her ethnic alter-
ity, but also an encapsulation of the aid she provides to her non-Colchian
guests. The term connotes the relationship of reciprocal benefit in which she
and Jason participate and reinforces the spirit of mutual consent that characterizes their marriage. This seduction differs fundamentally from the seductions
of Ixion, Ischys, and Peleus, for it forges—rather than dissolves—a guest-host
relationship and even successfully includes a female participant in it. Such a
model of seduction even parallels Pindar's conception of epinician poetry in
that it uses persuasion to build reciprocity.[100]

Conclusion

I began this chapter with an examination of gender and its significance for
ancient Greek poetry, pointing out that from the earliest poetry, female figures
have been used to express complicated relationships between poetry and truth.

---

99. See Segal 1986b, 53–54 and 62–64, who also notes this complementarity between Hera's and Aph-
    rodite's actions.
100. See Segal 1986b, 161–64, for how Medea and Jason mirror the poet's characteristics.

I then turned to Pindaric examples to show how female figures reflect both the gendered strands of earlier Greek poetry as well as the reciprocity-driven focus of Pindar's myths that I discussed in the previous chapter. The Ixion-myth of *Pythian* 2 suggests that the same emphasis on reciprocity that marks Pindaric alētheia informs the poet's presentations of falsehood as well. Furthermore, the poet infuses deception with female stereotypes, most obviously in the case of the Hera-cloud in Ixion's myth, which feminizes Zeus' act of deception by locating it in the body of a female figure. I continued with examinations of Coronis in *Pythian* 3 and Hippolyta in *Nemean* 5 to make the complementary point that female seduction is cast as deception. All three figures are culpable for deceptions that harm relationships of reciprocity. Thus, the poet's use of gender constructions has a specificity to his own poetry, which he presents as a form of reciprocity. His depictions of female falsehood and trickery emphasize the destructive role such forces play on reciprocal relationships like xenia. Such depiction of female seduction adheres somewhat to dominant female paradigms in ancient Greek poetry, but Pindar goes further by portraying these female figures as dangers to sacred institutions of reciprocity.[101]

These female figures are, furthermore, depicted in ways that evoke poetry itself. As a creation with her own creative capacity, the Hera-cloud reflects what poetic creation can do when devoid of the reciprocity concerns that govern Pindar's poetic activity. The Hera-cloud not only reflects stereotypes about female deception, she does so in a way that sheds light on how Pindar's reciprocity-driven epinician poetry works. Similarly, Coronis' secrecy and deception reflect negative female stereotypes, but in the context of *Pythian* 3 they also present a corrupted form of poetry's persuasive function. So, too, the context in which Hippolyta appears magnifies her relevance to poetry, and the language describing her deceptive traits puts them on the same continuum as Pindar's poetic activity. Such use of gender constructs demonstrates their signaling function, as they do not simply reflect male-female relations but rather point to the ways poetry operates. The Hera-cloud, Coronis, and Hippolyta belong in the tradition of Hesiod's Muses or Stesichorus' Helen in that the gender stereotypes they embody reflect poetic qualities (seemingly) unrelated to gender. In the context of Pindar's epinician, their relevance is specific to his particular poetic program.

---

101. Cf. McClure 1999, 32–69, who argues that verbal genres are gendered and that seductive persuasion is a specifically female mode of speech.

In their relation to truth, reciprocity, and poetry, these female figures complement many of Aeschylus' female characters who are central to his narratives of reciprocity. As in Pindar, reciprocity is figured as truth in Aeschylean tragedy; that is to say, Aeschylean instances of alētheia reflect principles of reciprocity. In Aeschylus, this truth-reciprocity combination has the effect of depicting the force of reciprocity as an inevitability. As in Pindar, Aeschylean truth is intertwined with a particular model of reciprocity relevant to his poetry, and female figures are embedded in this framework. A further complementarity is in the authorial function of many of Aeschylus' female characters. Like the female figures examined in this chapter, Aeschylus' female characters have a creative or verbal capacity that parallels the poet's own. But unlike Pindar's female figures, Aeschylus' perpetuate and articulate reciprocity rather than undermining it. Though both poets' female figures call attention to the poetic contexts in which they appear, Pindar's illustrate the delicacy of reciprocal relationships while Aeschylus' female characters reinforce their frameworks of reciprocity. The female characters of Pindar's and Aeschylus' poetry represent two sides of the same coin, reflecting the thematic complementarities between the two poets that ground this book.

CHAPTER 4

Women Know Best

Aeschylus' Seven against Thebes

As we turn to Aeschylus, we will see that complementary intertwinings of reciprocity, truth, and gender prevail. Like Pindaric epinician, Aeschylean tragedy revolves around reciprocity, an expectation that actions will be met by commensurate reactions. While Pindar tends to focus on the immediacy of reciprocity between guest and host or poet and patron, Aeschylean configurations emphasize the temporal continuity of reciprocity: past actions will be responsively duplicated in the future, for good or ill. Aeschylean plots provide a view of reciprocity that stretches across generations, a temporally expansive view that is well suited to the trilogy form that extant Aeschylean tragedy favors. Furthermore, the concept of reciprocity is entrenched enough to be figured as an inevitable truth. As I argued in previous chapters, both Pindar and Aeschylus shape alētheia, a word that for convenience's sake I loosely translate as "truth," to reflect the force of reciprocity. In Pindar alētheia denotes both objective truth ("what happens") as well as the obligation underlying epinician poetry. For Aeschylus, alētheia is often situated in contexts that foreground reciprocity and is used to connote the expectation of responsive reaction intrinsic to Aeschylean reciprocity.

Gender fits into this complex in that female figures reflect or refract this marriage of reciprocity and truth. Here we see a contrast between Pindar and Aeschylus: Pindar's female figures often undermine this relationship through their deceptive actions, while Aeschylus' female figures tend to possess unique avenues to truth and as such articulate or strengthen reciprocity, in both its amicable instantiations (a good for a good) and its hostile ones (retaliation or revenge). But both Pindar's and Aeschylus' female figures draw attention to the ways in which the reciprocity-truth relationship is constructed, the former through distortion of this relationship, the latter through reinforcement of it. Furthermore, though their actions and characterizations vary widely, female figures in both poets' works draw attention to the creative forces behind their narratives of reciprocity. They shed light on the poetry and poetic activity that give shape to their stories.

I begin my exploration of Aeschylean reciprocity, truth, and gender with *Seven against Thebes*, a difficult play that is missing its trilogic companions and thus leaves modern readers with a fragmented understanding of Aeschylus' House of Laius myth. Although it is the final play in a tragic trilogy, *Seven* does not provide satisfactory resolution the way the *Oresteia* famously does.[1] Instead, despair and confusion reign as the city remains standing but leaderless.[2] Although the city has been saved from destruction and enslavement by the Argive armies, the question of what to do after Eteocles' and Polyneices' deaths engenders further conflict; granted, some of this conflict is likely a product of the probable inauthenticity of the play's ending, but aporia dominates nonetheless.[3] The play begs resolution but provides no viable path to it.

Like the other Aeschylean tragedies I will examine, *Seven* presents challenging questions about the nature of truth and how to access it, both of which are gendered. In this chapter I examine how gender interacts with truth, in terms of both access to truth as well as reception and perception of truth-tellers. Ultimately, I argue that the Chorus of Theban Women have perceptive and interpretive abilities that afford them a big picture view of what is happening. Further, the dynamics of gender and truth shed light on the focus on reciprocity and retribution in Aeschylus' tragic plots. The Chorus perceive the patterns of reciprocity that thread through past, present, and future, and this narrative

---

1.   See Winnington-Ingram 1983, 19: "*Oresteia* leaves no loose ends. It is of course an assumption . . . that Aeschylus in 467 was writing trilogies upon the same principles of art and thought as in 458, but it is the assumption one prefers to make." See also Zeitlin 1992 and Winnington-Ingram 1983, 55–72, whose speculations on the Danaid trilogy are premised on comparisons with the *Oresteia*.

2.   Garvie 2014 argues that three passages in the ending allude to the alternative myth in which the Epigonoi march against Thebes. Seaford 2012, 167, however, sees the trilogy culminating and concluding with the completion of Oedipus' curse.

3.   The ending of *Seven* as we have it is in all likelihood a spurious interpolation informed by Sophocles' *Antigone*. See Brown 1976, Dawe 1967 and 1978, Flintoff 1980, Lloyd-Jones 1959, Orwin 1980, Otis 1960, and Taplin 1977, 169–91.

perception typifies Aeschylus' female characters. This is not to say that Aeschylus' male characters—in *Seven* or elsewhere—are utterly incapable of interpretation or perception; on the contrary, Eteocles interprets the message of each shield to form the basis of his countermeasure. He acknowledges, in other words, the power of interpretation and uses it to inform his battle strategy. He also tries at various points and to varying degrees to situate his own story within the history of Thebes.

But compared to the Chorus, he and the other male characters do not see as complete a picture. The Chorus demonstrate the fullest ability to situate *Seven* within the broader narrative in which it participates. Furthermore, by contextualizing in this way, the Chorus, more so than the other characters, make thematic sense of what happens and provide explanation for it. In effect, then, they channel the tragedian by articulating a framework for the story. In the following pages I will examine instances of interpretation, ultimately making the point that the Chorus' way of understanding affords them a bird's-eye view of the larger story. I will proceed through the play, beginning with Eteocles' opening lines in which he attempts to control the narrative. I will then discuss the Chorus' interaction with him and the contrasting perspectives it exposes. Hints of this contrast persist through the shield scene, which I discuss next. I conclude with an examination of what the Chorus say following Eteocles' final departure.

Eteocles' Attempt at Narrative Control

The opening lines of *Seven*, spoken by Eteocles, reflect the intergenerational history of Thebes. Eteocles calls on each and every citizen, "both the one who yet falls short of his youthful prime and the one who is past it" (καὶ τὸν ἐλλείποντ' ἔτι | ἥβης ἀκμαίας, καὶ τὸν ἔξηβον χρόνῳ, 10–11), to come "to the aid of your children and your Motherland, dearest nurse" (τέκνοις τε γῆ τε μητρί, φιλτάτῃ τροφῷ, 16). By characterizing Thebes as the people's mother, expansively addressing citizens in all stages of life, and making reference to their children, he evokes the temporal continuity of Thebes' history and alludes to the Theban autochthony myth. In so doing he tries to shape the present and future by understanding how it is dictated by the past.[4] With this opening speech

---

4.   Griffiths 2014, 729–32.

Eteocles also crafts his own characterization, as a leader concerned first and foremost for the city, which he lovingly personifies. He indicates respect for a city as a nurturer of her citizens (19) and accepts sole responsibility in the case of her destruction but credits the gods with any positive outcome (5–9)—a pious gratitude he expresses again when he attributes all good fortune thus far to the gods (21–23). Eteocles in this speech consistently puts on a show of noble leadership, gracious respect, conscientious humility, and devout piety, thus prompting a positive reception among some scholars, who view him as a man heroically but tragically facing a fate he is helpless to alter.[5] His attempts to control the narrative and shape his characterization evoke the similar tactics of the Danaids of *Suppliants*, as I will discuss in the next chapter.

But unlike the Danaids, Eteocles suffers from a crucial blind spot: although possessing laudable awareness of Thebes' autochthonous past, he makes no reference to his own familial history. The previous plays of this trilogy, *Laius* and *Oedipus*, must have dramatized the crimes and tragic fates of their title characters, yet Eteocles does not refer to them here. These lines initiate an opposition that one scholar sees in the play, between the myth of Theban autochthony and the myth of the House of Laius.[6] Eteocles' speech alludes to the former but not the latter, a move that can be read as ignorant and inept or as intentionally omissive, or both.[7] Such elision, whether or not intentional, indicates a certain tunnel vision on Eteocles' part that prevents him from viewing the bigger picture, even as he attempts to force the shape of that picture. As Froma Zeitlin writes, "his is a monocular gaze whose partial vision will betray him in the reading of the signs on the warriors' shields."[8] This limited perception is often shared by Aeschylus' male characters, who do not completely grasp the implications of their actions or the context of their circumstances. Eteocles does later refer to his father's curse: ὦ Ζεῦ τε καὶ Γῆ καὶ πολισσοῦχι θεοί, | Ἀρά τ'Ἐρινὺς

---

5.   E.g., Brown 1977; DeVito 1999; Griffiths 2014; Lawrence 2007. Their positive assessment of Eteocles is, of course, not a universal view. Cf. Burian 2009, 21, who argues that Eteocles' prominence and Polyneices' absence are not meant to suggest Eteocles' more righteous claim to justice but rather to emphasize the importance of his role as a ruler, and Winnington-Ingram 1983, 48: "if the sons were culpable—or thought culpable by their father—Eteocles was presumably no less so than his brother."

6.   See Zeitlin 2009, 15–16, who discusses the alternation of genos and polis as dominant voices in the play and Eteocles' failure to recognize the former in his opening speech.

7.   Zeitlin 2009, 16–18, attributes Eteocles' focus on autochthony to his rejection of his incestuous origins and his attempt to erase the role of women in the reproductive process. For a discussion of Eteocles' references to autochthony and their relevance to Theban identity, see Rader 2009, 10–13.

8.   Zeitlin 2009, 19.

πατρὸς ἡ μεγασθενής, | μή μοι πόλιν γε πρυμνόθεν πανώλεθρον | ἐκθαμνίσητε δηάλωτον Ἑλλάδος ("O Zeus and Earth and city-holding gods, and Curse, the great-hearted Erinys of my father, do not destroy my city, extirpating it root and branch from Greece," 69–72). But he does not seem to acknowledge his own part in fulfilling it and will only come to such a realization when he hears the description of Polyneices in the shield section. At this point he suffers from a blinkeredness that prevents him from fully recognizing the story in which he is situated and his role within that story.

The Chorus' Messengers

The Chorus, by contrast, are not so blinkered. We will see this most in the final third of the play, but there are hints of this perceptive ability from their first appearance, where they display their interpretive and visionary ability. They derive accurate meaning from the things they see and hear, despite the severely limited range of such things. Their ability to conjure so much meaning from so little information anticipates the profound capacity for insight that they demonstrate after the shield scene. Of course, the ability to interpret and envision is key to the plot of *Seven*, and it is not unique to the Chorus.[9] It is a necessary tool for all the characters, who must use any available information, whatever form it takes, to understand what is happening and what will happen.[10] Both Eteocles and the Chorus strive to understand the threat before them. But there is a gendered difference between their modes of knowledge, such as what we will see in *Agamemnon*. On the one hand, Eteocles revels in information provided to him by messenger figures, who report on what they have seen first-hand; on the other, the Chorus of *Seven* derive knowledge from their interpretations of sights and sounds that indirectly signal what is happening. Furthermore, gender affects how different speakers of truth are treated by their interlocutors.

Eteocles' speech ends by setting the scene for the first entrance of a mes-

9. Nagy 2000 argues for the generic significance of vision and visualization: he observes that *Seven* and Pindar's *Pythian* 8 present their respective, related mythic narratives as a vision, and that "the visual worlds of Aeschylus and Pindar can ultimately be described as epic in nature, and that the blazons visualized on the heroic shields of their 'neo-epic' and 'micro-epic' creations are in fact a shining example of epic pure and simple" (108–9).

10. Cf. Bacon 1964, 29: "The problem of knowing where the danger really is—who is really the stranger, the enemy, the outsider, haunts the play in many forms."

senger figure: <u>σκοποὺς</u> δὲ κἀγὼ καὶ <u>κατοπτῆρας</u> στρατοῦ | ἔπεμψα, τοὺς πέποιθα μὴ ματᾶν ὁδῷ· | καὶ τῶνδ᾿ ἀκούσας οὔ τι μὴ ληφθῶ <u>δόλῳ</u> ("And I sent *scouts* and *spies* of their army, whom I have trusted not to dally on the way; and when I hear these men, I will not be taken *by a trap*," 36–38). He uses language that stresses a messenger's capacity for sight (σκοποὺς, κατοπτῆρας) and casts this capacity as antithetical to deception (δόλῳ). When the Scout arrives, reporting the arrival of the Seven, he opens and closes his report with similar emphases on eyewitness knowledge, and the singularity of his own access to it:

ἥκω σαφῆ τἀκεῖθεν ἐκ στρατοῦ φέρων,
αὐτὸς <u>κατόπτης</u> δ᾿ εἴμ᾿ ἐγὼ τῶν πραγμάτων. (*Th.* 40–41)

I have come bearing from the army clear news from afar, and I myself am *eyewitness* of their deeds.[11]

κἀγὼ τὰ λοιπὰ πιστὸν ἡμεροσκόπον
<u>ὀφθαλμὸν</u> ἕξω, καὶ σαφηνείᾳ λόγου
εἰδὼς τὰ τῶν θύραθεν ἀβλαβὴς ἔσῃ. (66–68)

And I hereafter will keep my trusty *eye*, watching by day, and you will be unharmed, knowing by the clarity of my account what is happening outside.

Such privileging of eyewitness information resonates with other extant Aeschylean tragedies, which similarly depict male characters as partial to eyewitness testimony. The Scout emphasizes clarity (σαφῆ, 40; σαφηνείᾳ, 67) and the great distance between himself and Eteocles (τἀκεῖθεν, 40; θύραθεν, 68), thereby stressing his indispensability as Eteocles' sole source of such information. In closing, the Scout again stresses his importance, conjoining vision with knowledge (εἰδώς, 68) and promising safety (ἀβλαβὴς ἔσῃ, 68). Even in his confident assurances, however, there is a subtle hint of the limitations of what he can offer: what he reports is (only) what he can see in broad daylight (ἡμεροσκόπον, 66).[12]

---

11. Hutchinson 1985, 48 *ad* 41, notes this trope in Greek tragedy of a messenger stressing he is an eyewitness as proof of his veracity.

12. *Pace* Hutchinson 1985, 53 *ad* 66, who writes, "The element ἡμερο- *need not be significant* (my emphasis)."

The Chorus' histrionic fears of pain and suffering starkly contrast with the optimistic assurances of the Scout and hint at their alternative knowledge and authority:[13]

> θρεῦμαι φοβερὰ μεγάλ' ἄχη.
> μεθεῖται στρατὸς στρατόπεδον λιπών·
> ῥεῖ πολὺς ὅδε λεώς πρόδρομος ἱππότας·
> αἰθερία κόνις με πείθει φανεῖσ'
> ἄναυδος σαφὴς ἔτυμος ἄγγελος. (78–82)

I cry aloud great and fearful sorrows! The army has left the camp and is gone. This rushing crowd of horsemen flows full-stream! A cloud of dust on high appears and persuades me, a messenger *clear and true*, though voiceless.

Unlike the Scout, the Chorus must remain within the city walls and not venture beyond them. Their knowledge of the troops marching against Thebes is thus based on a more limited view than the Scout's as they do not lay eyes on the troops themselves, but only the cloud of dust raised by their footfalls (κόνις, 81). Their knowledge relies on what they can extrapolate from signs of the troops' approach, as they are not privy to the direct eyewitness accounts that only the Scout is privileged to possess. Despite these limitations, they refer to clear, persuasive vision (πείθει φανεῖσ', 81; σαφής, 82) reminiscent of the Scout's (σαφῆ, 40; κατόπτης, 41; πιστὸν ἡμεροσκόπον | ὀφθαλμὸν, 66–67; σαφηνεία, 67; εἰδὼς, 68). Their language evokes the "clarity of mantic clairvoyance" and links these passages with similarly functioning ones in Pindar.[14]

Etumos and Alēthēs

The Chorus compensate for their limited visual range by making inferences based on vestigial signals of military activity, and they form despairing conclusions based on these inferences. The vocabulary they use for this cloud, calling it a "messenger clear and true, though voiceless" (ἄναυδος σαφὴς ἔτυμος ἄγγελος, *Th.* 82) and noting its persuasiveness (πείθει, 81), pits the cloud against the Scout as an alternative source of truth. The use of etumos for this cloud

---

13. See Byrne 1997 on the Chorus' fear and its gendered implications.
14. Nagy 2000, 104–5.

resonates with an Aeschylean gender distinction that will appear in *Agamemnon*, in which an eyewitness account by a male messenger-figure is labeled alēthēs, while an interpretive account by a female figure is described as etumos. Indeed, the Chorus of *Seven* seem almost cognizant of this distinction when they term the cloud not only a "messenger," but a persuasive one (πείθει, 81). They acknowledge the persuasiveness of tragic messenger-figures, and appropriate it for their own alternative messenger. They invoke the trust that in Greek tragedy is usually granted only to (male) messenger-figures, and they interrogate the validity of this practice. Aeschylus' other female characters seem aware of this phenomenon too. In *Choephori*, when Electra sees a lock of hair and surmises it belongs to Orestes, she laments that it lacks the certainty of a messenger's report (εἴθ᾽ εἶχε φωνὴν ἔμφρον᾽ ἀγγέλου δίκην, | ὅπως δίφροντις οὖσα μὴ 'κινυσσόμην, "If only it had reasoned speech, *like a messenger*—so that I would not be of two minds and swayed back and forth," *Ch.* 195–96).

At first glance etumos and alēthēs seem synonymous in Aeschylus. By and large Aeschylean instances of alētheia and its cognates and compounds refer to verbal statements, a pattern that reflects a variation of Homeric usage. Similarly, etumos (and eteos and etētumos) can denote accuracy in reporting;[15] it also has a particular association with etymology.[16] But there is a distinction between etumos and alēthēs that Tilman Krischer has identified in Homer and that, I argue, is partly applicable here as well. According to Krischer, eteos, etumos, and etētumos are likely etymologically linked to εἶναι and have a broader application than alēthēs.[17] He observes that the range of alēthēs is limited to eyewitness accounts, specifically those that illuminate events that would otherwise remain unknown to the addressee. In contrast etumos refers more broadly to the whole of reality and does not connote anything about the speaker's source, which could be conjecture, dreams, or prophecy.[18] Etumos is thus more flexible than alēthēs in that it can be affixed to any claim of truth, whatever its source. A thorough examination of Aeschylean etumos and alēthēs yields similar findings. The application of etumos is generally broader than that of alēthēs

---

15. See, e.g., *Pers.* 513, *Pers.* 737, and *Supp.* 276, for examples of alēthēs and etumos characterizing verbal communications.
16. Wolhfarht 2004, 19. See, e.g., A. 682, where the Chorus etymologize Helen's name and characterize it with ἐτητύμως.
17. Krischer 1965, 166. On Hesiodic etumos and alēthēs as markers of local and Panhellenic traditions, respectively, see Nagy 1990, 421–22.
18. Krischer 1965, 167.

in that etumos can refer to nonverbal indicators of reality;[19] by contrast, alēthēs is typically applied to verbal statements, with some exceptions that I will discuss later. The use of etumos for the dust-cloud in *Seven* reflects this wider application. The Chorus implicitly acknowledge a difference between what an animate messenger offers and what the cloud brings when they describe the cloud as "voiceless" (ἄναυδος). But they assert the equal validity of the dust-cloud and, by implication, the women who interpret it, deeming the cloud's message σαφής.

The distinction between the Chorus and the Scout is most simply one of gender. As young, unmarried women of Thebes, the Chorus do not and cannot enjoy the kind of extradomestic access to the warfront that messengers do. Thus they must find their knowledge in less direct ways, interpreting the signs that they can access. Eteocles makes clear that this gendered distinction matters to him when he upbraids the women for breaching the confines of the domestic sphere: μέλει γὰρ ἀνδρί, μὴ γυνὴ βουλευέτω, | τἄξωθεν· ἔνδον δ' οὖσα μὴ βλάβην τίθει ("The affairs outside the home are the concern of a man. Let no woman deliberate them. Stay inside and do no harm," 200–201). While the Scout enjoys unrestricted movement between the interior and exterior of the city, the Chorus are stuck within the city's walls. Even their presence on the stage represents, as Zeitlin puts it, a "transgression of the norms . . . [a] challenge to masculine control that is often the focusing point for the dramatic conflict between the sexes; it is the tell-tale sign of the typical tragic situation and of the crisscrossing claims of male and female interests."[20]

Sight, Sound, and Interpretation

As the Chorus continue, they draw further inferences based on the sounds they hear, which they interpret as harbingers of the Argives' aggressive advent.[21] They describe the sound of the land being struck by hooves (83–84), the clashing of shields (100), the clatter of spears (103), the din of chariots (151), and the murderous whistle of the horses' bridles (122–23), interspersing such descriptions with visual images:

---

19. See *A.* 1296, *Eu.* 496, and *Th.* 82, for examples demonstrating this broader scope of etumos.
20. Zeitlin 1990, 109.
21. Bacon 1964, 29–30, suggests that their confinement informs their fears and perceptions, prompting them to focus more on external sounds as harbingers of danger, in contrast to Eteocles, who dwells on their cries themselves as dangers *within* the city's walls.

ὑπὲρ τειχέων ὁ λεύκασπις ὅρ-
νυται λαὸς εὐτρεπεῖς ἐπὶ πόλιν
διώκων <πόδας>. (90–92)[22]

The white shielded army rises over the walls, rushing on ready feet against the city.

κῦμα περὶ πτόλιν δοχμολόφων ἀνδρῶν
καχλάζει πνοαῖς Ἄρεος ὀρόμενον. (114–15)

A wave of men, helmed with nodding plumes, splashes around the city, urged on by the breaths of Ares.

These details—an army rising over the walls, a "wave" of men—are imagined; the Chorus have not actually seen them first-hand but instead are translating the sounds they hear into sights they envision. Their reliance on sound is a function of their limited view, which in turn is a product of their female gender and the restrictions on their mobility it imposes.

So blended are the sounds they hear with the images in their mind's eye that they even profess to *see* sound (κτύπον δέδορκα, "I see the din," 103).[23] They, furthermore, embed in their interpretations the seven Argives who have drawn lots for their assigned gates:

ἑπτὰ δ᾽ ἀγήνορες πρέποντες στρατοῦ
δορυσσοῖς σαγαῖς πύλαις †ἑβδόμαις†
προσίστανται πάλῳ λαχόντες. (124–26)

Seven conspicuous heroic men of the army have obtained their lots and stand against the seven gates with their spear-brandishing harnesses.

---

22. For simplicity's sake, I have adhered to the Oxford Classical Text of Page, but these lines are rife with textual difficulties. See Hutchinson 1985, 61, for discussion.

23. On the blending of sight and sound in this passage, see Gruber 2009, 165–66. See also Torrance 2007, 103, who observes that the mixture of sight and sound in this passage anticipates the description of the Argive warriors in the shield scene and argues for similarities between the content of the Chorus' ode and the Scout's reports. See also Bacon 1964, 29, who acknowledges that the shield scene, which primarily emphasizes visual elements, nevertheless also retains the descriptions of sound initiated by the Chorus.

In doing so, they blend their interpretations of what is happening outside the city's walls with the content of the Scout's eyewitness account. They even echo some of his language (πάλῳ λαχόντες, 126; cf. ὡς πάλῳ λαχών, 55). In this way they appropriate some of the Scout's authority as a reliable witness and create a blended model of knowledge formation in which they can participate, despite their intramural confinement. What this passage demonstrates is the Chorus' capacity for inferring significance from what they see and hear, for expanding their scope beyond the limited range of things they can see first-hand.

Eteocles does not credit them for such abilities, however. Though the Chorus' interpretations are correct, they are met with Eteocles' fierce and unrelenting disapproval:

> ὑμᾶς ἐρωτῶ, θρέμματ' οὐκ ἀνασχετά,
> ἤ ταῦτ' ἄριστα καὶ πόλει σωτήρια
> στρατῷ τε θάρσος τῷδε πυργηρουμένῳ,
> βρέτη πεσούσας πρὸς πολισσούχων θεῶν
> αὔειν, λακάζειν, σωφρόνων μισήματα;
> μήτ' ἐν κακοῖσι μήτ' ἐν εὐεστοῖ φίλη
> ξύνοικος εἴην τῷ γυναικείῳ γένει·
> κρατοῦσα μὲν γὰρ οὐχ ὁμιλητὸν θράσος,
> δείσασα δ' οἴκῳ καὶ πόλει πλέον κακόν.
> καὶ νῦν πολίταις τάσδε διαδρόμους φυγὰς
> θεῖσαι διερροθήσατ' ἄψυχον κάκην. (*Th.* 181–91)

You intolerable creatures, I ask you, are these things the best salvation for the city? Does it bring courage to this beleaguered army of ours for you to fall at the statues of the city's gods, crying and howling, hateful to those of sound mind? Neither in evils nor in fair good luck may I share a dwelling with the female race! For when she prevails her boldness has no peer, but when she's afraid, she's a greater evil for home and city. And now with these panicked flights you've inspired spiritless fear in the citizens with your clamor.

This scathing response by Eteocles seemingly adds nothing to the plot of *Seven* and is inconsistent with how he is characterized in the second half of the play.[24]

---

24. On which, see Bacon 1964, 30; Brown 1977, 301; Burian 2009, 21; Cameron 1970, 98–99; Edmunds 2017, 95; Gagarin 1976, 151–62; Hubbard 1992, 304–5; Hutchinson 1985, 74; Podlecki 1964, 282–99 esp. 287; Stehle 2005, 103–9; Vellacott 1979–1980; Winnington-Ingram 1983, 22.

But the very fact of his response is significant, given that choral songs are generally ignored by the next speaker.[25] Instead of ignoring or dismissing them, Eteocles excoriates them, and his outburst suggests that the Chorus' words are somehow significant. They have hit a nerve with him.

By paying such undue and unexpected attention to the Chorus, Eteocles serves in part to call attention to what they say and the alternative mode of knowledge they present. The Chorus enrich the Scout's direct, eyewitness accounts with their interpretations of the sounds they hear and the very limited range of things they can see, and they consider the implications of this information. Their seemingly irrational fears are actually the result of such consideration and prove to have some validity. As Peter Burian notes, "Despite the easy invocation of such topoi as the need for male dominance in the public sphere and the appropriateness of women's invisibility there (e.g., 200–201, 230–32), it is paradoxically the women's fears that make evident the full extent of the peril the polis now faces."[26] Granted, their worst fears—capture and enslavement of the city (253)—are not perfectly predictive; the city will ultimately avoid this fate. But by using the limited information available to them, the Chorus correctly perceive the dangers they face. Moreover, by speaking to them so harshly, Eteocles brings attention to what they say and the interpretive reasoning on which it is based, and he exposes his failure to recognize the validity of their knowledge.

Furthermore, he attributes their behavior to a female propensity for extreme and dangerous emotion. In so doing, he makes their gender the distinguishing feature of their knowledge as well as the basis for disregarding it. His derision of their emotion and their femaleness prevents him from seeing things the way they do and benefiting from the insights they can offer. Their interpretive and extrapolative mode reflects their wide scope; later in the play they will again demonstrate this capacity for an expansive vision that encompasses the broader implications of their present moment.

Danaus as Comparison

The interpretive mode of Seven's Chorus is not always the exclusive realm of female characters, but the derisive reaction it provokes is, as a similar situation

---

25. Foley 2001, 45; Hutchinson 1985, ad 182–202.
26. Burian 2009, 21. See also Foley 2001, 48: "Whatever we are to think of this scene in Seven against Thebes, however, the tables are eventually turned on the emphatically rational Eteocles."

in *Suppliants* makes clear. Danaus also communicates knowledge based on inferred data, using nearly identical language. Like the Chorus of *Seven* he refers to dust as a "voiceless messenger" signaling the arrival of an Argive army (ὁρῶ κόνιν, ἄναυδον ἄγγελον στρατοῦ, "I see *dust*, the *voiceless messenger* of an army," *Supp.* 180; cf. αἰθερία κόνις με πείθει φανεῖσ' | ἄναυδος σαφὴς ἔτυμος ἄγγελος, "A cloud of *dust* on high appears and persuades me, a *messenger* clear and true, though *voiceless*, *Th.* 81–82). He then describes the sounds of the wheels on their axles (181), thus, as the Chorus of *Seven* do, enmeshing sight and sound and extracting knowledge from limited information.

But in *Suppliants* Danaus experiences no scorn from his interlocutors, his own daughters. They are on the same side, and, what's more, they gladly welcome what the dust-cloud signals, namely, the arrival of the Argives from whom they will seek aid. Eteocles and the Chorus of *Seven*, of course, have no such positive attitude toward the Argives approaching their city, so for the Theban women of *Seven*, the dust-cloud they see represents nothing but danger. A further difference from the situation in *Suppliants* lies in the lack of solidarity between Eteocles and the Chorus. Despite their shared dread of the Argive threat, Eteocles and the Chorus are at odds with one another. He is not receptive to their interpretations of what the cloud of dust signifies. Indeed, the predominant conflict in this first part of *Seven* is not between Eteocles and Polyneices, but between Eteocles and the Chorus.[27] This comparison between Danaus and the Chorus of *Seven* demonstrates how gender matters when it comes to truth. While their similar interpretations of dust-clouds show that gender does not always determine how knowledge is formed, the contrasting reactions to their interpretations reveal the effect of gender on how a speaker is received. We will see similar dynamics at play in *Agamemnon*, where gender does not fully differentiate how characters access truth, but it affects their credibility.

The Shields: Partial Visions and Truths

My discussion of the dust-cloud is premised on a distinction between messenger-figures and alternative sources that require further interpretation of their significance. This distinction appears in other Aeschylean plays too,

---

27. Burian 2009, 21.

notably in *Agamemnon*, and it presumes that reports by messenger-figures are straightforward and reliable and do not require the further interpretive steps that signs like dust-clouds or footprints do to constitute knowledge. *Seven* then turns this distinction on its head in its famous shield section, which reveals how even eyewitness reports by messenger-figures require interpretation. The description of the shields spans nearly three hundred lines (375–652) in the middle of *Seven* and divides the play into a tripartite structure that mirrors the "genealogical triad" as well as the "trilogic form of the whole."[28] Visual description in this section functions in a number of ways. It replaces any physical action, thus, on a practical level, importing the action of an epic battle scene but obviating the need for physical actors to perform it.[29] It inscribes within the play the importance of visual symbols and interpretation of them. And it reveals the different types of sources that require interpretation of their significance: characters look both to the past and to visual symbols as indicators of the future.

The structure that repeats itself throughout this section is: (1) descriptive report of Argive and shield by the Scout; (2) response by Eteocles; (3) concluding response by the Chorus. Eteocles now engages in the kind of imaginative activity that he had earlier scorned the Chorus for indulging. His responses to each shield require interpretation of the images on them before he can rebut and debunk their assertions. The section functions as a kind of debate between Eteocles and the shields, which he personifies as avatars of their bearers. Zeitlin refers to the Scout's and Eteocles' speeches as forming "an antiphonal pair, opposite in content," followed by "a choral comment, which supports and strengthens the Theban cause and serves as the transition to the next gate."[30] William Thalmann similarly focuses on the symbolic significance of the Scout's descriptions, and to some extent, on Eteocles' response to them.[31]

Neither puts much stock in the choral responses, but I argue that some of them—though seemingly incidental—contain glimpses of the Chorus' superior insight. Furthermore, while Eteocles does become increasingly astute, the responses of the Chorus shed light on the lingering deficiencies of his under-

---

28. Zeitlin 2009, 8.

29. For a discussion of the influence of epic warrior ideology on *Seven*, see Torrance 2007, 64–67.

30. Zeitlin 2009, 81.

31. Thalmann 1978. Thalmann notes that the structure of pairing anticipates the final duel between Eteocles and Polyneices (Thalmann 1978, 105). His focus on pairs, however, elides the role of the Chorus.

standing.[32] Although Eteocles eventually becomes aware of his own imminent death and how it will occur, it is the Chorus who show hints of this expansive awareness from the beginning. As is characteristic of Aeschylean gender dynamics, it is the Chorus of Theban Women who possess the deepest understanding of what will happen and how it stems from the past.

Tydeus

The shield section and its system of symbols begin with Tydeus (375–96), whose shield depicts cosmological phenomena—sky, stars, night, moon—essentially representing the whole of the cosmos, reminiscent of the shield of Achilles in *Iliad* 18. The messenger also reports Tydeus' insults against Amphiaraus as a coward who fears death (383) and in general conveys the impression of Tydeus as a terrifyingly loud figure.[33] The shield itself is personified as "arrogant" and "overweening armor" (ὑπέρφρον σῆμ᾽, 387; ὑπερκόμποις σαγαῖς, 391), a personification that conflates the shield with its bearer.

Eteocles' response turns the force of the image back on Tydeus.[34] He predicts that Tydeus will experience in death the very night depicted on his shield. He sarcastically demeans Tydeus' clumsy use of symbolic imagery (400–406) and his failure to understand its destructive prophetic significance for himself.[35] In directing his argument against the image, Eteocles acknowledges the power of symbol. Like the Scout, he equates the image of the shield with its wielder, perhaps even ascribing too much significance to the images on Tydeus' shield.[36] He now engages willingly in imagination to inform his battle strategy, in contrast to his scornful dismissal of the Chorus' panic earlier, which was triggered by the sights and sounds foretelling the Argives' arrival.

He, furthermore, looks to the past to inform his present circumstances. Against Tydeus he stations Melanippus, whose autochthonous origins (412) he

---

32. See Bacon 1964, 27: "Both Patzer [1958] and Lesky [1960] have suggested that in the course of the play Eteocles progresses from uncertainty, or blindness, to knowledge about the workings of the family curse, and that in this progress the central messenger scene plays a crucial role."
33. Torrance 2007, 72.
34. Thus inaugurating his typical strategy in this scene. See Bacon 1964, 31: "He turns both the words and the visible symbols back on their originators so that they work to the destruction of the bearer."
35. Zeitlin 2009, 39. As Bacon 1964, 30, notes, Tydeus' words anticipate Eteocles' refusal to placate the fury, despite the Chorus' pleas.
36. Benardete 1968, 6, argues that at this point, Eteocles—and the messenger, to an extent— erroneously perceive arrogance in the symbolic imagery of Tydeus' shield: "Tydeus' presumption is more in what he says than in what he shows."

champions as filial loyalty to mother Thebes, which will be favored by justice rooted in kinship (Δίκη ὁμαίμων, 415); this is his first reference to dikē.[37] Eteocles' ability to link present to past—indeed, to narrativize the present in terms of the past—anticipates similar strategies by the Danaids in *Suppliants* that I will discuss in the next chapter. His words here recall his opening speech, in which he presents the past in an attempt to control the present.[38] But his otherwise expanding vision still has a blind spot, as he fails to recognize that the kinship dikē he claims for himself actually entails his own destruction. His imagined future does not extend to his own death.

The Chorus' response further exposes this blind spot. Although they cheer the defense of the city, their previous sense of foreboding continues: τρέμω δ' αἱματη- | φόρους μόρους ὑπὲρ φίλων | ὁλομένων ἰδέσθαι ("I tremble to see the bloody corpses of men, slain on behalf of their loved ones," 419–21). By referring to something that has not yet occurred, they expand Eteocles' field of vision to include more vivid consequences of the battle. Unlike Eteocles, who must rely on the actual, visible images on Tydeus' shield for his interpretive springboard, the Chorus are able to engage in true imagination. They make use of an image they see only in their mind's eye, thus revealing their more expansive view in comparison to the male characters, and what they see, the "bloody corpses of men, slain on behalf of their loved ones," eerily prefigures the mutual fratricide that will occur at the play's climax. Their expressions of fear stemming from this image recall their earlier hysterical reaction to the cloud of dust (78–82). In the present context, they function primarily as respondents rather than true interlocutors, so they do not meet with any harsh reaction as before. Instead, they simply introduce the next speech of the messenger, who never engages directly with them.

Capaneus and Eteoclus

The sections on Capaneus and Eteoclus reflect the similarity, even sameness, between Argive and Theban that will culminate in the final pairing between Eteocles and Polyneices. Eteocles shows some awareness of this sameness, but the Chorus more so.[39] Capaneus' shield depicts a naked man saying, "I will sack

---

37. As noted by Orwin 1980, 190.
38. See Griffiths 2014, 729–32.
39. This sameness, of course, is emphasized by the near homonymity between Eteoclus and Eteocles. Eteoclus "is one of the less stable elements in lists of the Seven" (Hutchinson 1985, 118 *ad* 457–85)

the city" (χρυσοῖς δὲ φωνεῖ γράμμασιν "πρήσω πόλιν," 434), which echoes the shield-bearer's own reported boasts of destruction to Thebes (424–28). Eteoclus' shield similarly illustrates a soldier scaling a city-wall while declaring his determination to do so (βοᾷ δὲ χοὗτος γραμμάτων ἐν ξυλλαβαῖς | ὡς οὐδ' ἂν Ἄρης σφ' ἐκβάλοι πυργωμάτων, "This man shouts in written syllables that not even Ares would throw him from the towered walls," 468–69). That their shields include both words and image allows Eteocles to respond directly to their verbal messages and skip the step of interpreting their visual symbols before responding.[40] He emphasizes Capaneus' boasting and the wrongheadedness it reveals (τῶν τοι ματαίων ἀνδράσιν φρονημάτων | ἡ γλῶσσ' ἀληθὴς γίγνεται κατήγορος | Καπανεὺς δ' ἀπειλεῖ δρᾶν παρεσκευασμένος, "The tongue is a *true accuser* of the vain thoughts of men. Capaneus makes threats, having been prepared to act," 438–40). His application of alēthēs to this statement is telling, as it dovetails with his emphasis on the verbal force of the shield and thus contrasts with the Chorus' earlier application of etumos to the dust-cloud (82), a purely visual image from which they extracted a meaningful message.

His words are atypically prophetic: his prediction that Capaneus will be struck down by a thunderbolt (πέποιθα δ' αὐτῷ ξὺν δίκῃ τὸν πυρφόρον | ἥξειν κεραυνόν οὐδὲν ἐξηκασμένον, "I trust that the fire-bearing thunderbolt will come to him, with justice," 444–45) accords with the mythological tradition (albeit post-Aeschylean) about Capaneus' fate.[41] Furthermore, Eteocles' reference to dikē (444) hints at the pattern of retribution that typifies Aeschylean tragedy. This moment shows his increasing perspicacity. His response to Eteoclus is similarly astute, but unwittingly so. Against his name-twin he pits Creon's son Megareus, who he claims will "either die and thereby pay in full his debt of nourishment to the land or take both the two men and the city on the shield" (ἢ θανὼν τροφεῖα πληρώσει χθονί | ἢ καὶ δύ' ἄνδρε καὶ πόλισμ' ἐπ' ἀσπίδος | ἑλὼν, 477–79).[42] The "two men" (δύ' ἄνδρε) ostensibly refers to Eteoclus and the man on his shield, but the use of the dual also evokes the near homonymity of Eteocles and Eteoclus. Eteocles' words have a double meaning, but not one that he seems to detect. He does not realize that he could easily be one of the "two men" to whom he refers.

---

and may even be an Aeschylean fabrication (Garvie 1978, 72–73), which serves the theme of sameness.

40. On the complex simultaneity of verbal and visual that ecphrasis entails, see Krieger 1992, 10–11.

41. See Gantz 1993 vol. 2, 518.

42. See Seaford 2012, 172, on the Thebans' intergenerational reciprocity with the land and the royal family's intergenerational debt to it.

The Chorus seemingly express simple agreement with Eteocles. They call for the death of those who threaten the city (452, 482–84) and their "maiden chambers" (πωλικῶν ἐδωλίων, 454–55). But their words are ambiguous, as they could refer just as easily to the Argives as to Eteocles and his fellow Theban warriors. By not naming Capaneus or Eteoclus in their responses, the Chorus generalize their statements to anyone who threatens the city and their womanhood, a group that includes not only Capaneus and Eteoclus, but also Eteocles. The ambiguity suggests their perception of sameness between the Thebans and Argives, thus anticipating the final brotherly face-off between Eteocles and Polyneices. Indeed, Eteocles himself activates an ambiguity when he says "even if he is excessively loud-mouthed" (κεἰ στόμαργός ἐστ' ἄγαν, 447), and it is unclear whether he refers to Capaneus or Polyphontes, whom he has pitted against Capaneus and whose name means "loud-sounding."[43] The ambiguity in the Chorus' response parallels this and reflects the increasing indistinguishability between the Argives and Thebans. They seem almost prescient of the stand-off that will ultimately occur between Polyneices and Eteocles.

Hippomedon and Parthenopaeus

The shields of Hippomedon and Parthenopaeus both feature myths whose significance Eteocles only partially comprehends. The Chorus, on the other hand, demonstrate comparatively greater understanding. Hippomedon's and Parthenopaeus' shields feature Typhon and the Sphinx, respectively. Typhon, as the monster who endangers Zeus' newly established reign in the beginning of the cosmos (Hesiod, *Th.* 821–68), represents the instability and potential disintegration of existing power structures.[44] Parthenopaeus' shield also depicts a monster, one with significance specifically for Thebes: the Sphinx.[45] Eteocles' choice of opponents for Hippomedon is obvious: he selects Hyperbius, whose shield depicts Zeus, the slayer of Typhon. This is the only instance where he describes a Theban shield to counter an Argive's. Thalmann observes that this

43. Most translators take Capaneus as its subject, but others argue that στόμαργος refers to Polyphontes and means "slow to speak" (Poochigian 2007, 3 and n. 15) or "no user of words" (Dawson 1970, 69–70). I take the disagreement as evidence of ambiguity.
44. See Clay 2003, 26–27; Goslin 2010; Mondi 1984, 334; Park 2014, 271–72; Walcot 1956, 198–206; West 1966, 24; and West 1997, 300–304, for the function of the Typhon myth within Hesiod's *Theogony*.
45. Commentators have noted the progressive specificity we see in the increasingly narrower focus of each shield. See Benardete 1968, 11; Thalmann 1978, 111–12 and 114–15; Torrance 2007, 83; Zeitlin 2009, 51.

pairing anticipates the failure of the Argive campaign: "As Eteocles asserts, since Zeus overcame Typhon there is good reason to expect that Hyperbius, the Theban, will prevail over Hippomedon. After this pair of speeches, the city's victory with the aid of Zeus cannot be in serious doubt."[46]

In contrast, Eteocles' response to Parthenopaeus is strikingly ineffective. He fails to deploy the simple and obvious counterargument to Parthenopaeus' Sphinx—that she was destroyed by Oedipus. This is a surprising oversight from the man astute enough to point out the deficiencies of Typhon as shield-image, but Seth Benardete sees cognizance in Eteocles' response:

> Eteocles considers the Sphinx to constitute a present danger to Thebes. He does not argue that as Zeus conquered Typhon, so Oedipus conquered the Sphinx, and hence the emblem augurs as well for Aktor as Hippomedon's emblem did for Aktor's brother Hyperbius (555). The Sphinx has to be destroyed again. (Benardete 1968, 12)

In Benardete's reading Eteocles sees the Sphinx as emblematic of the continuing curse on the family. Thalmann and Zeitlin offer similar interpretations.[47]

But in my view Eteocles' argumentative inconsistency here indicates his failure to understand the past. In omitting how the real Sphinx was destroyed, he reveals his blind spot about Thebes and his family's history and its continuity.[48] He does not understand the narrative of which he is a part. His evocation of Aeschylean truth further suggests his lacunose comprehension:

τῷ φέροντι μέμψεται,
πυκνοῦ κροτησμοῦ τυγχάνουσ᾽ ὑπὸ πτόλιν.
θεῶν θελόντων τὰν <u>ἀληθεύσαιμ</u>᾽ ἐγώ. (560–62)

---

46. Thalmann 1978, 106. For Thalmann, this section represents the culmination of the Argives' arrogance and the turning point at which Theban victory over the Argives seems to be decided (113–14).

47. Thalmann 1978, 114–15, and Zeitlin 2009, 68–73, who say that in her associations with Oedipus, the Sphinx also evokes his curse on his sons, and family strife in general.

48. It is possible that Aeschylus' version of the myth is one in which Oedipus does *not* conquer the Sphinx, given that she is the title character of the satyr play rounding out this tetralogy, but the later portions of *Seven* plainly refer to Oedipus' defeat of the Sphinx (775–77). Further, the satyr play concluding the tetralogy "plainly dealt with Oedipus' deliverance of Thebes from that monster" (Hutchinson 1985, xxvii; for the relevant fragments of *The Sphinx*, see Hutchinson 1985, xx–xxii).

She [the Sphinx] will find fault with the one who bears her when she meets with a relentless beating beneath the city's walls. *I would speak the truth*, should the gods be willing.

His use of the optative mood (ἀληθεύσαιμ', 562) undermines his confidence, and the narrow application of this truth-word to the fate awaiting Partheno-paeus accords with his narrow vision of truth: he does not use alētheia to encompass the causal linkages between past, present, and future. Eteocles suffers from a blinkered view that prevents him from seeing his own conflict with Polyneices and the polluting bloodshed that will result from it. The Chorus, by contrast, do sense that there is still disaster to come, even if they do not know the specifics. They are fearful and describe words piercing their breasts (563) and their hair standing on end (564), using the indicative mood to express their fears as fact (ἱκνεῖται, 563; ἵσταται, 564). They do express confidence for the first time in the Hippomedon section (521–25), and they pray here for death to the Argives (566–67)—prayers that are ultimately successful. But their lingering fears also evoke their earlier words and foreshadow the problems awaiting the city despite its salvation.

Amphiaraus

The description of Amphiaraus is the most telling and complex example of the interrelationship between truth and vision in *Seven against Thebes*. His shield has no image on it, yet he alone trades in prophetic vision. The Scout attributes the plainness of Amphiaraus' shield to his privileging of real over apparent excellence (592), but its lack of image seems also to criticize his comrades' misunderstanding and misappropriation of visual symbols.[49] Further, he is the only Argive shield-bearer whose direct speech is described:[50] the messenger details Amphiaraus' angry castigations against Tydeus for the violence he is about to inflict on Thebes and against Polyneices for his morally questionable actions (580–89). As both seer and warrior, he is personally invested in what he can

---

49. The most incisive scholarly treatment of the complexities and nuances of the Amphiaraus section is Zeitlin 2009, 79–90, who explicates the tensions, ambiguities, and divisions inherent in the character of Amphiaraus and his shield.

50. Zeitlin 2009, 81. See Uhlig 2019, 148–55, for discussion of Amphiaraus' speech.

foretell about the Argive expedition.[51] He predicts his own death and hopes to enrich the land of Thebes with the burial of his body there.[52]

Amphiaraus' characterization within *Seven* is at odds with his characterization without.[53] He is typically associated with Adrastus, who is usually one of the Seven and whose sister, Eriphyle, he marries (Pindar, *N.* 9.9–17). His son Alcmaeon participates in the next generation's revenge attack on Thebes.[54] Aeschylus' *Seven* alternately evokes and elides these details, thus stripping Amphiaraus of his usual associations and defining context.[55] As a result *Seven*'s Amphiaraus mainly functions to declare the Argive expedition unjust, thus affiliating himself with Eteocles. The Scout emphasizes Amphiaraus' prophetic ability (μάντιν … σοφόν, 382; μάντιν, 569; μάντις, 588; ὁ μάντις, 590), but his visions in Aeschylus are circumscribed. They serve the narrow purpose of criticizing Tydeus and Polyneices and do not reflect the wide scope of knowledge of the other Aeschylean seer, Cassandra.[56]

Amphiaraus does demonstrate some understanding of the intergenerational implications of the Argive expedition:

ἦ τοῖον ἔργον καὶ θεοῖσι προσφιλές,
καλόν τ᾽ ἀκοῦσαι καὶ λέγειν μεθυστέροις,
πόλιν πατρῴαν καὶ θεοὺς τοὺς ἐγγενεῖς
πορθεῖν, στράτευμ᾽ ἐπακτὸν ἐμβεβληκότα;
μητρός τε πηγὴν τίς κατασβέσει δίκη,
πατρίς τε γαῖα σῆς ὑπὸ σπουδῆς δορὶ
ἁλοῦσα πῶς σοι ξύμμαχος γενήσεται; (580–86)

Is such a deed pleasing to the gods as well, and good for posterity to hear and speak of, for a foreign army to attack and destroy your father's city and its native

51. This dual role is inscribed in Amphiaraus' characterization (ἀμφότερον μάντιν τ᾽ ἀγαθὸν καὶ δουρὶ μάρνασθαι, "both a seer and good at doing battle with a spear," Pindar, *O.* 6.17). Dillery 2005, 175–76, discusses the tensions inherent in Amphiaraus' dual warrior-seer identity.
52. This reference is presumably to the oracle of Amphiaraus at Thebes, but as Foster 2017 has convincingly argued, the reference is vague and possibly occludes the Theban specificity of the Amphiaraus myth.
53. Foster 2017 argues that Aeschylus strips Amphiaraus of his local, epichoric significance, suggesting that the Aeschylean myth of Amphiaraus is somewhat incomplete.
54. For a concise but thorough summary of the Epigonoi myth and its sources, see Gantz 1993 vol. 2, 522–25.
55. Foster 2017, 154–55.
56. *Pace* Hutchinson 1985, 133, whose respective assessments of Amphiaraus and Cassandra seemingly presume Polyneices' moral inferiority to Eteocles and differ slightly from mine: "The terrible clarity of his insight, like Cassandra's, extends to himself; but his heroic courage produces an effect of grandeur rather than of pathos."

gods? What justice will put out your mother's spring, and how will your fatherland be an ally to you if it is taken by spear because of your zeal?

Here he mirrors Eteocles and contrasts with Polyneices. In considering the
judgment of future generations (μεθυστέροις, 581) and repeatedly referring to
the land as a parent (πόλιν πατρῴαν, 583; μητρός πηγήν, 584; πατρίς γαῖα,
585), Amphiaraus invokes Theban autochthony myths, draws a direct line
between past and future, and criticizes Polyneices for failing to recognize this
temporal-causal relationship. He thus echoes Eteocles' opening speech, which
similarly personifies Thebes as mother and nurturer of her people (τέκνοις γῇ
τε μητρί, φιλτάτη τρόφῳ, 16). But like Eteocles, Amphiaraus' knowledge is
somewhat narrow or one-sided. Although he looks to the past to denounce
Polyneices' lack of complete vision and respect for Thebes (580–85), he fails to
predict either Eteocles' or Polyneices' deaths. Indeed, Amphiaraus' primary
function within the narrative of Seven is to serve as an advocate for Eteocles,
whose affinity for Amphiaraus is apparent in his response.[57] Amphiaraus'
criticism of Polyneices' sense of "justice" with respect to the land (584–85)
anticipates Eteocles' similar criticisms, which I will discuss further below
(οὐδ' ἐν πατρῴας μὴν χθονὸς κακουχίᾳ | οἶμαί νιν αὐτῷ νῦν παραστατεῖν
πέλας, "nor do I suppose that [Justice] now stands near him in his devastation of his fatherland," 668–69). Eteocles, predictably, praises Amphiaraus'
righteousness (δίκαιον, 598) and laments his unfortunate situation among the
Seven (597–614). In his embrace of Amphiaraus' views, he seems to see himself in Amphiaraus—a move that limits the scope and potential benefit of
Amphiaraus' knowledge. Amphiaraus predicts only the failure of the Argive
expedition, a prediction that attracts Eteocles and blinds him to its implication of his own death.

The Chorus' response is seemingly formulaic: they wish for the city's
well-being (κλύοντες θεοὶ δικαίους λιτὰς | ἁμετέρας τελεῖθ', ὡς πόλις
εὐτυχῇ, "Gods, hear and fulfill our just prayers, that the city may have good
fortune," 626–27). But their wishes contain deeper truths. Their prayers for

---

57. Scholars have observed parallels between Amphiaraus and Eteocles, but tend to overlook one
significant parallel, namely, that neither predicts Eteocles' own destruction. E.g., DeVito 1999
argues that both Eteocles and Amphiaraus acknowledge their own fate and work to fulfill it.
Other scholars (e.g., Otis 1960, 168; Thalmann 1978, 117–19; Zeitlin 2009, 84–88) argue that the
parallels between Eteocles and Amphiaraus serve to highlight the differences between them, thus
suggesting, in my view, that they credit Amphiaraus with greater prophetic ability than the text
of Seven itself warrants.

the city are embedded in dikē (δικαίους λιτάς, 626), thus anticipating the final shield description and the interrogation of dikē it prompts (see below). Further, by generalizing their concern to the city as a whole, rather than to Eteocles specifically, their prayers look forward to the final outcome of the play, in which the city stands but the brothers are dead. Thus, what are superficially their general concerns for safety are actually reflections of the Chorus' prescience. Their prayers are more accurate than Amphiaraus' predictions, which for all their specificity are nevertheless vitiated by crucial blind spots. We can view the Chorus' response here as broadening the applicability of Amphiaraus' prophecy.

Comparison with Amphiaraus' appearance in Pindar further exposes the limitations of his knowledge in Aeschylus. In *Pythian* 8 Amphiaraus is a figure from the past, delivering prophecies to the Epigonoi, the next generation of Argive attackers on Thebes (*P.* 8.39–56). Pindar's Amphiaraus, characterized in relation to his son and voicing sentiments about inherited virtues, represents a bridge between generations and advances the poet's ideology of intergenerational continuity and inherited excellence.[58] The comparison reveals a shortcoming in Aeschylus' Amphiaraus, who is not forward-looking the way Pindar's is. In *Seven* Amphiaraus' intergenerational significance mostly lies in his mirroring of both Eteocles and Oedipus.[59] Although he is the only truly prophetic character in *Seven*, his insights do not proceed further than the imminent Argive attack. The Chorus' superior capabilities in this respect are hinted at here and will be demonstrated later. They will predict that there are consequences to the brotherly conflict that stem from what has happened before.

Polyneices: Symmetry and Repetition

The description of Polyneices brings the shield section to a climactic end as it reveals the symmetries between the brothers that have been increasingly suggested and the awareness of their implications that Eteocles finally possesses. Yet even as he comes to his fullest realization of the threat before him, he still

---

58. Foster 2017, 156–57; see also Griffiths 2014, 748. See Uhlig 2019, 230–42, for the temporal complexities of *Pythian* 8. Foster 2017 reads Pindar's ode as a polemical response to Aeschylean tragedy: tragedy focuses on inherited destruction while epinician focuses on inherited excellence. Cf. Griffiths 2014, who argues that Aeschylus eschews the concept of inherited virtue and insists on one-man causality; thus he espouses an essentially democratic ideology, by contrast to Pindar's oligarchic and elitist promotion of inherited virtue.

59. Zeitlin 2009, 77–90.

has gaps in his knowledge. The Chorus' voicing of the themes that explain and define the various sections of the play—a function they have served at the margins of the play from its beginning—now comes to the center. This section unites reciprocity with dikē by bringing the symmetry of reciprocal action under its rubric. Polyneices initiates the use of repetitive language for the brotherly conflict, Eteocles increases it, and the Chorus bring it to a summary conclusion as they too take up this language and convey its significance within the larger themes of reciprocity and continuity that permeate the play.

Polyneices reportedly curses Thebes and Eteocles, proclaiming either joint death (κτανὼν θανεῖν, 636) or joint survival in which he would continue to torture Eteocles (637–38). His proclamations introduce the repetitive language that increasingly denotes the brothers' symmetry. His shield bears the image of a man led by Dikē personified, who declares, "I will bring this man back, and he will have his paternal city and full access to his home" (κατάξω δ' ἄνδρα τόνδε, καὶ πόλιν | ἕξει πατρῴαν δωμάτων τ' ἐπιστροφάς, 647–48). The strength of his shield lies in its explicitly verbal component, both in the written label of Dikē and in the words she speaks. Only now does Eteocles seem truly aware that his fraternal feud belongs to his family's history and finally express despair (653–55). Hints of his previous blind spots are still present: he rejects Polyneices' claims to dikē (662–71) insofar as it connotes objective righteousness, a rejection that implies his own sense of entitlement to an exclusive claim of dikē. But he also shows growing awareness of the system of reciprocity or retribution for previous action and of his own participation in this system.[60] His repeated use of polyptoton picks up and expands on Polyneices' to emphasize the symmetry of the brothers and their retributive stance: ἄρχοντί τ' ἄρχων καὶ κασιγνήτῳ κάσις, | ἐχθρὸς σὺν ἐχθρῷ στήσομαι ("I will stand, ruler against ruler, brother against brother, enemy against enemy," 674–75).[61] He even dubs his actions as "more within justice" (ἐνδικώτερος, 673), thus enfolding his retributive intent under the rubric of dikē.

The Chorus echo Eteocles' words but enrich and elaborate on them by relating their significance. They perceive Eteocles' folly and its situation within his

---

60. See Gagarin 1976, 137–38: "This *dikē* usually manifests in a conflict between individuals, and the modern tendency is to seek a sense of justice in such conflicts: which side is right, are punishment and reward properly distributed, is justice done? . . . such questions are misleading. In Aeschylean drama there are no Iagos. Each side has some validity, each individual claims the support of *dikē*."

61. Echoes of this symmetry appear in Sophocles' *Antigone*, when the Messenger describes Haemon's corpse entwined with Antigone's (κεῖται δὲ νεκρὸς περὶ νεκρῷ, "his corpse lies around hers," 1240).

intergenerational family saga, and they show us how fundamental the theme of reciprocity is in this play and its trilogy. Their ability to understand events as part of a connected timeline puts them in league with the other female characters of Aeschylean tragedy:

> This visionary quality in Aeschylean theater is assigned to women, whether to Clytemnestra in the beacon speech and the subsequent description of the fall of Troy, or to Cassandra, the priestess, who is truly the clairvoyant. It is Cassandra, like the chorus of the *Seven*, who can put together past, present, and future, where the chorus of male elders remains baffled and confused. (Zeitlin 1990, 111)

In the impassioned exchanges that ensue between Eteocles and the Chorus, Eteocles' scope of understanding broadens, and his use of alēthēs follows suit: he applies alēthēs to a vision that must be interpreted (ἄγαν δ᾽ ἀληθεῖς ἐνυπνίων φαντασμάτων | ὄψεις, πατρῴων χρημάτων δατήριοι, "Too *true* were the apparitions of my dream visions, which divided my father's wealth," 710–11). Further, he uses alēthēs to mark the applicability of the past to his present.

His comprehension of truth, while growing, is still incomplete, however, as it lacks the full temporal extent of the Chorus' insights. He sees his father's curse as fulfilled, while the Chorus see it as ongoing. Not only do they articulate the reflexivity of brotherly bloodshed (ἀλλ᾽ αὐτάδελφον αἷμα δρέψασθαι θέλεις; "But do you want to cull the blood *of your own brother*?" 718), they also consistently communicate its cyclical nature and the likelihood of future repetition and ramifications: ἀνδροῖν δ᾽ ὁμαίμοιν θάνατος ὧδ᾽ αὐτοκτόνος, | οὐκ ἔστι γῆρας τοῦδε τοῦ μιάσματος ("Mutual death by each other's hand to men of the same blood—there is no old age for this pollution," 681–82); ὠμοδακής σ᾽ ἄγαν ἵμερος ἐξοτρύ- | νει πικρόκαρπον ἀνδροκτασίαν τελεῖν | αἵματος οὐ θεμιστοῦ ("Fiercely gnawing desire excessively pushes you to carry out murder of blood not sanctioned, a murder that will bear bitter fruit," 692–94). Through repeated references to blood and fratricide, they note the permanent consequences of kin bloodshed and its replications in later generations. They situate the imminent fratricides squarely in the context of the House of Laius and its previous crimes, and they imply that the fratricides will produce further troubles. Furthermore, they cite their gender as a source of authority for their insights, thus drawing attention to the broader understanding it affords them: πείθου γυναιξὶ καίπερ οὐ στέργων ὅμως ("Obey us *women*, although you do not want to," 712).

The Chorus and the Continuity of Reciprocity

The Chorus continue to demonstrate this perceptiveness in their ode following Eteocles' final exit (720–91). Although *Seven* is the last play of a tragic trilogy, it contains hints of continuity into events to come after the deaths of the brothers. As I have mentioned, some of this lack of resolution stems from the confused ending, which most scholars now agree is a later interpolation informed by Sophocles' *Antigone* and not authentic to the original staging of *Seven* in 467 BCE.[62] But even before the problematic ending, there are frequent questions about the future of Thebes.[63] Whatever version of the myth *Seven* offers, the Chorus unquestionably situate Polyneices and Eteocles within the arc of the House of Laius story.[64] They articulate its retribution narrative as continuous and inevitable. Such continuity marks the singularity of the ode—no other passage of *Seven* looks to past generations to explain the present as explicitly as this one does.[65]

The Chorus begin with a reference to the Erinys that plagues the family of Oedipus:

πέφρικα τὰν ὠλεσίοικον
θεόν οὐ θεοῖς ὁμοίαν,
παναληθῆ κακόμαντιν
πατρὸς εὐκταίαν Ἐρινὺν
τελέσαι τὰς περιθύμους
κατάρας Οἰδιπόδα βλαψίφρονος·
παιδολέτωρ δ᾽ ἔρις ἅδ᾽ ὀτρύνει. (720–26)

I shudder at the house-destroying goddess who is not like other gods, an all-true prophet of evil, the Erinys invoked by the prayers of the father to fulfill the wrathful curses of crazy Oedipus; this child-murdering strife urges her on.

The Chorus understand Eteocles and Polyneices' conflict as a continuation of the family's saga. By associating the Erinys with Oedipus, they extend the

---

62. Taplin 1977, 169: "Most scholars, though by no means all, have accepted that 861–74 and 1005 ad fin. are later additions."
63. Garvie 2014 argues that *Seven* makes reference to the Epigonoi, the next generation of Argive attackers, though Edmunds 2017 claims that Polyneices and Eteocles are the last generation.
64. Winnington-Ingram 1983, 18: "[The Chorus] sing of the disobedience of Laius *and so place the present crisis in relation to the disastrous history of the house*" (emphasis mine).
65. Cf. Winnington-Ingram 1983, 19, and Zeitlin 2009, 8.

revenge narrative across generations and look to the past to explain the present.[66] They repeat this sentiment later, using language that again emphasizes Oedipus' role in the curse (πατρόθεν εὐκταία φάτις, "the spoken words [i.e., curse] invoked by the father," 841). Furthermore, their reference to "child-murdering strife" (παιδολέτωρ δ᾽ ἔρις, 726) ambiguously evokes both the filicidal impact of Oedipus' curse as well as the fratricidal result of the brothers' conflict. The ambiguity has the effect of interweaving and conflating the brothers' actions with their father's, thus suggesting the replications inherent in the House of Laius story.

Alēthēs

The Chorus' language of prophecy and truth suggests their affiliation with Cassandra, who, as I will discuss in chapter 6, has a similarly expansive understanding of truth. They invoke the Erinys of Oedipus, dubbing her the "all-true prophet of evil" (παναληθῆ κακόμαντιν, 722),[67] a phrase that resonates with Cassandra's self-designation as a "true prophet" (τὸ μέλλον ἥξει, καὶ σύ μ᾽ ἐν τάχει παρὼν | ἄγαν γ᾽ ἀληθόμαντιν οἰκτίρας ἐρεῖς, "The future will come, and you will soon be here, taking pity on me and calling me an exceedingly true prophet," A. 1240–41).[68] This use of alēthēs encompasses past, present, and future and is consistent with Cassandra's prophetic, visionary brand of truth. Her words occur just after she has predicted the death of Agamemnon as a consequence of Thyestes' cannibalism in the previous generation, and she uses the language of reciprocal retribution to designate this imminent consequence (ποινάς, A. 1223).[69] Like Cassandra, the Chorus of Seven refer to a retribution narrative as "truth" (παναληθῆ), invoking the same continuity of reciprocity that she did.

---

66. For the connection between fear and the Erinys, see Winnington-Ingram 1983, 29. He encapsulates the relationship between fear and certainty when he writes "The *fact* [emphasis mine] of the Erinys is a ground for fear" and surmises that Eteocles' fear of the Erinys has been present all along and is at the root of his initial reaction to the Chorus' very different fear, but it is a "vague and intermittent" fear and does not prevent his blind spots about his odds of survival and victory.

67. Gregory Nagy uses this passage to inform his reading of Eteocles' words at 709–11; in his view both passages are evidence for the link between vision and prophecy (2000, 113–14).

68. It also recalls *Iliad* 1.106, where Agamemnon berates the evil prophecies of Calchas (μάντι κακῶν οὐ πώ ποτέ μοι τὸ κρήγυον εἶπας, "prophet of evils, you've never yet said to me something agreeable").

69. On the nuances of ποινή, see Wilson 1999, 138–39.

While they are not actually seers, the Chorus' capacity to understand their current circumstances as part of an ongoing narrative affords them some predictive abilities. For example, even though it has not yet happened, they know the brothers will die by internecine bloodshed, and that further trouble will arise from it:

> ἐπεὶ δ' ἂν αὐτοκτόνως
> αὐτοδάικτοι θάνωσι καὶ γαῖα κόνις
> πίη μελαμπαγὲς αἷμα φοίνιον
> τίς ἂν καθαρμοὺς πόροι;
> τίς ἂν σφε λούσειεν; ὦ
> πόνοι δόμων νέοι παλαι-
> οἷσι συμμιγεῖς κακοῖς. (734–41)

But when they die, self-slain and self-slaying, and the dust of earth drinks their black-clotted red blood, who would provide purification? Who would cleanse them? Oh new toils of the house, mixed with old evils!

Their language connects their words now with previous things they have said and with words that will be spoken later. Their repeated use of αὐτο-words (αὐτοκτόνως | αὐτοδάικτοι, 734–35) echoes their earlier warnings to Eteocles against mutual fratricide (αὐτοκτόνος, 681; αὐτάδελφον, 718), reinforces their frequent reminders of the symmetry of bloodshed pervading the House of Laius, and anticipates the Messenger's announcement of the brothers' deaths (ἄνδρες τεθνᾶσιν ἐκ χερῶν αὐτοκτόνων, "the men have died by their self-slaying hands," 805).[70] The Chorus repeat this language when they see the brothers' corpses (τάδ' αὐτόδηλα, "these things are self-evident," 848), linking to their earlier words as well as to the Messenger's. Similarly, their reference to dust (γαῖα κόνις, 735) recalls their earlier fears of the dust-cloud as a true harbinger of imminent disaster (αἰθερία κόνις με πείθει φανεῖσ' | ἄναυδος σαφὴς ἔτυμος ἄγγελος, "A cloud of dust on high appears and persuades me, a messenger clear and true, though voiceless," 81–82), here naming the dust in apposition to the land and predicting the bloodshed that will occur on it. The circu-

---

70. Zeitlin 2009, 8, takes this reference as even more explicitly recalling symmetry and reciprocity; for her, "autoktony" evokes Oedipus' self-mutilation.

larity is striking: the dust, whose predictive value they were scorned for recognizing, now becomes the receptacle for the very destruction they correctly perceived it to signal.

Their reference to mutual fratricide and bloodshed mirrors their earlier fixation on the brothers' consanguinity (ὁμαίμοιν, 681; αὐτάδελφον αἷμα, 718), underscores sameness between the brothers and between present and past, and anticipates the Messenger's words (αὐτοὺς ἀδελφαῖς χερσὶν ἡναίρονθ' ἅμα, "they killed themselves at the same time by their brothers' hands," 811; πόλις σέσωται, βασιλέῳν δ' ὁμοσπόροιν | πέπωκεν αἷμα γαῖ' ὑπ' ἀλλήλων φόνῳ, "the city has been saved, but the earth has drunk the blood of same-sown kings by their murder of one another," 820–21).[71] So too does the reference to comingling of old and new calamities suggest a conflation of past and present (ὦ | πόνοι δόμων νέοι παλαι- | οῖσι συμμιγεῖς κακοῖς, "Oh new toils of the house, mixed with old evils!" 739–41).[72] Blood and the repetitive language of fratricide emphasize mythological continuity, the fraternity of the brothers, and the ancestral line they share. The Chorus, in juxtaposing new against old, interpret the brothers' imminent deaths as an expression of the ongoing myth, a consequence of prior events in the House of Laius. There are also subtle suggestions of the future implications of the brothers' deaths. When the Chorus describe the earth "drinking" the brothers' blood (πίῃ, 736), they anthropomorphize the land, thus recalling earlier personifications of Thebes as mother, and they suggest her continued nourishment from the fratricide. The phrase connotes continuity from, rather than finality in, the brothers' deaths. Likewise, they predict further troubles from the brothers' deaths when they worry about who will purify them.

The theme of continuity permeates the next antistrophe as they speak explicitly of Laius and Oedipus, whose earlier crimes, in the Chorus' view, have engendered the present situation. They describe Laius' defiance of the oracular injunction not to have children as a crime "born long ago" (παλαιγενῆ, 742), picking up the reference to the past in the previous strophe (παλαιοῖσι, 740–41).

71. Gantz 1982, 15–22, makes similar points about the symmetry between the two brothers, arguing that they share culpability for the troubles that befall them. Foley 2001, 49, too, makes the point that the Chorus' "lamentation pointedly blurs the moral distinction between the two brothers that Eteocles was so insistent to make in the shield scene."
72. See Seaford 2012, 172–74, on the interweaving of blood, incest, earth, and kin-killing that occurs in this and several other passages of *Seven*. He notes that this mixture (συμμιγεῖς) of old and new refers both to "temporal homogeneity" and to the permanent mixing of blood and earth (174). For other instances of blood mixing with earth, see Seaford 2012, 174–75.

Likewise, they refer to Oedipus as a "father-slayer" (πατροκτόνον, 752), which echoes αὐτοκτόνως (734) and further emphasizes the intergenerational pattern of familial murder, as does their designation of Oedipus' progeny as "bloody root" (ῥίζαν αἱματόεσσαν, 755), a metaphor that extends the theme of continuity from the previous strophe and connects the brothers' fate to Oedipus' crimes. The pervasive theme is continuity and seamless connectivity—even replication—between generations.

Again, Eteocles and Polyneices have not yet died, nor do any of the characters know for sure that they will. Only the audience truly know this. But the Chorus, though lacking any real prophetic ability, already speak correctly of the brothers' deaths as all but certain to occur. They situate the brothers' deaths within a timeline and overarching narrative, and their despair, particularly when they ask who might provide purification for the brothers (738–39), recalls the earlier hysteria (181–202) for which Eteocles chastised them but which now seems prescient. Their tone becomes more certain in lines 758–63, where they shift to the indicative mood to speak metaphorically about new waves crashing over the ship of the city (ἄγει, 758; ἀείρει, 759; καχλάζει, 760; τείνει, 763).

Furthermore, the Chorus are alone on stage when they voice this ode. This section parallels their earlier song at 287–368, which likewise expresses overwhelming fear and is sung in solitude.[73] In light of their theatrical solitude, it is difficult to understand their references to past, present, and future as anything other than a reflection of the tragedian's storytelling for the audience's benefit.[74] Their ode casts the narrative as one of intergenerational retribution. The audience, knowing the myth of *Seven*, would hear the Chorus' words as fact rather than speculation and as information from the tragedian himself. Of course, this is in keeping with the role tragic choruses often play of providing cohesive commentary on the actions and events they observe from the sidelines. But as I will discuss in subsequent chapters, the Chorus of *Suppliants* function similarly even though their role is much more protagonistic than the Chorus of *Seven*'s; so too do the nonchoral figures of Clytemnestra and Cassandra in *Agamemnon*. The cohesion the Chorus of *Seven* provide to the narrative is not

---

73. Taplin 1977, 166–67, observes this parallel but identifies a crucial shift between the two songs in that the former expresses the Chorus' fears for their own survival as well as the city's whereas in the latter "the chorus of Theban women terrified for their survival become instead mourners for the royal house and its terrible history" (166).

74. Edmunds 2017, 104–6, observes that the Chorus at 822–23 echo but rephrase 69, which Eteocles uttered outside of their hearing. Edmunds refers to this out-of-character revision as "communication by Aeschylus to the audience" (106).

simply a function of their choral role; it is also a function of their female gender. When they refer to the brothers' deaths as "fulfilled exchanges" (τέλειαι . . . καταλλαγαί, 766–67), they use the language of reciprocity to characterize the deaths as inevitable.[75] The symmetry of the fratricides reflects the retributive force that governs Aeschylean plots, which the female characters most often perceive and articulate.

The only flashes of uncertainty—or rather, of qualified or mitigated certainty—are in the Chorus' statements of fear: δέδοικα δὲ σὺν βασιλεῦσι | μὴ πόλις δαμασθῇ ("I fear that the city may be destroyed along with the kings," 764–65); νῦν δὲ τρέω | μὴ τελέσῃ καμψίπους Ἐρινύς ("And now I fear that the swift-running Erinys may fulfill it," 790–91). These expressions hearken back to their first appearance (78–202), where their nearly hysterical tone provoked Eteocles' castigations. Here their fears are grounded in their knowledge of the House of Laius myth and in their understanding of the fraternal conflict within the context of the family history. The Chorus contextualize their fears thus, situating them within the greater narrative of the myth and its continuing arc. In this light the Chorus, with all their fears, seem mindful and aware rather than hysterically timorous. They perceive how the past informs the present and future and how the advance of Polyneices' army actualizes retributive consequences of previous crimes, as well as Oedipus' own curse. They know that Eteocles and Polyneices will die. Indeed, this ode prompts reconsideration of their first appearance, in which they, in retrospect, now seem perspicacious rather than hysterical. Fear is now accurately predictive, analogous to prophecy.

It is important to note, too, that the Chorus' insights are never fully recognized by the male characters of *Seven*, and this seems to be a function of their female gender. Comparison with Amphiaraus brings this discrepancy out all the more. As others have already and perceptively noted, Amphiaraus is the Argive counterpart to Eteocles and even to Oedipus. But he parallels the Chorus in some ways too. More precisely, his predictions of doom accord with the Chorus' earlier fears (78–181), but their contrasting purposes differentiate them. Amphiaraus' predictions are couched in his criticism of Polyneices while the Chorus' are mainly rooted in concerns for their own and the city's welfare. Their receptions, too, bear sharp contrast. Eteocles is receptive to Amphiaraus' words because they align with his own biases, whereas he maligns the Chorus,

---

75. See Seaford 2012, 168, who notes that katallagē connotes "quittance or resolution. To say that the heavy *katallagai* of curses are *teleiai* is to imagine that curses create an imbalance or obligation that is resolved by suffering."

purportedly for inciting panic, but also for making predictions he finds less than credible. The Chorus never receive credit where it is due: unlike Amphiaraus with his reputation as a seer, the Chorus' perspicacity is never acknowledged. They are like the female characters of *Agamemnon*, who will meet with similar resistance in their interlocutors, as we will see in chapter 6. What we have in *Seven* is a Chorus whose female gender comes to define both their knowledge and the way such knowledge is treated by their male interlocutors. They are the most perceptive characters in *Seven*; they are the ones who perceive the big picture most completely. But their knowledge is always relegated to the margins. They are ever powerless against the preconceptions and willful blind spots of the male characters. Thus their function is primarily for the audience's benefit, as they shape the House of Laius myth into a unified whole and show, by their contrasting example, the brothers' failure to recognize it.

Conclusion

Aeschylus' *Seven* presents ways of formulating knowledge that rely on extrapolation from limited information. It is primarily through the Chorus of Theban Women that we see the arrangement of that information into a comprehensible narrative that strings together past, present, and future as interrelated and interconnected manifestations of one another. This responsiveness and continuity reflect the give-and-take pattern of reciprocity, which is figured as truth and is typical of Aeschylean storytelling. Furthermore, it is the Chorus who approximate a complete understanding of this pattern. Their perceptive ability is most evident in the final third of the play, but they reveal glimpses of it sooner, from their initial appearance onward.

That the Chorus of Theban Women are explicitly (and derogatively) gendered female affiliates them with the other female characters of Aeschylean tragedy. They further share a tendency to understand truth imaginatively and expansively. As we will see with the Danaids of *Suppliants* and with the female characters of *Agamemnon*, these characters comprehend the present and future in terms of the past, they understand the patterns of reciprocity that thread through the timeline, and they articulate this pattern as alētheia. In communicating the connective threads of the plot, the Chorus of *Seven* effectively act as a mouthpiece for the tragedian. Thus they draw attention to the story in which they are situated and nod to the creative processes behind that story.

In this way they resemble the Pindaric female figures I discussed in the previous chapter, who also function to draw attention to the poetic contexts in which they appear and to mirror poetic creativity in various ways. Furthermore, both Pindaric and Aeschylean narratives rely on reciprocity for their shape and articulate this reciprocity as alētheia, and female figures play the largest role in giving expression to this relationship. Of course, Pindar's female figures undermine that reciprocity through deception while the Chorus of *Seven* articulate and reinforce it as truth. But both, in inverse ways, draw attention to reciprocity, its configuration as truth, and its poetic contexts and thus share a characteristic that, as I will continue to argue, belongs predominantly to female figures in these two poets. In the chapters to come I will further draw out these relationships between reciprocity, truth, and gender in Aeschylus.

CHAPTER FIVE

Female Authorship

Forging Truth in Aeschylus' Suppliants

As the beginning of its tragic trilogy, *Suppliants* provides a glimpse into how Aeschylean tragedy weaves its reciprocity stories into larger tapestries.[1] Staged in the 460s BCE, *Suppliants* dramatizes the Danaids' flight from Egypt to Argos, where they appeal to the Argive king Pelasgus for protection from the cousins to whom they are unwillingly betrothed.[2] They claim kinship ties to Argos through their ancestress Io, ties that, they argue, obligate the Argives to help them; Pelasgus and the Argives are ultimately convinced. Establishing their shared ethnicity is crucial to this narrative as it links the Danaids to the Argives' past, which they hope will conscript the Argives to a shared future. The Danaids' story points up questions of ethnic identity, how it is constituted, and its implications for contemporaneous Athenian or Greek attitudes toward non-Athenians or non-Greeks.[3] The now lost subsequent plays of the trilogy presumably dramatized the failure of the Argives' protection, the Danaids' forced marriage to and subsequent murder of the Aegyptiads, and some kind of resolution.[4]

---

1. For simplicity's sake, I adopt the majority scholarly position that *Suppliants* is the first play of its trilogy (see Garvie 1969, 185–86), but there are arguments against this view, e.g., Rösler 1993 and Sommerstein 1995 (=2010b, 89–117).
2. As Burian 1991, xxiii, notes, the play itself is premised on an unanswered question about why the Danaids flee Egypt. For a summary of the various stances on this question, see Bachvarova 2009, 289n1; MacKinnon 1978; Murray 1958, 6–7; Turner 2001, 28; Winnington-Ingram 1983, 59–60. The Danaids answer this question themselves in the opening lines as they declare that they are not exiles for any bloodguilt (5–7) but refugees from "unholy marriage" to the Aegyptiads (γάμον Αἰγύπτου παίδων ἀσεβῆ, 10).
3. See Bakewell 1997 and 2013, Mitchell 2006, Vasunia 2001, 33–58, Wohl 2010.
4. More than one scholar (e.g., Winnington-Ingram 1983, 56; Zeitlin 1996, 162–63) has used the *Oresteia* to inform their speculations about the Danaid trilogy.

What is significant for my purposes is that the Danaids' arguments for asylum are premised on reciprocity, as they argue that the present and future should responsively echo the past. The efficacy of the Danaids' supplication rests on their convincing presentation of a narrative that interweaves their history and their future with that of the Argives. Furthermore, they use alētheia to articulate this argument, along with formulations of dikē, which closely parallels it. They typify Aeschylus' female characters in seeing their story as part of a timeline that includes cause-and-effect implications and in articulating this pattern as one of alētheia. In their identification with Io and their hope to replicate her story, they present the past, present, and future as intertwined and interrelated. The temporal progression they seek to establish—one that places their origins in Argos through Io—implies a trajectory of obligation, as the Danaids' arguments about Argive ancestry serve the purpose of securing Argive assistance in the present. Their supplication, premised on shared ethnicity, is not only a plea for help but also an argument that they are *owed* it. Like Pindar's epinician odes, the Danaid trilogy centers on reciprocity, not necessarily encapsulated explicitly as xenia or charis but more generally the idea that actions should be met with corresponding reactions.

Furthermore, the Danaids' role in communicating this roadmap of reciprocal action based on their ancestry is essentially an authorial one, as it is their task to construct a historical narrative. They must articulate a history that they share with the Argives, thus binding the Argives' interests to their own.[5] Their supplication involves crafting their story into one that Pelasgus will find credible as a compelling argument for Argive assistance. Through their scripting of the past and future, the Danaids become arbiters of truth in the sense that Aeschylean truth involves a long timeline that follows the rules of reciprocity, as I argued in chapter 1. They are the ones who determine what happened and propose what should happen, based on what has happened before. This conception of truth links past, present, and future not only sequentially, but also consequentially: in the Danaids' eyes the past should determine the future. They share with the Chorus of *Seven* a capacity to perceive this reciprocity-centered truth; they go beyond the women of *Seven* in their attempt also to shape it.

The Danaids must recruit male allies to enact the story they craft. In this

---

5.   A role similarly assumed later by Euripides' Medea: see Boedeker 1991, 109 and Rabinowitz 1992, 49 and 1993, 145.

way they emulate the tragedian, for they construct their narrative by prescribing others' actions to their own specifications. Within the context of a tragic trilogy, the Danaids' (ultimately unsuccessful) attempt to control their future mimics an authorial hand in that they influence the behavior of other characters to try to shape the unfolding trilogy. Moreover, the narrative they construct is a typically Aeschylean one in that it presents their current circumstances within a cyclical timeline in which past events precipitate future reverberations—in other words, a timeline based in reciprocity. By drawing attention to the contours of their story and the mechanics of storytelling, the Danaids reflect a tradition of female figures allegorizing poetic or literary creativity, a tradition that includes the Chorus of *Seven* as well as the Muses of the *Theogony*, Stesichorus' *Helen*, and the female figures of Pindaric epinician that I discussed in chapter 3. Furthermore, they share with Pindar's female figures the function of drawing attention to poetic contexts that foreground reciprocity specifically, in one way or the other.

In the sections that follow I examine the Danaids' language of truth and dikē as a reflection of the temporal and causal continuity typical of Aeschylean tragedy. I explore how this conception of truth, for the Danaids, involves carefully constructing an identity and narrative that makes the most of their hybrid origins and the varying degrees of agency their position affords them, to serve their purpose of securing Argive aid. I will examine their interaction with Pelasgus as a part of their strategy of controlling and shaping a truth that replicates the past in the present and future. My final section discusses the limits of this type of authorial control and the Danaids' inevitable recourse to a violent form of reciprocity.

Truth and Time

Direct references to truth are rare in *Suppliants*, and those that do occur may seem unremarkable; for example, adverbial forms like ἀληθῶς, ἐτήτυμως, and ἐτύμως are typically used for simple emphasis, like English "really" or "truly."[6] But some instances are telling. Several passages reflect the need for female speakers to establish their reliability, a phenomenon we will also see in *Agamemnon*. Furthermore, such contexts reveal the Danaids' conception of truth as a

---

6.   E.g., *Supp.* 315, 736.

convergence of past, present, and future—that is to say, a conception of truth that essentially parallels reciprocity, in that events of the past catalyze responsive replications in the future. We have already seen in chapter 1 an example of how the Danaids conjoin truth and reciprocity:

ἄγε δή λέξωμεν ἐπ᾽ Ἀργείοις
εὐχὰς ἀγαθὰς ἀγαθῶν ποινάς·
Ζεὺς δ᾽ ἐφορεύοι ξένιος ξενίου
στόματος τιμὰς †ἐπ᾽ ἀληθείᾳ
τέρμον᾽ ἀμέμπτων πρὸς ἅπαντα† (625–29)

Come, indeed, and let us speak good prayers for the Argives, returns for good deeds. May Zeus, god of strangers, look upon offerings from a stranger's mouth, in truth, in service to every goal of the blameless.

As I discussed in that chapter, the collocation of verbal repetitions (ἀγαθὰς ἀγαθῶν, 626; ξένιος ξενίου, 627), reciprocal returns (ποινάς, 626), and alētheia (628) all serve to articulate a union of reciprocity and truth that parallels what we see in Pindar. What I did not articulate in chapter 1 is the significance of the Danaids speaking these lines. Their words and actions here and throughout *Suppliants* underscores the role Aeschylus' female characters play as the primary articulators of the association between reciprocity and truth. As such, they are inversions of Pindar's female figures, who call attention to this association by undermining it through their deceptions.

Furthermore, female characters in Aeschylus are key to articulating the temporal aspect of reciprocity: the action-reaction pattern occurs across time. The Danaids do not always use alētheia specifically to designate this pattern, but their articulations of past, present, and future connectedness cleave to the patterns of alētheia and reciprocity that I discussed in chapter 1. For the Danaids, the cyclical modes in which they envision time are premised on reciprocal obligation. In the context of *Suppliants* this pattern has implications for Greek identity, which the Danaids establish through their history. They appeal to the Argives to protect them, out of duty or obligation based on their shared Greekness.

Connected to this intertwining of reciprocity and truth is the general requirement for Aeschylus' female characters to validate their claims. When the Danaids introduce themselves, they punctuate their tale of descent from Io and Epaphus with a promise to provide confirmation:

ὄντ' ἐπιλεξαμένα
νῦν ἐν ποιονόμοις ματρὸς ἀρχαίας τόποις τῶν
πρόσθε πόνων μνασαμένα, τάδε νῦν ἐπιδείξω
πιστὰ τεκμήρια, γαιονόμοισι δ᾽ ἄελπτά περ ὄντα φανεῖται·
γνώσεται δὲ λόγου τις ἐν μάκει. (49–56)[7]

Having called him [Epaphus] by name, remembering the past toils of our ancient mother while we now stand in her rich grassy fields, I will show these trusty proofs, and they—although unexpected—will become clear to the inhabitants. Anyone will come to an understanding in the length of the speech.

Significantly, the Danaids are alone at this point, speaking only to the audience; they have not yet engaged with Pelasgus, their main Argive interlocutor. But their language is already defensive, preemptively so. Aware that they will encounter incredulity, they promise "trusty proofs" (πιστὰ τεκμήρια) of their claims about Io and Epaphus as their ancestors (40–46); this phrase resonates with several moments in *Agamemnon* in which female speakers must similarly prove their reliability. Twice do the Chorus of *Agamemnon* use such terms as they demand and accept proof of Clytemnestra's claims (τί γὰρ τὸ <u>πιστόν</u>; ἔστι τῶνδέ σοι <u>τέκμαρ</u>; "For what is the *proof*? Do you have *evidence* of these things?" *A.* 272; ἐγὼ δ᾽ ἀκούσας <u>πιστά</u> σου <u>τεκμήρια</u>, "I, having heard your *trusty proofs*," *A.* 352).[8] Laura McClure has identified such language as a feature of persuasive female speech in Aeschylean tragedy, as it borrows male courtroom speech to convey authority.[9] The Danaids' defensiveness is justified, as it turns out, for Pelasgus will specifically describe their claims as "untrustworthy" (ἄπιστα, 278).

Furthermore, the Danaids possess a temporally expansive conception of their story that we saw with the Chorus of *Seven* and will see in *Agamemnon*'s Cassandra and Clytemnestra as well. When they invoke Io, they interweave her

---

7. I reproduce Page's Oxford Classical Text. West's Teubner edition varies slightly; see West 1990b, 128–29, especially for discussion of colometry. See also Friis Johansen and Whittle 1980 vol. 2, 49–52 for further discussion of textual corruption in lines 53–55. I defer to their assessment that "the general sense of these lines is clear enough: the Danaids will produce evidence (that they are of Argive origin), and this evidence will prove trustworthy although it is not expected to seem so at first" (Friis Johansen and Whittle 1980 vol. 2, 49 *ad* 53–55).

8. Sommerstein 2019, 169 *ad* 276 also notes the parallel with *A.* 272. For the invoking of "proofs" in general, see also *A.* 1366; *Ch.* 205, 667; *Eu.* 244, 447, 485.

9. McClure 1999, 72–80; McClure discusses here specifically the character of Clytemnestra in *Agamemnon*, who shifts between a masculine, public, civic, and judicial mode of speech, and a feminine mode typified by claims of marital fidelity and social and ritual propriety.

story with theirs and imply that her past should inform their present and future. As Froma Zeitlin notes, "The suppliants, bound to their past by the myth of their ancestor, Io, view time precisely in this mode of repetition, and yearn for nothing more than the impossible wish to relive and repeat her story (e.g., νέωσον εὔφρον αἶνον, *Su.* 534)."[10] Zeitlin also observes how the Danaids script their present in terms of the past, bringing the primordial time of myth into the present time of tragedy.[11] In doing so they situate themselves in an ongoing narrative in which the experiences of their ancestress will be replicated in their own.[12] Their continued existence is dependent on their knowledge of and close relationship to the past, and their ability to communicate this knowledge and relationship persuasively to the Argives.

This view of their past and future as corresponding to one another is intrinsically bound to the rules of reciprocity, which stipulate responsive and commensurate reaction to past actions and events. Furthermore, the knowledge that serves to establish a credible link between the Danaids' history and that of the Argives is figured as truth, and it is vital to the validity of their supplication that the Argives owe them aid. When they meet Pelasgus, they claim Argive identity, posit a shared history, and promise confirmation of their claims:

Χο. βραχὺς τορός θ' ὁ μῦθος· Ἀργεῖαι γένος
ἐξευχόμεσθα, σπέρματ' εὐτέκνου βοός·
καὶ τῷδ' ἀληθῆ πάντα προσφύσω λόγῳ. (274–76)

Our story is short and clear: we boast to be Argives by race, descendants of the cow blessed with offspring. And I'll confirm all things as *true* with this speech.

Line 276 is plagued with textual difficulties, but in all of its proposed variations, the Danaids assure Pelasgus of the demonstrable validity of their account.[13] West's Teubner edition even infuses their speech with the courtroom language of the previous passage I discussed (χὼς ταῦτ' ἀληθῆ, πιστὰ προσφύσω λόγῳ

---

10. Zeitlin 1990, 111.
11. Zeitlin 1996, 160–64.
12. Gödde 2000, 197, makes a comparable point that the Danaids' supplication does not merely address the present situation but situates them in a historical context.
13. What is printed above comes from Page's Oxford Classical Text. Bowen has καὶ ταῦτ' ἀληθῆ πάντα προσθήσω λόγον (Bowen 2013, 74, and 204 for discussion); Friis Johansen and Whittle have καὶ ταῦτ' ἀληθῆ· πάντα προσφύσω λόγον ("and this is true: I shall add the whole story," Friis Johansen and Whittle 1980 vol. 2, 218–19).

("and to show that this is true, we will add *proofs* to what we have said").[14] What is significant for my purposes is that the Danaids contextualize their experiences in a timeline and designate them as alētheia. They apply ἀληθῆ to a narrative that—as in the previous passage—bridges and intertwines past and present. This temporally expansive configuration of alētheia is one that implies that the present both does and *should* correspond to the past, and it will ultimately serve their claims that the Argives are obligated to help them.

In a similar vein they use the language of truth in a passage about the birth of Epaphus from Io:

λαβοῦσα δ᾽ ἕρμα Δῖον <u>ἀψευδεῖ</u> λόγῳ
γείνατο παῖδ᾽ ἀμεμφῆ
δι᾽ αἰῶνος μακροῦ πάνολβον·
ἔνθεν πᾶσα βοᾷ χθών
"φυσιζόου γένος τόδε
Ζηνός ἐστιν <u>ἀληθῶς</u>."
τίς γὰρ ἂν κατέπαυσεν Ἥ-
ρας νόσους ἐπιβούλους;
Διὸς τόδ᾽ ἔργον, καὶ τόδ᾽ ἂν γένος λέγων
ἐξ Ἐπάφου κυρήσαις. (580–99)

And having conceived by Zeus, by an account *not false*, she gave birth to a blameless son, completely happy through his long life. Then the whole earth shouts, "*Truly* this is the progeny of life-producing Zeus!" For who could have stopped the treacherous plagues of Hera? You would be right if you said that this deed was of Zeus and this race comes from Epaphus.

By embedding truth-words in the story of Epaphus' birth (ἀψευδεῖ, 580; ἀληθῶς, 585), the Chorus situate them in a context that stresses intergenerational continuity and longevity. They associate truth with temporal progression, in keeping with their vision of their own truth as part of an ongoing story.

---

14. West 1990a, 141; Translation of Sommerstein 2008 vol. 1, 323. West (1990b, 138) bases his text in part on the argument of Sommerstein 1977, 69, who posits χὼς ταῦτ᾽ ἀληθῆ, <u>πάντα</u> προσφύσω λόγῳ ("And <to prove> that this is true, I shall add the whole story"). Sommerstein eventually replaces πάντα with πιστὰ (2008 vol. 1, 322; 2019, 60), following West's Teubner. Sommerstein explicitly draws the courtroom parallel in his discussion of this line (2019, 169 *ad* 276; 1977, 69).

Truth and Dikē

Adjacent to the Danaids' conception of truth is their conception of dikē, which they repeatedly invoke without explicitly defining.[15] As Michael Gagarin observes, although the Danaids frequently express confidence that dikē and Zeus are on their side, the Aegyptiads ultimately prevail militarily and their herald makes similar claims to dikē.[16] The Danaids' assertions, therefore, must be read as "an expression of their own feelings but not necessarily an objective statement of fact."[17] Yet their articulation of dikē, like their configuration of alētheia, adeptly obscures its subjectivity as they embed it in the language of vision and fate:

> ἀλλά θεοὶ γενέται κλύετ' εὖ <u>τὸ δίκαιον ἰδόντες</u>
> †ἥβᾳ μὴ τέλεον† δόντες ἔχειν <u>παρ' αἶσαν</u>,
> ὕβριν δ' ἐτύμως στυγοῦντες
> πέλοιτ' ἂν <u>ἔνδικοι</u> γάμοις.[18]
> ἔστιν κἀκ πολέμου τειρομένοις
> βωμὸς ἀρῆς φυγάσιν
> ῥῦμα, δαιμόνων σέβας. (79–85)

> But, gods of our race, hear us favorably after *seeing what is just*: by not granting to the youth to have something accomplished *contrary to fate*, and by truly hating violence, you would be *righteous* toward marriages. There is an altar, a defense for those fleeing ruin and worn out from war, an object of holiness of the gods.

This is a difficult passage, not least for the textual uncertainty of ἥβᾳ (80), to which some editors prefer ἥβαν.[19] Further, there is disagreement about whether

---

15. See Robertson 1936, on the convergence of abstract and technical senses of dikē in *Suppliants*. Robertson 1936, 104n3, catalogues instances of legal language that complement a general sense of equity underlying dikē.
16. Gagarin 1976, 129–30. The Danaids' claims to dikē include *Supp.* 78, 343, 395, 406, 430, 437; the Aegyptiads' claims occur in 916, 934–37 (Gagarin 1976, 129–30, 134).
17. Gagarin 1976, 130. But he does acknowledge (1976, 129), that the Danaids' claims to dikē indicate an awareness of their governing narrative.
18. The text ἔνδικοι γάμοις is suspect, appearing in the manuscripts but corrected by various editors to ἔνδικος γάμος (Obadick, adopted by Friis Johansen and Whittle) or ἔνδικοι νόμοις (Hermann, Wilamowitz, Hartung), the problem being that ἔνδικοι does not typically govern a dative. See Friis Johansen and Whittle 1980 vol. 2, 78–79 *ad* 82 for thorough explanation and discussion. Whatever the correct text, it is clear that the Danaids are seeking to apply the notion of justice to marriage.
19. Bowen 2013, 58; Sommerstein 2019, 53.

ἥβα/ἥβαν ("youth") refers to the Danaids or to the Aegyptiads.[20] But the basic meaning is clear: the Danaids equate justice with fate (τὸ δίκαιον, 79; αἶσαν, 80), and they assert an opposition between their unwanted marriage and what is fated and just. When they call on the gods to see the just (τὸ δίκαιον ἰδόντες, 79), which they compare to fate (αἶσαν, 80), they present their version of dikē as something manifestly apparent. This is in keeping with the general tendency of Aeschylus' characters when they lay claim to dikē: they seem to imagine an external, divine force that will set things right and produce a satisfactory outcome for the moral wrongs committed. As Alexis Pinchard argues, there is a cosmic aspect to Aeschylean dikē, which connotes an underlying law of all behavior, whether human or animal. This law is premised on assumed equivalence between crime and punishment and on hereditary guilt for past crimes.[21] This conception of dikē aligns with the thinking of Anaximander and other Presocratics who imply that Dikē or causal law in general rules the universe.[22]

Thus dikē dictates what will happen, which will correspond to what has happened before. In its temporal scope it overlaps with alētheia, an unsurprising association given the history of dikē in earlier poetry, which often presents it in ways similar to truth. As Marcel Detienne has observed, Hesiod's *Theogony* specifically links dikē with alētheia through the figure of Nereus:

Νηρέα δ' ἀψευδέα καὶ ἀληθέα γείνατο Πόντος
πρεσβύτατον παίδων· αὐτὰρ καλέουσι γέροντα,
οὕνεκα νημερτής τε καὶ ἤπιος, οὐδὲ θεμίστων
λήθεται, ἀλλὰ δίκαια καὶ ἤπια δήνεα οἶδεν. (233–36)

Pontus begot Nereus, without lies and truthful, the oldest of his children. But they call him the old man because he is infallible and kind, and he does not forget divine law, but knows just and gentle counsels.

Nereus' various characteristics include truthfulness, primogeniture, infallibility, kindness, piety, and good judgment. Seeking to illuminate the connections among these wide-ranging qualities, Detienne observes, "In religious thought a distinction does not exist between the domains of justice and truth. The many

---

20. Bowen 2013, 163 *ad* 80–82 and West 1990b, 132–33 prefer the Aegyptiads; Sommerstein 2019, 117–18 *ad* 79–80 prefers the Danaids.
21. Pinchard 2016. Pinchard's larger argument is that similarities between Aeschylean and Orphic conceptions of dikē suggest an Indo-European precedent for a sense of cosmic justice that governs everything and is not merely a human social value.
22. Lloyd-Jones 1971, 79–80.

affinities between *Dikē* and *Alētheia* are well attested."[23] He cites examples from sources ranging from the Archaic through Roman periods, from anecdotes describing Alētheia and Dikē living among the gods to instances in Archaic poetry where alētheia is described as just (ἀληθείη δὲ παρέστω | σοὶ καὶ ἐμοί, πάντων χρῆμα δικαιότατον, "Let truth be present for you and me, the most just possession of all," Mimnermus, Fr. 8 West). Detienne further includes examples where dikē is described with language reminiscent of alētheia, such as this fragment of Solon:

οὐδὲ φυλάσσονται σεμνὰ Δίκης θέμεθλα,
ἣ σιγῶσα σύνοιδε τὰ γιγνόμενα πρό τ' ἐόντα,
τῷ δὲ χρόνῳ πάντως ἦλθ' ἀποτεισομένη. (Solon, Fr. 4.14–16 West)

and they do not guard the holy foundations of Justice, who silently knows what is happening and what has happened before, and at all events comes for payback in time.

Dikē's knowledge of the present and past is a common trait of alētheia, as Detienne notes. He identifies a line of thought in which knowledge of past, present, and future is also associated with a sense that what happens responds and corresponds to a previous act, that actions are followed by consequences.[24]

Like Detienne, Pinchard identifies an alignment between truth and justice in ancient Greek thought. He argues, among other things, that Aeschylus' treatment of dikē is consonant with Indo-Iranian as well as other Greek traditions and reflects a general belief that some events are controlled at the cosmic level as responses to one another. Examining these various traditions he writes, "Both Justice and Truth are basically the same thing. To know truly the things means to know them as they *should* be because what should happen will really happen. Therefore, every fault is due to ignorance."[25] This truth-justice correspondence suggests that truth—"what happens"—is determined by the patterns of dikē. Aeschylus' characters share an expectation of reciprocal justice that is so strong as to be described in terms of truth.

---

23. Detienne 1996, 55.
24. Detienne's full catalogue of examples, some of which contain no clear references to either alētheia or dikē, is not invariably compelling, but his broader point about associations between the two is convincing.
25. Pinchard 2016, 280. Pinchard argues specifically for a concomitant belief in human responsibility to seek and know this truth-justice because of human capacity for logos.

In the case of the Danaids, their convictions about reciprocal justice are such that they must convince others to adopt the same understanding. This is in keeping with the gendered aspect of reciprocity and truth in Aeschylus: female characters, in various ways, have uniquely nuanced understandings of the reciprocity-truth combination, but they are not always readily believed. The Danaids' polemic—what Richard Buxton has identified as a contrast between peitho and bia—demonstrates their control of their narrative.[26] Repeated references to dikē (τὸ δίκαιον, *Supp.* 79; ἔνδικοι, 82) are interlaced with references to peaceful marriage and reflect the Danaids' shaping of dikē to serve their refusal to marry the Aegyptiads. The equation of dikē and fate, furthermore, demonstrates that the Danaids present what ought to happen as what will happen.

Inherent in this conceptualization is a sense that dikē occupies a trajectory or timeline that the Danaids alone can access. Thus they are in company with *Agamemnon*'s Cassandra and the Chorus of *Seven*, who share similar visionary qualities.[27] But the Danaids actually want to enact what they see. They function somewhere in between the two female characters of *Agamemnon* I will discuss in the next chapter: Cassandra, who sees the future clearly but is powerless to effect or affect it, and Clytemnestra, who both envisions and enacts the future she desires. Bridging these two poles, the Danaids' agency resides in their ability to sway their male interlocutors. They lack the objective certainty of Clytemnestra and Cassandra and possess only a hopeful conviction about what *should* happen—which is something they cannot enact by themselves. When Danaus advises them to delay no further, he points to the disconnect between the Danaids' will and their capacity for action: "Do not loiter now, but let there be force to your intent" (μή νυν σχόλαζε, μηχανῆς δ' ἔστω κράτος, 209). Essentially, the Danaids must author their own story and craft the characters within it to serve that story.

Pelasgus is their foil. While they have vision without agency, Pelasgus has the capacity for action but lacks their conviction. He yearns for clarity (407–17) and a "clear-sighted eye to go to the depths in the manner of a diver" (δίκην κολυμβητῆρος, ἐς βυθὸν μοθεῖν | δεδορκὸς ὄμμα, 408–9). His use of dikē (here, "manner" or "custom") recalls the justice that the Danaids continually invoke.[28]

---

26. Buxton 1982, 69–70.
27. Zeitlin 1990, 111.
28. This Aeschylean convergence of the prepositional use of δίκην with its more general connotations of "order, custom, justice, revenge" is well documented in the *Oresteia*. See O'Neill 1941, 295; Wilson 2006. *Pace* Garvie 1986, 94.

But while they are resolute, Pelasgus constantly deliberates, searching for salvation in the form of insight (φροντίδος σωτηρίου, 407, 417), a solution that will innocuously carry out what the gods deem just. His anxiety stems from his hope to avoid the violence the Chorus' vision requires and his increasing certainty in the legitimacy of the Chorus' request. Indeed, it becomes clear that Pelasgus' uncertainty is really a mask for avoidance when, at one point in his frustration, he even expresses a preference for ignorance over knowledge (453–54).

The Danaids as Autobiographers

The Danaids' convictions rest on their ability to construct their own identity and history. As they bridge past and present they also bridge geographic space to produce an explanation for their hybrid or dual identity as both Greek and Egyptian.[29] Thus the hybrid identity they constantly work to create blends Greek and Egyptian, past and present, in a way that parallels the temporal patterns of Aeschylean truth, which encompasses and indeed compresses past, present, and future. From the very beginning of the play, the Chorus of Danaids harmonize their birth in and journey from a non-Greek land with their appeals to the Greek god Zeus:

Ζεὺς μὲν ἀφίκτωρ ἐπίδοι προφρόνως
στόλον ἡμέτερον νάιον ἀρθέντ᾽
ἀπὸ προστομίων λεπτοψαμάθων
Νείλου· Δίαν δὲ λιποῦσαι
χθόνα σύγχορτον Συρίᾳ φεύγομεν. (1–5)

May Zeus, god of suppliants, look readily upon our group, conveyed by ship from the Nile's mouth with its fine sands. Having left the land of Zeus bordering on Syria, we are fugitives.

---

29. A hybridity that possibly reflects the evolving political climate in Athens. See Mitchell 2006, 206, who argues that this blending of Greek and non-Greek identities may reflect the fairly amicable Greek-Persian relations of the 460s; Turner 2001, who posits that *Suppliants* complicates the simple Greek-foreigner dichotomy of *Persians*, possibly as a symptom of its contemporary sociopolitical context; Bakewell 2013, 5, who sees *Suppliants* as a reflection of conflicted attitudes toward foreigners in contemporaneous Athens; see also his earlier article (Bakewell 1997), where he argues that the popularity of *Suppliants* in Athens may be attributable to the successful harmonization of polis-identity-preservation and traditional hospitality that the play presents and to which Athens would aspire.

Their dual references to Zeus as god of suppliants (Ζεὺς ἀφίκτωρ) and of Egypt (Δίαν . . . χθόνα σύγχορτον Συρίᾳ) emphasize the universal authority of the god whose protection they invoke.[30] They manage to make Zeus both an Egyptian and a Greek god, to whom they entrust their protection at their Egyptian port of departure and their Greek point of arrival.

Their dual Greek-Egyptian identity is further premised on their identification with Io:

Δαναὸς δὲ πατὴρ καὶ βούλαρχος
καὶ στασίαρχος τάδε πεσσονομῶν
κύδιστ᾿ ἀχέων ἐπέκρανεν
φεύγειν ἀνέδην διὰ κῦμ᾿ ἅλιον,
κέλσαι δ᾿ Ἄργους γαῖαν, ὅθεν δὴ
γένος ἡμέτερον τῆς οἰστροδόνου
βοὸς ἐξ ἐπαφῆς κἀξ ἐπιπνοίας
Διὸς εὐχόμενον τετέλεσται. (11–18)

Danaus, our father, deviser of our plan, and chief of our band, took in the situation like a board game, and brought about these as the most noble of our pains, to flee pell-mell over the salt sea and put to shore at the land of Argos, where indeed our race originates, boasting it comes from the touch and breath of Zeus upon the cow driven round by the gadfly.

Their claim of descent from Io functions as evidence of their Argive identity and, as Richard Seaford notes, aligns them with a female figure whose story of transition from parthenos to consort of Zeus similarly involves her own geographic movement from center to periphery.[31] In claiming descent from Io, they attempt to mitigate their foreignness to Argos and merge their Egyptian and Greek roots, a theme that will permeate the play. Their supplication itself is premised, of course, on their outsider status, but it is granted to them because of their ability to blend outsider with insider qualities.[32]

Their frequent deployment of the myth of Io (40–56, 291–314, 531–89)

---

30. As Zeitlin 1992, 221, notes, the Danaids' characterization of Zeus generally "blends Greek, barbarian, and universal attributes."
31. Seaford 2012, 140–44.
32. See Vasunia 2001, 41: "the Danaids retain a dual ethnicity and claim, or have imputed to them (933), either one according to situation or need." *Pace* Turner 2001, who argues that the Danaids' success stems solely from their threat of suicide at 455–67.

reflects not only their constructed Greco-Egyptian identity but also their capacity for myth-making as they shape their ancestress' story in a way that suits their interests. They present Zeus, for example, as a beneficent presence in Io's life, a characterization that serves their self-professed reliance on his protection. When they describe Epaphus' conception as occurring merely from the touch of Zeus' hand (καὶ Ζεὺς γ᾽ ἐφάπτωρ χειρὶ φιτύει γόνον, "And Zeus laying hold of her with his hand begot a child," 313), they sanitize Zeus' involvement with Io so that her "experience seems to promise both sexuality and childbirth . . . without pain."[33] What is noteworthy is that the Danaids seem aware of Zeus' more violent actions—they have twice referred to Zeus and Io copulating both before and after her metamorphosis (295–96; 301)—but they blend the traditional account with this anodyne one.[34] They do hint at Zeus' rape of Io: their description of him as ἐφάπτωρ could denote benign "touching" or more forceful "seizing."[35]

The Danaids explicitly frame their story as part of Io's. At line 524 they begin a hymn to Zeus in which they relay the myth of Io while also constantly inserting and asserting themselves within its continuing arc. Their ode anticipates the seamless linking of past, present, and future that Cassandra's discourse will deploy in Agamemnon (see chapter 6) and is typical of Aeschylus' female characters. Indeed, they explicitly assert their reenactment of Io's story as they claim Zeus and Io as ancestors (536, 539) and point out that they quite literally follow in her footsteps (παλαιὸν δ᾽ εἰς ἴχνος μετέσταν, | ματέρος ἀνθονόμους ἐπωπάς, | λειμῶνα βούχιλον, ἔνθεν Ἰώ, "I departed to the ancient track, the spot where my mother was watched over as she grazed on flowers, the cow-pasturing meadow, from which Io [fled]," 538–39). They thus employ the known past of Io to script their own unknown future, a process that infuses their rhetoric with a fictive or creative function. Their authorial hand becomes ever clearer as they characterize the relationship between Zeus and Io as an affectionate one.[36]

33. Zeitlin 1996, 152.
34. See Friis Johansen and Whittle 1980 vol. 2, 235–36 ad 295, for other versions in which Zeus and Io copulate before her metamorphosis. They surmise that the failure to conceive may reflect Aeschylus "amalgamating two distinct versions of Zeus' union with Io and procreation of Epaphus, but the account of Zeus' possessing Io while she still inhabits Argos (which may be inferred from this passage to belong to ancient Argive tradition) is in any case contextually relevant" since it lends strength to their case for Argive heritage.
35. As Wohl 2010, 425, similarly observes. Pace Belfiore 2000, 48, who, even with the latter meaning, sees a positive connotation in ἐφάπτωρ, in keeping with what she sees as the "benevolent force" of Zeus, in contrast to the violent rapacity of the Aegyptiads.
36. Belfiore 2000, 47, observes that "Zeus in Suppliants is portrayed as consistently benevolent toward Io." She further asserts, however, "we see no suggestions that [the Danaids'] account is partial or

Their positive characterization of this relationship speaks to their own capacity for myth-making to suit their purposes.

The Danaids' willfully positive depiction of Zeus reflects the control they exercise over their rhetoric in their attempt to persuade him. Notably, they are alone at this point and not engaging with any interlocutors who are physically present. Their hymn is solely addressed to Zeus and functions to secure his protection.[37] Thus they address Zeus in the most flattering terms possible and obfuscate his role in Io's suffering.[38] Such obfuscation is particularly striking when they characterize Io's tormented flight from the gadfly as fated (ἐν αἴσᾳ, 545) rather than instigated by Zeus and Hera. They later place the blame for the gadfly entirely on Hera (564) and describe Zeus as the source of Io's salvation:

<δι'> αἰῶνος κρέων ἀπαύστου
Ζεὺς < >
†βία† δ' ἀπημάντῳ σθένει
καὶ θείαις ἐπιπνοίαις
παύεται. (574–78)

Lord Zeus, through unceasing time, . . . by innocuous strength and divine breaths she was stopped.

This revisionism dovetails with their ultimate goal to present their own future as fated, and reflects their own authorial hand or even sleight-of-hand in their characterization of Zeus. Their depictions of him serve their need for his benevolence. That they alone craft Zeus' characterization while also being at his mercy makes their relationship akin to that between Stesichorus and Helen: Stesichorus too controls his words to cater to Helen's liking.

The Danaids make full use of their narrative control, the only control they

---

distorted, and it is in fact confirmed by Pelasgos (310)." But as I will argue, line 310 (καὶ ταῦτ' ἔλεξας πάντα συγκόλλως ἐμοί, "And all these things you said are in accordance with my own opinion") does not unequivocally belong to Pelasgus and is better viewed as evidence of his recruitment to the Danaids' myth-making agenda.

37. See Gödde 2000, 195–96, for the praise function of this passage. She notes that the Io myth in *Suppliants* serves not only to convince Pelasgus of the Danaids' Argive identity but also to secure Zeus' protection.

38. Zeitlin 1996, 152–53, discusses their "curious rewriting" of the story as a "merging [of] desire, sexuality, and childbirth" with any associated pain displaced. *Pace* Belfiore 2000, 47, who takes the Danaids' depiction of the Io-Zeus relationship at face value: "In spite of the clear evidence in the text, scholars have frequently misunderstood the nature of Zeus's relationship with Io. Some assume that it is involuntary on her part."

have in the absence of physical control over their well-being. In so doing they claim an active stance in crafting a past, present, and future that are responsive to and reflective of one another. They not only perceive what will happen, they also actively forge it. By blending their Greek and Egyptian identities, and by crafting a myth of Io that substantiates this blending, they are able to script the past as well as the present and to intertwine the two. Their story is one that represents the Aeschylean truth I argue for: it occupies a temporal continuum of action followed by reciprocal reaction. The Danaids themselves are arbiters of this truth, as they shape this past-present-future continuity through their narrative craft. In this respect they are analogous to the tragedian himself and thus also evoke creative figures like Helen in *Iliad* 3, who weaves a tapestry reflecting the Trojan War story in which she exists, and the female figures in Pindar discussed in chapter 3, whose creative capacities parallel the poet's.

The analogy with the tragedian obtains in the Danaids' interactions with their father too. Their relationship with him reflects the careful balance they strike between relying on male authority and controlling their own stories. Danaus' purpose in the trilogy is confusing at best, given that his own physical safety is not obviously endangered.[39] But his interaction with his daughters conjures an intricate interplay of power and helplessness that mirrors both the Danaids' power over their narrative and the limits of this power. As Sheila Murnaghan observes, their references to their father as βούλαρχος (11) and στασίαρχος (12) evoke the role of a chorēgos.[40] They thus set up both a contrast and an affiliation between themselves and Danaus, as his leadership position is premised on membership in their group. They hold him up as their father and leader and ascribe to him authorship of their escape plan (βούλαρχος, 11), using a term that also connotes desire for rule.[41] They acknowledge his authority over them, but by characterizing him as their leader they assert their own kind of authority.[42]

---

39. There may be something in the mythic backdrop to *Suppliants* that explains Danaus' supportive presence in his daughters' flight. Sommerstein 2010b, 89–117 (= Sommerstein 1995, relying on Rösler 1993 and Sicherl 1986) argues that *Suppliants* is preceded by *Egyptians* and predicated on an oracle that Danaus will be felled by a future son-in-law, an oracle that he does not share with his daughters.

40. Murnaghan 2005, 191.

41. See Sommerstein 1977, 67 and Zeitlin 1992, 220–21, who both point out that the terms βούλαρχος and στασίαρχος imply a desire to rule by provoking civil unrest.

42. See Zeitlin 1992, 205–6 on the interrogation of power in the Danaid trilogy. Vernant and Vidal-Naquet 1981, 14–15, discusses the tension and ambiguity inherent in this type of power, noting that kratos in *Suppliants* is used variously to denote legitimate authority or brute force.

By the same token, the chorēgos analogy ascribes to Danaus a creative role, yet it is the Danaids themselves who are behind this formulation, authors both of the characterization of their father as leader and of their self-characterization as followers. Danaus uses his authority to choreograph their words and gestures (194–203), impressing on them the importance of clear speech, humility, and understated equanimity—along with innocence—in a successful rhetorical strategy. He prescribes a balance between assertiveness and reticence, in accordance with their dual roles as Argives and outsiders.[43] Their interaction reveals the choreography behind the Danaids' rhetoric. In advising them Danaus empowers the Danaids to take charge of their identity and by extension their continuing story. But, paradoxically, what he advises requires reliance on Greek male support. Thus the Danaids are both empowered and dependent. They have the ability to craft their story, but it is one that requires the support of male allies. Their relationship to their father further brings out this circularity or paradox. They rely on him for his advice, but his authority to advise comes from the Danaids themselves. In the interaction between father and daughters there is a confusion and constant shifting of agency, a choreographed dance in the balance of power. Ultimately the source of this power comes from the Danaids, who craft their identity in service to the agenda they advance. They depend on their father's leadership, but it is they who have granted him this authority.

Much of this confusion between active and passive, powerful and subordinate, is premised on the Danaids' careful deployment of their female identity. As they invoke various entities for protection, they make clear that they are vulnerable as parthenoi, but they do not stress their identification as such:

ὦ πόλις, ὦ γῆ καὶ λευκὸν ὕδωρ,
ὕπατοί τε θεοὶ καὶ βαρυτίμους
χθόνιοι θήκας κατέχοντες,
καὶ Ζεὺς σωτὴρ τρίτος, οἰκοφύλαξ
ὁσίων ἀνδρῶν, δέξασθ᾽ ἱκέτην
τὸν θηλυγενῆ στόλον αἰδοίῳ
πνεύματι χώρας· ἀρσενοπληθῆ δ᾽
ἑσμὸν ὑβριστὴν Αἰγυπτογενῆ,
πρὶν πόδα χέρσῳ τῇδ᾽ ἐν ἀσώδει

---

43. Wohl 2010, 420–22, makes similar observations about the balancing act the Danaids must play, ultimately misrepresenting themselves as subservient to and dependent on male power.

θεῖναι, ξὺν ὄχῳ ταχυήρει
πέμψατε πόντονδ᾽· ἔνθα δὲ λαίλαπι
χειμωνοτύπῳ βροντῇ στεροπῇ τ᾽
ὀμβροφόροισίν τ᾽ ἀνέμοις ἀγρίας
ἁλὸς ἀντήσαντες ὄλοιντο,
πρίν ποτε λέκτρων ὧν θέμις εἴργει
σφετεριξάμενοι πατραδέλφειαν
τήνδ᾽ ἀεκόντων ἐπιβῆναι. (23–39)

O city, O land, and clear water, gods both on high and those beneath the earth who possess severely punishing tombs, and third, Zeus Savior, guardian of the household of holy men, receive our female suppliant group into the land with your compassionate breath. Before they set foot on this muddy land, send the insolent, crowding swarm of men born of Aegyptus to sea, with a fast-rowing ship. There by a storming hurricane, by thunder and lightning, and by rain-bringing winds may they meet with the savage sea and be destroyed before they appropriate their cousins and mount their unwilling beds, from which divine law excludes them.

Just as they curate their hybrid ethnicity, so too their presentation as women. While they call attention to their female gender (θηλυγενῆ, 28) and cast their cousins as rapists who would "mount unwilling beds" against divine law (λέκτρων . . . ἀεκόντων ἐπιβῆναι, 37–39), they stop short of declaring themselves parthenoi, a term that appears only once in Suppliants, in the mouth of Pelasgus (480). This avoidance dovetails with their dependence on Zeus, who is the very god who raped their ancestress Io and thus cannot be considered particularly sensitive to parthenoi.[44] Yet their descent from Zeus and their appeals to his protection are central to their justification for asylum; thus, they do not emphatically identify as parthenoi. This balancing act demonstrates how carefully they curate their self-presentation and the shape of their narrative.

The Danaids and Pelasgus: Forging Collaboration

Such careful control also serves their persuasive strategy with Pelasgus, whose support they require. Their rhetorical skill is most clearly visible here, as their

---

44. Gantz 1978a, 279, makes a similar point, that the Danaids' position is paradoxical since they make an "appeal to Zeus to save them from the lust of the Egyptians . . . in the name of his own lust for their ancestor."

interactions with Pelasgus ultimately fashion him as their collaborator.[45] By crafting a narrative that blends their identity with his, they seek to cultivate solidarity. As they interact with Pelasgus, they must not only present their story to him in a way that he will find credible, they must also present a justifiable case for the Argives to assume the risk of protecting them from the Aegyptiads. They essentially forge the truth as they tell it, interweaving their story of Argive ancestry with the necessity of Argive assistance against their violent pursuers. They enfold the various aspects of their identity into their supplication as they attempt to convince Pelasgus of who they are and why he must harbor them. By engineering how they will be perceived, they influence his actions and reactions, as well as the shape of the narrative. Their appeals to Pelasgus ultimately make him the male proxy for implementing the agenda they script, one in which he plays an integral part. They circumvent the laws or customs that limit their bodily autonomy by recruiting him to act on their behalf.

They are hindered by both their ethnicity and their gender. Pelasgus is skeptical of their claims to Argive identity: ἄπιστα μυθεῖσθ᾽, ὦ ξέναι, κλύειν ἐμοί, | ὅπως τόδ᾽ ὑμῖν ἐστιν Ἀργεῖον γένος ("Foreign women, you say things unbelievable for me to hear, that this race of yours is Argive," 278–79).[46] And in taking stock of their non-Greek appearance, he catalogues the different ethnicities of women to whom the Danaids might be compared: Libyan, Egyptian, Cyprian, Indian, and Amazon (279–87). Further, instead of merely guessing they are Cyprian, Pelasgus supposes they might have been forged in the *image* of Cyprian identity by a male craftsman: Κύπριος χαρακτήρ τ᾽ ἐν γυναικείοις τύποις | εἰκὼς πέπληκται τεκτόνων πρὸς ἀρσένων ("A Cyprian stamp has *seemingly* been struck on female forms *by male artisans*," 282–83). Although it anticipates the Danaids' characterization of Zeus as τέκτων (592), this couplet is textually problematic and has been rejected on linguistic grounds as well as for reasons of sense.[47] Notably, Cyprian does not obviously belong in the catalogue of non-Greek identities, although there is some evidence that fifth-century Cyprus was a melting pot of various ethnicities and was not considered part of Greece.[48]

---

45. Cf. Wohl 2010, 420, on the astounding degree of political agency the Danaids exercise in their interactions with Pelasgus as their proxenos rather than kyrios.

46. For an interpretation of these lines see Bakewell 1997, 217–18.

47. Zeitlin 1996, 153–54, notes the resonance with line 592. For arguments for excising the couplet, see Bowen 2013, 204–6; Friis Johansen and Whittle 1975, 21–25; and Sommerstein 2019, 170–71.

48. See Friis Johansen and Whittle 1980 vol. 2, 224 and 226; Sommerstein 1977, 69–71. I should make clear, however, that Friis Johansen and Whittle ultimately reject lines 282–83 and were the first to argue that they were interpolated from another play (Friis Johansen and Whittle 1975, 20–21). Further, Sommerstein's most recent arguments seem to reject his 1977 stance (Sommerstein 2019, 170–71 *ad* 282–83).

Their problematic nature aside, the fact remains that the lines have been preserved in the manuscripts and have thus become part of the tradition that shapes the reception of this play, for better or worse. As it stands, the couplet has Pelasgus channeling a tradition of male artisanship of female characters as he uses the language of likeness and male creation to describe the Danaids' distinctive appearance.[49] These lines parallel the instances of blended male and female creativity (and deception) that I discussed in previous chapters, in which a male figure creates deceptive female figures like Pandora and the Hera-cloud of the Ixion myth, who are replicas of other things (ἵκελον, Hes., *Th.* 572; εἶδος, Pi., *P.* 2.38), products of a male creator but given their own agency for deception and destruction. Pelasgus' accusation converges with a tradition of infusing male creativity with female deception and hints at the Danaids' potential to create a false narrative. He caps his list with the "manless Amazons" (ἀνάνδρους . . . Ἀμαζόνας, 287), thus explicitly coloring his catalogue of ethnicities with one that is exclusively female.[50] With this final comparison to the Amazons, he crystallizes his conflation of ethnicity and gender as dual justifications for undermining and marginalizing the Danaids.[51]

At the start of the play, the Danaids' promises to confirm their claims may have seemed unnecessary (49–56). Now as they face Pelasgus, such promises seem a prescient anticipation of gender-based disbelief. Their preemptive tactics allow them to exploit the various facets of their identity to seize some degree of agency over their stories and their bodies. Eventually they draw Pelasgus in as a collaborator in their narrative as they build a shared history and a shared future. Acquiring his physical alliance necessitates forging an authorial one as well. When he asks them their story, they do not simply retell the Io myth. Instead, details of the myth unfold in quick stichomythia between them (291–346). By engaging Pelasgus in this exchange of questions and answers, the Chorus enlist him as an ally in the construction of their identity, making him

---

49. Wohl 2010, 418, sees an analogy between gender and nature/culture here: "The metaphor of impression (probably a coinage metaphor) in 282–83 suggests that ethnicity is a cultural (masculine) stamp upon a natural (feminine) material."

50. Bakewell 1997, 217–18, argues that this comparison to the Amazons expresses Pelasgus' perceptive concern about the Danaids' potential to harm the city; he credits Pelasgus with correctly understanding the Danaids' proclivity to violence. Bakewell adduces interesting textual resonances, but ascribes too much perceptiveness to Pelasgus.

51. In an examination of the ethnic stereotyping of Egyptians in Greek tragedy, Phiroze Vasunia makes a similar observation about the intersection of gender and ethnicity in Aeschylus' *Suppliants*: "we might rather state that the Danaids' detestation of their cousins is framed by their aversion to the idea of marriage and to the violence of men. The representation of the Egyptian men is part of this representation of a conflict between the sexes and is colored by the representation of that conflict" (Vasunia 2001, 55).

an active participant in the formation of the Io myth as a link between the Argives and Danaids. His increasing belief in their claims about Io stems partly from his own participation in crafting them.

Their exchange reveals a number of details about Io's myth: her connection to Argos as a priestess of Hera; Zeus' relationship to her; her transformation into a cow by Hera's hand; Zeus' own transformation into a bull for copulation with Io; her watchman Argus; the gadfly sent to torment her; her travels to Egypt; and the descent of the Danaids from her. Texts and translations put most or all of the questions in Pelasgus' mouth, but the manuscripts are confusing enough that editors and commentators disagree about which lines belong to him or to the Chorus. Textual certainty is impossible, but this lack of certainty is, paradoxically, illuminating, for the obscurity in the texts parallels what must have been the jumbled state of rapid-fire exchange between Pelasgus and the Chorus in live performance. For the audience, it was probably not always clear or salient who was speaking which lines in such a section, where rapidity would have blurred the distinctions between knowledge-provider and knowledge-seeker.[52]

This heightened excitement and diminished clarity become especially marked in the ambiguity of line 310, which some editors assign to the Chorus and others to Pelasgus: καὶ ταῦτ᾽ ἔλεξας πάντα συγκόλλως ἐμοί ("And all these things you said are in accordance with my own opinion").[53] In either case, both speaker and addressee are cast as collaborators in—rather than mere inquirers of—the Chorus' story. In this back and forth, the Chorus and Pelasgus work together to discover the truth of their lineages that binds them together and forges their fates into mutually influential and dependent ones. The Chorus thus enfold Pelasgus into their story and make him its coauthor. Together they forge the connections between past, present, and future that form the basis of Aeschylean reciprocity and truth.

As they forge this narrative, the Danaids must also convince Pelasgus that they have a right to Argive protection from the Aegyptiads. Kinship alone is an insufficient basis for this argument given that the Aegyptiads are also descended

---

52. Rosenmeyer 1982, 203, points out that the effect of this passage is ultimately to provide information, whoever the speakers of individual lines may be. Cf. Ireland 1974, for Aeschylus' use of stichomythia to construct and develop complex ideas, and Thomson 1967, 189, for the sometimes riddling function of stichomythia.

53. Burian 1991 and Page 1972 assign 310 to the Chorus; Bowen 2013, Friis Johansen and Whittle 1980, West 1990a, and Sommerstein 2019 assign it to Pelasgus. See West 1990b, 140–41 for further discussion.

from Io.[54] What the Danaids must do is argue that marriage to their cousins is wrong, but they lack a legal basis for this argument. When Pelasgus inquires whether it is personal enmity or illegality that motivates their flight, they do not answer directly:

> Βα. πότερα κατ' ἔχθραν ἢ τὸ μὴ θέμις λέγεις;
> Χο. τίς δ' ἂν φίλους ὄνοιτο τοὺς κεκτημένους; (336–37)

> PELASGUS: Do you speak out of hostility or because of something not right?
> CHORUS: Who could fault friends who have purchased them?

Pelasgus fallaciously presumes that a divinely lawful marriage could occur without their approval and affection, a fallacy the Danaids' response addresses.[55] Textual difficulties plague line 337 and prevent its sure translation, but all the proposed variants juxtapose affection and ownership, indicating the innately fraught position from which the Danaids' supplication originates.[56] In phrasing their response in the form of a question, the Danaids deflect, suggesting that Pelasgus' question is itself faulty.[57] When he points out that their case may have no legal basis, either in Egypt or Greece (387–91), the Danaids deflect again.[58] Instead of answering directly, the Danaids vow never to accept the dominance of men (392–93), thus, as Alan Sommerstein notes, evading the question and tacitly admitting that there is no legal basis for their appeals.[59]

In effect their deflections interrogate the validity of legal arguments surrounding marriage. By extension they interrogate the validity of marriage itself, at least the type of forced marriage they flee. Their refusal to marry the Aegyptiads may be unexplained, but it is frequent and consistent—a telling indication

---

54. As Vasunia 2001, 41, observes, however, the Aegyptiads are not explicitly characterized as having hybrid identity.

55. As Belfiore 2000, 57, observes, Pelasgus presents a false antithesis between enmity and themis: "It is *themis* that forbids the barbarian marriage sought by the Aigyptiads, in which the bride is an unwilling partner."

56. See Bowen 2013, 218–19 *ad* 337, Friis Johansen and Whittle 1980 vol. 2, 271–73 *ad* 337, and Sommerstein 2019, 186–87 *ad* 337, for the various possibilities, along with their respective strengths and weaknesses.

57. Cf. Bowen 2013, 218 *ad* 337 and Gruber 2009, 240.

58. On the legal controversy surrounding the Danaids' flight, see Garvie 1969, 216–21; MacKinnon 1978, 77–79; Turner 2001, 33–34.

59. Sommerstein 2008 vol. 1, 341n80 and 2019, 203 *ad* 392–96. Cf. Bowen 2013, 231 *ad* 392–96; Gagarin 1976, 129, who notes that "they are notably evasive when pressed by Pelasgus for specific facts to support their case (336–39), and they use threats of suicide rather than legal or moral arguments to sway his decision."

that legal definitions of marriage are themselves faulty.[60] The Danaids' probable lack of legal recourse points to a flaw in the system of marriage, which affords no agency to the bride or her advocates. This flaw is all the more glaring when we consider that their father Danaus too is forced to flee. His seeming lack of authority over his daughters' marriages is at odds with fifth-century Athenian marriage law, which vested male guardians with such authority and would have informed the contemporary audience's reception of this play.[61]

They reinforce their objections with claims about dikē (ἀλλ' ἡ Δίκη γε ξυμμάχων ὑπερστατεῖ, "But Justice protects allies," 343; ξύμμαχον δ' ἑλόμενος Δίκαν | κρῖνε σέβας τὸ πρὸς θεῶν, "Choose Justice as your ally and make a decision for what is holy in the eyes of the gods," 395–96). They thus infuse dikē with questions about the nature of marriage, as well as the duties of allies to protect women from unwanted marriage. Such an interrogation of marriage complements their identification with Io and their sanitized version of her relationship with Zeus. The protective quality they associate with dikē blends it with supplication and obligation, to serve both the past they construct and the present and future they hope will spring from it. Furthermore, it is Pelasgus himself who unwittingly initiates this blend of supplication and dikē; the Danaids simply capitalize on it. While he expresses doubt about their claims to Justice (εἴπερ γ' ἀπ' ἀρχῆς πραγμάτων κοινωνὸς ἦν, "Yes, if [Justice] was a companion in your affairs from the beginning," 344), he also expresses concern about Zeus Hiketios (345–47). The Danaids' attempts to align themselves with Pelasgus begin to work as he comes to accept their claims of hybrid identity and the right to asylum it affords. He refers to the Danaids as ἀστοξένων (356), a term that denotes "foreigners connected by race with the city"[62] and suggests that he is increasingly convinced of their right to Argive protection.

The Danaids' treatment of dikē is inherently informed by their female gender. The arguments they craft, blending supplication with dikē and Egyptian identity with Argive, are necessitated by the position they are in as parthenoi.

---

60. Friis Johansen and Whittle 1980 vol. 1, 29–30, document the Danaids' consistent and repeated expressions of antipathy toward marriage and their cousins: "Throughout they express their aversion to the marriage (39, 332 (corrupt), 394, 788–805, 1031–32, 1063–64) and also to the Aegyptiads (511, 790); they further represent both as characterized by ὕβρις (30, 81, 104, 426, 528, 817, 845), the Aegyptiads as possessed by ἄτη (106–11), and the marriage as impious (9–10), contrary to θέμις (37), to αἶσα (80; see n.) and to δίκη (82), and equivalent to bondage (335; cf. 221, 392–93, 791)."

61. On such customs and regulations concerning marriage in Athens, see Foxhall 2013, 32–35; Pomeroy 1995, 62–65; Patterson 1991, esp. 48–53.

62. Friis Johansen and Whittle 1980 vol. 2, 285 ad loc.

So, too, are the more aggressive moves they take in service to their supplication. What brings Pelasgus decisively to their side is their threat of suicide (455–67), which will bring pollution on Argos and is morally questionable, as scholars have noted.[63] But it forces visual clarity on Pelasgus, who is thus far unable (or unwilling) to find it. What they threaten specifically is to use their girdles to hang themselves from the statues of the gods (465), but they prolong this announcement over several lines, beginning simply with pointing to their girdles, then slowly illustrating for Pelasgus their potential function. This prolonged threat might seem an excessively manipulative and riddling tactic, but their presentation of it in such a visual way lends strength to their argument that their verbal appeals lacked.

Gesturing to their girdles, furthermore, draws attention to their female gender and makes visible its heretofore invisible power.[64] It is a brilliant encapsulation of their defining paradox: the very femaleness that prevents them from refusing marriage to their cousins also enables them to obtain the male assistance that will help them against the Aegyptiads. As Pelasgus registers shock when he finally realizes what they have in mind, the Danaids respond, "You understand! For I have made it more *clear to your eye!*" (ξυνῆκας· ὠμμάτωσα γὰρ σαφέστερον, 467), again invoking vision as a source of authority and legitimacy. Although manipulative, their tactics reflect their own clear-sighted determination and provide Pelasgus with a model of clarity to adopt.[65] Their threat has the effect of bringing Pelasgus to their cause.[66]

The Danaids' tactics and Pelasgus' hesitation reflect a gap between their interests, a gap that the Danaids must close. Pelasgus' primary concern is for the safety of his city. He appears sympathetic to the Danaids and simply wishes to harmonize their needs with his own. The Danaids' task is thus to blend their interests with his and to convince him that what is good for them is good for Argos too. Their threat is the negative counterpart to this argument: what is bad

---

63. See, e.g., Gagarin 1976, 129 and Turner 2001, 35. This threat plays on ancient Greek gender tropes of virgin suicide (Wohl 2010, 427, citing Loraux 1987, 7–30). Bednarowski 2010, 195, summarizes the scholarly animus against the Danaids; he offers a more forgiving argument that the Athenian audience would have perceived the Danaids as sincerely desperate to avoid capture and forced marriage.

64. Cf. Zeitlin 1992, 229, who notes that their threatened removal of their girdles also alludes to the surrender of their virginity. See also Bakewell 2013, 71–73, on the eroticism and exoticism of the Danaids.

65. As Lesky 1966, 80, notes, Pelasgus' decision to help the Danaids results from both their coercion and his own careful consideration.

66. Cf. Buxton 1982, 75: "At 478–9 [Pelasgus] accepts the weight of the case which the maidens have been pressing all along. . . . Linguistically as well as morally he appropriates the Danaids' stance and makes it his own."

for them is bad for Argos. It dovetails with their efforts to forge a shared identity with the Argives, which entails both a shared past and a shared future, even if that future is a bleak one. Their threat is an extreme iteration of how they recruit male agents to their cause. As parthenoi, they have no legal authority over their own bodies. They must rely on—even hijack—the authority of potential male protectors like Pelasgus, who, though shocked, can use this threat himself in his own case to the Argive populace for the Danaids' protection.

The Limits of Female Narrative Control

Once Argive aid for the Danaids is secured, the Aegyptiads' imminent arrival tests and reveals the limits of the Danaids' narrative strategy. Their authorial power disintegrates under physical threat, and they must ultimately inflict physical violence in the next play. Their reliance on male agents to enact their vision of a shared future demonstrates the uncertainty and tension underlying *Suppliants*.[67] The Danaids can exercise some control in the verbal realm: as long as they can persuade Pelasgus and the Argives to their cause, they can align their hopes with their fates. But once they secure the Argives' commitment, they have no control over the violence that will ensue between the Argives and Aegyptiads.[68] Indeed, their physical control in *Suppliants* is limited to their potential for suicide. Fear takes hold of them as they realize that their female gender, previously just an obstacle to immediate access to the king and Argives, now becomes a physical detriment as they are not equipped to engage physically with their male pursuers: μόνην δὲ μὴ πρόλειπε, λίσσομαι, πάτερ· | γυνὴ μονωθεῖσ᾽ οὐδέν· οὐκ ἔνεστ᾽ Ἄρης ("Do not leave me alone, father, I beg you! A woman left alone is nothing. There is no Ares in her," 748–49).

As the Danaids lose their conviction, Pelasgus gains it. Their enlistment of Pelasgus not only as ally but as coauthor of their story is now complete, as he assumes full control of the situation and the certainty that previously was theirs alone. Persuaded at last by the Danaids' appeals, he unites their words with his

---

67. Gantz 1978a, esp. 287, takes their visionary limitations further when he argues that the Danaids' rejection of the Aegyptiads is myopic in its failure to recognize the necessity of sexual union to the very perpetuation of life itself. His argument, however, seems premised on a basic antipathy for the Danaids, but others—for example, Robertson 1924, Winnington-Ingram 1983, 59–61, and Bednarowski 2010—are more sympathetic to them.

68. Wohl 2010, taking Spivak 1994 as her springboard, discusses the transformation of the Danaids' "unfamiliar narrative—foreign girls enter into negotiations for political asylum with a Greek king . . . into a reassuring tale of Greek men saving Egyptian women from Egyptian men" (422) and the parallels between this story and the US justification for war in Aghanistan.

ability for physical action. The final scene devolves into chaos as the Chorus scream and the Herald of the Aegyptiads threatens violence if they do not board the ship (882–84). As Pelasgus chastises the Herald for his barbaric behavior and warns him that disrespecting Argive asylum will result in harm to the Aegyptiads (911–15), he brings the Danaids into the full privilege and protection of Greek identity. Further, he adopts their arguments about reciprocity in his interactions with the Herald, chastising him for his failure to recognize xenia (ξένος μὲν εἶναι πρῶτον οὐκ ἐπίστασαι, "First, you do not know how to be a guest-friend," 917).

The final sections of the play demonstrate both the efficacy of the Danaids' strategy and its limitations. While they have succeeded in appropriating Pelasgus' agency by crafting an identity and a narrative that binds him to them, they have now exhausted the possibilities of their rhetoric and must rely solely on him for survival. Pelasgus ultimately adopts some of the Danaids' persuasive practices in his engagement with the Herald. He cites the supreme authority of argument when he tells the Herald that he can take the Danaids if he can persuade them to go willingly (940–41). In his interactions with the Herald, Pelasgus assumes a posture of conviction, speaks with the authority of the Argives behind him (942–44), and asserts the masculinity of this authority, thus co-opting the verbal persuasiveness of the Danaids but joining to it the physical strength of the male: ἀλλ᾿ ἄρσενάς τοι τῆσδε γῆς οἰκήτορας | εὑρήσετ᾿, οὐ πίνοντας ἐκ κριθῶν μέθυ ("But you will find men as inhabitants of this land, not drinkers of barley-wine," 952–53).

As the play closes, however, the uncertainty of the future arises, while visual clarity dissipates: σὺ δέ γ᾿ οὐκ οἶσθα τὸ μέλλον. | τί δὲ μέλλω φρένα Δίαν | καθορᾶν, ὄψιν ἄβυσσον; ("You do not know the future. How am I going to see the mind of Zeus, the unfathomable sight?" 1056–58). It is unclear who the speaker of these lines is—the Danaids? A new Chorus of Handmaidens? Have the Danaids split into two half-choruses? Do they argue with an Argive leader?[69] The state of the manuscripts obscures the identities of the speakers, but the end of the play reminds us that the trilogy and its arc of dikē and reciprocity will continue:

69. See Sommerstein 2010b, 101, esp. nn44–46, for a list of the various positions. See also Bednarowski 2011 for an assessment of the scholarly communis opinio along with his own argument that the final song is sung by the Danaids split into half-choruses that complement rather than oppose one another.

Ζεὺς ἄναξ ἀποστεροί-
η γάμον δυσάνορα
δάιον, ὅσπερ Ἰὼ
πημονᾶς ἐλύσατ᾽ εὖ
χειρὶ παιωνίᾳ κατασχεθών,
εὐμενῆ βίαν κτίσας,

καὶ κράτος νέμοι γυναι-
ξίν. τὸ βέλτερον κακοῦ
καὶ τὸ δίμοιρον αἰνῶ
καὶ <u>δίκᾳ δίκας</u> ἕπε-
σθαι ξὺν εὐχαῖς ἐμαῖς λυτηρίοις
μαχαναῖς θεοῦ πάρα. (1062–73)

May lord Zeus avert hateful marriage to a bad husband, he who set Io free from her miseries by holding them back with his healing hand and making force kindly. And may he dispense power to women. I acquiesce in what is better than evil, the two-thirds share, and in *justice following justice* with my prayers, by the contrivances of the god that provide deliverance.

While this arc of retribution is certain, how it will be revealed is not (for the characters). Whether the Danaids are divided or united at this point, these lines point to a consistent thought among at least some of them that their fates mirror Io's—again linking past, present, and future—and that Zeus engineers this fate to be kind to women, a thought consistent with their formulation of the Zeus-Io relationship as an affectionate one.[70]

Their repetition of dikē (δίκᾳ δίκας, 1071) echoes the formulations of Pindaric and Aeschylean reciprocity I discussed in chapter 1 and underscores their belief in a reciprocity-driven outcome commensurate with previous actions. While they do not know the specifics of what will happen, they do know that the future will respond—and correspond—to the present and past. This is the truth they believe in and have actively forged from the beginning of the play. This truth mirrors Aeschylean conceptions of reciprocity as a governing force and reflects the way Aeschylus' stories work. Further, they have been the pri-

---

70. Lines 576–78 contain a comparable sentiment, as Sommerstein 2008 vol. 1, 429n224 observes. In lines 575–79, the Danaids claim Zeus put an end to Io's tormented travels.

mary perceivers and arbiters of this truth, in keeping with Aeschylus' general characterization of female figures, who have a preternatural ability to detect the larger narrative in which they are situated.

The Danaids will not cleave to merely rhetorical strategies in authoring their narrative. We know they will, with the exception of Hypermnestra, kill their Egyptian cousin-husbands, thus taking into their hands the violence that is normally the realm of men. The uncertainty they express at the end of the play reveals the limits of their narrative control. It dissolves in the face of real, physical danger to them, it becomes transferred to Pelasgus—enforced by Argive physical strength—and in the end the Danaids must abandon rhetoric and resort to physical force, which is still premised on reciprocity, but of a different kind. Their plan to escape the Aegyptiads with Argive assistance will fail, and they themselves will engage in a murderous violence that belies their self-presentation to Pelasgus and departs from the narrative they had scripted with him.

Until now the Danaids' strategy has been to control the narrative by constructing a past history and arguing that the present and future should replicate it. This strategy has implications for Aeschylean truth, which is premised on reciprocity in that past events precipitate future replications. As we will see in the *Oresteia*, these replications are violent, one murderous act responding to a previous one. In *Suppliants* the Danaids present a truth that has the same repetitive pattern, but their aim is a reciprocity in which kindness precipitates further kindness. The Danaids are not only cognizant of this truth but actively assert it and attempt to impose it on their own narrative. This strategy breaks down in the next play, when they yield to the type of hostile reciprocity we will see in the *Oresteia* and kill their husbands. As Winnington-Ingram observes,

> The victims of violence in *Supplices* become violent agents in the sequel, for violence breeds violence, *hubris* breeds *hubris*. Even in *Supplices*, for all their claims to *sophrosune*, the Danaids showed a potentiality of violence. There they threatened to kill themselves rather than submit to wedlock: in the outcome they kill their bridegrooms. Thus the themes of *bia* and *hubris*, prominent in *Supplices*, were carried over into the later plays. (1983, 57)

Winnington-Ingram here encapsulates what Aeschylean reciprocity will become in the rest of the trilogy. The narrative the Danaids have thus far crafted, the timeline of cyclical repetitions of acts of kindness, will ultimately give way to the reciprocity of violence.

Conclusion

The various strategies the Danaids employ for their own survival involve shaping their story—their history and future—and presenting it as truth. In this way they are akin to an author, and thus reflect some of the creative abilities of figures like Hesiod's Muses, Stesichorus' Helen-cloud, and Pindar's Hera-cloud. Lacking their own legal authority or physical agency, the Danaids must enact their wishes through a persuasive strategy that empowers them to choreograph the actions of male characters. They envision a plot, one they script as fated and inevitable, and, like Hesiod's Muses or Stesichorus' Helen, they rely on male agents to actualize it. These characteristics situate them in a poetic tradition that interweaves female gender with poetic creativity, but with a specificity to Aeschylean tragedy. They emulate the tragedian himself, who likewise has the ability to script the story, but the inability to enact it himself—he must rely on his actors. In this way the Danaids—and other Aeschylean female characters— can be seen as analogues for the poet himself. They parallel the Pindaric female figures I discuss in chapter 3 who, though quite distinct from the Danaids in most respects, share the function of calling attention to the poetic contexts in which they exist.

Furthermore, the Danaids display their narrative abilities in a reciprocity-driven context that typifies Aeschylean tragedy and complements Pindaric reciprocities. With his ongoing narratives predicated on replication of the past in a present and future that respond to it, Aeschylus constructs plots that are shaped by the forces of reciprocity, and he casts his female characters as the detectors and articulators of these forces. The Danaids make every attempt to construe this reciprocity as inevitable; they present the past as a catalyst of obligations that should and will shape the future, and they configure this phenomenon as truth. Thus, like the Chorus of *Seven*, they put formulations of reciprocity and truth at the center of the story in which they exist.

CHAPTER 6

Truth, Gender, and Revenge
in Aeschylus' *Oresteia*

As I discussed in previous chapters, alētheia encapsulates the reciprocity principles that shape Pindaric and Aeschylean poetry. In Aeschylus this principle involves connectedness between past, present, and future: what occurs and will occur is premised on what happened before. This cause-and-effect order is one that Aeschylus associates with reciprocity, of action that compels reaction. Aeschylus' intertwining of truth and reciprocity is most apparent in *Agamemnon*, which introduces the pattern of revenge that will govern the *Oresteia* trilogy, a pattern based on the principle of reciprocity and articulated with alētheia and with language denoting symmetry between actions and their consequences. After ten years at war, Agamemnon returns home from Troy with his concubine Cassandra, both of whom are killed by his wife Clytemnestra and her lover (his cousin) Aegisthus. Their deaths answer for and correspond to previous losses—notably, the sacrifice of Iphigenia—and will be replicated in the next play where, at the hands of Orestes, Clytemnestra and Aegisthus meet the same death they inflicted on Agamemnon. The cycle of violence comes to an end in *Eumenides*.

Gender informs nearly every aspect of the trilogy. Each conflict parallels a male-female opposition whose starkness and inherent fallacies are revealed in the perpetuation and eventual resolution of conflict. As Michael Gagarin writes, "That there is sexual conflict in some sense in the *Oresteia* is obvious, since the basic pattern of action and retributive reaction (*drasanti pathein*) unfolds in the trilogy as an alternation of male and female agents: Agamemnon, Clytemnestra, Orestes, and the Furies."[1] In a similar vein, Brooke Holmes notes the *Ores-*

---

1. Gagarin 1976, 87. See also Winnington-Ingram 1983, 101: "It will not be disputed that the rela-

teia's use of gender conflict to illustrate various power differentials: "The *Oresteia* shows the extent to which gender functions in Greek mythology as a way of organising relationships of power in the cosmos, the city and the family."[2]

As I will argue, consideration of gender illuminates not only the conflicts themselves but the theme of reciprocity giving narrative coherence to those conflicts. I will begin with *Agamemnon*, which follows the general Aeschylean trend of casting female characters who are aware of the reciprocity that governs their narrative. As in the other Aeschylean works I have examined, it is *Agamemnon*'s female rather than male characters who understand the pattern of action-reaction that permeates the narrative in which they are situated. Both Clytemnestra and Cassandra display an expansive understanding rooted in the unique sources of their knowledge: Clytemnestra relies on the beacon-fires announcing the fall of Troy, and Cassandra has prophetic visions. Both sources require interpretation before their meanings can be understood. Through these interpreted sources Clytemnestra and Cassandra gain a comprehension of truth that encompasses its temporal and causal dimensions. They understand their story as part of a continuing arc in which past and present instances of violence result in future consequences, and they see acts of revenge as responsive to and mirroring previous wrongs. Furthermore, they use alētheia to describe the sovereignty and inevitability of retribution. Cassandra and Clytemnestra essentially articulate themes shaping their story and thus call attention to the nature of those themes. I will then proceed to a discussion of *Choephori* and *Eumenides*, which complicate the relationship between reciprocity and truth set forth in *Agamemnon* and further call attention to what forces shape the narrative.

Clytemnestra and the Herald: Different Sources of Truth

Male and female characters in *Agamemnon* have different conceptions of truth. They discover and react to the truth differently, and their gender affects how

---

tionship between the sexes was a subject of great interest to Aeschylus." Other provocative studies of gender in the *Oresteia* include Foley 2001, 202–34; Goldhill 1984; McClure 1999, 70–111; Wohl 1998, 59–117; Zeitlin 1996, 87–119.

2.   Holmes 2012, 128. See also Zeitlin 1996, 100, who observes the inextricability of gender from the main preoccupation of the *Oresteia*: "by posing the son's action in separating himself from his mother as a crime, *the issue of justice and the issue of the female are inextricably blended* [my emphasis]."

they are perceived and treated by their interlocutors. In other words, truth in *Agamemnon* is gendered. The play shows the relationship of gender to knowledge and the implications thereof for the articulation of revenge in Aeschylean tragedy. We first see this gendering of truth in the contrasting examples of Clytemnestra and the Herald. Clytemnestra has attracted scholarly attention for her craftiness, cunning use of language, and subversion of gender roles.[3] As I will show here, her way of accessing and deriving knowledge also deserves attention. She demonstrates an ability to extrapolate detailed, accurate messages about the fate of Troy and the return of Agamemnon from a source that does not inherently contain such detail, namely, the beacon-fires that signal the fall of Troy.

Although it is a Watchman who awaits the light of those fires at the beginning of the play, it is Clytemnestra who has determined their significance. She is the one who has stationed the Watchman (10–11), who himself expresses some uncertainty about the fires' message when he sees them (εἴπερ Ἰλίου πόλις | ἑάλωκεν, ὡς ὁ φρυκτὸς ἀγγέλλων πρέπει, "if the city of Troy has been taken, as the signal-fire appears to be reporting," *A.* 29–30). Clytemnestra, by contrast, is more confident that the fires are evidence of the Greeks' victory, but she meets with the skepticism and derision of the Chorus of Argive Elders when she announces the news. They constantly question her and demand evidence (πῶς φῄς; πέφευγε τοὔπος ἐξ ἀπιστίας, "What are you saying? From disbelief your word has escaped me," *A.* 268; τί γὰρ τὸ πιστόν; ἔστι τῶνδέ σοι τέκμαρ; "For what is it that's trustworthy? Do you have evidence of this?" 272). They then speculate that whatever her evidence may be, it is likely questionable at best (πότερα δ᾽ ὀνείρων φάσματ᾽ εὐπιθῆ σέβεις; "Do you respect the visions of dreams as persuasive?" 274; ἀλλ᾽ ἦ σ᾽ ἐπίανέν τις ἄπτερος φάτις; "But is it some wingless rumor exciting you?" 276; καὶ τίς τόδ᾽ ἐξίκοιτ᾽ ἂν ἀγγέλων τάχος; "And which of the messengers could arrive so quickly?" 280).[4]

Clytemnestra does eventually gain their trust, first by specifying Hephaestus as her source (281) and explaining the beacon-fires' system of message-

---

3. See, e.g., Betensky 1978; Fletcher 1999, 21–23; Foley 2001, 201–34; Goldhill 1984, 33–42, 48–57; McClure 1999, 70–100; Winnington-Ingram 1983, 101–31; Wohl 1998, 103–10; Zeitlin 1996, 87–98. I have found very helpful Wohlfarht 2004, a dissertation on truth in Aeschylus. Its insights about Clytemnestra and Cassandra overlap with some of my own, which focus on gender and reciprocity.

4. The Chorus do pledge allegiance to her (258–60), but they make clear that their allegiance is a function of her marriage to Agamemnon, whose absence makes her his proxy. See Goldhill 1984, 34: "[Clytemnestra's] power is because of the lack not just of the ruler but of the 'male.'"

transmission (281–316). By attributing the fires to Hephaestus, she casts the relay of beacon-fires as a single and divine entity;[5] she thus imposes unity on a message that is by its very nature fragmented through its transmission. Furthermore, she goes beyond the simple message that Troy has fallen. Just as the Chorus of *Seven* interpret dust-clouds and sounds to imagine details of the Argive advance, Clytemnestra extracts from the fires a bigger, more elaborate picture, effectively using them as a springboard to tell a story. She speaks of the sights and sounds at Troy, the distinctive shouts of victors and defeated (βοὴν ἄμικτον, 321; καὶ τῶν ἁλόντων καὶ κρατησάντων δίχα | φθογγάς, 324–25), the fallen bodies (325–27), the lamentations of the newly enslaved Trojan elders (328), and the toils of the Greek conquerors who can finally sleep comfortably and at ease (330–37). By her own admission these details are imagined (οἶμαι, 321) and not witnessed firsthand. As R. D. Dawe observes, "She cannot possibly have known what conditions were actually like there but she speaks with the authority of a messenger and the insight of Kassandra."[6] Indeed, another critic describes Clytemnestra's speech as "almost mantic."[7] From the simple message of the beacon-fires she derives a much more elaborate one that reflects her capacity for interpretation and even empathy. Her account includes not only the sights and sounds of Troy, but also the feelings from which they originate or which they provoke.[8] This ability to imagine and narrativize dovetails with the long view she will take later in the play.[9]

Though imagined in its details, her account is realistic enough to persuade the Chorus of its validity. Her credibility stems from her ability to articulate what she imagines: she verbalizes the nonverbal message of the beacon-fires.[10] In so doing she presents her truth as a quality of her speech rather than her

---

5. For the use of personification here, see Goldhill 1984, 38 and Lloyd-Jones 1979, 15. For post-classical parallels of this rhetorical use of divinity as authority, see Rothschild 2004, 185–212. Swift 2018, 127, sees generic mixture in the passages on the beacon-fires: "Clytemnestra's response to the beacon redefines the paeanic language [of the Chorus' response to the beacons] into epinician mode, by imagining the light as an athletic torch race (312–4)."

6. Dawe 1963, 51. See also Zeitlin 1990, 111 and Schein 1982, 15, for the visionary qualities of Cassandra and other Aeschylean female characters.

7. Conacher 1987, 33. See also Goward 2005, 64 and Fraenkel 1950 vol. 2, 333, who note the degree of speculative detail in Clytemnestra's account.

8. See also Foley 2001, 207–9, on Clytemnestra's persuasiveness in these lines. Wohl 1998, 106, sees these lines as Clytemnestra's "reassuring alternative to the horrors imagined by the chorus."

9. Cf. Wolhfarht 2004, 8, who asserts that the beacon-fires signify different things for different characters: for the Watchman, the fires represent the end of the war and the return of Agamemnon; for the Chorus, "a future full of hope"; for Clytemnestra, her vengeance on Agamemnon for Iphigenia's death.

10. Goldhill 1984, 38–39.

imagination, bringing specificity to the abstract and putting the message in terms that the Chorus finally understand and believe. They express their trust in specifically gendered terms and ascribe it to the quality of her speech:[11]

γύναι, κατ' ἄνδρα σώφρον' εὐφρόνως λέγεις·
ἐγὼ δ' ἀκούσας πιστά σου τεκμήρια
θεοὺς προσειπεῖν εὖ παρασκευάζομαι. (351–53)

Woman, you speak wisely, in the manner of a prudent man. I have heard your trusty proofs and am prepared to address the gods piously.

As Laura McClure has observed, the Chorus' initial skepticism and subsequent approval reflect a contrast between a masculine concern for legalistic arguments, encapsulated by πιστὰ τεκμήρια (352), and "less reliable, and therefore more feminine, forms of speech."[12] McClure further argues that Clytemnestra blends masculine and feminine discourses to build the Chorus' trust in her.[13] Clytemnestra has been double-gendered like this from the beginning when the Watchman characterizes her authority as the "man-minded hopeful heart of a woman" (γυναικὸς ἀνδρόβουλον ἐλπίζον κέαρ, 11). What is clear from her interaction with the Chorus is that her credibility (or lack thereof) is inherently connected to her gender, both as the Chorus define it and as she redefines it in reaction.[14] Although she is broadly telling the truth—Agamemnon indeed has defeated the Trojans and will return home—she must "prove" it by infusing the abstract message of the beacon-fires with specific details that, though imagined, nevertheless cleave to a legalistic framework persuasive to the Chorus.

Gendered Truths: Etumos and Alēthēs

Further, the very words for truth that the Chorus use point to a distinction and disparity in how they perceive male and female truth. Clytemnestra's interpre-

---

11. *Pace* Denniston and Page 1957, *ad* 352, who think the Chorus' praise "is not to be taken seriously; nothing Clytemnestra has said affords evidence, let alone 'convincing proof,' that the beacons betoken the fall of Troy."
12. McClure 1999, 74; see also McClure 1999, 74n10, citing Goldhill 1984, 39, who identifies a feminine mode of visible proof and a masculine mode of "conceptualisation in language." For an examination of legal imagery in the *Agamemnon*, see Daube 1941.
13. McClure 1999, 74. This blending occurs when Clytemnestra uses the masculine discourse of proofs and logic but caps her speech with a clear statement of her womanhood (348).
14. For Clytemnestra's gender-subversion, see Foley 2001, 203–34; Goldhill 1984, 56; Winnington-Ingram 1983, 101–31; Wohl 1998, 103–10.

tive truths do not sustain the Chorus' belief. They revert to doubt that is very
clearly rooted in Clytemnestra's female gender:

πυρὸς δ' ὑπ' εὐαγγέλου
πόλιν διήκει θοὰ
βάξις· εἰ δ' ἐτήτυμος,
τίς οἶδεν, ἤ τι θεῖόν ἐστί πῃ ψύθος;
τίς ὧδε παιδνὸς ἤ φρενῶν κεκομμένος,
φλογὸς παραγγέλμασιν
νέοις πυρωθέντα καρδίαν, ἔπειτ'
    ἀλλαγᾷ λόγου καμεῖν;
γυναικὸς αἰχμᾷ πρέπει
πρὸ τοῦ φανέντος χάριν ξυναινέσαι·
πιθανὸς ἄγαν ὁ θῆλυς ὅρος ἐπινέμεται
ταχύπορος· ἀλλὰ ταχύμορον
γυναικογήρυτον ὄλλυται κλέος. (475–87)

From the fire of good news swift rumor pervades the city. Who knows if it is
true or if it is some godly lie? Who is so immature or senseless that he gets
excited at the new reports of the flame, and then crestfallen when the story
changes? It suits a woman's temper to give thanks for something before it happens. Too credulous, the boundary of a woman's mind spreads quickly; but
quickly does a rumor voiced by a woman die.

Their sudden reversal is confusing, to say the least. As Denniston and Page
note, "There is nothing in this play or any other properly comparable with the
present example, in which the foundations of a whole stasimon are undermined
in the epode with sudden and total ruin."[15] Eduard Fraenkel posits a "certain
looseness in the psychological texture of the Chorus" as an explanation.[16] R. P.
Winnington-Ingram conjectures that the Chorus, having just expressed anxiety
over the negative consequences of war for its victors, are now relieved that the
news of Troy's fall may still be false.[17] Whatever the psychological motivation
may be for the reversal, it is clear that Clytemnestra's female gender continues
to inform the Chorus' perceptions of her.

Their language reinforces the gendered basis of their skepticism: they use a

15. Denniston and Page 1957, 114.
16. Fraenkel 1950 vol. 2, 249.
17. Winnington-Ingram 1983, 104.

cognate of etumos rather than alēthēs to designate the type of truth in Clytemnestra's account, if she *is* telling the truth. As I discussed in chapter 4, this distinction is significant and parallels the distinction that Tilman Krischer has identified in Homer, in which alēthēs is limited to eyewitness accounts while etētumos/etumos/eteos is broader and can be more flexibly applied to any kind of source.[18] Etumos can even be applied to false claims. This Homeric distinction suggests itself here as well and has implications for how the Chorus view the truth-value of the beacon-fires. For them, the fires do not carry the authority of a speaking messenger who communicates a true report based on what he has witnessed first-hand. Instead, it is a nonverbal signal whose message is determined by the interpreter.

In this context the Chorus' use of etumos suggests a lesser degree of trust than what they would afford a messenger's eyewitness account, which they term alēthēs:

τάχ' εἰσόμεθα λαμπάδων φαεσφόρων
φρυκτωριῶν τε καὶ πυρὸς παραλλαγάς,
εἴτ' οὖν <u>ἀληθεῖς</u> εἴτ' ὀνειράτων δίκην
τερπνὸν τόδ' ἐλθὸν φῶς ἐφήλωσεν φρένας·
κῆρυκ' ἀπ' ἀκτῆς τόνδ' ὁρῶ κατάσκιον
κλάδοις ἐλαίας. (489–94)

Soon we will know about the transmissions of the light-bearing torches of the beacons and flames, whether they are *true* or whether this light that came bringing joy deceived our minds like dreams. I see this herald from the shore, covered with twigs of olive.[19]

Their anticipation of the Herald's arrival contrasts with their skepticism about Clytemnestra's reliability.[20] They immediately commit to trusting him unconditionally, and by switching to alēthēs, they express and reinforce their view that

---

18. Krischer 1965, 166–67.
19. Page's OCT and Lloyd-Jones 1979 give these lines to Clytemnestra in accordance with the manuscripts (see Scott 1978, who argues for this stance), but most other editions and translations, including West's Teubner, attribute them to the Chorus (see Fraenkel 1950 vol. 2, 252–53, for discussion).
20. Fraenkel 1950 vol. 2, 248: "The moment which the poet has chosen for the utterance of the Elders' doubts was dictated to him by considerations of dramatic structure, that is to say the need for an effectual foil to the Herald's speech."

he is the ultimate arbiter of the fires' validity. All he ends up doing is corroborating Clytemnestra's account but adducing different sources; yet for the Chorus, her interpretation of the beacon-fires can be confirmed as alēthēs (rather than etumos) only by the Herald's report. It is noteworthy that the Chorus' use of alēthēs differs markedly from Clytemnestra's and Cassandra's, as I will discuss later.

The obvious difference between Clytemnestra's and the Herald's accounts lies in the nature of their sources. Whereas Clytemnestra makes inferences based on the beacon-fires, the Herald's information comes from his own eyewitness experience of actual events and is thus immediately privileged for its presumed validity.[21] As the only one who can provide a firsthand account of what happened at Troy, he is not asked to provide evidence either for his report or for his character. Nevertheless, he emphasizes the validity of his account with claims of its veracity (οὐ ψευδῆ λέγω, "I do not speak false things," 625), quantity of information (πάντ' ἔχεις λόγον, "You have the whole story," 582), or both (τοσαῦτ' ἀκούσας ἴσθι τἀληθῆ κλύων, "Know that, having heard so much, you hear the truth," 680).[22] His account is consistent with Clytemnestra's, but the Chorus believe him without question: νικώμενος λόγοισιν οὐκ ἀναίνομαι, | ἀεὶ γὰρ ἡβᾷ τοῖς γέρουσιν εὐμαθεῖν ("Won over by your words, I do not reject them; for in old men learning well is always young," 583–84). The difference in tone is obvious. They immediately value the news the Herald offers them, while they are constantly skeptical of Clytemnestra. This is an understandable difference, of course. The Herald's knowledge comes from first-hand experience, while Clytemnestra's account is purely imagined.

The Chorus' interaction with the Herald reflects a general privileging of information from messengers, particularly those in Aeschylus, as knowledgeable figures who deliver information unknown or unknowable to the characters about "events that happened in the (near or distant) past, and in a locale not included in the play area."[23] Sophocles' and Euripides' messenger speeches generally report nearby deaths or gruesome manglings that would not effectively be depicted in live-action, but Aeschylus' messengers report on events that are far less gory but far more distant, such as in *Persians* 266–67, where the Herald

---

21. See Wians 2009, 182–85, on the Archaic privileging of first-hand experience that forms the backdrop to this passage. Cf. Thumiger 2013, 225.
22. Cf. Barrett 2002, 11: "The model of truthful speech he employs here is one predicated upon fullness of description based on his own status as an eyewitness observer."
23. Rosenmeyer 1982, 197.

introduces his report about Salamis with assurances that it comes from his own eyewitness knowledge.[24]

Furthermore, the trust in Aeschylean messenger-figures comes not only from their firsthand knowledge but also from their intellectual capacity, which nonverbal sources of information lack. The Chorus draw this specific contrast between the beacon-fires' voiceless inscrutability and the Herald's verbal clarity:

μαρτυρεῖ δέ μοι κάσις
πηλοῦ ξύνουρος διψία κόνις τάδε,
ὡς οὔτ᾽ ἄναυδος οὔτε σοι δαίων φλόγα
ὕλης ὀρείας σημανεῖ καπνῷ πυρός
ἀλλ᾽ ἢ τὸ χαίρειν μᾶλλον ἐκβάξει λέγων ... (494–98)

Thirsty dust, the twin sibling of the mud, bears witness to these things for me, that neither voicelessly nor kindling a flame of mountain wood for you will [the Herald] signal with the smoke of fire, but speaking he will bid us either to rejoice more ...

There is a curious adaptation in these lines of the dust as voiceless messenger that we see in Seven (81–82) and in Suppliants (180), which I discussed in chapter 4. Like the Theban women and Danaus, the Chorus of Agamemnon see the dust as a sign of someone's arrival, but they apply the descriptor ἄναυδος ("voiceless") to the beacon-fires instead, in a way that is critical. In Choephori Electra draws a similar distinction. She laments that Orestes' lock of hair does not possess the intellect and verbal ability of a messenger and thus cannot convey a clear message (εἴθ᾽ εἶχε φωνὴν ἔμφρον᾽ ἀγγέλου δίκην, | ὅπως δίφροντις οὖσα μὴ ᾽κινυσσόμην | ἀλλ᾽ εὖ σάφ᾽ ᾔνει, "If only it had reasoned speech, like a messenger—so that I would not be of two minds and swayed back and forth—but it said clearly" Ch. 195–97). These lines suggest that on some level it is not only their eyewitness experience that gives messenger-figures their credibility but also their sentience. Clytemnestra, by contrast, does not gain the same credibility for her intellectual capacity, which indeed the Chorus think she

---

24. Although it is a commonplace in ancient Greek drama for a messenger-figure to report offstage action, the Aeschylean messenger is distinct for his comparative rarity and for reporting events that have occurred prior to, rather than simultaneously with, the events of the play. See Taplin 1977, 83. The notable exception is the angelos at Th. 792.

lacks. Instead they consistently mock her for trusting in nonverbal sources. Their skepticism of such sources, furthermore, is ultimately proved to be unfounded, both in *Choephori* when Electra meets Orestes face-to-face and in *Agamemnon*, where Clytemnestra is vindicated and mocks the Chorus' disbelief and their misogyny accordingly (587–92).

A significant difference between Clytemnestra and the Herald is the degree to which they are personally affected by the implications of their similar reports. Clytemnestra is plotting revenge against her husband. As Winnington-Ingram observes, "The return of her husband is a threat. Yet so great is she that she does not fear his return, but rather longs passionately for it, because it will give her the opportunity of avenging herself and of demonstrating her superiority."[25] Thus her interest in his return qualitatively differs from the Herald's. The Chorus point out that Clytemnestra's belief in Agamemnon's return overlaps with her hope for it (483–84), and she herself hints as much in lines replete with irony: "For what light is sweeter for a woman to look upon than this, to open the gates when a god has saved her husband from war?" (τί γὰρ | γυναικὶ τούτου φέγγος ἥδιον δρακεῖν, | ἀπὸ στρατείας ἄνδρα σώσαντος θεοῦ | πύλας ἀνοῖξαι; 601–4).

This difference is a gendered one. Clytemnestra, as the wife who stays home while her husband goes to war, would have a personal interest in his return, although here, of course, this interest perversely conflates homecoming with revenge. By contrast, messenger-figures such as the Herald are not family members and are invariably male. The Herald's role is thus emotionally detached and, furthermore, allows him access to both the domestic spaces at home and the battlefields abroad. His maleness is a given, a prerequisite for his role as messenger, which in turn affords him the unique ability to obtain and report firsthand knowledge. Accordingly, the Chorus do not fixate on his gender the way they do with Clytemnestra, nor do they express skepticism. Indeed, they do not mention his gender at all, effectively making the Herald gender neutral, a status that male characters often enjoy in tragedy. Gender in tragedy most often emerges via reference to female gender; male gender is typically a by-product of discussing and defining female difference. In effect the Herald's genderlessness is itself an unspoken affirmation of his maleness.

---

25. Winnington-Ingram 1983, 106.

Cassandra: Truth in Prophecy

As we turn to Cassandra, the links not only between truth and gender, but also between reciprocity, truth, and gender become clearer. Like Clytemnestra, Cassandra meets with the Chorus' fluctuating reactions to her words, and she shares with Clytemnestra a capacity to envision the truth—here, via prophecy. Cassandra is unique as a seer who is female, non-Greek, and a captured concubine.[26] Her brand of prophecy is also unique, as it does not involve interpretation of external omens but rather originates from her mind's eye and includes her own bloody demise.[27] She has occupied considerable space in scholarship because of her puzzling role in the play and trilogy—her death does not fit into the narrative of familial intergenerational revenge, nor does she have clear influence on the rest of the *Oresteia*'s plot.[28] As I will argue, Cassandra's visions align her with Clytemnestra; both "see" things, and both demonstrate a similar depth of understanding about the inevitability of reciprocity. Clytemnestra resembles the Chorus of *Seven* in that she demonstrates in the early part of the play an ability to extract vivid truths based on limited information, and later reveals an ability to understand the events of the play in the context of a larger narrative. Cassandra, with her visionary ability along with her view of the past, present, and future of the House of Atreus, helps shed light on these two aspects of Clytemnestra's knowledge. It is through Cassandra and Clytemnestra that we see how Aeschylus figures reciprocity as truth.

The Chorus are reluctant or unable to accept what Cassandra says and alternately believe and fail to understand her.[29] When she speaks of the bloody past of the House of Atreus—the familial murders, the cannibalizing of Thyestes' children—they recognize the events to which she refers and are quick to ascribe prophetic ability to her (1090–99). But when her utterances become predictive rather than reflective, they have trouble. Their admiration dissipates into confusion at her revelations of plotting within the house (1100–106). She is well

---

26. As noted in Brault 2009, 198.

27. Schein 1982, 11–12.

28. The most comprehensive survey of the scholarship on Cassandra is in Mitchell-Boyask 2006, 270n2, whose list includes but is not limited to Fletcher 1999, 23–32; Fontenrose 1971, 107–9; Fraenkel 1964: 375–87; Goldhill 1984: 81–88; Jones 1962, 132–34; Knox 1972, 109–21; Lebeck 1971, 28–39, 47–56, 61–62, 84–85; Mason 1959, 84–86; Mazzoldi 2001; McClure 1999, 92–97; Neitzel 1984; Rehm 1994, 44, 50–52; Roberts 1984, 65–66; Seaford 1987; Sider 1978, 15–18; Taplin 1977, 304–6, 317–19; Thalmann 1985, 228; Whallon 1980, 55–59; Wohl 1998, 110–14; Zeitlin 1965. More recently, Pillinger 2019, 28–73.

29. See Lebeck 1971, 52–58.

received only as long as what she says relates to the past and is thus already familiar to her listeners. When she describes the immediate future, the Chorus are stopped short, claiming ignorance (ἄιδρις, 1105).[30]

As she proceeds to detail Agamemnon's death and her own (1107–48), she continues to be incomprehensible to the Chorus, but she does achieve another moment of clarity with them when she describes the events at Troy that she herself has witnessed (1156–66). She is akin to the Herald here, since at this point her visions come from the kind of eyewitness experience that the Chorus recognize as credible. Further, some of this credibility can stem from establishing a link between her history and theirs. When she alludes to Paris, her visions align with the Chorus' own knowledge and experience and make them more receptive to her prophetic utterances. As Anne Lebeck has noted, Cassandra interweaves her own fate with Agamemnon's, and the destruction of Troy with the curse upon the Atreids.[31] Even when she describes events in the House of Atreus at which she was not present (1178–97), the Chorus believe her because she speaks as if she were: θαυμάζω δέ σου, | πόντου πέραν τραφεῖσαν ἀλλόθρουν πόλιν | κυρεῖν λέγουσαν ὥσπερ εἰ παρεστάτεις ("But I marvel at you, that though bred beyond the sea you hit the mark in speaking of a foreign city, *as if you had been present*," 1199–201). The authority with which she delivers these accounts is akin to what a messenger-figure would have. The Chorus' alternation between belief and disbelief indicates the credibility they assign to information that is familiar to them, particularly when it is reported by someone who seems to have eyewitness experience.

The key difference between Cassandra's truth and a messenger's lies in temporal scope. She sees past, present, and future alike, whereas a messenger can report only on the past.[32] This broader scope is encapsulated in Cassandra's use of alēthēs:

τὸ μέλλον ἥξει, καὶ σύ μ᾽ ἐν τάχει παρὼν
ἄγαν γ᾽ ἀληθόμαντιν οἰκτίρας ἐρεῖς. (1240–41)

---

30. Pillinger 2019, 47–48, also makes this observation.
31. Lebeck 1971, 51–58.
32. Cf. Zeitlin 1990, 111: "It is Cassandra . . . who can put together past, present, and future, where the chorus of male elders remains baffled and confused." Zeitlin compares Cassandra to the Chorus of *Seven against Thebes*: they, like Cassandra, conceive of a bigger picture, in contrast to their male interlocutor Eteocles, who shortsightedly looks only to the present and consequently meets his doom.

The future will come, and you will soon be here, taking pity on me and calling me an exceedingly *true prophet.*

Here alēthēs refers to her prophecies of the future, in contrast to previous instances in the play where it referred to, for example, the Herald's anticipated reportage of past events (491). The Chorus' response to her reflects their more limited understanding of alētheia:

τὴν μὲν Θυέστου δαῖτα παιδείων κρεῶν
ξυνῆκα καὶ πέφρικα, καὶ φόβος μ᾽ ἔχει
κλύοντ᾽ ἀληθῶς οὐδὲν ἐξῃκασμένα. (A. 1242–44)

I understand the feast of Thyestes on the flesh of his children and I shudder, and fear takes hold of me as I hear it *truly and not mere semblances.*

Again, they comprehend when she speaks of events they recognize, and they apply alētheia in its adverbial form to a report of past events. They explicitly pit comprehensible reality against resemblance, suggesting that their understanding requires the visual imagery they see as her typical mode to be translated into a *verbal* representation of a past event with which they are already familiar. The way Cassandra understands truth, by contrast, lacks temporal distinction. As Pascale-Anne Brault writes, "the introduction of the prophetic [i.e., via Cassandra] compresses past, present, and future into the narrative, thus creating tension between the three."[33] This is what sets her apart from the other characters and makes her so difficult for the Chorus to comprehend.

Cassandra as Mirror: Time, Truth, Reciprocity

Furthermore, the temporal simultaneity of Cassandra's visions should be considered in the context of the *Oresteia* as what she sees aligns with the action-reaction pattern of the trilogy. The past, present, and future truth that she perceives reflects the self-perpetuating nature of revenge, the defining force of the plot conceived by Aeschylus. Cassandra affords us glimpses of the events that will be dramatized in *Choephori*.[34] She thus functions as a window into the continuing plot of the trilogy and occupies an intermediary position between

---

33. Brault 2009, 202.
34. Cf. Leahy 1969, 145.

the interior and exterior of the drama. As Judith Fletcher argues, Cassandra's all-encompassing knowledge of events both on and off stage aligns her with audience and spectator.[35] Seth Schein similarly notes that Cassandra functions as an interpretive aide of sorts: "[Cassandra's] imagination has clarified many of the enigmas and obscurities of what had happened earlier in the play, told us where the drama is going (though even she cannot foresee the action of *Eumenides* in which the Furies do leave the house), and helped reveal a meaning, albeit a painful one, in the sequence of events. . . . She compresses and condenses the imagery and ideas of the play."[36]

Ancient Greek literature frequently assigns predictive abilities to female figures who stand to be personally affected by their predictions. For example, the female servants of Hector's house preemptively mourn his death (*Il.* 6.500–502); Andromache foresees Astyanax's demise along with Troy's fall (*Il.* 24.727–29); Artemisia predicts the destruction of Xerxes' fleet at Salamis (Herodotus 8.68). As our earliest extant textual source to document Cassandra's prophetic ability, *Agamemnon* participates in this literary tradition of female perception in a way that sheds light on the contours of the story in which Cassandra is situated.[37] By relating what she experiences and predicts to past events, she draws attention to the ongoing narrative. Furthermore, her history with Apollo infuses her character with suggestions of poetic self-reflection in that her story resonates with that of Coronis as a fellow young female consort of Apollo who eventually rejects him and ultimately dies for doing so; Cassandra even cites Apollo as the source of her demise (1080–82, 1085–86).[38] As I argued in chapter 3, Coronis is one of several female characters in Pindar's myths who draws attention to the poetic context in which she appears. Cassandra serves a similar mirroring function, here by providing details both for the background and the aftermath of *Agamemnon*, and thus exposing the centrality of reciprocity in Aeschylean tragedy.[39]

---

35. See Fletcher 1999, 23–32, who sees Cassandra as an analog for the audience in light of their shared knowledge of the myth.

36. Schein 1982, 15.

37. Neither the *Iliad* nor the *Odyssey* mentions Cassandra's prophetic ability, although she seems to have prophetic powers in the *Cypria* (Proclus, *Chrestomathia* 1). Cassandra's wide-ranging vision does have its limits: as already noted, it does not include the plot of *Eumenides* (Schein 1982, 15), and it also, by excluding Iphigenia and Helen, "is almost exclusively male-centered" (Wohl 1998, 112).

38. Kuhns 1962, 40–41, argues on the basis of A. 1206–8 that Cassandra "violated the covenant of marriage." Mitchell-Boyask 2006, 271, also characterizes Cassandra and Apollo's relationship as a marriage. Leahy 1969 uses the similarities between Cassandra and Coronis to argue that Cassandra's death in *Agamemnon* is in part punishment for her rejection of Apollo.

39. Cassandra's association with Apollo, the source of her prophetic visions, anticipates his role in *Choephori* and *Eumenides*, as Robin Mitchell-Boyask observes (Mitchell-Boyask 2006, 271).

The prophetic ability Cassandra receives from Apollo shares some characteristics of poetic composition. As Paolo Wolhfarht observes, the temporal scope of Cassandra's vision recalls both a Homeric prophet, Calchas, who is credited with knowledge of past, present, and future alike (ὃς ᾔδη τά τ' ἐόντα τά τ' ἐσσόμενα πρό τ' ἐόντα, "who knew the things that are and the things that will be and were before," *Il.* 1.70), as well as Hesiod's Muses, the divine embodiments of poetry who possess the same temporally expansive knowledge (εἴρουσαι τά τ' ἐόντα τά τ' ἐσσόμενα πρό τ' ἐόντα, "saying the things that are and the things that will be and were before," *Th.* 38).[40] These lines are echoed in Solon, who ascribes this type of knowledge to Dikē, a suggestive association given the links between dikē and reciprocity that I discussed in chapter 5: οὐδὲ φυλάσσονται σεμνὰ Δίκης θέμεθλα, | ἢ σιγῶσα σύνοιδε τὰ γιγνόμενα πρό τ' ἐόντα ("They do not protect the sacred halls of Dikē, who silently knows what is happening and what happened before," Fr. 4.14–15).[41]

Cassandra sees the causal links between past, present, and future. This quality gives her truth poetic significance as her ramblings refer to revenge and retaliation and thus reflect the tragic narrative in which she is trapped. Her understanding of temporal progression is also an understanding of causality as she interweaves references to past carnage with allusions to future consequences:

καὶ μὴν πεπωκώς γ', ὡς θρασύνεσθαι πλέον,
βρότειον αἷμα κῶμος ἐν δόμοις μένει,
δύσπεμπτος ἔξω, συγγόνων Ἐρινύων·
ὑμνοῦσι δ' ὕμνον δώμασιν προσήμεναι
πρώταρχον ἄτην, ἐν μέρει δ' ἀπέπτυσαν
εὐνὰς ἀδελφοῦ τῷ πατοῦντι δυσμενεῖς. (1188–93)

And having drunk human blood so as to become bolder, a band remains in the house, hard to banish, a band of *kindred Erinyes*. Setting upon the house, they sing a song of *original ruin*, and in turn they spit, disgusted with the man frequenting his brother's marriage bed.

---

40. Wolhfarht 2004, 88 and 90, notes these parallels between Cassandra, Calchas, and Hesiod's Muses.
41. See Detienne 1996, 55, for further discussion.

By making reference to the "original ruin" of Thyestes' and Atreus' crimes (πρώταρχον ἄτην, 1192) and the "kindred Erinyes" (συγγόνων Ἐρινύων, 1190) who still occupy the house, Cassandra hints at Agamemnon's imminent murder and links it to past crimes within the family. She anticipates the Erinyes' appearance in *Choephori* and *Eumenides*, and she casts them as intrinsic to the family they plague.

These hints of Cassandra's broad awareness become explicit later when she refers to the reciprocity of Atreid carnage as she foretells the deaths that will result from her own:[42]

οὔτοι δυσοίζω θάμνον ὡς ὄρνις φόβῳ,
ἄλλως· θανούσῃ μαρτυρεῖτέ μοι τόδε,[43]
ὅταν γυνὴ γυναικὸς ἀντ᾽ ἐμοῦ θάνῃ
ἀνήρ τε δυσδάμαρτος ἀντ᾽ ἀνδρὸς πέσῃ. (1316–19)

I do not tremble like a bird at a bush; when I die bear witness to me of this, when a *woman* dies in place of a *woman*, me, and a *man* falls in place of an ill-wedded *man*.

Cassandra's use of polyptoton (γυνὴ γυναικὸς, ἀνήρ . . . ἀνδρὸς) brings out the symmetrical, responsive nature of reciprocity. The repetitions are typical of Pindaric and Aeschylean formulations of reciprocity, as I discussed in chapter 1, but while Pindaric reciprocity is generally immediate, Cassandra's formulation occupies a longer timeline. Her gift of sight enfolds prediction in causality as she ties past, present, and future together. The Chorus, however, do not readily perceive the future implications of past violence, instead noting only the accuracy of her references to Atreus and Thyestes. As Timothy Gantz has argued, the Chorus' blind spot results from their refusal to accept the "logical ἀνάγκη of Agamemnon's death."[44] To extend the point made by Gantz, the Chorus, in their avoidance of unpleasant knowledge, effectively curtail awareness of revenge as the narrative force behind the trilogy.

---

42. On the transactional nature of Cassandra's death, see Wohl 1998, 110–12.
43. My text and translation of 1317 here adhere to West's Teubner, which adopts various emendations that make sense of the manuscript reading (preserved in Page's OCT), which has ἀλλ᾽ ὡς θανούσῃ μαρτυρῆτέ μοι τόδε.
44. Gantz 1983, 82; supported by Winnington-Ingram 1954, 26.

Female Truth and Tragedy

In essence Cassandra's foretelling maps out the events to come in the trilogy. By giving voice and shape to the ensuing plot, she acts as a mouthpiece for the tragedian. Clytemnestra too perceives and envisions the larger narrative in which she exists.[45] Denied by their male interlocutors of any claims to alētheia, Cassandra and Clytemnestra nonetheless appropriate the term to designate not only their own claims of accurate knowledge but also their fundamental and unique understanding of the narrative forces shaping their plots.[46] Both characters demonstrate awareness of the sovereignty of revenge. Truth for them is not a mere expression of fact but an understanding that revenge is self-perpetuating. Male knowledge, limited to discrete events from the past, precludes perception of the ongoing revenge narrative. Unlike the Herald, Cassandra contextualizes truth within a narrative of reciprocity and retribution. Because she sees the past just as she sees the present and the future, she understands events as connected and related to one another and thus has access to a truth that is specifically oriented to revenge.

Cassandra essentially functions as a window into Aeschylean myth-making and plot-devising. It is her visions that encapsulate the plot and background of the *Oresteia*, presenting the events of *Agamemnon* as intertwined with the past of the House of Atreus as well as with the events to occur in *Choephori*.[47] In this function she overlaps with the *Iliad*'s Helen, who is in the midst of weaving a tapestry depicting "the many struggles of the Trojan horse-tamers and bronze-clad Achaeans" (πολέας δ' ἐνέπασσεν ἀέθλους | Τρώων θ' ἱπποδάμων καὶ Ἀχαιῶν χαλκοχιτώνων, *Il.* 3.126–27) when Iris calls upon her to "see the marvelous deeds of the Trojan horse-tamers and bronze-clad Achaeans" (ἵνα θέσκελα ἔργα ἴδηαι | Τρώων θ' ἱπποδάμων καὶ Ἀχαιῶν χαλκοχιτώνων, 130–31). Helen's tapestry mirrors the story in which it appears; Iris' words in turn adaptively parrot the description of Helen's tapestry. In effect the passage presents a circu-

---

45. For the sake of argumentative economy, I have not examined Cassandra's communicative tendencies in great detail, nor her interaction with Clytemnestra, but an insightful treatment of both can be found in Pillinger 2019, 28–73.

46. *Pace* Fletcher 1999, 25, who limits this ability to Cassandra alone, excluding Clytemnestra: "No character in the drama has such a comprehensive understanding of the fortunes of the house of Atreus. Agamemnon is simply purblind; Clytemnestra and Aegisthus are limited to understanding events directly connected to their revenge; the Chorus can only think back to the immediate events surrounding the Trojan War."

47. She does suffer from a certain tunnel vision, however; as Wohl 1998, 112–14, points out, Cassandra's prophecies are androcentric, and even her suffering is conflated with Agamemnon's.

larity and identity in Helen's and the poet's creations, which mutually echo and articulate one another. Helen, a character within a poem, mirrors the poet's creation with her own. This kind of circularity calls attention to the created context in which the story and characters exist, and it is often female characters who activate this circularity. Aeschylus' Cassandra belongs to this tradition. By articulating the story in which she finds herself, she calls attention to that story, its characteristics, and its thematic continuities. Cassandra differs from Helen in that her visions not only mirror her story but exceed its bounds. As I said above, her understanding of reciprocity resonates with Pindar's formulations but crosses generational boundaries; so too does it cross the limits of *Agamemnon*, as she speaks to events that precede and proceed from the events of the play. Indeed, her visions predate and postdate her own life.

Clytemnestra, too, possesses an ability that calls attention to events outside the scope of *Agamemnon*. She acknowledges as truth the probability that her gruesome actions will be met with corresponding and equal reactions. As I noted in chapter 1, the Chorus foretell the aftermath of Agamemnon's death, but it is Clytemnestra who encapsulates this repetitive pattern as one of alētheia:

> Χο. ὄνειδος ἥκει τόδ' ἀντ' ὀνείδους,
> δύσμαχα δ' ἐστι κρῖναι.
> φέρει φέροντ', ἐκτίνει δ' ὁ καίνων·
> μίμνει δὲ μίμνοντος ἐν θρόνῳ Διὸς
> παθεῖν τὸν ἔρξαντα· θέσμιον γάρ.
> τίς ἂν γονὰν ἀραῖον ἐκβάλοι δόμων;
> κεκόλληται γένος πρὸς ἄτᾳ.
> Κλ. ἐς τόνδ' ἐνέβης ξὺν ἀληθείᾳ
> χρησμόν. (1560–68)

> CHORUS: This *reproach* has come to answer *reproach*, and it is difficult to judge. Someone *robs the robber*, and the killer pays the penalty. It *awaits* the doer to suffer while Zeus *awaits* on his throne, for it is the way things work. Who would throw the accursed seed from the house? The race has been affixed to ruin.
> CLYTEMNESTRA: You came upon this prophecy *with truth*.

The Chorus' repetitive language emphasizes the symmetry of reciprocity (ὄνειδος ... ὀνείδους, 1560; φέρει φέροντ', 1562; μίμνει δὲ μίμνοντος, 1563) and recalls Cassandra's language in lines 1318–19 (γυνὴ γυναικὸς, ἀνήρ . . . ἀνδρὸς).[48] But it is Clytemnestra who acknowledges the inevitability of consequences and designates it alētheia.[49] Her application of alētheia to the Chorus' language of revenge complements her earlier trust in the beacon-fires, which are described in similar language: she uses polyptoton to illustrate the relay system of the beacon-fires (φρυκτὸς δὲ φρυκτὸν . . . ἔπεμπεν, "beacon sent beacon," 282–83), which can be seen as an "elaborate allegory" for the process of intergenerational retribution.[50] Taken together, the two passages reflect Clytemnestra's understanding of truth in systems that rely on repetition.

Her admission here dovetails with her earlier attribution of Agamemnon's death to a "spirit of vengeance against Atreus" (ἀλάστωρ Ἀτρέως, 1501–2)—an attempt to remove her own agency for the deed and contextualize it within the fraught history of the Atreids.[51] Like Cassandra, she communicates a conception of truth that situates events in a cause-and-effect chain. More than simply conveying accuracy, alētheia characterizes the certainty of reprisal for murder, a reprisal that will unfold as the trilogy continues, ensured by divine law. Clytemnestra is not fully acquiescent to this certainty. As Helene Foley notes, "Clytemnestra takes the choral response on the one hand as a concession of sorts on the question of justice and on the other as a challenge difficult to meet."[52] She continues with a proposal for circumventing revenge (1568–76) and in *Choephori* will similarly attempt, in vain, to alter this course of retribution, an attempt that demonstrates her understanding of inevitability even as she tries to resist it, as reflected in her adaptive use of the polyptoton characterizing reciprocity: "Let us see whether we *will conquer* or *be conquered*," she says, as she faces off against Orestes (εἰδῶμεν εἰ νικῶμεν ἢ νικώμεθα, *Ch.* 890).[53]

---

48. Käppel 1998, 177, observes that the Chorus (perhaps unwittingly) attribute Clytemnestra and Aegisthus' actions to some type of underlying and all-powerful law of revenge.

49. *Pace* Wians 2009, 191, who does not credit Clytemnestra with such awareness: "For all her devious use of the truth, Clytemnestra is deceived about her role in the larger history of events. Both she and Agamemnon are participants in a story still unfolding; both are the objects of a lesson being taught, the victims of Aeschylus's sacrificial drama, not those who are meant to benefit from it."

50. Gantz 1977, 31. Clytemnestra also uses such language later, to describe the symmetry of Agamemnon's and Clytemnestra's deaths (ἀνάξια δράσας | ἄξια πάσχων, "having done unworthy things, he suffers worthy ones," 1526–27), as observed by Foley 2001, 225.

51. For thorough discussion of this claim, see Foley 2001, 217–22, who concludes that Clytemnestra ultimately does not deny her own responsibility for the murder and its consequences. See also Devereux 1976, 188, who notes that the Chorus refute this defense and will acknowledge only that this vengeful spirit may have aided and abetted her, but she committed the act of murder (1505–8).

52. Foley 2001, 227.

53. This steady acknowledgment, the understanding that her own decisive actions work in tandem with a "natural" course of things, reflects the way she generally wields power. As Aya Betensky

Aegisthus: Revenge without Truth

Aegisthus' contrasting view of revenge brings out Cassandra's and Clytemnestra's perceptiveness all the more and suggests that the ability to see revenge as truth is a female trait. Like the Chorus and the Herald, he does not take the long view that Clytemnestra and Cassandra do. Granted, he does see Agamemnon's murder as the consequence of a series of crimes. He seeks to justify his part in Agamemnon's demise by detailing the wrongs committed against his father Thyestes by Atreus (1577–1611). Such details supplement Cassandra's previous allusions (1090–92, 1191–93, 1217–22) and expand the revenge plot beyond Clytemnestra's antipathy for her husband.[54] His speech is marked by triumphant elation and the equivalence he draws between retributive justice and his own personal satisfaction.

But a crucial difference is that he seems to think the series concludes with Agamemnon's death; he does not perceive the implications of his own murderous role. His shortsightedness here recalls *Odyssey* 1.37–41, where Zeus claims the gods had advised Aegisthus against adultery and homicide, informing him about Orestes' future revenge. To him, revenge is not inevitable but a function of individual decision combined with the righteousness of Dikē (κἀγὼ δίκαιος τοῦδε τοῦ φόνου ῥαφεύς, "And I am the just planner of this murder," *A.* 1604; τραφέντα δ᾽ αὖθις ἡ Δίκη κατήγαγεν, | καὶ τοῦδε τἀνδρὸς ἡψάμην θυραῖος ὤν, | πᾶσαν ξυνάψας μηχανὴν δυσβουλίας, "Dikē led me back after I'd grown up, and I attacked this man while I was an exile, having put together every contrivance of ill-will," 1607–10). Although Aegisthus claims to be content to die now that his revenge has been enacted (1610–11), he—unlike Clytemnestra or Cassandra—demonstrates no real awareness of his own death as part of a vengeful cycle. When the Chorus warn him of consequences (1615–18), Aegisthus is dismissive.[55]

notes, Clytemnestra's "power is based on the connections she makes between herself, her own sexuality, and the elements of the natural world. . . . As much as Achilles or Ajax or Antigone, she finds that society's values do not fit her; she can change her circumstances, but not, any more than they, prevent the consequences" (1978, 13).

54. Käppel 1998, 172–77, examines the role of Aegisthus in supplementing the revenge plot so that it is not centered solely on Clytemnestra and Iphigenia. Aegisthus does not provide a complete account; see Fraenkel 1950 vol. 3, 745 *ad* 1585: "It is rather the case that a veil is deliberately drawn here over all details. We can hardly expect Aegisthus to accuse his own father: so this account avoids the subject of Thyestes' adultery, which, however, the poet assumes to be known to his audience (1193)."

55. Foley 2001, 206–7, makes a related point: the contrast between Aegisthus' and Clytemnestra's respective interactions with the Chorus brings out the greater complexity and moral ambiguity of Clytemnestra's character.

Gender has been a constant refrain in the play, but its implications for truth and knowledge might seem unclear at first. On the one hand, it is clear that gender is a salient feature of how characters are perceived and defined. The Watchman comments on Clytemnestra's "man-minded hopeful heart" (ἀνδρόβουλον ἐλπίζον κέαρ, 11), the Chorus accuse Aegisthus of effeminacy (1625),[56] they constantly bring up female gender in their interactions with Clytemnestra (351–53, 483–84), and the whole person of Cassandra herself—spurned consort of Apollo, captured concubine of Agamemnon—is a function of her female gender as she would not play these roles if she were male. On the other hand, it could be argued that gender is not relevant to these characters' ways of accessing the truth. Comparison with only the Herald alone might suggest that Cassandra's and Clytemnestra's comparatively long view of events is a function not of their gender but of their particular roles in the drama. The Herald's role is circumscribed, limited to reporting what he has seen without speculation about why. Further, he is not a member of the royal family, he has no personal investment in what befalls them, and he has no reason to contextualize what he has seen within a longer narrative. He exists outside of the cyclical revenge patterns that plague the House of Atreus. Clytemnestra and Cassandra, by contrast, see their own lives and deaths as part of that narrative. They are naturally more inclined to take a bigger picture view than the Herald is, given their personal stakes in the drama. But the character of Aegisthus suggests that personal investment alone does not produce the kind of clear-sightedness that Clytemnestra and Cassandra share. Like them, he is intimately embedded and invested in the House of Atreus drama. The cyclical revenge patterns of this House involve not only his implementation of vengeful actions but also what will befall him; he stands to be directly affected by what Cassandra foresees and what the Chorus warn. Yet he does not see the writing on the wall for him. For whatever reason he, unlike Clytemnestra and Cassandra, does not understand the imminent consequences of his actions and how his story fits into an ongoing narrative.

---

56. See Zeitlin 1996, 92, for further discussion.

The Evolution of Reciprocity and Truth in Choephori *and* Eumenides

Similar patterns of gender, knowledge, and reciprocity continue in *Choephori*, but the relationship between reciprocity and truth evolves. Clytemnestra infers information based on images or visions that require interpretation, this information pertains to the ongoing narrative of reciprocal return, and the Chorus will continue to articulate the repetitive language that emphasizes the symmetrical and duplicative nature of reciprocal violence. In addition the play activates resonances with other Aeschylean templates of gender and reciprocity; most notably, the Chorus of (female) Libation Bearers parallel the Chorus of Danaids in *Suppliants* in that both articulate the way reciprocity works and convince their interlocutors of the validity of this system. *Choephori* reflects the continued interlocking of gender conflict and revenge: Orestes kills his mother and her lover in the same way that they killed Agamemnon, then is hounded by the female Erinyes as punishment; the genders of the agents and targets of revenge are the reverse of what they were in *Agamemnon*, making the two plays and their revenge plots complements of one another. It is clear that revenge continues to be intertwined with gender. What is conspicuously absent, however, is an explicit connection between revenge and truth. The continuing cycle of reciprocity is sometimes spoken of as an inevitability, but terms like alēthēs or alētheia are no longer used to describe this cycle.

The passages describing Clytemnestra's dream show us the evolution of the characters' attitudes toward interpretive knowledge and reciprocity.[57] The Chorus briefly mention the dream early on (33–41) and later provide more detail in response to Orestes' query (526): Clytemnestra has dreamt of giving birth to a serpent, swaddling it, nursing it, and then being bitten by it (527–33). The poetic origin of the dream seems to be Stesichorus' *Oresteia*, in which Clytemnestra dreams of a bloody snake:[58]

---

57. On the "both polyvalent and direct" relationship of Clytemnestra's dream to the climax of *Choephori*, see Catenaccio 2011, 211–21.
58. On the multivalent significance of the serpent, see Whallon 1958. O'Neill 1998 argues for Homer as an additional model for the dream of Clytemnestra; in the *Iliad* Hecuba bares her breast to Hector, who is subsequently compared to a snake (22.82–85, 92–96).

τᾷ δὲ δράκων ἐδόκησεν μολεῖν κάρα βεβροτωμένος ἄκρον,
ἐκ δ᾽ ἄρα τοῦ βασιλεὺς Πλεισθενίδας ἐφάνη (Plut., *De Sera Numinis Vindicta*
555a = *PMG* 219 = Finglass 180)

The snake seemed to her to approach, stained with gore on the top of its head,
and a Pleisthenid king appeared from it.

The Stesichorean dream-snake could represent Agamemnon or Orestes.[59]
Aeschylus adapts the dream to feature the mother-son conflict, but the ambiguity in its Stesichorean source prompts a comparison between Orestes and
Agamemnon and between the plot of *Choephori* and the events of *Agamemnon*
that precede and precipitate it.

Like Cassandra's visions, the dream provides a script for the continuing
revenge narrative and reflects its intergenerational aspect.[60] The credence Clytemnestra gives to this dream parallels the validity she ascribes to the beacon-
fires of *Agamemnon* in that both the dream and the fires are sources that must
be interpreted. Unlike the Argive Elders of *Agamemnon*, the Chorus of this play
are receptive to Clytemnestra's interpretation, that the dream sprang from the
discontent of the murdered (38–41). The predictive accuracy of the dream
seems to be widely accepted, in sharp contrast to *Agamemnon*, where only Clytemnestra and Cassandra fully understand the inexorable force of retribution.
The Chorus of *Choephori*, tasked by Clytemnestra with pouring libations of
atonement at Agamemnon's tomb, express despair over the futility of doing so
(44–47). They regard further retaliation as inevitable and refer to their libations
as χάριν ἀχάριτον ("graceless favor," 44), a phrase that both evokes the symmetry of reciprocal action and disparages Clytemnestra's attempt to avert the violence due to her: "The cognate privative epithet shows that the essential meaning of its noun [χάριν] is to be denied."[61] The Chorus' view, which the play will
eventually bear out, is that the law of revenge is supreme: δι᾽ αἷμᾰτ᾽ ἐκποθένθ᾽
ὑπὸ χθονὸς τροφοῦ | τίτας φόνος πέπηγεν οὐ διαρρύδαν ("On account of
blood drunk by the nourishing earth, vengeful slaughter sticks fast and does
not flow away," 66–67).

---

59. See Garvie 1986, xix, for the ambiguity in this fragment; he argues that the Pleisthenid king refers
   to Agamemnon rather than Orestes. It may intentionally present ambiguity between Agamemnon and Orestes, however; see Mueller-Goldingen 2000, 10–11.
60. On the parallels between dreams and Cassandra's visions, see Catenaccio 2011, 209–10.
61. Garvie 1986, 58–59 *ad* 43–46.

Over the course of *Choephori*, all the characters comprehend and accept the dream's implications.[62] With Electra's and the Chorus' help, Orestes comes to understand what the dream means and his own role that it foretells.[63] He repeatedly expresses his determination to engineer its actualization (οὔτοι μάταιον ἂν τόδ᾽ ὄψανον πέλοι, "This vision would *not* be idle!" 534; ἀλλ᾽ εὔχομαι γῇ τῇδε καὶ πατρὸς τάφῳ | τοὔνειρον εἶναι τοῦτ᾽ ἐμοὶ τελεσφόρον, "But I pray by this land and by my father's grave that this dream be fulfilled in me," 540–41).[64] As Philip Vellacott writes, "The steadily intensifying excitement brings its effect: Orestes is now ready to hear Clytemnestra's dream, to seize on it point by point, and with a fascinated eagerness (526–534, 540–550) to see himself as the son, once nursed at the breast, now grown to be his mother's killer."[65] Orestes consciously inserts himself into the role scripted for him by the dream. As she faces Orestes Clytemnestra looks back on her dream as an accurate premonition: "Alas, I gave birth to and nurtured this snake! The fear from the dream was truly a prophet" (οἲ 'γώ, τεκοῦσα τόνδ᾽ ὄφιν ἐθρεψάμην· | ἦ κάρτα μάντις οὐξ ὀνειράτων φόβος, 928–29).

While the dream provides a template for what will happen, the Chorus play a critical role in ensuring it does. In Electra's first interchange with them, they prod her toward a desire for vengeance as something not only possible but necessary:

Ηλ. τί φῶ; δίδασκ᾽ ἄπειρον ἐξηγουμένη.

Χο. ἐλθεῖν τιν᾽ αὐτοῖς δαίμον᾽ ἢ βροτῶν τινα.

Ηλ. πότερα δικαστὴν ἢ δικηφόρον λέγεις;

Χο. ἁπλωστὶ φράζουσ᾽, ὅστις ἀνταποκτενεῖ.

Ηλ. καὶ ταῦτά μούστιν εὐσεβῆ θεῶν πάρα;

Χο. πῶς δ᾽ οὔ, τὸν ἐχθρὸν ἀνταμείβεσθαι κακοῖς; (118–23)

ELECTRA. What should I say? Explain, teach me, as I am inexperienced.

CHORUS. Pray that some god or man may come to them.

---

62. Cf. Lawrence 2013, 90: "Therefore, right up until Orestes' hesitation over the deed (899), there is an overwhelming sense of the rightness and virtual inevitability of the talio which entails the slaughter of Aegisthus and Clytemnestra." My reading of *Choephori*, though, on the whole differs from that of Lawrence, who seems to see in the play an unequivocal assertion of Orestes' righteousness.

63. Zeitlin 1996, 358; Catenaccio 2011, 217–19. Cf. Foley 2001, 35, who notes that "in the *kommos* the chorus and Electra play the dominant role in generating revenge through their lament."

64. Cf. Lawrence 2013, 93: "he takes [the dream], rightly, not only as a symbolic statement of his imminent deed, but also as a command to perform it (540–50)."

65. Vellacott 1984, 152.

ELECTRA. Do you mean a judge or an avenger?
CHORUS. Say it simply: someone to kill in return.
ELECTRA. And are these holy things for me to ask from the gods?
CHORUS. Why not, to repay an enemy with harm?

This passage reflects the crucial role of the Chorus in articulating the role of reciprocity in securing justice.[66] They are the first to speak explicitly of matricide to begin with,[67] and they contextualize it within a cycle of return violence (ἀνταποκτενεῖ, 121; ἀνταμείβεσθαι, 123). They dismiss the distinction Electra tries to make between a "judge" (δικαστήν) and an "avenger" (δικηφόρον), presenting simple reciprocal action as the only course worthy of consideration.

The Chorus continue in this vein in the kommos, their climactic lamentation with Orestes:

ἀντὶ μὲν ἐχθρᾶς γλώσσης ἐχθρὰ
γλῶσσα τελείσθω· τοὐφειλόμενον
πράσσουσα Δίκη μέγ᾽ ἀυτεῖ·
ἀντὶ δὲ πληγῆς φονίας φονίαν
πληγὴν τινέτω. δράσαντα παθεῖν,
τριγέρων μῦθος τάδε φωνεῖ. (309–15)

Let *evil tongue* be paid for *evil tongue*. In doing what is due Justice cries loudly, "Let one pay *bloody stroke for bloody stroke*." "That the doer suffer," is a story thrice-told.

Here the Chorus utter the famous phrase δράσαντα παθεῖν ("that the doer suffer"), which comes to define the *Oresteia*.[68] Their repetitive language of revenge (ἐχθρᾶς ... ἐχθρά; γλώσσης ... γλῶσσα; πληγῆς ... πληγήν; φονίας φονίαν) recalls the warnings of the Argive Elders to Clytemnestra that I discussed above (ὄνειδος ... ὀνείδους, A. 1560; φέρει φέροντ᾽, 1562; μίμνει δὲ μίμνοντος, 1563) and exemplifies the language both Pindar and Aeschylus use to articulate the symmetries of reciprocal action. Furthermore, the Chorus of Libation Bearers conceptualize this retributive pattern as one sanctioned by Dikē. They build on

---

66. On the agency of the Chorus in *Choephori*, see Foley 2001, 33–36 and 157; McCall 1990; Rosenmeyer 1982, 163–64.
67. Vellacott 1984, 150.
68. Cf. Blundell 1989, 29; Gagarin 1976, 66.

this association between dikē and reciprocal violence when they refer to the Erinys as the face of the cycle they describe:

ἀλλὰ νόμος μὲν φονίας σταγόνας
χυμένας ἐς πέδον ἄλλο προσαιτεῖν
αἷμα· βοᾷ γὰρ λοιγὸς Ἐρινὺν
παρὰ τῶν πρότερον φθιμένων ἄτην
ἑτέραν ἐπάγουσαν ἐπ' ἄτῃ. (400–404)

But it is law that bloody drops poured to the ground demand another murder. For the havoc from those killed before cries out for the Erinys who brings *one ruin upon another*.

Again, the Chorus use the repetitive language of reciprocity to emphasize the symmetry of revenge (ἄτην . . . ἄτῃ, 403–4), they link past events with present to make a case for self-perpetuating revenge (παρὰ τῶν πρότερον φθιμένων, 403),[69] and they couch this self-perpetuation in terms of nomos (400), which infuses vengeance with the force of natural law.[70] Prodded by Electra and the Chorus in the kommos, Orestes comes to parrot their repetitive language (Ἄρης Ἄρει ξυμβαλεῖ, Δίκᾳ Δίκα, "Ares will fight Ares, Justice with Justice," 461).[71] As he plots his revenge, he stresses that the deceptive actions Clytemnestra and Aegisthus took to carry out Agamemnon's murder will be visited upon them, too (ὡς ἂν δόλῳ κτείναντες ἄνδρα τίμιον | δόλῳ γε καὶ ληφθῶσιν, ἐν ταὐτῷ βρόχῳ | θανόντες, "so that those who killed a worthy man *by a trick* be apprehended as well *by a trick*, dying in the same snare," 556–58[72]). Within the revenge narrative, deception becomes both the charge against Clytemnestra

---

69. Helene Foley too notes the Chorus' role as temporal bridge: "Lamentation, with its strong generation of emotion, focuses the power and desire to carry through revenge in a communal setting that builds connections between past, present, and future members of the group" (Foley 2001, 34).

70. Vellacott 1984, 151–52, notes that these lines "equate Orestes' vengeance with Clytemnestra's by prompting him to become the same kind of 'doer' as she."

71. As Foley 2001, 33–34 notes, the extent to which the kommos influences Orestes' decision is disputed among scholars, but its significance cannot be denied given that it occasions Orestes' interpretation of Clytemnestra's dream as well as his first lamentation for his father.

72. Lebeck 1971, 113–14, sees this repetitive language as an indicator of Orestes' awareness that his actions are simultaneously (and paradoxically) both right and wrong. The degree to which Orestes feels personal responsibility for the matricide is a matter of debate, but it is clear from the text that he at the very least consciously assumes the role of Apollo's agent. On Orestes' guilt and decisive agency, see Dodds 1960, 30, who argues that Orestes is aware of its criminality when he opts to commit murder, while Winnington-Ingram 1983, 143–45, rebuts the view that Orestes is in such masterful control of his situation.

and Aegisthus, and the means by which they will die, a double-edged sword of crime and punishment.

In *Choephori* we see that the predictions Cassandra made in *Agamemnon* will come true, after characters like Electra and Orestes engage in a collaborative, even dialectical process with the Chorus, who articulate the pattern of reciprocal vengeance and sway them toward actions that will reinforce it.[73] They do not merely express the way the world generally works and try to make sense of the events of the drama—a typical function of a chorus when they are alone and addressing only the audience. Instead, Orestes and Electra share the stage with them. The Chorus' words are delivered to them at this crucial moment during which the decision for matricide is taking shape. The reciprocity of revenge is now widely accepted and even consciously adopted as the governing principle by which the Chorus and characters shape their words and actions. What we see in *Choephori* is both a shift away from *Agamemnon* as well as a continuation of its themes. Like Cassandra or Clytemnestra in *Agamemnon*, the Chorus of female Libation Bearers expose retribution as the governing force behind the plot. But they are doing so contemporaneously with the plot; they do not merely predict it, they script it in real time as Electra and Orestes play along. Their knowledge of the future is linked to their subsequent role in its execution. The Chorus function like the Danaids of *Suppliants*, who play a similar role in articulating the rules of reciprocity and convincing their interlocutors to follow them.

The difference is that *Choephori* does not use alētheia or alēthēs to designate the force of these rules. The closest approximation of the reciprocity-truth associations of *Agamemnon* comes in the role of Apollo, whom Orestes credits with his revenge plan: ἦ καὶ Λοξίας ἐφήμισεν | ἄναξ Ἀπόλλων, μάντις ἀψευδὴς τὸ πρίν ("[dying in the same snare,] in the way even Loxias, lord Apollo, declared, a prophet who has been without deceit in the past," 558–59). By characterizing Apollo as an "unlying prophet" or "a prophet without deceit" (μάντις ἀψευδής), Orestes evokes the associations between prophecy and truth embodied in the figure of Cassandra in *Agamemnon*, who herself had a history with Apollo; by making this characterization in the context of his revenge plans, he evokes the further associations between reciprocity and truth also represented in Cassandra. But Orestes uses the alpha-privative apseudēs rather than alēthēs to char-

---

73. Cf. Fraenkel 1950 vol. 3, 626 *ad* 1178–1330, who notes the crucial role of Aeschylean stichomythiae in revealing critical information in *A.* 1202ff., *Ch.* 166ff., 908ff., and *Eu.* 892ff.

acterize Apollo. His characterization resonates with Pindar's, in which Apollo is a god who "does not touch falsehoods" (ψευδέων δ᾽ οὐχ ἅπτεται, P. 3.29).[74] It is worth noting that the Pindaric characterization does not promise a truthful Apollo; rather, in the context of the myth of Coronis, which I discussed in chapter 3, it refers to Apollo's ability to discern and reject her falsehoods. The resonance is fitting given the paradox in the *Choephori* passage of Orestes invoking an "unlying" god to authorize his deceptive plans. Further, Orestes claims Apollo has been apseudēs (only) "in the past" (τὸ πρίν, 555). As A. F. Garvie notes, "Orestes does not mean to imply that Apollo is likely to tell lies in the future, but in *Eum.* his veracity will be called into question."[75] Orestes unwittingly hints at questions about Apollo's credibility and, more generally, the moral uncertainties that will be at issue in the final play of the tragic trilogy.

It is useful to think of Apollo as an adaptive replacement of alētheia in the relationship between reciprocity and truth that was established in *Agamemnon*. As the trilogy progresses, it becomes clear that the inexorability of reciprocity will come to fruition in *Choephori* via the oracular injunction of Apollo and the decisions of the characters to follow it. The vengeful decisions and actions of Orestes and Electra—sanctioned and even prescribed by Apollo—give specific, defined form to the vague predictions of payback expressed in *Agamemnon* by Cassandra (1316–20) and the Argive Elders (1560–66) and defined as alētheia by Clytemnestra (1567). The term alētheia, however, itself recedes to the background and loses its association with reciprocity in *Choephori*.

This is a significant departure from *Agamemnon*, whose two female characters understand the cycle of reciprocity as a manifestation of truth. While all the characters of *Choephori* understand sooner or later that reciprocal vengeance will occur, none of them conceive of its occurrence in terms of alētheia; the absence of this term from articulations of reciprocity suggests a waning sense of its inevitability. Furthermore, unlike the Argive Elders of *Agamemnon* the Chorus of Libation Bearers do not articulate the rules of reciprocity as a warning of what is to come but as an injunction to Orestes and Electra to act. If they articulate the inevitability of the force of revenge, it is at least partly to instigate or facilitate the actualization of the revenge plot.[76] The absence of

---

74. The line also recalls the *Homeric Hymn to Hermes*, where Hermes claims not to know how to speak falsehoods (οὐκ οἶδα ψεύδεσθαι, 369), undoubtedly mimicking a common attribute of Apollo.

75. Garvie 1986, 195 *ad* 559.

76. In seeing the Chorus as a parallel for the tragedian in terms of articulating and crafting the plot, I differ somewhat from Rosenmeyer, Thiel, and Podlecki, whose views are summarized in Wolh-

terms for truth from the discourse of reciprocity is indicative of this shift, and it portends the end of the revenge cycle that will occur in the final play of the *Oresteia* trilogy.

The slow disappearance of alētheia from reciprocity culminates in *Eumenides*, where the Erinyes and Apollo, unspeaking and unembodied in *Choephori*, now appear in the flesh and at odds with one another.[77] Their conflict represents larger questions about whether a matricide is worse than husband-killing, whether blood relations trump marriage, whether a mother is less of a parent than a father, and whether the older Erinyes should have more authority than the younger Apollo. Ultimately, their case is referred to arbitration in Athens, Orestes is acquitted by Athena's deciding vote, and the Erinyes are given an Athenian cult and incorporated into the city's new murder court system established by Athena.[78]

There is evidence that the Erinyes have been present all along, the latent force behind each act of retribution in the *Oresteia*.[79] Cassandra describes seeing them entrenched in the house (*A.* 1186–88), suggesting their influence over Clytemnestra's murder of Agamemnon.[80] And of course, Orestes sees them at the end of *Choephori*.[81] Their embodiment in *Eumenides* should ostensibly personify the action-reaction pattern that has defined the *Oresteia* thus far: "Their very function is to perpetuate, forever, the ineluctable, dialectical mechanism underlying reciprocal violence."[82] But curiously, the Erinyes do not situate Orestes' crime within a longer history of familial vengeance. Instead, they decontextualize it and extract it from the narrative arc of retribution originally

---

farht 2004, 113n33: "On the risk of confusing the voices of the Chorus and of the author in Aeschylus' plays, see Rosenmeyer 1982, 61 ff., [and 166–69,] Thiel 1993, 1 ff., and more recently Podlecki 2003, 12–13: 'It is dangerous to take these choral comments as authoritative, much less as authorial.'"

77. I adopt the communis opinio that the Erinyes did not have a physical presence on the stage of *Choephori*. For a subtle discussion of the relationship between the invisible Erinyes of *Choephori* and the visible Chorus of *Eumenides*, see Brown 1983.

78. Some would argue, based on the title of the play, that the Erinyes are also renamed the Eumenides, but Brown 1984, 267–76, points out that the word Eumenides never occurs in the play and convincingly argues that the title given to the play (at the end of the fifth century or later) is not Aeschylus' own.

79. See Käppel 1998, 172–78, who argues for a "Rachedaimon" (revenge god) as an ever present force shaping the plot.

80. On the significance of *A.* 1186–93, see Brown 1983, 14: "This confirms that the forces whose operation has been deduced by others from events in the human world have an objective existence within the framework of the play."

81. See Brown 1983 for the relationship between the invisible Erinyes at the end of *Choephori* and the embodied Erinyes in *Eumenides*.

82. Hall 2015, 254.

scripted in *Agamemnon* and acknowledged as "truth" by Clytemnestra. When the Chorus first present their grievance to Athena, they elide any of Orestes' motives, thus characterizing it as simple murder without the larger context in which it occurred:

Χο. φονεὺς γὰρ εἶναι μητρὸς ἠξιώσατο.
Αθ. ἀλλ' ἢ 'ξ ἀνάγκης, ἢ τινος τρέων κότον;
Χο. ποῦ γὰρ τοσοῦτο κέντρον ὡς μητροκτονεῖν;
Αθ. δυοῖν παρόντοιν ἥμισυς λόγου πάρα. (425–28)

CHORUS: For he deemed it right to be his mother's murderer.
ATHENA: But out of necessity, or in fear of someone's ill-will?
CHORUS: Where is there a goad so great as for a man to murder his mother?
ATHENA: Although two parties are present, only half of the story is.

The Erinyes disjoin Orestes' crime from its predecessors, thus extricating it from the events of *Agamemnon* as well as the prior history of the House of Atreus.[83] Their conception of revenge diverges from what has been articulated in the earlier plays. Whereas Clytemnestra and Cassandra each demonstrate an understanding that contextualizes violent actions within a narrative of reciprocal reactions, and the characters of *Choephori* follow suit, the Erinyes prefer, paradoxically and impossibly, to consider retribution extracontextually; they have hinted at this disposition when they tell Apollo the narrow criterion that guides their vengeance (Απ. τί γὰρ, γυναικὸς ἥτις ἄνδρα νοσφίσῃ; | Χο. οὐκ ἂν γένοιθ' ὅμαιμος αὐθέντης φόνος, "Apollo: What of a woman who kills her husband? Chorus: It would not be a same-blood murder by a kinsman," 211–12). Athena immediately detects this logical fallacy, recognizing that actions do not occur in a vacuum.

The other side deploys similar tactics: Apollo, too, decontextualizes Orestes' matricide from the longer history of reciprocal violence that has plagued the House of Atreus. He takes responsibility for Orestes' actions (*Eu.* 84, 579–80) and removes them from the chain of murders in the House of Atreus by making no mention of Clytemnestra's motives for killing Agamemnon; and, of course, he even extricates Orestes' crime from a pattern of familial bloodshed by deny-

---

83. Cf. Sommerstein 1989, 157 *ad* 426–27: "Athena's first thought, on learning of the crime, is to ask whether there were mitigating circumstances; but for the Erinyes no circumstances can mitigate matricide."

ing Clytemnestra's maternal parenthood (657–66).[84] Accompanying this shift is the near absence of the repetitive language that characterizes the symmetry of reciprocal action in both *Agamemnon* and *Choephori*. The Erinyes make ample reference to punishment (e.g., 261–75), but neither they nor Apollo make use of polyptoton to characterize reciprocal violence, as was common in the previous plays. Only Orestes does, in a way that reminds us of his motives in *Choephori*: ἔκτεινα τὴν τεκοῦσαν, οὐκ ἀρνήσομαι, | ἀντικτόνοις ποιναῖσι φιλτάτου πατρός ("I *killed* the woman who bore me, I will not deny it, as punishment *in return for killing* my beloved father," 463–64). But he now feels uncertain and asks for Athena's judgment (467–69); this is a hint that *Eumenides* will deliver a restructuring of the role and force of the reciprocity principle.

The intertwining of reciprocity and truth is undone in this third play in which the causal connectivity between acts of violence is undermined and ultimately discarded. The unraveling begins in *Choephori* where the revenge narrative is adopted by the characters but is nowhere equated with truth. The middle play of the *Oresteia* trilogy subtly undermines the idea that reciprocal return is inevitable. *Eumenides* does away with it altogether, as evident in the acquittal of Orestes, but also in the changing use of the language of reciprocity. This change accompanies the transformation of dikē that occurs over the course of the trilogy, from individual revenge to court-based justice.[85] Such a transformation follows a shift in the nature of revenge and its agents. Over the course of the trilogy, we see a transition from individual agents of revenge (Clytemnestra in *Agamemnon*) to a blend of individual and collective agents (Electra, Orestes, and the Chorus of *Choephori*) to retributive punishment being located solely within the collective body of the Chorus of Erinyes in *Eumenides*.[86]

What results is a divorce of truth from reciprocity. Truth as "what happens" still encompasses past, present, and future. But without revenge as its conjoined twin, this is simply a temporal progression and not a causal one: we can no longer see the present and future as automatic responsive echoes of past actions, particularly in light of the increasingly prescriptive (rather than merely predic-

---

84. For a bibliographical survey on Apollo's famously specious argument, see Chesi 2014, 147n228.

85. Or an integration of divine Dikē with its mortal instantiations; see Podlecki 1966, 63, who sees this integration as the product of ambiguity: "In precisely this ambiguity [of *dikē*] Aeschylus found the means of solving the problem he had set himself: the Justice of the gods could only become efficacious for men in this world through the workings of Law." See also Kitto 1971, 94. Rosenmeyer 1982, 356, on the other hand, sees an increasing separation of human from divine in the new "Right."

86. This transition reflects the Chorus' increasing agency over the course of the trilogy. See McCall 1990, 27.

tive) nature of Apollo's oracle. The interventions of Apollo and Athena, along with the embodiment of the Erinyes, expose and undermine the unspoken assumption that truth and revenge exist as a higher power independent of the gods. Ultimately, it is through gender that the complexities of reciprocity and truth are exposed. While the propensity of female characters to understand truth in *Agamemnon* does not persist, unchanged, in the subsequent plays of the trilogy, what does remain consistent are the gendered interactions from which new revelations about reciprocity emerge. The conflict between Apollo and the Erinyes is a gendered one, hinging on questions about the nature of family relationships that are impossible to engage without considering gender.

This conflict generates insights about the changing role of reciprocity within the tragic plot, and it prompts consideration of what forces form the substance of that plot. In *Agamemnon* Cassandra's predictions and Clytemnestra's understanding of revenge shed light not only on what would happen to them, but also on the continuing plot of the *Oresteia*. In this way these two characters could be seen as a mouthpiece for the tragedian. The Chorus of *Choephori* take up this role in articulating what reciprocity looks like for the characters of *Choephori*. But as has been noted, Cassandra's predictions do not extend beyond the plot of *Choephori*,[87] nor does Clytemnestra foresee anything beyond the second play. This, too, also draws attention to tragic composition, for in providing and then retracting voices that predict the events of his plays, the tragedian invites consideration and interrogation of the reciprocity principles on which those predictions are premised. The disappearance of such voices leaves us wondering what role reciprocity will now play in the new landscape of *Eumenides*. In this final play it is not so much female characters specifically that shed light on tragic composition; rather, it is male-female conflict that engenders reflection on the role reciprocity played in the previous parts of the story and on what will replace it as the story concludes.

Conclusion

The salience of gender in the conflicts and violence of *Agamemnon* is not in and of itself surprising. But there is also a certain gendering of *understanding* that operates in the play, uniting characters of the same gender even as everything

---

87. Schein 1982, 15.

else divides them. Cassandra and Clytemnestra—two very different characters on different sides of the revenge act—nevertheless both recognize a continuing narrative of retribution.[88] By contrast, the male characters Aegisthus, the Herald, and the Chorus of Argive Elders—also very different from one another—share the tendency to overlook, disregard, or otherwise misapprehend the inevitability of retribution. Put simply, the female characters understand revenge as truth, envisioning it as part of the natural and inevitable course of events, and the male characters do not.

Reciprocity and truth are intertwined in *Agamemnon*, as the intergenerational cycle of retributive violence is characterized by an inevitability that is cast as truth (alētheia). The female characters of *Agamemnon* demonstrate the greatest awareness of this relationship between reciprocity and truth. Clytemnestra and Cassandra are conscious that action is met by reaction, cause is followed by effect, and that their own lives and fates are embedded in this pattern. That they understand the story they are in and how it will unfold puts them in league with the Choruses of *Seven* and *Suppliants*, who share similar characteristics. In all three plays truth is figured as a timeline in which events occur as responses to and replications of each other, and in all three plays female characters demonstrate the greatest awareness of the larger narrative that encompasses what they see and experience. Their awareness is gained in various ways and has various effects, but one key similarity is that the female characters somehow give voice to the reciprocity themes that govern their stories and thus provide a framework for understanding them.

Inherent in the conclusion to the *Oresteia* is an interrogation of this framework. The pattern that initially plays out is one of violence and return violence, a pattern so predictable that it is figured as truth. But as the trilogy progresses, Aeschylus prompts us to question this pattern and its predictability. He does so first by removing the designation of alētheia from this pattern in *Choephori*. In *Eumenides* the pattern itself loses its prominence. As a trilogy that establishes reciprocity as its governing rule at the beginning but removes it by the end, the *Oresteia* raises questions about the nature of its story, how it is scripted, who determines the pattern it should follow. All of these questions are prompted by the words of the various female characters or by their interactions with male

---

88. Wohl 1998, 100–117, also sees a complementarity between Clytemnestra and Cassandra, although in a very different way: "If Clytemnestra embodies and punishes the commodity fetish, Cassandra forgives the violence of exchange and offers sympathy for its disastrous consequences" (Wohl 1998, 102).

characters or both. It is through them that we understand what the revenge plot looks like and how it is supposed to work. It is through them that we begin to understand revenge as the truth governing the narrative. And it is through them that we also see the dissolution of this truth as they variously articulate and then reject the processes of reciprocity.

The symmetrical pattern of Aeschylean reciprocity along with its configuration as truth resonates with what we see in Pindar and helps reveal the complementarity between the two contemporaries. Further, the role of Aeschylus' female characters in giving voice to this framework recalls the Pindaric female figures of chapter 3, who also call attention to the themes of the poetry in which they are situated. More specifically, both Aeschylus' and Pindar's female characters shed light on the forces of reciprocity shaping their narratives and on the relationship between reciprocity and truth. Aeschylus' female characters express and reinforce this relationship; Pindar's female characters perform deceptive acts that undermine it. This inversion points to a complementarity between Pindar and Aeschylus, who draw on different aspects of reciprocity for their myth-making and poetic creation. Ultimately, the female characters of the *Oresteia* show us how Aeschylean storytelling works, by shining a light on the connections between reciprocity and truth, and where those connections fail. Thus they parallel Pindar's female figures who perform a similar function, and they help reveal the complementary ways the two poets intertwine reciprocity, truth, and gender.

Epilogue

This book has examined truth, reciprocity, and gender in Pindar and Aeschylus and has argued for a complementarity in their treatments of these three concepts. This complementarity takes into account—indeed, is premised on—both the similarities and the differences between the two poets. Although ostensibly quite different, Pindar and Aeschylus are surprisingly comparable in their articulations of reciprocity, their use of reciprocity to frame their poetry or narratives, their conception of truth as both objective reality and as a manifestation of reciprocity, and their depictions of female characters who shine light on the linkages between reciprocity and truth. Both poets share a thematic concern for principles of equal exchange—whether for good or ill. By understanding Pindar's relationship with his patron as one of equal and respectful exchange, we understand his use of myth—along with the various details within his myths—as a way of reinforcing this principle. Analogously, the correspondence between past and future—the latter being an equivalent reaction to the former—is a form of reciprocity that is at the core of Aeschylean tragedy. Furthermore, the quid pro quo nature of reciprocity informs both poets' conceptions of truth and depictions of gender.

For Pindar and Aeschylus, truth, while signaling some kind of objective reality (i.e., "what happens"), is also informed by the reciprocity themes that pervade their works. Both poets use the language of truth, alētheia, to designate what happens, and what happens is shaped by the rule of reciprocity. Pindar's poetry revolves around the reciprocity of friendship or guest-friendship by which he defines his relationship to his patron. This relationship is premised on mutual, beneficial, and symmetrical exchange, is allegorized in the mythologi-

cal exempla of his odes, and generates certain obligations between its participants. For the epinician poet, the obligation in question is to praise his patron,
which can come into conflict with his obligation to tell the truth. Pindar balances and harmonizes these potentially conflicting obligations by presenting
alētheia as a principle that encompasses both. A variation of this type of reciprocity operates in Aeschylean tragedy, which portrays narratives of action followed by corresponding reaction, whether amicable or hostile. Aeschylus too
marries truth to the narratives of reciprocity and retribution that he portrays in
his tragedies. Aeschylean truth encompasses a temporal span of past, present,
and future as well as the causality between events that occur along this timeline.
The present and future do not simply follow the past but follow *from* it as events
respond and correspond to prior ones. Alētheia in Aeschylus denotes both the
events themselves and the cause-and-effect pattern they follow.

These connections between truth and reciprocity become ever clearer when
we consider depictions of gender. While Pindaric epinician focuses on the positive aspects of reciprocity, he deploys deceptive female figures to undermine
them. Female figures like the Hera-cloud, Coronis, and Hippolyta incorporate
existing stereotypes about lying, manipulative women to illustrate the harms of
deception to relationships of reciprocity, which require truthfulness. At the
same time they display persuasiveness and creativity, both of which are compo-
nents of effective poetry. They thus are suggestive of how Pindar conceives of
poetry and reflects on its potential for harm. In this way they follow in the tradition of Hesiod's Muses, who articulate the existence of both truth and falsehood and yet aestheticize them to the point of obscuring this distinction. Gender in Pindar is not a frequently cultivated field of study. I hope to have sown
the seeds here for consideration of how Pindar's gender constructs are situated
within a long poetic tradition of interweaving female gender and poetic creativity, and of problematizing the potential of such creativity. Aeschylean tragedy
depicts female figures who perceive and perpetuate reciprocity and articulate it
as a type of truth. They provide the clearest expression of Aeschylean truth as a
function of reciprocity, as many of them share a capacity to perceive the big
picture of not only "what happens" but also "how what happens is related to
what happened before and what will happen next." Some characters even display the ability to *shape* the bigger picture. Pindar's and Aeschylus' female figures are distinct from and sometimes even at odds with one another, but when
considered in light of their relationship to reciprocity and truth, the two poets'
treatments of such figures are complementary. Aeschylus' female characters

articulate the truth of reciprocity while Pindar's engage in deception that undermines it, but both ultimately call attention to the relationship between reciprocity and truth.

What we see in Pindar and Aeschylus suggests that truth and gender are paradoxically both fixed and malleable. Both poets refer to truth as if it is an objective and fixed reality, and their references to it reflect the traditions that precede them. Yet Pindar also embeds this idea within his obligations as a xenos to his laudandus—indeed, he even suggests that the obligations of reciprocity constitute the strongest foundation for delivering truth. In the same vein Aeschylus refers to truth as "what happens," but he also presents truth as a chain of events connected to and stemming from one another based on the reciprocity principle. The amalgamation of objectivity and contextual specificity in each poet's rendering of truth prompts questions about how "objective" truth really is, and whether or how easily we can observe this phenomenon in other poetry or indeed in any genre.

So too with gender. Like truth, gender in Pindar and Aeschylus reflects the conventions of previous Greek poetic, mythological, and intellectual traditions. Gender constructs are surprisingly consistent across ancient Greek texts despite the vast span of time and space these texts cover. Thus deceptiveness, allure, enigma, incomprehensibility—these are female traits found in the earliest Greek texts, and they find a home in Pindar and Aeschylus too. One recognizes the women of Pindar and Aeschylus because they are based on widely familiar tropes. But as Pindar and Aeschylus incorporate these gender constructs in ways very specific to their own poetic works, there arise opportunities for broader reflection on the relationship between gender and context. If Pindar's and Aeschylus' depictions of female characters are specific to their poetic contexts, paying attention to this specificity can shed light on the way their respective poetry works. The perspicacity of Aeschylus' female characters who perceive the story in which they exist, the specific noxiousness of Pindar's female characters who inflict harm on reciprocal relationships analogous to poet-patron reciprocity—ultimately they are revealing of the intertwined relationship between poetry itself and its subject matter.

Even reciprocity is subject to some scrutiny. By identifying reciprocity as a shared feature of Pindaric and Aeschylean poetry, we see how both poets simultaneously focus on and interrogate it. Pindar's poet-patron relationships shape his notions of truth and his conceptions of what poetry should do. He depicts deception as antithetical to truth and reciprocity, yet his characterizations of such deception sometimes overlap with the positive aspects of poetry. Thus he interrogates truth and the function and effect of poetry. He presents reciprocity as the force that would keep things on a straight course, but this argument is not always believable; Pindar draws attention to the alignment between reciprocity and truth but in various ways also prompts scrutiny of it. Likewise, we see the problems that arise from the action-reaction pattern in Aeschylean tragedy. Various characters try to buck it, for example, Eteocles in *Seven against Thebes*, who only gradually begins to understand how his family history will have reverberations in his generation. The female Chorus, by contrast, are well aware of what the inexorable force of reciprocity means for Polyneices and Eteocles, yet they are powerless to stop it, making the deaths of the brothers all the more devastating. The Danaids of *Suppliants* will find that imposing frameworks of amicable reciprocity on their story can only take them so far before they must resort to violence. The *Oresteia* eventually puts an end to the reciprocity cycle that has generated repeated murder in the House of Atreus. Aeschylus' plays establish a relationship between reciprocity and truth by presenting reciprocity as the force governing how things will turn out, but they also interrogate this relationship by presenting the failures of reciprocity.

I started this book by advancing three claims: first, that Pindar and Aeschylus frame their poetry using similar principles of reciprocity; second, that each poet depicts truth in a way that is specific to those reciprocity principles; and third, that their depictions of gender are shaped by this intertwining of truth and reciprocity. Comparing Pindar and Aeschylus in terms of truth, reciprocity, and gender reveals their similar intertwinings of these concepts and invites consideration of the convergences between the two poets that exist and persist despite their very different poetic forms. I have proposed complementarity as a way of making sense of both their similar presentations of reciprocity and truth, and the different ways they use gender to reinforce the intertwining of these two concepts. I have aimed to advance understanding of each poet, both on their own and in relation to one another. By illuminating the complementary ways these two poets treat reciprocity, truth, and gender, I hope to have presented Pindar and Aeschylus as two pieces of a puzzle, inhabitants of a shared poetic ecosystem that produces similar thematic intertwinings.

What all this means, then, is that we can see the effects of context on representations of truth and of gender, but we can also understand contexts more clearly if we examine it through the lens of truth or gender, or both. I have relied on reciprocity as the stable, fixed principle from which I have undertaken my examinations of truth and gender in Pindar and Aeschylus, but as I conclude this work I will provide some provocations about what we can learn if we remove reciprocity as the linchpin of our study. The pervasiveness of gender and the insights into poetry that emerge from considering gender in Pindar and Aeschylus should prompt reflection on whether gender could provide similar interpretive benefits for other Greek poets as well. I would like for scholars of ancient Greek literature to at least consider the role of gender when beginning their inquiries into the texts. Truth, too, is pervasive in the work of the ancient Greek poets, and when there are poetic references to truth, it behooves us to interrogate their meanings and the multiple implications thereof. Identifying conceptions of poetry—what poets think the purpose of their work is—is a typical goal of scholarship on ancient Greek poetry. Part of this goal could include consideration of whether, to what extent, and in what ways truth figures into these conceptions. Conceptions and constructions of truth and the ways poets relate to it can inform literary scholarship just as they inform philosophical inquiries. Conversely, we can think of poets like Pindar and Aeschylus and others under the rubric of philosophical study for what they can reveal to us about human tendencies, concerns, and behavior. Ultimately, this study invites interrogation of how poetry works, how it reveals its inner workings, and how truth and gender play into these revelations.

Bibliography

Adkins, A. W. H. 1972. "Truth, ΚΟΣΜΟΣ, and ΑΡΕΤΗ in the Homeric Poems." *Classical Quarterly* 22.1:5–18.

Ahlert, Paulheinz. 1942. *Mädchen und Frauen in Pindars Dichtung*. Philologus Supplement 34.1. Leipzig: Dieterich.

Andújar, Rosa, Thomas R. P. Coward, and Theodora A. Hadjimichael, eds. 2018. *Paths of Song: The Lyric Dimension of Greek Tragedy*. Berlin: De Gruyter.

Arthur, Marylin B. 1982. "Cultural Strategies in Hesiod's *Theogony*: Law, Family, Society." *Arethusa* 15.1:63–82.

Athanassaki, Lucia. 2004. "Deixis, Performance, and Poetics in Pindar's *First Olympian Ode*." *Arethusa* 37.3:317–41.

Athanassaki, Lucia. 2010. "Giving Wings to the Aeginetan Sculptures: The Panhellenic Aspirations of Pindar's *Eighth Olympian*." In *Aegina: Contexts for Choral Lyric Poetry; Myth, History, and Identity in the Fifth Century BC*, edited by David Fearn, 257–92. Oxford: Oxford University Press.

Austin, Norman. 1994. *Helen of Troy and Her Shameless Phantom*. Ithaca: Cornell University Press.

Bachvarova, Mary R. 2009. "Suppliant Danaids and Argive Nymphs in Aeschylus." *Classical Journal* 104.4:289–310.

Bacon, Helen H. 1964. "The Shield of Eteocles." *Arion* 3.3:27–38.

Bakewell, Geoffrey W. 1997. "Μετοικία in the *Supplices* of Aeschylus." *Classical Antiquity* 16.2:209–28.

Bakewell, Geoffrey W. 2013. *Aeschylus's "Suppliant Women": The Tragedy of Immigration*. Madison: University of Wisconsin Press.

Barclay, Laurie J., David B. Whiteside, and Karl Aquino. 2014. "To Avenge or Not to Avenge? Exploring the Interactive Effects of Moral Identity and the Negative Reciprocity Norm." *Journal of Business Ethics* 121:15–28.

Barrett, James. 2002. *Staged Narrative: Poetics and the Messenger in Greek Tragedy*. Berkeley: University of California Press.

Bassi, Karen. 1993. "Helen and the Discourse of Denial in Stesichorus' Palinode." *Arethusa* 26:51–75.

Bednarowski, K. Paul. 2010. "The Danaids' Threat: Obscurity, Suspense and the Shedding of Tradition in Aeschylus' *Suppliants.*" *Classical Journal* 105.3:193–212.

Bednarowski, K. Paul. 2011. "When the *Exodos* Is Not the End: The Closing Song of Aeschylus' *Suppliants.*" *Greek, Roman, and Byzantine Studies* 51:552–78.

Beecroft, Alexander J. 2006. "'This Is Not a True Story': Stesichorus's *Palinode* and the Revenge of the Epichoric." *Transactions of the American Philological Association* 136:47–69.

Beidelman, T. 1989. "Agonistic Exchange: Homeric Reciprocity and the Heritage of Simmel and Mauss." *Cultural Anthropology* 4:227–59.

Belfiore, Elizabeth. 1985. "'Lies Unlike the Truth': Plato on Hesiod, *Theogony* 27." *Transactions of the American Philological Association* 115:47–57.

Belfiore, Elizabeth. 1998. "Harming Friends: Problematic Reciprocity in Greek Tragedy." In Gill, Postlethwaite, and Seaford 1998, 139–58.

Belfiore, Elizabeth S. 2000. *Murder among Friends: Violation of* Philia *in Greek Tragedy.* Oxford: Oxford University Press.

Bell, John M. 1984. "God, Man, and Animal in Pindar's Second Pythian." In *Greek Poetry and Philosophy: Studies in Honour of Leonard Woodbury*, edited by Douglas E. Gerber, 1–31. Chico: Scholars Press.

Benardete, Seth. 1968. "Two Notes on Aeschylus' Septem (2nd Part)." *Wiener Studien* 81:5–17.

Benardete, Seth G., trans. 1991. "*The Suppliant Maidens and the Persians.*" In *The Complete Greek Tragedies Aeschylus II*, edited by David Grene and Richmond Lattimore. Chicago: University of Chicago Press.

Bergren, Ann. 1983. "Language and the Female in Early Greek Thought." *Arethusa* 16:69–95. = Bergren 2008, 13–40.

Bergren, Ann. 1992. "Architecture Gender Philosophy." In *Innovations of Antiquity*, edited by Ralph Hexter and Daniel Selden, 253–305. New York: Routledge. = Bergren 2008, 242–303.

Bergren, Ann. 2008. *Weaving Truth: Essays on Language and the Female in Greek Thought.* Hellenic Studies 19. Cambridge, MA: Harvard University Press.

Betensky, Aya. 1978. "Aeschylus' *Oresteia*: The Power of Clytemnestra." *Ramus* 7:11–25.

Black-Michaud, Jacob. 1975. *Cohesive Force: Feud in the Ancient Mediterranean and the Middle East.* Oxford: Blackwell.

Blanchard, Alain. 2003. "Sémonide, fr. 7, v. 1–95: Pourquoi les femmes ne ressemblent-elles pas davantage aux hommes!" In *La poésie grecque antique: Actes du 13ème colloque de la Villa Kérylos à Beaulieu-sur-Mer les 18 & 19 octobre 2002*, edited by Jacques Jouanna and Jean Leclant, 77–88. Cahiers de la Villa Kérylos 14. Paris: Académie des Inscriptions et Belles-Lettres.

Blondell, Ruby. 2013. *Helen of Troy: Beauty, Myth, Devastation.* Oxford: Oxford University Press.

Blümer, Wilhelm. 2001. *Interpretation archaischer Dichtung: Die mythologischen Partien der "Erga" Hesiods.* 2 vols. Münster: Aschendorff.

Blundell, Mary Whitlock. 1989. *Helping Friends and Harming Enemies: A Study in Sophocles and Greek Ethics.* Cambridge: Cambridge University Press.

Boedeker, Deborah. 1991. "Euripides' Medea and the Vanity of Logoi." *Classical Philology* 86:95–112.

Bordo, Susan. 1993. *Unbearable Weight: Feminism, Western Culture, and the Body.* Berkeley: University of California Press.

Bourdieu, Pierre. 1977. *Outline of a Theory of Practice.* Translated by Richard Nice. Cambridge: Cambridge University Press.

Bowen, A. J. 2013. *Aeschylus, "Suppliant Women."* Oxford: Oxbow Books.

Bowie, E. L. 1993. "Lies, Fiction and Slander in Early Greek Poetry." In *Lies and Fiction in the Ancient World,* edited by Christopher Gill and T. P. Wiseman, 1–37. Exeter: University of Exeter Press.

Braswell, Bruce Karl. 1988. *A Commentary on the "Fourth Pythian" Ode of Pindar.* Berlin: De Gruyter.

Brault, Pascale-Anne. 2009. "Playing the Cassandra: Prophecies of the Feminine in the *Polis* and Beyond." In McCoskey and Zakin 2009, 197–220.

Bremer, Dieter. 1976. *Licht und Dunkel in der frühgriechischen Dichtung.* Bonn: Bouvier.

Brillante, Carlo. 1995. "Amore senza χάρις: Pind. *Pyth.* II 42–48." *Quaderni Urbinati di Cultura Classica,* N.S., 49.1:33–38.

Brown, A. L. 1976. "The End of the *Seven against Thebes.*" *Classical Quarterly,* N.S., 26.2:206–19.

Brown, A. L. 1977. "Eteocles and the Chorus in the *Seven against Thebes.*" *Phoenix* 31.4:300–318.

Brown, A. L. 1983. "The Erinyes in the *Oresteia*: Real Life, the Supernatural, and the Stage." *Journal of Hellenic Studies* 103:13–34.

Brown, A. L. 1984. "Eumenides in Greek Tragedy." *Classical Quarterly* 34.2:260–81.

Brown, Christopher G. 2018. "Picturing a Truth: Beast Fable, Early *Iambos,* and Semonides on the Creation of Women." *Mouseion,* ser. 3, 15:29–47.

Brown, Donald E. 1991. *Human Universals.* New York: McGraw-Hill.

Bundy, Elroy L. 1986. *Studia Pindarica.* Berkeley: University of California Press. (= 1962. *Studia Pindarica, I–II.* Berkeley: University of California Press).

Burgess, Dana L. 1993. "Food, Sex, Money and Poetry in 'Olympian' 1." *Hermes* 121.1:35–44.

Burian, Peter, trans. 1991. *Aeschylus, "The Suppliants."* Princeton: Princeton University Press.

Burian, Peter. 2009. "City, Farewell! *Genos, Polis,* and Gender in Aeschylus' *Seven against Thebes* and Euripides' *Phoenician Women.*" In McCoskey and Zakin 2009, 15–45.

Burke, Kenneth. 1966. *Language as Symbolic Action: Essays on Life, Literature, and Method.* Berkeley: University of California Press.

Burton, R. W. B. 1962. *Pindar's "Pythian Odes": Essays in Interpretation*. Oxford: Oxford University Press.

Butler, Judith. 1993. *Bodies That Matter: On the Discursive Limits of "Sex."* New York: Routledge.

Butler, Judith. 1999. *Gender Trouble: Feminism and the Subversion of Identity*. New York: Routledge.

Buxton, R. G. A. 1982. *Persuasion in Greek Tragedy: A Study of* Peitho. Cambridge: Cambridge University Press.

Byrne, Lucy. 1997. "Fear in the *Seven against Thebes*." In *Rape in Antiquity: Sexual Violence in the Greek and Roman Worlds*, edited by Susan Deacy and Karen Pierce, 143–62. London: Duckworth.

Cairns, D. L., and J. G. Howie. 2010. *Bacchylides: Five "Epinician Odes."* Cambridge: Francis Cairns.

Cameron, H. D. 1970. "The Power of Words in the *Seven against Thebes*." *Transactions of the American Philological Association* 101:95–118.

Campbell, David A. 1982. *Greek Lyric Poetry: A Selection of Early Greek Lyric, Elegiac and Iambic Poetry*. Bristol: Bristol Classical Press.

Carey, C. 1976. "Pindar's Eighth Nemean Ode." *Proceedings of the Cambridge Philological Society* 22:26–41.

Carey, C. 1981. *A Commentary on Five Odes of Pindar: "Pythian" 2, "Pythian" 9, "Nemean" 1, "Nemean" 7, "Isthmian" 8*. New York: Arno Press.

Carnes, Jeffrey S. 1996. "The Ends of the Earth: Fathers, Ephebes, and Wild Women in *Nemean* 4 and 5." *Arethusa* 29:15–55.

Catenaccio, Claire. 2011. "Dream as Image and Action in Aeschylus' *Oresteia*." *Greek, Roman, and Byzantine Studies* 51:202–31.

Chesi, Giulia Maria. 2014. *The Play of Words: Blood Ties and Power Relations in Aeschylus' "Oresteia."* Berlin: De Gruyter.

Cingano, Ettore. 1982. "Quante testimonianze sulle palinodie di Stesicoro?" *Quaderni Urbinati di Cultura Classica*, N.S., 12:21–33.

Clay, Jenny Strauss. 2003. *Hesiod's Cosmos*. Cambridge: Cambridge University Press.

Cole, Thomas. 1983. "Archaic Truth." *Quaderni Urbinati di Cultura Classica* 42:7–28.

Conacher, D. J. 1987. *Aeschylus' "Oresteia": A Literary Commentary*. Toronto: University of Toronto Press.

Cook, Erwin. 2016. "Homeric Reciprocities." *Journal of Mediterranean Archaeology* 29.1:94–104.

Crotty, Kevin. 1994. *The Poetics of Supplication: Homer's "Iliad" and "Odyssey."* Ithaca: Cornell University Press.

Currie, Bruno. 2005. *Pindar and the Cult of Heroes*. Oxford: Oxford University Press.

d'Alfonso, Francesa. 1993–1994. "Stesicoro corale nelle due principali testimonianze sulla 'Palinodia' (Isocr. *Hel.* 64; Plat. *Phaedr.* 243a)." *Helikon* 33–34:419–29.

Daube, Benjamin. 1941. *Zu den Rechtsproblemen in Aischylos' "Agamemnon."* Zürich: Niehans.

Davies, Malcolm. 1987. "Aeschylus' Clytemnestra: Sword or Axe?" *Classical Quarterly*, N.S., 37.1:65–75.

Davies, Malcolm. 1988. "Monody, Choral Lyric, and the Tyranny of the Hand-Book." *Classical Quarterly*, N.S., 38.1:52–64.

Davies, Malcolm, and Patrick J. Finglass. 2014. *Stesichorus: The Poems*. Edited with introduction, translation and commentary. Cambridge: Cambridge University Press.

Dawe, R. D. 1963. "Inconsistency of Plot and Character in Aeschylus." *Proceedings of the Cambridge Philological Society*, N.S., 9:21–62.

Dawe, R. D. 1967. "The End of *Seven against Thebes.*" *Classical Quarterly*, N.S., 17.1:16–28.

Dawe, R. D. 1978. "The End of *Seven against Thebes* Yet Again." In Dawe, Diggle, and Easterling 1978, 87–103.

Dawe, R. D., J. Diggle, and P. E. Easterling, eds. 1978. *Dionysiaca: Nine Studies in Greek Poetry by Former Pupils, Presented to Sir Denys Page on His Seventieth Birthday*. Cambridge: Cambridge University Library.

Dawson, Christopher M. 1970. *"The Seven against Thebes": A Translation with Commentary*. Englewood Cliffs, NJ: Prentice-Hall.

De Boer, Katherine R. 2017. "Pindar's Peaceful Rapes." *Helios* 44.1:1–27.

Denniston, John Dewar, and Denys Page. 1957. *Aeschylus, "Agamemnon."* Oxford: Oxford University Press.

Detienne, Marcel. 1967. *Les maîtres de vérité dans la Grèce archaïque*. Paris: Maspero.

Detienne, Marcel. 1996. *The Masters of Truth in Archaic Greece*. Translated by Janet Lloyd. New York: Zone Books. (Translation of Detienne 1967).

Devereux, George. 1976. *Dreams in Greek Tragedy: An Ethno-Psycho-Analytical Study*. Oxford: Basil Blackwell.

DeVito, Ann. 1999. "Eteocles, Amphiaraus, and Necessity in Aeschylus' 'Seven against Thebes.'" *Hermes* 127.2:165–71.

Dillery, John. 2005. "Chresmologues and *Manteis*: Independent Diviners and the Problem of Authority." In *Mantikê: Studies in Ancient Divination*, edited by Sarah Iles Johnston and Peter T. Struck, 167–231. Leiden: Brill.

Dodds, E. R. 1960. "Morals and Politics in the *Oresteia.*" *Proceedings of the Cambridge Philological Society*, N.S., 6:19–31.

Donlan, Walter. 1982. "Reciprocities in Homer." *Classical World* 75.3:137–75.

Donlan, Walter. 1997. "The Homeric Economy." In *A New Companion to Homer*, edited by Ian Morris and Barry Powell, 649–67. Leiden: Brill.

Drachmann, A. B., ed. 1997 (=1903). *Scholia vetera in Pindari "Carmina."* 3 vols. Stuttgart: Teubner.

duBois, Page. 1991. *Torture and Truth*. New York: Routledge.

duBois, Page. 1992. "Eros and the Woman." *Ramus* 21:97–116.

Duchemin, Jacqueline. 1970. "Pindare et la Sicile: Réflexions sur quelques thèmes mythiques." In *Hommages à M. Delcourt*, 78–91. Collection Latomus 114. Brussels: Revue d'études latines.

Edmunds, Lowell. 2016. *Stealing Helen: The Myth of the Abducted Wife in Comparative Perspective*. Princeton: Princeton University Press.

Edmunds, Lowell. 2017. "Eteocles and Thebes in Aeschylus' *Seven against Thebes*." In *Aeschylus and War: Comparative Perspectives on "Seven against Thebes,"* edited by Isabelle Torrance, 91–113. Abingdon: Routledge.

Faraone, Christopher A. 1993. "The Wheel, the Whip and Other Implements of Torture: Erotic Magic in Pindar *Pythian* 4.213–19." *Classical Journal* 89.1:1–19.

Farnell, Lewis Richard. 1932. *The Works of Pindar*. Translated, with literary and critical commentaries. Vol. 2. London: Macmillan.

Fausto-Sterling, Anne. 1993. "The Five Sexes: Why Male and Female Are Not Enough." *Sciences* 33:20–25.

Fearn, David. 2013. "Kleos versus Stone? Lyric Poetry and Context for Memorialization." In *Inscriptions and Their Uses in Greek and Latin Literature*, edited by Peter Liddel and Polly Low, 231–53. Oxford: Oxford University Press.

Felson Rubin, Nancy. 1984. "The Epinician Speaker in Pindar's First Olympian: Toward a Model for Analyzing Character in Ancient Choral Lyric." *Poetics Today* 5:377–97.

Finglass, P. J. 2007. *Pindar, "Pythian" Eleven*. Cambridge: Cambridge University Press.

Finglass, P. J. 2015. "Stesichorus, Master of Narrative." In *Stesichorus in Context*, edited by P. J. Finglass and Adrian Kelly, 83–97. Cambridge: Cambridge University Press.

Finkelberg, Margalit. 1998. *The Birth of Literary Fiction in Ancient Greece*. Oxford: Oxford University Press.

Finkelberg, Margalit. 2005. *Greeks and Pre-Greeks: Aegean Prehistory and Greek Heroic Tradition*. Cambridge: Cambridge University Press.

Finley, John H., Jr. 1955. *Pindar and Aeschylus*. Cambridge, MA: Harvard University Press.

Finley, M. I. 1954. *The World of Odysseus*. New York: Viking Press.

Finley, M. I. 1981. *Economy and Society in Ancient Greece*. Edited by Brent Shaw and Richard Saller. New York: Viking Press.

Fitch, Edward. 1924. "Pindar and Homer." *Classical Philology* 19.1:57–65.

Fitzgerald, William. 1987. *Agonistic Poetry: The Pindaric Mode in Pindar, Horace, Hölderlin, and the English Ode*. Berkeley: University of California Press.

Fletcher, Judith. 1999. "Exchanging Glances: Vision and Representation in Aeschylus' *Agamemnon*." *Helios* 26.1:11–34.

Flintoff, Everard. 1980. "The Ending of the *Seven against Thebes*." *Mnemosyne*, 4th ser., 33.3/4:244–71.

Foley, Helene P. 1981. "The Concept of Women in Athenian Drama." In *Reflections of Women in Antiquity*, edited by Helene P. Foley, 127–68. New York: Gordon and Break.

Foley, Helene P. 1992. "*Anodos* Dramas: Euripides' *Alcestis* and *Helen*." In *Innovations of Antiquity*, edited by Ralph Hexter and Daniel Selden, 133–60. New York: Routledge.

Foley, Helene P. 2001. *Female Acts in Greek Tragedy*. Princeton: Princeton University Press.

Fontenrose, Joseph. 1971. "Gods and Men in the *Oresteia*." *Transactions of the American Philological Association* 102:71–109.

Ford, Andrew. 2006. "The Genre of Genres: Paenas and *Paian* in Early Greek Poetry." *Poetica* 38.3/4:278–96.

Foster, Margaret. 2017. "Fathers and Sons in War: *Seven against Thebes, Pythian* 8, and the Polemics of Genre." In *Aeschylus and War: Comparative Perspectives on "Seven against Thebes*," edited by Isabelle Torrance, 150–72. Abingdon: Routledge.

Foxhall, Lin. 2013. *Studying Gender in Classical Antiquity*. Cambridge: Cambridge University Press.

Fraenkel, Eduard. 1950. *Aeschylus, "Agamemnon."* 3 vols. Oxford: Oxford University Press.

Fraenkel, Eduard. 1954. "Vermutungen zum Aetna-Festspiel des Aeschylus." *Eranos* 52:61–75. = 1964. *Kleine Beiträge zur klassischen Philologie*. Erster Band, 249–62. Rome: Edizioni di Storia e Letteratura.

Fraenkel, Eduard. 1964. "Die Kassandraszene der Orestie." In *Kleine Beiträge zur klassischen Philologie*. Erster Band, 375–87. Rome: Edizioni di Storia e Letteratura.

Friis Johansen, H., and E. W. Whittle. 1975. "Textual Notes on Aeschylus' *Supplices* 1–503." *Symbolae Osloenses* 50.1:5–41.

Friis Johansen, H., and E. W. Whittle. 1980. *Aeschylus, "The Suppliants."* 3 vols. Copenhagen: Gyldendal.

Fry, Douglas P. 2006. "Reciprocity: The Foundation Stone of Morality." In *Handbook of Moral Development*, edited by Melanie Killen and Judith G. Smetana, 399–422. Mahwah, NJ: Lawrence Erlbaum Associates.

Gagarin, Michael. 1976. *Aeschylean Drama*. Berkeley: University of California Press.

Gantz, Timothy Nolan. 1977. "The Fires of the *Oresteia*." *Journal of Hellenic Studies* 97:28–38.

Gantz, Timothy. 1978a. "Love and Death in the *Suppliants* of Aischylos." *Phoenix* 32.4:278–87.

Gantz, Timothy Nolan. 1978b. "Pindar's Second Pythian: The Myth of Ixion." *Hermes* 106:14–26.

Gantz, Timothy. 1982. "Inherited Guilt in Aischylos." *Classical Journal* 78.1:1–23.

Gantz, Timothy. 1983. "The Chorus of Aischylos' *Agamemnon*." *Harvard Studies in Classical Philology* 87:65–86.

Gantz, Timothy. 1993. *Early Greek Myth: A Guide to Literary and Artistic Sources*. 2 vols. Baltimore: Johns Hopkins University Press.

Garland, Robert. 1990. *The Greek Way of Life: From Conception to Old Age*. Ithaca: Cornell University Press.

Garvie, A. F. 1969. *Aeschylus' "Supplices": Play and Trilogy*. Cambridge: Cambridge University Press.

Garvie, A. F. 1978. "Aeschylus' Simple Plots." In Dawe, Diggle, and Easterling 1978, 63–86.

Garvie, A. F. 1986. *Aeschylus, "Choephori."* With introduction and commentary. Oxford: Oxford University Press.

Garvie, A. F. 2014. "Closure or Indeterminacy in *Septem* and Other Plays?" *Journal of Hellenic Studies* 134:23–40.

Gentili, Bruno. 1981. "Verità e accordo contrattuale (σύνθεσις) in Pindaro, fr. 205 Sn.-Maehl." *Illinois Classical Studies* 6:215–20.

Gerber, Douglas E. 1962. "What Time Can Do (Pindar, *Nemean* 1.46–47)." *Transactions of the American Philological Association* 93:30–33.

Gerber, Douglas E. 1982. *Pindar's "Olympian" One: A Commentary.* Toronto: University of Toronto Press.

Gernet, Louis. 1981. *The Anthropology of Ancient Greece.* Translated by John D. B. Hamilton and Blaise Nagy. Baltimore: Johns Hopkins University Press. = Translation of 1968. *Anthropologie de la Grèce antique.* Paris: François Maspero.

Gildersleeve, Basil L. 1885. *Pindar: The "Olympian" and "Pythian" Odes.* New York: American Book Company.

Gill, Christopher. 1996. *Personality in Greek Epic, Tragedy and Philosophy: The Self in Dialogue.* Oxford: Oxford University Press.

Gill, Christopher, Norman Postlethwaite, and Richard Seaford, eds. 1998. *Reciprocity in Ancient Greece.* Oxford: Oxford University Press.

Gill, Christopher, and T. P. Wiseman, eds. 1993. *Lies and Fiction in the Ancient World.* Exeter: University of Exeter Press.

Gödde, Susanne. 2000. *Das Drama der Hikesie: Ritual und Rhetorik in Aischylos' "Hiketiden."* Münster: Aschendorff.

Goldhill, Simon. 1984. *Language, Sexuality, Narrative: The "Oresteia."* Cambridge: Cambridge University Press.

Goldhill, Simon. 1986. *Reading Greek Tragedy.* Cambridge: Cambridge University Press.

Goldman, Shalom. 1995. *The Wiles of Women, the Wiles of Men: Joseph and Potiphar's Wife in Ancient Near Eastern, Jewish, and Islamic Folklore.* Albany: State University of New York Press.

Goslin, Owen. 2010. "Hesiod's Typhonomachy and the Ordering of Sound." *Transactions of the American Philological Association* 140:351–73.

Gouldner, Alvin W. 1960. "The Norm of Reciprocity: A Preliminary Statement." *American Sociological Review* 25.2:161–78.

Gow, A. S. F. 1934. "ΙΥΓΞ, ΡΟΜΒΟΣ, *Rhombus, Turbo.*" *Journal of Hellenic Studies* 54:1–13.

Goward, Barbara. 2005. *Aeschylus, "Agamemnon."* London: Duckworth.

Griffith, Mark. 1976. *The Authenticity of Prometheus Bound.* Cambridge: Cambridge University Press.

Griffiths, E. M. 2014. "View from Vanishing Point: Kairos and the Meta-City in Aeschylus' *Seven against Thebes* and Pindar's *Pythian* 8." *Mnemosyne* 67:725–61.

Grosz, Elizabeth A. 1994. *Volatile Bodies: Toward a Corporeal Feminism*. Bloomington: Indiana University Press.

Gruber, Markus A. 2009. *Der Chor in den Tragödien des Aischylos*. Tübingen: Gunter Narr.

Hall, Edith. 2015. "Peaceful Conflict Resolution and Its Discontents in Aeschylus's *Eumenides.*" *Common Knowledge* 21.2:253–69.

Harris, Edward M. 2006. *Democracy and the Rule of Law in Classical Athens: Essays on Law, Society, and Politics*. Cambridge: Cambridge University Press.

Harvey, A. E. 1955. "The Classification of Greek Lyric Poetry." *Classical Quarterly*, N.S., 5.3/4:157–75.

Heitsch, Ernst. 1962. "Die nicht-philosophische ΑΛΗΘΕΙΑ." *Hermes* 90:24–33.

Heitsch, Ernst. 1963. "Wahrheit als Erinnerung." *Hermes* 91:36–52.

Herington, C. J. 1970. *The Author of the Prometheus Bound*. Austin: University of Texas Press.

Herington, John. 1984. "Pindar's Eleventh Pythian Ode and Aeschylus' *Agamemnon.*" In *Greek Poetry and Philosophy: Studies in Honor of Leonard Woodbury*, edited by D. Gerber, 137–46. Chico: Scholars Press.

Herington, John. 1985. *Poetry into Drama: Early Tragedy and the Greek Poetic Tradition*. Berkeley: University of California Press.

Herman, Gabriel. 1987. *Ritualised Friendship and the Greek City*. Cambridge: Cambridge University Press.

Holmes, Brooke. 2012. *Gender: Antiquity and Its Legacy*. Oxford: Oxford University Press.

Hornblower, Simon. 2004. *Thucydides and Pindar: Historical Narrative and the World of Epinikian Poetry*. Oxford: Oxford University Press.

Howie, J. G. 1983. "The Revision of Myth in Pindar *Olympian* 1." *Papers of the Liverpool Latin Seminar* 4:277–313.

Hubbard, Thomas K. 1985. *The Pindaric Mind: A Study of Logical Structure in Early Greek Poetry*. Leiden: Brill.

Hubbard, Thomas K. 1986. "The Subject/Object-Relation in Pindar's Second *Pythian* and Seventh *Nemean.*" *Quaderni Urbinati di Cultura Classica*, N.S., 22.1:53–72.

Hubbard, Thomas K. 1987. "The 'Cooking' of Pelops: Pindar and the Process of Mythological Revisionism." *Helios* 14:3–21.

Hubbard, Thomas K. 1992. "Tragic Preludes: Aeschylus *Seven against Thebes* 4–8." *Phoenix* 46.4:299–308.

Hutchinson, G. O. 1985. *Aeschylus, "Septem contra Thebas."* Edited with introduction and commentary. Oxford: Oxford University Press.

Instone, Stephen. 1996. *Selected Odes: "Olympian" One, "Pythian" Nine, "Nemeans" Two and Three, "Isthmian" One*. Warminster: Aris and Phillips.

Ireland, Stanley. 1974. "Stichomythia in Aeschylus: The Dramatic Role of Syntax and Connecting Particles." *Hermes* 102.4:509–24.

Italie, G. 1955. *Index Aeschyleus*. Leiden: Brill.

Jones, John. 1962. *On Aristotle and Greek Tragedy*. Oxford: Oxford University Press.

Kannicht, Richard. 1969. *Euripides, "Helena."* 2 vols. Heidelberg: Carl Winter Universitätsverlag.

Käppel, Lutz. 1998. *Die Konstruktion der Handlung in der "Orestie" des Aischylos: Die Makrostruktur des 'Plot' als Sinnträger in der Darstellung des Geschlechterfluchs*. Munich: C. H. Beck.

Katz, Joshua T., and Katharina Volk. 2000. "'Mere Bellies'? A New Look at *Theogony* 26–8." *Journal of Hellenic Studies* 120:122–31.

Katz, Marilyn A. 1994. "The Character of Tragedy: Women and the Greek Imagination." *Arethusa* 27:81–103.

Kelly, Adrian. 2007. "Stesikhoros and Helen." *Museum Helveticum* 64.1:1–21.

Killen, Melanie, and Frans B. M. de Waal. 2000. "The Evolution and Development of Morality." In *Natural Conflict Resolution*, edited by Filippo Aureli and Frans B. M. de Waal, 352–72. Berkeley: University of California Press.

Kirkwood, G. M. 1982. *Selections from Pindar*. Edited with an introduction and commentary. Chico: Scholars Press.

Kitto, H. D. F. 1971. *Greek Tragedy: A Literary Study*. 3rd ed. London: Methuen. Reprint of 1961.

Knox, Bernard M. W. 1972. "Aeschylus and the Third Actor." *American Journal of Philology* 93:104–24.

Köhnken, Adolf. 1974. "Pindar as Innovator: Poseidon Hippios and the Relevance of the Pelops Story in Olympian 1." *Classical Quarterly*, n.s., 27:199–206.

Komornicka, A. M. 1972. "Quelques remarques sur la notion d' ΑΛΑΘΕΙΑ et de ΨΕΥΔΟΣ chez Pindare." *Eos* 60:235–53.

Komornicka, A. M. 1976. "La notion du temps chez Pindare: Divers emplois et aspects du terme χρόνος." *Eos* 64:5–15.

Komornicka, A. M. 1979. *Étude sur Pindare et la lyrique archaïque grecque: Termes désignant le vrai et le faux*. Lodz: Lodz University.

Komornicka, A. M. 1981. "Termes déterminant le Vrai et le Faux chez Pindare." In *Aischylos und Pindar: Studien zu werk und Nachwirkung*, edited by Ernst Günther Schmidt, 81–89. Berlin: Akademie-Verlag.

Konstan, David. 1998. "The Invention of Fiction." In *Ancient Fiction and Early Christian Narrative*, edited by Ronald F. Hock, J. Bradley Chance, and Judith Perkin, 3–17. Atlanta: Society of Biblical Literature.

Krieger, Murray. 1992. *Ekphrasis: The Illusion of the Natural Sign*. Baltimore: Johns Hopkins University Press.

Krischer, Tilman. 1965. "ΕΤΥΜΟΣ und ΑΛΗΘΗΣ." *Philologus* 109:161–74.

Kromer, Gretchen. 1976. "The Value of Time in Pindar's *Olympian* 10." *Hermes* 104:420–36.

Kuhns, Richard. 1962. *The House, the City, and the Judge*. Indianapolis: Bobbs-Merrill.

Kurke, Leslie. 1991. *The Traffic in Praise: Pindar and the Poetics of Social Economy*. Ithaca: Cornell University Press.

Kurke, Leslie. 2013. "Pindar's Pythian 11 and the *Oresteia*: Contestatory Ritual Poetics in the 5th c. BCE." *Classical Antiquity* 32.1:101–75.

Kyriakou, Poulheria. 1994. "Images of Women in Pindar." *Materiali e discussioni per l'analisi dei testi classici* 32:31–54.

Lamarque, Peter, and Stein Haugom Olsen. 1994. *Truth, Fiction, and Literature: A Philosophical Perspective*. Oxford: Oxford University Press.

Laqueur, Thomas Walter. 1990. *Making Sex: Body and Gender from the Greeks to Freud*. Cambridge, MA: Harvard University Press.

Lardinois, André, and Laura McClure, eds. 2001. *Making Silence Speak: Women's Voices in Greek Literature and Society*. Princeton: Princeton University Press.

Larsson Lovén, Lena, and Aneta Strömberg, eds. 2010. *Ancient Marriage in Myth and Reality*. Newcastle upon Tyne: Cambridge Scholars Publishing.

Latte, Kurt. 1946. "Hesiods Dichterweihe." *Antike und Abendland* 2:152–63.

Lawrence, Stuart E. 2007. "Eteocles' Moral Awareness in Aeschylus' *Seven*." *Classical World* 100.4:335–53.

Lawrence, Stuart. 2013. *Moral Awareness in Greek Tragedy*. Oxford: Oxford University Press.

Leahy, D. M. 1969. "The Role of Cassandra in the *Oresteia* of Aeschylus." *Bulletin of the John Rylands Library* 52:144–77.

Lebeck, Anne. 1971. *The "Oresteia": A Study in Language and Structure*. Cambridge, MA: Harvard University Press.

Ledbetter, Grace M. 2003. *Poetics before Plato*. Princeton: Princeton University Press.

Lefkowitz, Mary R. 1991. *First-Person Fictions: Pindar's Poetic "I."* Oxford: Oxford University Press.

Leone, Pietro. 1964. "La Palinodia di Stesicoro." *Annali della Facoltà di lettere e filosofia dell' Università di Napoli* 11:5–28.

Lesky, Albin. 1960. "Eteokles in den Sieben gegen Theben." *Wiener Studien* 73:5–17.

Lesky, Albin. 1966. "Decision and Responsibility in the Tragedy of Aeschylus." *Journal of Hellenic Studies* 86:78–85.

LeVen, Pauline Anaïs. 2014. *The Many-Headed Muse: Tradition and Innovation in Late Classical Greek Lyric Poetry*. Cambridge: Cambridge University Press.

Lévi-Strauss, Claude. 1966. *The Elementary Structures of Kinship*. 2nd ed. Translated by James Bell, John Sturmer, and Rodney Needham. Edited by Rodney Needham. Boston: Beacon Press. Translation of 1949. *Les structures élémentaires de parenté*.

Liapis, Vayos. 2020. "Payback Time: Metamorphoses of Debt and Commodity in Pindar's *Olympian* 10." *Greece and Rome* 67.1:5–27.

Lloyd-Jones, Hugh. 1959. "The End of the *Seven against Thebes*." *Classical Quarterly*, N.S., 9.1:80–115.

Lloyd-Jones, Hugh. 1971. *The Justice of Zeus*. Berkeley: University of California Press.

Lloyd-Jones, Hugh. 1973. "Modern Interpretation of Pindar: The Second Pythian and Seventh Nemean Odes." *Journal of Hellenic Studies* 93:109–37.

Lloyd-Jones, Hugh. 1975. *Females of the Species: Semonides on Women*. London: Duckworth.

Lloyd-Jones, Hugh, trans. 1979. *Aeschylus, "Oresteia."* Berkeley: University of California Press.

Loraux, Nicole. 1978. "Sur la race des femmes et quelques-unes de ses tribus." *Arethusa* 11.1/2:43–87. = Loraux 1993, 72–110.

Loraux, Nicole. 1987. *Tragic Ways of Killing a Woman*. Translated by Anthony Forster. Cambridge, MA: Harvard University Press.

Loraux, Nicole. 1993. *The Children of Athena*. Translated by Caroline Levine. Princeton: Princeton University Press.

Lowe, N. J. 2000. "Comic Plots and the Invention of Fiction." In *The Rivals of Aristophanes: Studies in Athenian Old Comedy*, edited by David Harvey and John Wilkins, 259–72. London: Duckworth and the Classical Press of Wales.

Luther, Wilhelm. 1966. *Wahrheit, Licht und Erkenntnis in der griechischen Philosophie bis Demokrit*. Archiv für Begriffsgeschichte, vol. 10. Bonn: H. Bouvier.

Lyons, Deborah. 2003. "Dangerous Gifts: Ideologies of Marriage and Exchange in Ancient Greece." *Classical Antiquity* 22.1:93–134.

Lyons, Deborah. 2012. *Dangerous Gifts: Gender and Exchange in Ancient Greece*. Austin: University of Texas Press.

MacKinnon, J. K. 1978. "The Reason for the Danaids' Flight." *Classical Quarterly*, N.S., 28.1:74–82.

MacLachlan, Bonnie. 1993. *The Age of Grace: Charis in Early Greek Poetry*. Princeton: Princeton University Press.

Malinowski, Bronislaw. 1922. *Argonauts of the Western Pacific*. New York: E. P. Dutton.

Malinowski, Bronislaw. 1932. *Crime and Custom in Savage Society*. London: Paul, Trench, Trubner.

Marquardt, Patricia A. 1982. "Hesiod's Ambiguous View of Woman." *Classical Philology* 77.4:283–91.

Maslov, Boris. 2015. *Pindar and the Emergence of Literature*. Cambridge: Cambridge University Press.

Mason, P. G. 1959. "Kassandra." *Journal of Hellenic Studies* 79:80–93.

Massimilla, Giulio. 1990. "L'Elena di Stesicoro quale premessa ad una ritrattazione." *La Parola del Passato* 45:370–81.

Masterson, Mark, Nancy Sorkin Rabinowitz, James Robson, and Lloyd Llewellyn-Jones. 2014. "Introduction." In Robson, Rabinowitz, and Masterson 2014, 1–12.

Mauss, Marcel. 1925. "Essai sur le don: Forme et raison de l'échange dans les sociétés archaïques." *Année Sociologie* 1:30–186.

Mauss, Marcel. 1967. *The Gift*. Translated by Ian Cunnison. New York: Norton. = Translation of Mauss 1925.

Mazzoldi, Sabina. 2001. "Lo scotto di Cassandra μάντις: Aesch. *Ag.* 1275–1276." *Quaderni Urbinati di Cultura Classica* 68:93–98.

McCall, Marsh. 1990. "The Chorus of Aeschylus' *Choephori.*" In *Cabinet of the Muses: Essays on Classical and Comparative Literature in Honor of Thomas G. Rosenmeyer*, edited by Mark Griffith and Donald J. Mastronarde, 17–30. Atlanta: Scholars Press.

McClure, Laura. 1999. *Spoken Like a Woman: Speech and Gender in Athenian Drama.* Princeton: Princeton University Press.

McCoskey, Denise Eileen, and Emily Zakin, eds. 2009. *Bound by the City: Greek Tragedy, Sexual Difference, and the Formation of the Polis.* Albany: State University of New York Press.

McLaughlin, Gráinne. 2004. "Professional Foul: Persona in Pindar." In *Games and Festivals in Classical Antiquity: Proceedings of the Conference Held in Edinburgh 10–12 July 2000*, edited by Sinclair Bell and Glenys Davies, 25–32. Oxford: Archaeopress.

Michelini, Ann Norris. 1987. *Euripides and the Tragic Tradition.* Madison: University of Wisconsin Press.

Miller, Andrew M. 1982. "*Phthonos* and *Parphasis*: The Argument of *Nemean* 8.19–34." *Greek, Roman, and Byzantine Studies* 23.2:111–20.

Mitchell, Lynette G. 2006. "Greeks, Barbarians and Aeschylus' *Suppliants.*" *Greece and Rome* 53.2:205–23.

Mitchell-Boyask, Robin. 2006. "The Marriage of Cassandra and the *Oresteia*: Text, Image, Performance." *Transactions of the American Philological Association* 136:269–97.

Molm, Linda D., Jessica L. Collett, and David R. Schaefer. 2007. "Building Solidarity through Generalized Exchange: A Theory of Reciprocity." *American Journal of Sociology* 113.1:205–42.

Mondi, Robert. 1984. "The Ascension of Zeus and the Composition of Hesiod's Theogony." *Greek, Roman, and Byzantine Studies* 225:325–44.

Morgan, Kathryn A. 2015. *Pindar and the Construction of Syracusan Monarchy in the Fifth Century B.C.* Oxford: Oxford University Press.

Morgan, Teresa J. 2005. "The Wisdom of Semonides Fr. 7." *Proceedings of the Cambridge Philological Society* 51:72–85.

Morrison, A. D. 2007. *The Narrator in Archaic Greek and Hellenistic Poetry.* Cambridge: Cambridge University Press.

Most, Glenn W. 1985. *The Measures of Praise: Structure and Function in Pindar's Second "Pythian" and Seventh "Nemean" Odes.* Göttingen: Vandenhoeck und Ruprecht.

Mueller, Melissa. 2001. "The Language of Reciprocity in Euripides' *Medea.*" *American Journal of Philology* 122:471–504.

Mueller-Goldingen, Christian. 2000. "Tradition und Innovation zu Stesichoros' Umgang mit dem Mythos." *L'Antiquité Classique* 69:1–19.

Murnaghan, Sheila. 2005. "Women in Groups: Aeschylus's *Suppliants* and the Female Choruses of Greek Tragedy." In *The Soul of Tragedy: Essays on Athenian Drama,* edited by Victoria Pedrick and Steven M. Oberhelman, 183–98. Chicago: University of Chicago Press.

Murray, Robert Duff, Jr. 1958. *The Motif of Io in Aeschylus' "Suppliants."* Princeton: Princeton University Press.

Nagy, Gregory. 1986. "Pindar's *Olympian* 1 and the Aetiology of the Olympic Games." *Transactions of the American Philological Association* 116:71–88.

Nagy, Gregory. 1990. *Pindar's Homer: The Lyric Possession of an Epic Past*. Baltimore: Johns Hopkins University Press.

Nagy, Gregory. 1996. *Homeric Questions*. Austin: University of Texas Press.

Nagy, Gregory. 2000. "'Dream of a Shade': Refractions of Epic Vision in Pindar's *Pythian* 8 and Aeschylus' *Seven against Thebes*." *Harvard Studies in Classical Philology* 100:97–118.

Naiden, F. S. 2006. *Ancient Supplication*. Oxford: Oxford University Press.

Nassen, Paula J. 1975. "A Literary Study of Pindar's *Olympian* 10." *Transactions of the American Philological Association* 105:219–40.

Neitzel, Heinz. 1984. "Agamemnons Ermordung in Kassandras Vision (A. *Ag.* 1125–1129)." *Hermes* 112:271–81.

Nicholson, Nigel. 1998. "The Truth of Pederasty: A Supplement to Foucault's Genealogy of the Relation between Truth and Desire in Ancient Greece." *Intertexts* 2.1:26–45.

Nicholson, Nigel. 2016. *The Poetics of Victory in the Greek West: Epinician, Oral Tradition, and the Deinomenid Empire*. Oxford: Oxford University Press.

Nietzsche, Friedrich. 2017 (1886). *The Essential Nietzsche: Beyond Good and Evil; A Genealogy of Morals*. Translated by Helen Zimmern. New York: Quarto Group.

Nisetich, Frank J. 1989. *Pindar and Homer*. Baltimore: Johns Hopkins University Press.

Norwood, Gilbert. 1945. *Pindar*. Berkeley: University of California Press.

Obbink, Dirk. 2001. "The Genre of Plataea: Generic Unity in the New Simonides." In *The New Simonides: Contexts of Praise and Desire*, edited by Deborah Boedeker and David Sider, 65–85. Oxford: Oxford University Press.

O'Neill, Eugene G., Jr. 1941. "The Prologue of the *Troades* of Euripides." *Transactions of the American Philological Association* 72:288–320.

O'Neill, K. 1998. "Aeschylus, Homer, and the Serpent at the Breast." *Phoenix* 52.3/4:216–29.

Ormand, Kirk. 1999. *Exchange and the Maiden: Marriage in Sophoclean Tragedy*. Austin: University of Texas Press.

Ortega, Alfonso. 1970. "Poesía y verdad en Píndaro." *Helmantica* 21:353–72.

Orwin, Clifford. 1980. "Feminine Justice: The End of the *Seven against Thebes*." *Classical Philology* 75.3:187–96.

Osborne, Robin. 2001. "The Use of Abuse: Semonides 7." *Proceedings of the Cambridge Philological Society* 47:47–64.

Otis, Brooks. 1960. "The Unity of the *Seven against Thebes*." *Greek, Roman, and Byzantine Studies* 3.4:153–74.

Page, Denys, ed. 1972. *Aeschyli septem quae supersunt tragoedias.* Oxford: Oxford University Press.

Park, Arum. 2013. "Truth and Genre in Pindar." *Classical Quarterly,* N.S., 63.1:17–36.

Park, Arum. 2014. "Parthenogenesis in Hesiod's *Theogony.*" *Preternature: Critical and Historical Studies on the Preternatural* 3.2:261–83.

Park, Arum. 2017. "Reality, Illusion, or Both? Cloud-Women in Stesichorus and Pindar." In *Resemblance and Reality in Greek Thought: Essays in Honor of Peter M. Smith,* edited by Arum Park, 65–79. Abingdon: Routledge.

Patterson, Cynthia P. 1991. "Marriage and the Married Woman in Athenian Law." In *Women's History and Ancient History,* edited by Sarah B. Pomeroy, 48–72. Chapel Hill: University of North Carolina Press.

Patzer, Harald. 1958. "Die dramatische Handlung der Sieben gegen Theben." *Harvard Studies in Classical Philology* 63:97–119.

Pellicia, Hayden. 1987. "Pindarus Homericus: *Pythian* 3.1–80." *Harvard Studies in Classical Philology* 91:39–63.

Pillinger, Emily. 2019. *Cassandra and the Poetics of Prophecy in Greek and Latin Literature.* Cambridge: Cambridge University Press.

Pinchard, Alexis. 2016. "Dikē as Global World Order: An Orphic Inheritance in Aeschylus?" *Trends in Classics* 8.2:242–81.

Podlecki, Anthony J. 1964. "The Character of Eteocles in Aeschylus' *Septem.*" *Transactions of the American Philological Association* 95:283–99.

Podlecki, Anthony J. 1966. *The Political Background of Aeschylean Tragedy.* Ann Arbor: University of Michigan Press.

Podlecki, A. J. 1971. "Stesichoreia." *Athenaeum* 49:313–27.

Podlecki, A. J. 2003. "Watching, Waiting, Witchcraft: The Chorus of the *Oresteia.*" In *Theatres of Action: Papers for Chris Dearden,* edited by John Davidson and Arthur Pomeroy, 12–33. Auckland: Polygraphia.

Pomeroy, Sarah B. 1995. *Goddesses, Whores, Wives, and Slaves: Women in Classical Antiquity.* New York: Schocken Books.

Poochigian, Aaron. 2007. "Arguments from Silence: Text and Stage in Aischylos' *Seven against Thebes.*" *Classical Journal* 103.1:1–11.

Postlethwaite, Norman. 1998. "Akhilleus and Agamemnon: Generalized Reciprocity." In Gill, Postlethwaite, and Seaford 1998, 93–104.

Prag, A. J. N. W. 1991. "Clytemnestra's Weapon Yet Once More." *Classical Quarterly,* N.S., 41.1:242–46.

Pratt, Louise H. 1993. *Lying and Poetry from Homer to Pindar: Falsehood and Deception in Archaic Greek Poetics.* Ann Arbor: University of Michigan Press.

Pucci, Pietro. 1977. *Hesiod and the Language of Poetry.* Baltimore: Johns Hopkins University Press.

Puelma, Mario. 1989. "Der Dichter und die Wahrheit in der griechischen Poetik von Homer bis Aristoteles." *Museum Helveticum* 46:65–100.

Rabinowitz, Nancy Sorkin. 1992. "Tragedy and the Politics of Containment." In *Pornography and Representation in Greece and Rome*, edited by Amy Richlin, 36–52. New York: Oxford University Press.

Rabinowitz, Nancy Sorkin. 1993. *Anxiety Veiled: Euripides and the Traffic in Women*. Ithaca: Cornell University Press.

Race, William H. 1986. *Pindar*. Boston: Twayne Publishers.

Race, William H. 1990. *Style and Rhetoric in Pindar's Odes*. Atlanta: Scholars Press.

Race, William H. 1997. *Pindar, "Olympian" Odes. "Pythian" Odes. "Nemean" Odes. "Isthmian" Odes. Fragments*. 2 vols. Cambridge, MA: Harvard University Press.

Rader, Richard. 2009. "'And Whatever It Is, It Is You': The Autochthonous Self in Aeschylus's *Seven against Thebes*." *Arethusa* 42.1:1–44.

Raeburn, David, and Oliver Thomas. 2011. *The "Agamemnon" of Aeschylus: A Commentary for Students*. Oxford: Oxford University Press.

Reden, Sitta von. 1995. *Exchange in Ancient Greece*. London: Duckworth.

Rehm, Rush. 1994. *Marriage to Death: The Conflation of Wedding and Funeral Rituals in Greek Tragedy*. Princeton: Princeton University Press.

Roberts, Deborah H. 1984. *Apollo and His Oracle in the "Oresteia."* Göttingen: Vandenhoeck und Ruprecht.

Robertson, D. S. 1924. "The End of the *Supplices* Trilogy of Aeschylus." *Classical Review* 38:51–53.

Robertson, H. G. 1936. "Δίκη and Ὕβρις in Aeschylus' *Suppliants*." *Classical Review* 50.3:104–9.

Robson, James, Nancy Sorkin Rabinowitz, and Mark Masterson, eds. 2014. *Sex in Antiquity: Exploring Gender and Sexuality in the Ancient World*. Abingdon: Routledge.

Rose, Peter. 1982. "Towards a Dialectical Hermeneutic of Pindar's *Pythian* X." *Helios*, N.S., 9:47–73. = Rose 1992, 165–84.

Rose, Peter W. 1992. *Sons of the Gods, Children of Earth: Ideology and Literary Form in Ancient Greece*. Ithaca: Cornell University Press.

Rosenmeyer, Thomas G. 1982. *The Art of Aeschylus*. Berkeley: University of California Press.

Rösler, Wolfgang. 1980. "Entdeckung der Fiktionalität in der Antike." *Poetica* 12:283–319.

Rösler, W. 1993. "Der Schluß der 'Hiketiden' und die Danaiden-Trilogie des Aischylos." *Rheinisches Museum* 136:1–22.

Roth, Paul. 1993. "The Theme of Corrupted *Xenia* in Aeschylus' *Oresteia*." *Mnemosyne* 46.1:1–17.

Rothschild, Clare K. 2004. *Luke–Acts and the Rhetoric of History: An Investigation of Early Christian Historiography*. Tübingen: Mohr Siebeck.

Rubin, Gayle. 2011. "The Traffic in Women: Notes on the 'Political Economy' of Sex." In *Deviations: A Gayle Rubin Reader*, 33–65. Durham: Duke University Press. = 1975. *Toward an Anthropology of Women*, edited by Rayna Reiter, 157–210. New York:

Monthly Review Press. = 1990. *Women, Class, and the Feminist Imagination*, edited by Karen Hansen and Ilene Philipson, 74–113. Philadelphia: Temple University Press.

Sahlins, Marshall D. 1965. "On the Sociology of Primitive Exchange." In *The Relevance of Models for Social Anthropology*, edited by Michael Banton, 139–236. London: Tavistock.

Sahlins, Marshall. 1972. *Stone Age Economics*. Chicago: Aldine-Atherton.

Sailor, Dylan, and Sarah Culpepper Stroup. 1999. "ΦΘΟΝΟΣ Δ' ΑΠΕΣΤΩ: The Translation of Transgression in Aiskhylos' *Agamemnon*." *Classical Antiquity* 18:153–82.

Schein, Seth L. 1982. "The Cassandra Scene in Aeschylus' *Agamemnon*." *Greece and Rome*, 2nd ser., 29.1:11–16.

Scott, Joan W. 1986. "Gender: A Useful Category of Historical Analysis." *American Historical Review* 91.5:1053–75.

Scott, William C. 1978. "Lines for Clytemnestra (*Agamemnon* 489–502)." *Transactions of the American Philological Association* 108:259–69.

Seaford, Richard. 1987. "The Tragic Wedding." *Journal of Hellenic Studies* 107:106–30.

Seaford, Richard. 1994. *Reciprocity and Ritual: Homer and Tragedy in the Developing City-State*. Oxford: Oxford University Press.

Seaford, Richard. 1998. "Introduction." In Gill, Postlethwaite, and Seaford 1998, 1–11.

Seaford, Richard. 2012. *Cosmology and the Polis: The Social Construction of Space and Time in the Tragedies of Aeschylus*. Cambridge: Cambridge University Press.

Segal, Charles. 1967. "Pindar's *Seventh Nemean*." *Transactions of the American Philological Association* 98:431–80.

Segal, Charles. 1986a. "Naming, Truth, and Creation in the Poetics of Pindar." *Diacritics* 16.2:65–83.

Segal, Charles. 1986b. *Pindar's Mythmaking: The Fourth "Pythian" Ode*. Princeton: Princeton University Press.

Sicherl, M. 1986. "Die Tragik der Danaiden." *Museum Helveticum* 43:81–110.

Sider, David. 1978. "Stagecraft in the *Oresteia*." *American Journal of Philology* 99:12–27.

Sider, David. 1989. "The Blinding of Stesichorus." *Hermes* 117:423–31.

Sigelman, Asya C. 2016. *Pindar's Poetics of Immortality*. Cambridge: Cambridge University Press.

Sikes, E. E. 1931. *The Greek View of Poetry*. London: Methuen.

Silk, Michael. 2013. "The Greek Dramatic Genres: Theoretical Perspectives." In *Greek Comedy and the Discourse of Genres*, edited by Emmanuela Bakola, Lucia Prauscello, and Mario Telò, 15–39. Cambridge: Cambridge University Press.

Slater, William J. 1969. *Lexicon to Pindar*. Berlin: De Gruyter.

Slater, William J. 1979. "Pindar and Hypothekai." *Proceedings, Second International Conference on Boiotian Antiquities*, 79–82. Montreal: McGill University.

Slater, William J. 1988. "Pindar's *Pythian* 3: Structure and Purpose." *Quaderni Urbinati di Cultura Classica*, N.S., 29:51–61.

Snell, Bruno. 1975. "ΑΛΗΘΕΙΑ." *Würzburger Jahrbücher für die Altertumswissenschaft* 1:9–17.

Snell, B., and H. Maehler, eds. 1997 (=1987). *Pindari Carmina cum Fragmentis. Pars 1, Epinicia.* Stuttgart: Teubner.

Sommerstein, Alan H. 1977. "Notes on Aeschylus' *Suppliants.*" *Bulletin of the Institute of Classical Studies* 24:67–82.

Sommerstein, Alan H. 1989. *Eumenides.* Cambridge: Cambridge University Press.

Sommerstein, Alan H. 1995. "The Beginning and the End of Aeschylus' Danaid Trilogy." In *Griechischrömische Komödie und Tragödie,* edited by B. Zimmermann, 111–34. Stuttgart: Springer-Verlag. = Sommerstein 2010b, 89–117.

Sommerstein, Alan H. 2008. *Aeschylus.* 2 vols. Cambridge, MA: Harvard University Press.

Sommerstein, Alan H. 2010a. *Aeschylean Tragedy.* London: Duckworth.

Sommerstein, Alan H. 2010b. *The Tangled Ways of Zeus and Other Studies in and around Greek Tragedy.* Oxford: Oxford University Press.

Sommerstein, Alan H. 2019. *Aeschylus, "Suppliants."* Cambridge: Cambridge University Press.

Spelman, Henry L. 2018. *Pindar and the Poetics of Permanence.* Oxford: Oxford University Press.

Spivak, Gayatri Chakravorty. 1994. "Can the Subaltern Speak?" In *Colonial Discourse and Post-Colonial Theory,* edited by Patrick Williams and Laura Chrisman, 66–111. New York: Columbia University Press.

Stamatopoulou, Zoe. 2017. *Hesiod and Classical Greek Poetry: Reception and Transformation in the Fifth Century BCE.* Cambridge: Cambridge University Press.

Starr, Chester G. 1968. "Ideas of Truth in Early Greece." *La Parola del Passato* 23:348–59.

Stehle, Eva. 2005. "Prayer and Curse in Aeschylus' *Seven against Thebes.*" *Classical Philology* 100.2:101–22.

Steiner, Deborah. 1994. *The Tyrant's Writ: Myths and Images of Writing in Ancient Greece.* Princeton: Princeton University Press.

Steiner, Deborah. 2004. "Catullan Excavations: Pindar's *Olympian* 10 and Catullus 68." *Harvard Studies in Classical Philology* 102:275–97.

Steiner, D. 2010. "The Immeasures of Praise: The Epinician Celebration of Agamemnon's Return." *Hermes* 138.1:22–37.

Sussman, Linda S. 1978. "The Birth of the Gods: Sexuality, Conflict and Cosmic Structure in Hesiod's *Theogony.*" *Ramus* 7.1:61–77.

Svenbro, Jesper. 1984. "Vengeance et société en Grèce archaïque: A Propos de la fin de l'*Odyssée.*" In *La Vengeance: Études d'ethnologie, d'histoire et de philosophie.* Vol. 3, edited by R. Verdier and J. P. Poly, 47–64. Paris: Cujas.

Swift, L. A. 2010. *The Hidden Chorus: Echoes of Genre in Tragic Lyric.* Oxford: Oxford University Press.

Swift, Laura. 2018. "Competing Generic Narratives in Aeschylus' *Oresteia*." In Andújar, Coward, and Hadjimichael 2018, 119–36.

Taplin, Oliver. 1977. *The Stagecraft of Aeschylus: The Dramatic Use of Exits and Entrances in Greek Tragedy*. Oxford: Oxford University Press.

Tatsi, Anna. 2008. "On the Meaning of χρόνος in Pindar's *Nemean* 1.46." *Mnemosyne* 61:120–29.

Thalmann, William G. 1978. *Dramatic Art in Aeschylus' "Seven against Thebes."* New Haven: Yale University Press.

Thalmann, W. G. 1985. "Speech and Silence in the *Oresteia* 2." *Phoenix* 39.3:221–37.

Theunissen, Michael. 2000. *Pindar: Menschenlos und Wende der Zeit*. Munich: Beck.

Thomas, Rosalind. 1989. *Oral Tradition and Written Record in Classical Athens*. Cambridge: Cambridge University Press.

Thomas, Rosalind. 2007. "Fame, Memorial, and Choral Poetry: The Origins of Epinikian Poetry—an Historical Study." In *Pindar's Poetry, Patrons, and Festivals: From Archaic Greece to the Roman Empire*, edited by Simon Hornblower and Catherine Morgan, 141–66. Oxford: Oxford University Press.

Thomson, George, ed. 1966. *The "Oresteia" of Aeschylus*. 2 vols. Amsterdam: Adolf J. Hakkert.

Thomson, George. 1967. *Aeschylus and Athens: A Study in the Social Origins of Drama*. 2nd ed. New York: Haskell House.

Thumiger, Chiara. 2013. "Vision and Knowledge in Greek Tragedy." *Helios* 40:223–45.

Tor, Shaul. 2017. *Mortal and Divine in Early Greek Epistemology: A Study of Hesiod, Xenophanes and Parmenides*. Cambridge: Cambridge University Press.

Torrance, Isabelle. 2007. *Aeschylus, "Seven against Thebes."* London: Duckworth.

Tsitsibakou-Vasalos, Evanthia. 2010. "Brightness and Darkness in Pindar's Pythian 3." In *Light and Darkness in Ancient Greek Myth and Religion*, edited by Menelaos Christopoulos, Efimia D. Karakantza, and Olga Levaniouk, 30–76. Lanham, MD: Lexington Books.

Turner, Chad. 2001. "Perverted Supplication and Other Inversions in Aeschylus' Danaid Trilogy." *Classical Journal* 97.1:27–50.

Uhlig, Anna. 2019. *Theatrical Reenactment in Pindar and Aeschylus*. Cambridge: Cambridge University Press.

van Wees, Hans. 1998. "The Law of Gratitude: Reciprocity in Anthropological Theory." In Gill, Postlethwaite, and Seaford 1998, 13–49.

Vasunia, Phiroze. 2001. *The Gift of the Nile: Hellenizing Egypt from Aeschylus to Alexander*. Berkeley: University of California Press.

Vellacott, Philip. 1979–1980. "Aeschylus' *Seven against Thebes*." *Classical World* 73.4:211–19.

Vellacott, Philip. 1984. "Aeschylus' Orestes." *Classical World* 77.3:145–57.

Verdenius, W. J. 1972. "Notes on the Proem of Hesiod's *Theogony*." *Mnemosyne* 25.3:225–60.

Verdenius, W. J. 1988. *Commentaries on Pindar*. Vol. 2, *"Olympian" Odes 1, 10, 11, "Nemean" 11, "Isthmian" 2*. Leiden: Brill.

Vernant, Jean-Pierre, and Pierre Vidal-Naquet. 1981. *Tragedy and Myth in Ancient Greece*. Translated by Janet Lloyd. Sussex: Harvester Press.

Vivante, Paolo. 1972. "On Time in Pindar." *Arethusa* 5:107–31.

Walcot, P. 1956. "The Text of Hesiod's Theogony and the Hittite Epic of Kumarbi." *Classical Quarterly*, N.S., 6.3–4:198–206.

Walcot, P. 1987. "Romantic Love and True Love: Greek Attitudes to Marriage." *Ancient Society* 18:5–33.

Wells, James. 2009. *Pindar's Verbal Art: An Ethnographic Study of Epinician Style*. Cambridge, MA: Harvard University Press.

West, M. L. 1966. *Hesiod, "Theogony."* Edited with prolegomena and commentary. Oxford: Oxford University Press.

West, M. L., ed. 1990a. *Aeschyli Tragoediae cum Incerti Poetae "Prometheo."* Stuttgart: Teubner.

West, M. L. 1990b. *Studies in Aeschylus*. Stuttgart: Teubner.

West, M. L. 1997. *The East Face of Helicon*. Oxford: Oxford University Press.

Westermarck, Edward. 1906. *The Origin and Development of the Moral Ideas*. 2 vols. London: Macmillan.

Whallon, William. 1958. "The Serpent at the Breast." *Transactions of the American Philological Association* 89:271–75.

Whallon, William. 1980. *Problem and Spectacle: Studies in the "Oresteia."* Heidelberg: Carl Winter Universitätsverlag.

Wians, William. 2009. "The Agamemnon and Human Knowledge." In *Logos and Muthos: Philosophical Essays in Greek Literature*, edited by William Wians, 181–98. Albany: State University of New York Press.

Wilamowitz-Moellendorff, Ulrich von. 1922. *Pindaros*. Berlin: Weidmann.

Williams, Bernard. 2002. *Truth and Truthfulness*. Princeton: Princeton University Press.

Wilson, Donna. 1999. "Symbolic Violence in Iliad Book 9." *Classical World* 93.2:131–47.

Wilson, Donna. 2002. *Ransom, Revenge, and Heroic Identity in the "Iliad."* Cambridge: Cambridge University Press.

Wilson, Peter. 2006. *"Dikēn* in the Oresteia of Aeschylus." In "Greek Drama III: Essays in Honour of Kevin Lee," 187–201. Supplement 87, *Bulletin of the Institute of Classical Studies*.

Winnington-Ingram, R. P. 1954. "Aeschylus, Agamemnon 1343–71." *Classical Quarterly*, N.S., 4:23–30.

Winnington-Ingram, R. P. 1983. *Studies in Aeschylus*. Cambridge: Cambridge University Press.

Wohl, Victoria. 1998. *Intimate Commerce: Exchange, Gender, and Subjectivity in Greek Tragedy*. Austin: University of Texas Press.

Wohl, Victoria. 2010. "Suppliant Women and the Democratic State: White Men Saving

Brown Women from Brown Men." In *When Worlds Elide: Classics, Politics, Culture*, edited by Karen Bassi and J. Peter Euben, 409–35. Lanham, MD: Lexington Books.

Wolhfarht, Paolo. 2004. "The Ambiguous Discourse of Truth in Aeschylus' *Agamemnon*." PhD diss., University of British Columbia.

Woodbury, Leonard. 1967. "Helen and the Palinode." *Phoenix* 21.3:157–76.

Woodbury, Leonard. 1968. "Pindar and the Mercenary Muse: *I*. 2.1–13." *Transactions of the American Philological Association* 99:527–42.

Woodbury, Leonard. 1969. "Truth and the Song: Bacchylides 3.96–98." *Phoenix* 23.4:331–35.

Worman, Nancy. 1997. "The Body as Argument: Helen in Four Greek Texts." *Classical Antiquity* 16.1:151–203.

Worman, Nancy. 2002. *The Cast of Character: Style in Greek Literature*. Austin: University of Texas Press.

Young, David C. 1968. *Three Odes of Pindar: "Pythian" 11, "Pythian" 3, and "Olympian" 7*. Leiden: Brill.

Young, David C. 1970. "Pindar *Nemean* 7: Some Preliminary Remarks (vv. 1–20)." *Transactions of the American Philological Association* 101:633–43.

Young, David C. 1983. "Pindar *Pythians* 2 and 3: Inscriptional ποτέ and the 'Poetic Epistle.'" *Harvard Studies in Classical Philology* 87:31–48.

Zanker, Graham. 1998. "Beyond Reciprocity: The Akhilleus-Priam Scene in *Iliad* 24." In Gill, Postlethwaite, and Seaford 1998, 73–92.

Zarecki, Jonathan P. 2007. "Pandora and the Good Eris in Hesiod." *Greek, Roman, and Byzantine Studies* 47:5–29.

Zeitlin, Froma I. 1965. "The Motif of the Corrupted Sacrifice in Aeschylus' *Oresteia*." *Transactions of the American Philological Association* 96:463–508.

Zeitlin, Froma I. 1990. "Patterns of Gender in Aeschylean Drama: *Seven against Thebes* and the Danaid Trilogy." In *Cabinet of the Muses: Essays on Classical and Comparative Literature in Honor of Thomas G. Rosenmeyer*, edited by Mark Griffith and Donald J. Mastronarde, 103–15. Atlanta: Scholars Press.

Zeitlin, Froma I. 1992. "The Politics of Eros in the Danaid Trilogy of Aeschylus." In *Innovations of Antiquity*, edited by Ralph Hexter and Daniel Selden, 203–52. New York: Routledge. Revised in Zeitlin 1996, 123–71.

Zeitlin, Froma I. 1996. *Playing the Other: Gender and Society in Classical Greek Literature*. Chicago: University of Chicago Press.

Zeitlin, Froma I. 2009. *Under the Sign of the Shield: Semiotics and Aeschylus' "Seven against Thebes"*. Lanham, MD: Lexington Books. Originally published 1982. Rome: Edizioni dell' Ateneo.

Index Locorum

General Index

Achilles, 11–12, 26, 59, 62, 65, 122, 189n53
Aegina, 50, 94, 100n85
Aegisthus, 73, 99–100, 102, 170, 186n46, 188n48, 189–90, 193n62, 195–96, 202
Aegyptiads, 33n81, 38n93,141, 148–49, 151, 154, 158–59, 161–66, 168; ethnicity of, 162n54
Agamemnon, 11, 40, 42, 90n63, 100–101, 134, 170, 172, 173n9, 174, 179, 181, 185, 186nn46–47, 187–92, 195, 198–99
Ajax, 31n77, 59, 62–68, 72, 189n53
alētheia/alatheia, 16–17, 149–50; in Aeschylus, 12, 27–42, 70, 108, 115, 127, 139–40, 142, 144, 147–49, 170–71, 182, 186–88, 202, 204–5; in Homer, 16–17, 36, 37; personification of, 19–27, 47, 150; in Pindar, 12, 16–27, 34n82, 41, 43, 45–46, 47n7, 48n10, 49, 51–52, 59, 61, 64, 68, 70, 71, 79, 80, 87–88, 91, 95–96, 98, 106, 108, 140, 204–5. See also alēthēs; truth
alēthēs, 17n25, 75, 146–47; in Aeschylus, 114–16, 124, 132, 134, 174, 176–77, 181–82; in Homer, 16n22; in Pindar, 18, 21–22, 36–37, 53–54. See also alētheia; truth
Amphiaraus, 122, 127–30, 138–39
Andromache, 73, 183
Aphrodite, 73n4, 83, 85, 103–5
Apollo, 88–91, 93–94, 183–84, 190, 195n72, 196–201
Argives in Suppliants, 33–34, 120, 141–47; 159, 161, 163, 165–66, 168
Asclepius, 88, 92–93
Athena, 83, 85, 198–201
Atreus, 180–81, 185–86, 188–90, 199, 207

Augeas, 25, 46, 47–49, 51, 68, 71–72, 79, 82

Cassandra, 8, 28n65, 30, 91n64, 94, 100–101, 128, 132, 134, 137, 145, 151, 154, 170–71, 172n3, 173, 177, 180–90, 192, 196–99, 201–2. See also vision: of Cassandra
Centaurus, 77, 81–82, 86
charis, 9, 13–15, 18–19, 26, 31n77, 48, 53–55, 58, 77, 81–82, 86–87, 104, 142, 192
Chiron, 88, 92–94, 104n98
Chorus of *Agamemnon*, 36–37, 39n94, 42, 43, 73, 115n16, 145, 172–82, 185, 186n46, 187–90, 192, 194, 197, 202
Chorus of *Choephori*, 30–31, 32, 41, 191–97, 200–201
Chorus of *Eumenides*. See Erinyes
Chorus of *Seven*: alternative mode of knowledge, 7–8, 112–18, 173, 180; awareness of reciprocity, 30–31, 110, 133–40, 142–43, 145, 151, 169, 181n32, 202; conflict with Eteocles, 118–19; interpretation of shields, 121–33. See also vision: of Theban Women
Chorus of *Suppliants*, 8, 30–31, 33–36, 43, 73n6, 111, 120, 123, 137, 139, 141–49, 151–69, 191, 196, 202, 207; authorial agency of, 142–43, 151, 154–55, 157, 159–61, 165, 168–69; ethnicity of, 141–44, 146, 152–54, 155n37, 156–60, 163–66. See also vision: of Danaids
Clytemnestra, 8, 29, 38–43, 73, 90n63, 99–103, 132, 137, 145, 151, 170–80, 186–202. See also vision: of Clytemnestra

239